Praise for *Rage*

'Washington's most eminent journalist dissects his first term and ... concludes he is simply «the wrong man for the job». In a devastating critique ... he lambasts him for reveling in "perpetual rage". A riveting read.' **Tony Rennell**, *Daily Mail*

'Even in a news landscape where it feels like nothing is shocking anymore, the first excerpts from the new Bob Woodward book still landed like a pair of hydrogen bombs.' *Vanity Fair*

'*Rage* may be Bob Woodward's most important book since All the President's Men.' **Peter Bergen**, *CNN*

'The book possesses more than a patina of similarity to the famous televised interviews between David Frost and Richard Nixon, the president Woodward and Carl Bernstein brought down with their reporting on Watergate nearly a half-century ago.' *Guardian*

'Woodward's prose offers readers that delicious, vicarious sense of being an insider, right there in the room with Bob, a witness to presidential sulks and boasts.' **Rosa Brooks**, *Washington Post*

'[T]his revealing look at an embattled presidency facing a pandemic, racial unrest and a suffering economy ... the book's details have been explosive.' *USA Today*

'Rage is essential reading for anyone hoping to understand Trump.' **Walter Clemons**, *New York Journal of Books*

'Damning ... Unlike most Tr
tell us something new abou
confirming what we
Michelle Goldb

D1331667

RAGE

BOB WOODWARD

**SIMON &
SCHUSTER**

London · New York · Sydney · Toronto · New Delhi

First published in the United States by Simon & Schuster Inc., 2020
First published in Great Britain by Simon & Schuster UK Ltd, 2020
This edition published in Great Britain by Simon & Schuster UK Ltd, 2021

3 5 7 9 10 8 6 4 2

Simon & Schuster UK Ltd
1st Floor
222 Gray's Inn Road
London WC1X 8HB

www.simonandschuster.co.uk
www.simonandschuster.com.au
www.simonandschuster.co.in

Simon & Schuster Australia, Sydney
Simon & Schuster India, New Delhi

A CIP catalogue record for this book
is available from the British Library

Paperback ISBN: 978-1-4711-9774-1
eBook ISBN: 978-1-4711-9772-7

Interior design by Lewelin Polanco

Printed in the UK by CPI Group (UK) Ltd, Croydon, CR0 4YY

MIX
Paper from
responsible sources
FSC® C020471

To Alice Mayhew, who edited every one of my 19 previous books over 44 years and gave me a lifetime of wisdom and love, and to Carolyn Reidy, our revered and steady captain at Simon & Schuster. I miss them both.

And to the next generation:
Diana Woodward
Tali Woodward
son-in-law Gabe Roth
grandchildren Zadie and Theo

Contents

Author's Personal Note

Evelyn M. Duffy has now assisted me on six books over 13 years on four presidents. A remarkable woman of depth and integrity, she believes that everyone should be held accountable, including and especially me. She is an organizational genius who effectively has acquired multiple PhDs in the presidency, government, journalism and modern life. She insisted that everyone in this book get the fairest treatment possible, including President Trump. She kept her eyes on that prize and worked tirelessly to see it fulfilled. Cheerful and authentic, she has the stamina of half a dozen. As the nominal boss, I realize that her level of engagement is not something that can be required or purchased. It is only something she could give. She did. For Evelyn, it is a way of life. Once again she served as full collaborator and in the spirit—and with the level of effort—of a coauthor.

Steve Reilly came to work with Evelyn and myself just under a year ago. He is one of the hardest workers I've ever seen. "Do you mind if I come in and work Sunday?" was a common request. "Okay," I'd say, without hesitation. He gives new life and meaning to the archetypal image of the dogged, relentless investigative reporter staying all night in the newsroom. He has a gentle and pleasant demeanor, and inwardly is tough as steel. He insists on verification for everything; no fact or nuance goes unchecked. Steve spent five years on *USA Today*'s investigative team and was a finalist for the 2017 Pulitzer Prize for Investigative Reporting. He has innate integrity, kindness and creativity. He is a true digger and searcher of the truth, and I thank him for his immeasurable contributions to this book. He has a great future in journalism, the profession I know he loves.

"I bring rage out. I do bring rage out. I always have. I don't know if that's an asset or a liability, but whatever it is, I do."

Presidential candidate Donald J. Trump in an interview with Bob Woodward and Robert Costa on March 31, 2016, at the Old Post Office Pavilion, Trump International Hotel, Washington, D.C.

"This is when you said to us: 'I bring out rage in people. I bring rage out. I always have. I don't know if it's an asset or a liability. But whatever it is, I do.' Is that true?"

"Yes," Trump said. "Sometimes. I do more things than other people are able to get done. And that, sometimes, can make my opponents unhappy. They view me differently than they view other presidents. A lot of other presidents that you've covered didn't get a lot done, Bob."

President Donald J. Trump in an interview with Bob Woodward for this book, June 22, 2020.

PROLOGUE

◆———◆

During the Top Secret President's Daily Brief the afternoon of Tuesday, January 28, 2020, discussion in the Oval Office turned to a mysterious pneumonia-like virus outbreak in China. Public health officials and President Trump himself were telling the public the virus was low-risk for the United States.

"This will be the biggest national security threat you face in your presidency," Robert O'Brien, the national security adviser, told Trump, expressing a jarring, contrarian view as deliberately and as strongly as possible.

Trump's head popped up. He asked the intelligence PDB briefer, Beth Sanner, several questions. She said China was worried, and the intelligence community was monitoring it, but it looked like this would not be anything nearly as serious as the deadly 2003 Severe Acute Respiratory Syndrome (SARS) outbreak.

"This is going to be the roughest thing you face," persisted O'Brien from his seat around the Resolute Desk, well aware that Trump was only midway through his impeachment trial in the Senate, which had begun twelve days earlier and was consuming his attention. O'Brien believed the national security adviser had to try to see around corners, a duty to warn of an impending disaster. And this problem was urgent, not some geopolitical issue that might happen three years down the road. This virus could develop very quickly in the United States.

O'Brien, 53, a lawyer, author and former international hostage negotiator, was Trump's fourth national security adviser. He had been in the key post only four months and did not consider himself a pound-your-fist-on-the-table kind of person, but he felt passionate that the outbreak was a real threat.

"I agree with that conclusion," said Matt Pottinger, the deputy national security adviser, from a couch further back in the Oval Office. Trump knew Pottinger, 46, who had been with the National Security Council staff for three years since the beginning of the Trump presidency, was uniquely, almost perfectly, qualified to deliver such an assessment.

His warning was authoritative and carried great weight. Pottinger had lived in China seven years and been a *Wall Street Journal* reporter there during the SARS outbreak. A China scholar, he spoke fluent Mandarin.

Affable, profane and a workaholic, Pottinger also was a decorated former Marine intelligence officer, a job that culminated in coauthoring an influential report about the inadequacies of U.S. intelligence agencies.

Pottinger knew firsthand that the Chinese were masters at concealing trouble and covering it up. He had written over 30 stories about SARS and how the Chinese had intentionally withheld information for months about its seriousness and vastly understated its spread, a mishandling that allowed SARS to move around the globe. The *Journal* had submitted his work for a Pulitzer Prize.

"What do you know?" Trump asked Pottinger.

For the last four days, Pottinger said he had been working the phones calling doctors in China and Hong Kong he had maintained contact with and who understood the science. He'd also been reading Chinese social media.

"Is this going to be as bad as '03?" he had asked one of his contacts in China.

"Don't think SARS 2003," the expert replied. "Think influenza pandemic 1918."

Pottinger said he had been floored. The so-called Spanish Flu pandemic of 1918 killed an estimated 50 million people worldwide with about 675,000 deaths in the United States.

"Why do you think it will be worse than 2003?" asked the president.

Pottinger's contacts told him three factors were dramatically accelerating the transmission of the new disease. Contrary to official hedged reports from the Chinese government, people were getting the disease easily from other people, not just animals; this is called human-to-human spread. He had just learned that morning it was being spread by people who didn't show any symptoms; this is called asymptomatic spread. His best, most authoritative source said 50 percent were infected but showed no symptoms. This meant a once-in-a-lifetime health emergency, a virus out of control with a vast amount of the spread not immediately detectable. And it had already traveled far from Wuhan, China, where the outbreak apparently began. To Pottinger, these were the three alarms of a three-alarm fire.

Most troubling, Pottinger said, the Chinese had essentially quarantined Wuhan, a city of 11 million people, larger than any American city. People could not travel within China, say from Wuhan to Beijing. But they had not cut off travel from China to the rest of the world, including the United States. That meant a highly infectious and devastating virus was probably already silently streaming into the U.S.

"What do we do about it?" the president asked.

Cut off travel from China to the United States, Pottinger said.

Pottinger was confident the information from his sources was solid, based on hard data, not speculation. He'd launched an in-depth examination of the new virus. The first case outside China had been reported on January 13 in Thailand. Clearly the virus was spreading human-to-human.

Top officials at the Centers for Disease Control, the nation's chief public health agency, had also been reporting with increasing alarm to Pottinger that they had been trying for weeks to send the crack U.S. disease detectives from the Epidemic Intelligence Service to China to see what was going on. The Chinese had stonewalled, refusing to cooperate and share samples of the virus as required by international agreement.

The head of the Chinese CDC had sounded like a hostage in one phone call, and the Chinese health minister also refused U.S. assistance.

Pottinger had seen this movie before. He picked up the pace of his calls the weekend of January 24–26. "I came out of that weekend with my hair standing on end," Pottinger said privately.

Several Chinese elites well connected with the Communist Party and government signaled that they thought China had a sinister goal: "China's not going to be the only one to suffer from this." If China was the only country to have mass infections on the scale of the 1918 pandemic, they would be at a massive economic disadvantage. It was a suspicion, but one held by the people who knew the regime best. A frightening possibility. Pottinger, a China hawk, was not ready to make a judgment on China's intent one way or the other. Most likely the outbreak was accidental. But he was certain the United States was in for an unparalleled health onslaught. And China's lack of transparency would only make it worse. With SARS the Chinese had egregiously concealed the outbreak of a dangerous new infectious disease for three months.

Three days later, on January 31, the president did impose restrictions on travelers from China, a move opposed by a number of his cabinet members. But his public attention was focused on just about everything except the virus: the upcoming Super Bowl, the technological meltdown in the Democratic caucuses in Iowa, his State of the Union address and, most importantly, the impeachment trial in the Senate. When the highly infectious respiratory disease caused by the novel coronavirus, known as Covid-19, did come up in settings where he had an opportunity to reach a large number of Americans, Trump continued to reassure the public they faced little risk.

"How concerned are you" about coronavirus? Fox's Sean Hannity asked Trump on February 2 near the end of a pre–Super Bowl game interview focused largely on the unfairness of impeachment and his 2020 Democratic rivals.

"We pretty much shut it down coming in from China," Trump said. Something of a pregame presidential tradition, the interview drew the largest ever audience for the controversial and popular talk show host. "We're offering tremendous help. We have the best in the world for that. . . . But we can't have thousands of people coming in who may have this problem, the coronavirus."

That morning, even National Security Adviser O'Brien, who had issued the ominous warning just days earlier, had said on CBS's *Face the Nation*, "Right now, there's no reason for Americans to panic. This is something that is a low-risk, we think, in the U.S."

Two days later on February 4, nearly 40 million Americans tuned in to watch the president's annual State of the Union address, a constitutionally mandated update to Congress about the most pressing issues facing the country. The speech is the highest visibility moment for a president to address matters of great importance. About halfway through the lengthy speech, Trump mentioned coronavirus in one short paragraph. "Protecting Americans' health also means fighting infectious diseases. We are coordinating with the Chinese government and working closely together on the coronavirus outbreak in China," Trump said. "My administration will take all necessary steps to safeguard our citizens from this threat."

That did not, however, include sharing any part of the warning he had received with the public.

When I later asked the president about the warning from O'Brien, he said he didn't recall it. "You know, I'm sure he said it," Trump said. "Nice guy."

And in an interview with President Trump on March 19, six weeks before I learned of O'Brien's and Pottinger's warnings, the president said his statements in the early weeks of the virus had been deliberately designed to not draw attention to it.

"I wanted to always play it down," Trump told me. "I still like playing it down, because I don't want to create a panic."

Trump called me at home about 9:00 p.m. on Friday, February 7, 2020. Since he had been acquitted in the Senate impeachment trial two days earlier, I expected he would be in a good mood.

"Now we've got a little bit of an interesting setback with the virus going in China," he said. He had spoken with President Xi Jinping of China the night before.

"Setback?" I was surprised the virus was on his mind, rather than his acquittal. There were only 12 confirmed cases in the United States. The first reported coronavirus death in the United States was three weeks away. The news had been all impeachment all the time.

The Chinese were very focused on the virus, Trump said.

"I think that that goes away in two months with the heat,"

Trump said. "You know as it gets hotter that tends to kill the virus. You know, you hope."

He added, "We had a great talk for a long time. But we have a good relationship. I think we like each other a lot."

I reminded the president that in earlier interviews for this book he had told me he had harshly confronted President Xi about the Made in China 2025 plan to overtake the United States and become the world's leading producer in high-tech manufacturing in 10 industries from driverless cars to biomedicine. "That's very insulting to me," Trump had told Xi. The president had also said with fierce pride that he was "breaking China's ass on trade" and caused China's annual economic growth rate to go negative.

"Oh, yeah, we've had some arguments," Trump acknowledged.

So what had President Xi said yesterday?

"Oh, we were talking mostly about the virus," Trump said.

Why? I wondered. "Mostly?"

"And I think he's going to have it in good shape," Trump said, "but you know, it's a very tricky situation."

What made it "tricky"?

"It goes through air," Trump said. "That's always tougher than the touch. You don't have to touch things. Right? But the air, you just breathe the air and that's how it's passed. And so that's a very tricky one. That's a very delicate one. It's also more deadly than even your strenuous flus."

"Deadly" was a very strong word. Something was obviously going on here that I was not focused on. Over the next month I would make trips to Florida and the West Coast, oblivious to the mounting pandemic. At this point I also was not aware O'Brien had told the president that the virus "will be the biggest national security threat you face in your presidency." I'd heard no one calling for any change in Americans' behavior other than not traveling to China. Americans went about their daily lives, including more than 60 million who traveled by air domestically that month.

In our call, Trump had surprising detail about the virus.

Trump continued, "Pretty amazing. This is more deadly" than the flu, maybe five times more so.

"This is deadly stuff," Trump repeated. He praised President Xi. "I think he's going to do a good job. He built a number of hospitals in record-setting time. They know what they're doing. They're very organized. And we'll see. We're working with them. We're sending them things, in terms of equipment and lots of other things. And the relationship is very good. Much better than before. It was strained because of the [trade] deal."

My first book on his presidency, *Fear: Trump in the White House*, had been published 17 months before this February 7 phone call. *Fear* described Trump as "an emotionally overwrought, mercurial and unpredictable leader" who had created a governing crisis and "a nervous breakdown of the executive power of the most powerful country in the world."

While discussing *Fear* on television, I was asked for my bottom-line summary of Trump's leadership. "Let's hope to God we don't have a crisis," I said.

Trump had declined to be interviewed for *Fear* but regularly told aides he wished he had cooperated. So for this book he agreed to be interviewed. By February 7, we were on our sixth of what would be 17 interviews.

I asked, "What's the plan for the next eight to 10 months?"

"Just do well," Trump replied. "Just do well. Run the country well."

"Help me define 'well,'" I said.

"Look," Trump said, "when you're running a country it's full of surprises. *There's dynamite behind every door.*"

Years ago, I had once heard a similar expression used by military forces to describe the hazards and nerve-racking emotions of house-to-house searches in a violent combat zone.

I was surprised at this "dynamite behind every door" language from Trump. Instead of being his usual upbeat, cheerleading or angry self, the president sounded foreboding, even unconfident with a touch of unexpected fatalism.

"You want to say, good, but then something happens," Trump continued. "Boeing happens, as an example. Boeing was the greatest company in the world, and all the sudden it has a big, big misstep. And it hurts the country." Boeing is still reeling from problems with its 737-MAX airplane, which had been grounded in 2019 after back-to-back fatal crashes within five months in Indonesia and Ethiopia, killing all 346 people on board.

"General Motors goes out on strike," Trump said, giving another example. Nearly 50,000 autoworkers had held a 40-day strike in the fall of 2019. "They shouldn't have gone. They should have been able to work that out. But they couldn't do it. They go on strike. Hundreds of thousands of people aren't working. All of this stuff happens. And you have to make it good."

"There's dynamite behind every door" seemed the most self-aware statement about the jeopardy, pressures and responsibilities of the presidency I had heard Trump make in public or private.

Yet the unexpected headline from the call was also his detailed knowledge of the virus and his description of it as so deadly so early in February, more than a month before it began to engulf him, his presidency and the United States. And so at odds with his public tone.

The details from his call with Xi were troubling. I only later learned that much more had been hidden: that his top White House national security advisers had warned him of impending disaster in the U.S. and believed China and Xi could not be trusted; that his top health advisers had tried desperately to get their medical team into China to investigate; that Trump himself had offered to help Xi and been personally rebuffed.

Xi was concealing a lot. So was Trump.

Who was responsible for the failure to warn the American

public of the coming pandemic? Where was the breakdown? What leadership decisions did Trump make or fail to make in the crucial early weeks? It would take me months to get answers to those questions.

After reporting *Fear*, I thought it was likely the potential crisis I worried about might arise from foreign affairs where Trump had the least experience and took the greatest risks. So when I began my new reporting for this book last year, well before the arrival of the virus, I decided to look again and more deeply at the national security team he recruited and built in the first months after his election in 2016.

I now see that Trump's handling of the virus—certainly the greatest test for him and his presidency, at least so far—reflects the instincts, habits and style acquired in the first years as president and over the course of a lifetime.

One of the great questions of any presidency is: How does it end? But so is the question: How did it begin? So we turn there.

ONE

◆————◆

Shortly before the Thanksgiving holiday of 2016, retired Marine General James Mattis saw a call from an unknown Indiana number flash on his cell phone screen. Not knowing anyone from there, he ignored it.

He was volunteering at the local Tri-Cities Food Bank in Richland, Washington, his childhood home on the Columbia River, where his mother and brother still lived.

When a second call came from Indiana, he answered.

"This is Mike Pence."

Mattis didn't know a Mike Pence, but quickly realized he was speaking with the vice president–elect.

The president-elect would like to talk to you about the secretary of defense job, Pence said.

I am happy to give him my advice, Mattis said, but I am not eligible. To preserve strict civilian control, the law prohibits anyone who has been a military officer in the last seven years from serving as defense secretary. The only exception had been World War II General George Marshall, who had received a waiver in 1950 and been a national hero.

Given the raging partisan divisions in Washington, Mattis privately believed Democrats in Congress would never support such a waiver.

But Mattis did want to talk to Trump, and agreed to fly east. He wanted to persuade Trump to question his positions on NATO and torture. Trump had called the military alliance "obsolete" and promised to bring back the "enhanced interrogation techniques" on suspected terrorists that President Barack Obama had banned. Mattis thought Trump was wrong on both counts.

One thing was clear in Mattis's mind: He did not want the job. Mattis had boundless love for the Marine Corps, but not Washington, D.C. Mattis had been commander of U.S. Central Command, known as CentCom, from 2010 to 2013, overseeing the wars in Iraq and Afghanistan. He was fired by Obama due to his aggressiveness toward Iran when Obama was negotiating a nuclear deal with Iran.

Shortly after arriving at Trump's golf club in Bedminster, New Jersey, on Saturday, November 19, Mattis was escorted to an informal gathering around a table with Trump, Pence, chief strategist Steve Bannon, Ivanka Trump and Trump's son-in-law, Jared Kushner.

Mattis had a stoic Marine exterior and attention-getting ramrod posture, but his bright, open and inviting smile softened his presence.

Right up front, Trump questioned the value of NATO, which had been formed by ten European countries, the United States and Canada at the end of World War II as a safeguard against Soviet aggression. In 2016 there were 28 member nations.

The other countries of NATO, these European allies, are taking us to the cleaners, Trump said. The United States didn't need NATO. We pay and they get protected. They take us for all we're worth and they're not giving enough in exchange.

No, Mattis insisted, if we didn't have NATO we would have to invent it and build it because we need it so badly. You know how you build your big, tall buildings? You'd build NATO.

Huh? said Trump.

The NATO countries, which pledge that an attack against one is an attack against all, went to war after your hometown of New York City was attacked, Mattis reminded him. NATO troops were sent to Afghanistan after the 9/11 terrorist attacks on the United States. Several of those countries have lost more boys per capita in Afghanistan than we have. They've been bleeding.

Yes, they have to do more, Mattis said. You're absolutely right they need to spend more of their GDP on defense. You're absolutely right to press them. I'll even tell you how I'd take the message to them. We need to let them know that we are not going to keep telling American parents they have to care more about protecting European kids than Europeans care.

But, Mattis continued, NATO held the line against Soviet aggression during the Cold War until the internal rot of the Soviet Union collapsed upon itself. NATO prevented real war on the European continent. We need NATO.

To Mattis's surprise, Trump did not argue. He seemed to be listening.

The president-elect next voiced approval of torture as the quickest way to obtain information from captured terrorists.

Mattis didn't want to spend time explaining the origins of his personal philosophy. He subscribed to the beliefs of General John Lejeune, the legendary World War I general often described as the greatest Marine of all time. Lejeune believed the Corps not only had to make efficient fighters, but return better citizens to society. Inflicting torture caused spiritual damage and produced horrible people, Mattis believed. It undermined the country's moral authority.

Instead, he only said to Trump, "We have to recognize that torture damages us. With a cup of coffee and a cigarette you can get just as much out of them."

Trump was listening attentively, and Mattis was again somewhat surprised.

Next up was the intelligence community, another subject of Trump's criticism during the campaign.

"We have the best spies in the world," Mattis said. "I'm probably the first general in history—for three years at CentCom I was never surprised on a strategic or operational matter. Not once."

Ivanka Trump, the president-elect's daughter, asked how long it would take to review and rewrite the strategy to defeat ISIS, the violent Islamic State of Iraq and Syria terrorist group which had sprung from the remnants of al Qaeda in Iraq and spread into Syria as it tried to create a caliphate in the Arab world.

Trump had promised in the campaign to "knock the hell out of" ISIS. Mattis, surprised the question had come from Ivanka, said it would take months to review. The strategy needed to radically change from a slow war of attrition to one of "annihilation." Time was a key issue. Slow wars were losing ones for the United States.

Mattis could see Trump was proud Ivanka had weighed in.

"Is your name Mad Dog?" Trump asked. "Your nickname?"

"No, sir."

"What is it?"

"Chaos."

"I don't like that name," said Trump.

"Well, that's my name."

"I thought it was Mad Dog."

No, that came from someone else. Mattis blamed the media.

"Do you mind if I change your name to Mad Dog?"

"You can sort of do whatever you want."

"Mad Dog Mattis," Trump said. "That works out great." Can you do the job?

Government service in any form, Mattis believed, was both an honor and an obligation. He hadn't wanted the job, but when the commander in chief called, you accepted without hesitation—no Hamlet wringing his hands at the wall, debating with himself, "To be or not to be."

He said he could. But Trump did not want to announce it publicly yet. Getting a waiver should be easy, he said.

After the 40-minute interview, Trump said they were going to appear before the press. Did Mattis want to say anything?

No, thank you.

Steve Bannon had arranged for the photo of Trump and Mattis to resemble 10 Downing Street—the British prime minister before a large door. The media would be across the street and Trump would be the leader.

"All I can say is he is the real deal!" Trump said to the press. Mattis stood coolly silent.

Trump later tweeted: "General James 'Mad Dog' Mattis, who is being considered for Secretary of Defense, was very impressive yesterday."

Mattis had a general operating philosophy which he articulated many times over the years: "You don't always control your circumstances, but you can control your response."

He called his mother, Lucille, who was 94 years old. She had served in Army intelligence in World War II. He knew she hated Trump.

"How can you work for that man?" she asked.

"Ma, last time I checked, I work for the Constitution. I'll go back and read it again."

"All right," she said. "All right."

TWO

———————◆———————

Right after the election, Rex Tillerson, the longtime CEO of ExxonMobil, received phone messages from Steve Bannon and Jared Kushner. Tillerson, who had run the largest publicly traded oil and gas company in the world for nearly eleven years, was the embodiment of Big Oil. A Texan with a smooth voice and easy laugh, he was a highly disciplined rider and breeder of cutting horses on his 83-acre ranch near Dallas. He ignored their calls.

Then Vice President–elect Pence called. Tillerson decided to take the call.

"The president-elect's been told you know a lot of world leaders," Pence said, "and you know a lot about the current situation around the world. Would you be willing to come up and give him a briefing?"

"I'll be happy to do that," Tillerson said. He often briefed presidents, but he wasn't keen on making a high-visibility walk through the lobby of Trump Tower. "I'm not going to come through those front doors by those gilded elevators and do the press walk."

Pence promised they would slip him in discreetly.

Tillerson, 64, arrived at Trump Tower on December 6 and rode up on the private elevator. With a swept-back mane of gray hair and a big Texas drawl, he stood out. Bannon and the designated White House chief of staff Reince Priebus greeted and escorted him into a side conference room.

"You're not a Never Trumper are you?" Priebus asked.

Tillerson wasn't absolutely sure what that was, but got the idea, and said no.

"Have you ever said anything negative about the president-elect?" Bannon asked.

"Not that I recall, Steve."

"We noticed you didn't contribute anything."

"I don't do political contributions," Tillerson replied, trying to sidestep the question. "I've found it's not particularly healthy in the job I'm in." He was a lifelong Republican. His wife, Renda, had paid $2,500 to go to a Trump lunch.

Records show Tillerson made more than $100,000 in contributions in the 2016 election cycle, including $2,700 to Trump's competitor Jeb Bush. Since 2000 he has made more than $400,000 in contributions.

"Did you vote in the election?"

"Yes."

"Who'd you vote for?"

"I voted for President-elect Trump."

Okay, okay, let's go in and see him.

Tillerson found the political vetting heavy-handed and slightly weird.

Trump was sitting at his desk and rose to greet his visitor. Trump had been such a dominant television presence that to see him in person was a little jarring.

Campaign material—stuffed animals and hats—littered the office. Disneyland, Tillerson thought.

Everyone sat down. Jared Kushner joined them.

"So tell me what's going on around the world," Trump asked.

"You've been dealt a really difficult hand in foreign affairs," Tillerson said. As Exxon's CEO, he traveled the world and met with heads of state. "I've been listening to these world leaders for the last eight years" during the Obama presidency. "The challenges now are as serious as any president has faced in my lifetime."

Tillerson said his closest relationship was with Russian president Vladimir Putin, whom he visited regularly. Oil and gas amounted to over 60 percent of Russia's exports, and Russia was Exxon's biggest oil exploration area in the world, with holdings of more than 60 million acres. Exxon had a 30 percent interest in a Russian production-sharing agreement that produced oil and gas from fields in the Russian Far East. Exxon also had 7.5 percent ownership of a pipeline that transported oil from Kazakhstan to a Russian port on the Black Sea.

Let me tell you a story, Tillerson said, about a meeting with Putin two years before the U.S. presidential election.

"We were down in Sochi having a lunch, and I would always just try to ask questions to Putin and let him do the talking," Tillerson said. It was not hard to get the Russian president to speak openly given Putin's interest in the energy markets and new technologies.

"Well," Putin said, "I've given up on your President Obama. He doesn't do anything he says he's going to do. I can't deal with someone who won't follow through on his promises. I'll wait for your next president." Tillerson said Putin looked directly at him, adding, "I know when that is."

Seeing Trump had visibly perked up at the mention of Putin, Tillerson described an earlier conversation when Putin had said he disagreed with Obama's decision in 2011 to intervene in the Libyan civil war, which resulted in the gruesome death of Libyan leader Muammar al-Qaddafi and the widespread upheaval and civil war it unleashed.

Putin said he had warned Obama. "I said to Obama, I understand you don't like Qaddafi, but what comes after him? He couldn't answer that. So I told him, well, until you can answer that, you shouldn't go in," Tillerson quoted Putin.

"The issue came before the United Nations Security Council," Tillerson continued. "Putin could have blocked it. And Putin told me, 'I called Obama. I told him I'm going to abstain for you.' So Putin I think was trying to say to me, I was trying to work with this guy.

"So fast-forward to Syria," Tillerson continued. "And when Obama drew the red line over the use of chemicals. Putin and Obama talked again. And Putin said, 'Okay, I understand if you think you have to respond to that. But I'm not going to allow you to make the same mistake in Syria that you made in Libya because I have a stake in Syria. So let's understand one another.' That's what Putin told me he said to Obama. So somewhere in the midst of that, Putin came to the conclusion this guy's never going to fix anything. All he does is make it worse.

"Now Libya has turned into a mess," Tillerson said to Trump. "The question you always have to ask yourself is do you know what's going to come next? And of course we know the Libyan revolution helped ISIS. All the bad guys that formed ISIS, Muammar Qaddafi had them locked up in his prison."

Tillerson added, "Putin feels like we treat Russia like a banana republic." The year before, Tillerson said he had been tooling around the Black Sea on Putin's yacht. "And he said to me, 'You need to remember we're a nuclear power. As powerful as you. You Americans think you won the Cold War. You did not win the Cold War. We never fought that war. We could have, but we didn't.' And that put chills up my spine."

There is a significant opportunity here, Tillerson said. "When Putin said the breakup of the Soviet Union was the greatest tragedy of the twentieth century, it wasn't because he loved communism. It was because Russia's stature had been destroyed.

"Anybody who tries to think about Russia in terms of the Soviet era doesn't know a thing about Russia. The seventy years of Soviet rule was a speed bump in Russian history and it had no lasting effect.

"If you want to understand Russia, they haven't changed much culturally in 1,000 years. They are the most fatalistic people on the face of the earth, which is why they're willing to live under lousy leaders. If you ask them about it, they'd say they don't like it, but they'd say 'Das Russia'—'That's Russia.' They'd shrug their shoulders. I would talk to my Russian employees about it. Only one time did Russians rise up in revolution. And that didn't turn out so well. So they look back on that and they say, Don't do that again."

Bottom line, Tillerson said, "You can deal with Putin. Obama was never able to. There is just a fundamental dislike of one another. Putin is a terrible racist, as we all know. All Russians are, generally. And Obama had a terrible disdain for Putin."

Putin has a goal for Russia, Tillerson said. "They want recognition of their role in the global order. And Putin wants respect as a leader of a great country. We've never been willing to give him either.

"Now they view their role in the global world order as equivalent to ours. That's what they seek."

Trump seemed rapt at all this firsthand information about Putin.

Tillerson turned to Asia. "China is a different challenge for you. On the one hand, China's rise, their economy, the lifting of 500 million people out of poverty to middle-class status, all of the economic benefits to the rest of the world—those are all good things.

"But China has gone too far in the South China Sea with the island building." For years, the Chinese had been building military bases on the islands. They had vastly expanded their footprint by dumping sand and muck dredged from the ocean on top of the rock and reef formations, building man-made islands in order to set up more bases with an alarming array of military installations in the highly valuable international trade passage that threatened the U.S. Navy's Pacific domination. Other countries in the region, most notably Japan, lay claim to part of the sea.

"That's going to be your problem," Tillerson said. Also, Hong Kong and Taiwan, he said. "You're going to have to deal with a conflict with China over those.

"Russia is an immediate challenge to you. China is a long-term challenge."

Tillerson continued his round-the-world tour. He talked extensively about the Middle East, where he also knew the leaders. He told Trump how some fifteen years ago he had been talking to Sheikh Mohammed bin Zayed, the powerful crown prince of the Emirates. "He was a pretty young guy. We were talking in his house. And he says, we don't need nuclear weapons. As long as we have friends who have them." The protective nuclear American umbrella was crucial.

The United States still had a dominant role in the world, Tillerson told Trump. "All the aces are still in the cards on the table." In his view the four aces were military strength, economic strength, democracy and freedom, but Trump did not ask what they were.

"Your job is to draw every one of them out with the right politics and tactics," he said, adding confidently, "Those aces belong to the United States of America."

Ivanka Trump came into the room and Trump introduced her. She sat down and Trump stood up theatrically behind his desk.

"I really like everything you said," Trump declared to Tillerson. "You clearly are a guy that knows the world. You've got these relationships. I'm sure you've been following the press. I've been talking to a lot of people about serving in my cabinet. I've got a lot of people that want some of these high-profile jobs."

Uh-oh, Tillerson thought, here it comes, perhaps secretary of energy, a job that would be real easy to decline.

"You're the perfect guy to be my secretary of state," the president-elect said.

Tillerson lurched back.

"You're surprised?" said Bannon.

"Yes, I am surprised," Tillerson said, though he had—perhaps even intentionally—pushed all the buttons on Trump's console, especially on the pathway to Putin. Tillerson then took a breath. "I've got a job," he told Trump.

"But you're going to retire pretty soon," Trump said. He apparently had been prepped that Tillerson was three months away from Exxon's mandatory retirement age of 65. His successor had already been picked and the transition was under way. "This is just three months early," Trump added.

"This will be really hard to do," Tillerson said. "It will be really hard for you. I would not be an easy person to get confirmed, you know. Chairman and CEO of ExxonMobil. We're not exactly the most loved corporation in the world," adding defensively, "undeservedly."

"I really need you," Trump said. "You're the guy."

Now Tillerson, like so many before him, was experiencing the almost irresistible call to presidential service.

"I've got to think this over. I would need to talk to my board, obviously. Look, it's not a simple matter for me. Just personally and financially and my obligations to the ExxonMobil corporation"—40 years. "I don't know if it's doable." He was worth hundreds of millions of dollars and was looking forward to retiring to the horse ranch he and his wife ran.

"When do you think you could give me an answer?" Trump asked.

It was now Tuesday, December 6. "I will commit to give you an answer by Friday."

"I can hold off that long."

Tillerson called his wife, Renda, from the car and said, "You're not going to believe what just happened."

"He asked you to be secretary of state," she said.

"Well, how'd you know?"

"I told you God's not through with you."

In the car, Tillerson took stock and settled in for a little intro-spection. Had he failed to conceal a yearning from Renda? This was the job held by Jefferson, Madison, Monroe, Marshall. Fourth in line to the presidency. Had he hid his ambition even from him-self? What did he really want? Whose interests should he serve? Could he find the proper version of all his obligations? To Renda, Exxon, the country and now, of all things, Donald Trump?

Back home, Renda had some answers. As you've approached retirement you've become irritable, she said. Subconsciously, she believed, he was worried about that terrible question: What am I going to do?

"Look," she told him, "you've been in training for this for the last twenty years. You are supposed to help this man. He needs your help. You need to go help him."

Tillerson thought he had every reason in the world not to take the job. If Renda had not said all that to him, he believed he would have talked himself out of it.

He had not served in the military and always felt uneasy about that. Was this his time to serve his country? For the moment, he had the upper hand. Trump was waiting for his answer. So he called Reince Priebus.

"I've got three questions for the president-elect," he said.

"Okay, shoot. What are they?"

"Reince, I'm not going to give them to you. I've got to ask them of the president face-to-face. I have to see his answers."

Priebus arranged for Tillerson to see Trump at his residence in New York on Saturday.

Tillerson meanwhile talked to longtime Republican friends who had served as secretary of state—Condoleezza Rice (four years for George W. Bush), James A. Baker III (three years for George H. W. Bush) and George Shultz (six years for Ronald Reagan). He reminded them he was coming from Big Oil and he did not want to cause a problem for himself or the newly elected president. They were public service mavens. The advice was unanimous: You must do it. When the president asks, if it is in the realm of the possible and if it is legal, you respond with a yes.

Tillerson visited Trump at his residence in private.

"I want the freedom to pick my own people," he asked the president-elect. "I understand if there's somebody that's just highly objectionable to you," Tillerson said. In the end, it was the president's decision and responsibility to nominate someone. "But I hope I'll have the freedom to put the team together that I feel I'll need to help you."

"Done," Trump said.

"The second question, I want your assurance that when we get into this, you will never withdraw my nomination. Because I'm going to be a very difficult confirmation." He was aware that presidents often folded when controversy hit. The Big Oil executive would inevitably draw fire. "And I don't want you spending any of your political capital on me. I'll get this done myself, or I won't get it done. And if they vote me down, it's not the end of my life. I'll go home and pick up where I left off. You've got to assure me you won't give up and give in."

"Okay," Trump said. "They're going to confirm you. It's not going to be a big deal. Don't even worry about that."

Third, Tillerson said, "I want you to promise me that we are never going to have a public dispute, because that doesn't serve anyone."

In the New York real estate world, Trump had built a decades-long reputation for disparaging former business and romantic partners in the tabloid press after relationships turned sour.

"If you're unhappy with me, call me and ream my ass out," Tillerson said. "It's all behind closed doors. Because when I walk out that door, I serve you and the American people. I will not disparage anybody. It's just not in my nature."

"Don't worry," Trump said, "we're going to get along splendidly."

THREE

On December 1, in Cincinnati at his first rally on his election "thank you" tour, Trump announced, "We are going to appoint Mad Dog Mattis as our secretary of Defense." The name Mad Dog was going to stick.

For his second "thank you" rally, in Fayetteville, North Carolina, the following week, the president-elect asked Mattis to join him as he formally introduced him as his nominee for secretary of defense on December 6. The event was being held near Fort Bragg, the home of the Army Special Operations Command and the famed 82nd Airborne Division. Bad weather kept them from flying in, so Mattis joined Trump for the long car ride in the rain through the North Carolina woods.

At one point, Trump confided he had chosen Rex Tillerson to be his secretary of state.

Tillerson will be great, perfect, Trump said, gushing about the Exxon CEO. This man has presence. He'd run one of the world's largest, most successful organizations. Not part of the Washington establishment, untainted by the swamp. He was a dealmaker who negotiated oil contracts all over the world, including billions with Russia. For years he has negotiated with Putin, who awarded him the Russian Order of Friendship. Trump spoke as if he had hired the Michael Jordan of diplomacy. He loved that the Tillerson pick would defy all the conventional wisdom.

Mattis had never heard Trump talk about anyone with such admiration and respect.

God, Mattis thought, this is going to be great.

Since his retirement from the Marines three years earlier, Mattis had spent a good deal of time as a research fellow at the Hoover Institution, a conservative public policy think tank at Stanford University. Hoover had begun as a library started by President Herbert Hoover and was a comfortable perch for Mattis, who had 7,000 books in his personal library and was often referred to as the "Warrior Monk."

At Hoover, he had befriended George Shultz, treasury secretary under Nixon and secretary of state under Reagan. Mattis was struck by an admonition in Shultz's memoir about the necessity of having a stiff spine. When you disagreed with the president you served, you had to preserve your independence and hold your ground.

"To do the job well, you can't want it too much," Shultz told Mattis as he left Hoover.

After spending Christmas with his mother in Richland, Washington, Mattis flew to Washington, D.C. He heard Tillerson was in town too, and called him at his hotel on December 28.

"This is Jim Mattis," he said. They hadn't met, but "we might be working together."

"Let me buy you dinner," Tillerson said. "I'm living at the Jefferson Hotel. Why don't you come on over tonight?"

Mattis, habitually early, was the first to arrive at the hotel's

Michelin-starred Plume restaurant. He slid into his seat at a special table set aside by staff in a discreet alcove in the back to give them privacy.

When Tillerson arrived and was shown to the alcove, he noticed Mattis was wearing a white shirt and a tie but no jacket. When Mattis stood, Tillerson glanced at his blue jeans and tennis shoes. "You and I are going to get along," Tillerson said.

Tillerson believed you needed to know someone's life story, their early years, to really understand who they were. He shared his. Raised in a lower-middle-class family in Texas, Tillerson had worked as a busboy and a janitor and had picked cotton on the weekends. His father delivered milk in a truck. Central to his life, Tillerson said, were the Boy Scouts. He had been an Eagle Scout and most recently president of the national Boy Scouts.

"Have you got family that are coming back to Washington with you?" Tillerson asked.

"Never been married," Mattis said. "I was married to the Marine Corps." He gave a summary of his 40-year career from the very bottom to four stars.

In some ways, Tillerson had also been wed to one institution. "At Exxon, I was always just so pleased to get a paycheck every two weeks," Tillerson said. "They moved me around so much. By the time that I'd started figuring what I was doing, they'd move me to something I knew nothing about. And I'd have to start all over."

They turned to their international experience. Mattis had served in the Gulf War and in Afghanistan and Iraq before rising to CentCom commander. Tillerson said he knew the world, having lived in Yemen, where he had run Exxon operations. "It's almost like I've been on a 40-year listening tour."

On Russia, Tillerson told Mattis about his longtime relationship with Putin, providing a shorter version than the one he had given Trump. But his bottom line was the same: The new president would have an opening with Putin and could perhaps even develop a constructive relationship.

Mattis did not agree with Tillerson. For him Russia, especially when it aligned with China, remained an ongoing threat and was not to be trusted.

Mattis and Tillerson were on a path neither could have possibly imagined six weeks earlier. They gingerly acknowledged that Trump might be a difficult boss. The new president was a student of Roy Cohn's epic counterattacks, a bankrupt casino owner, a womanizer and a reality television star of *The Apprentice* who clearly relished bestowing the trademark "You're fired!" on contestants.

Mattis proposed an idea born of experience.

Over the last 40 years, Mattis said, there had been some years when relations between the secretary of state and secretary of defense had been so bad they did not speak to each other or even so much as cross the Potomac River and shake hands.

"Jim," Tillerson said, "how can that be? I understand they might not like each other," but a collapsed working relationship seemed impossible and counterproductive.

Mattis explained there was nearly always tension between State and Defense.

For example, Secretary of State George Shultz complained privately that Defense Secretary Caspar Weinberger was wary and reluctant to use the military other than to deter the Soviet Union and prevent World War III. Even as the leader of the Defense Department he wanted diplomacy to solve all other problems around the world.

Shultz, in contrast, believed power and diplomacy needed to work in tandem. He characterized his difference with Weinberger as "a battle royal."

Mattis said the one exception he had witnessed to State-Defense combat occurred when he was a colonel and military assistant to Secretaries of Defense William Perry and William Cohen during the later Bill Clinton years from 1996 to 1998. At the time, Madeleine Albright was secretary of state and Sandy Berger was national security adviser. The trio of Albright, Cohen and Berger had regular lunches and meetings. "Every week they settled things," Mattis said.

Because President Clinton was focused on domestic matters and then later consumed by the Whitewater investigation and his eventual impeachment for lying about an affair with White House intern Monica Lewinsky, foreign and defense policy received little presidential attention. If the three—Cohen, Albright and Berger—presented a united front with a recommended course of action, Clinton would approve.

"The issues were probably appropriate that they be settled that way," Mattis told Tillerson. The process served the interests, Mattis believed, of both Clinton and the foreign policy team.

A vivid example occurred in the middle of the impeachment of Clinton in December 1998. Iraqi dictator Saddam Hussein had repeatedly refused to admit weapons inspectors into facilities suspected of making weapons of mass destruction as required by a United Nations resolution. Cohen and the others told Clinton he had to bomb Iraq to establish his credibility and prove the United States was serious. The secretary of defense proposed an operation called Desert Fox, consisting of 650 bomber or missile sorties against 100 targets. This was no pinprick like Reagan's 11-minute bombing of Libya by 30 Air Force and Navy bombers.

Clintonites in the White House were worried such a military action would be seen as a "wag the dog" tactic to distract from impeachment.

Cohen, backed by Albright and Berger, argued the opposite. "A failure to take action now will undercut our credibility," Secretary Cohen told Clinton at a National Security Council meeting. "Our word is at stake. If we don't carry it out, we're going to be tested in the future. If you don't act here, the next argument will be that you're paralyzed" by the impeachment proceedings.

Clinton acquiesced. "I can't consider anything else," he said. "I have no choice."

Desert Fox lasted three days. The operation killed or wounded 1,400 Iraqi military personnel, according to U.S. estimates. Saddam's ambitions were tamed for several years.

We should work together in a similar way, Mattis said. "I think our foreign policy has been militarized over the last twenty years." Too many wars, too many military actions. "I have seen too many boys die."

Mattis had a startling proposal for Tillerson. "I want you in the lead on foreign policy. I'll tell you what we can do, what I can't do. I'll tell you the risks. But when we get done, I don't want the White House sorting it out between the two of us. You and I will sort it all out. And so let's meet weekly. Let's talk as often as necessary. When we walk in the White House, we're joined at the hip." Mattis held two fingers together to illustrate the unity. "That's the way it is."

Tillerson loved the plan. "I promise," he said. "I don't know how to even begin to formulate solutions to some of our foreign policy challenges if I don't have the military standing right up against my back." He arched his back and placed his hand on his spine for support. "Otherwise the guys"—the foreign diplomats—"I'm talking to aren't going to pay a bit of attention to me."

"You're going to be in the driver's seat for foreign policy," Mattis said. "The bus would be driven by State Department diplomats." Mattis would enhance the power of the diplomats by pressuring the military side, being tough. "Any country dealing with us would listen to their diplomats, because they didn't want to deal with me"—Mattis and the powerful U.S. military.

Tillerson saw they had quickly closed on a working agreement. State and Defense would never go into a National Security Council meeting without having worked out a common position. If an open issue existed, they would find a common position.

As a general, Mattis's job had been to carry out orders from the civilians—president, secretary of defense and National Security Council. But now he had to shift. He was no longer there just to carry out policy—"no cheery aye-aye, sir." Tillerson and he were there to construct policy.

Mattis was surprised how simpatico he felt with Tillerson. He just knew he could work with him. Sometimes you sit down with someone and you know you can trust them.

Mattis continued, "My job is to try to keep the peace, or what passes for peace in this troubled world." Mattis often liked to say, "Keep the peace one more year, one more month, one more day, one more hour as you guys [diplomats] work your magic." America is still an inspiration, he added, but "Intimidation is necessary. That's what I exist for. But it should generally be the last resort."

Both men left Plume confident they would make it work between State and Defense.

Mattis spent the first three weeks in Washington preparing for his confirmation hearings, a period normally focused on meetings with senators who would vote on his nomination. Republican senators found him appealing, a consummate professional. But he quickly met a wall of silence from the Democrats in Congress. Not even routine courtesy calls. Then endorsements came from former Republican defense secretaries Donald Rumsfeld and Robert Gates, and former Democratic defense secretary Leon Panetta. Word began to spread that Mattis was the "good" Trump nominee.

Suddenly Senate Democratic Leader Chuck Schumer opened the door. Mattis experienced an unexpected flood of attention. The Democrats couldn't see enough of him. He even met with democratic socialist Bernie Sanders and Mazie Hirono of Hawaii, bringing to about 50 the number of senators he met with from both parties. He seemed to be on a good footing for his confirmation.

During the confirmation process, the CIA and Defense Intelligence Agency gave him in-depth briefings, but protocol prevented any real contact with senior military leaders in the Pentagon. He could not presume he would be confirmed. But Mattis kept asking for the strategy. What was the plan? What was the current theory of the case for defending the United States? Trump made many promises during the campaign. How would they fit into the overall strategy?

But Mattis was not getting any answers. If he had learned one thing from his 40 years on active duty, it was essential to think these matters through, weigh them, debate them, test them against history. It was gut-wrenching to be shut off from such critical matters.

Mattis received his waiver and the Senate confirmed him, 98 to 1.

Later Tillerson was confirmed by the Senate 56 to 43, winning four votes from the Democratic Caucus. Trump gave him his personal cell phone number and said he could call him 24/7 and he would take the call. Trump also agreed to give Tillerson an hour on Tuesdays and Thursdays when the two of them would meet alone. Also, on Fridays, Trump would have lunch with both Tillerson and Mattis when all were in town.

FOUR

Just days after the election, Senator Dan Coats, an Indiana Republican, also received a call from Pence, one of his closest friends and confidants.

A calm and gentlemanly devout Christian, the 73-year-old Coats had served sixteen years in the Senate.

"You want a job?" Pence, a born-again Christian himself, asked Coats.

"No, no," Coats said, "I don't want a job!"

Pence knew Coats was on a different path. Pence, when governor of Indiana, had invited Coats and his wife, Marsha, to stop by for dinner with him and his wife, Karen, at Aynes House, the governor's retreat in a rolling, wooded area about 45 minutes outside Indianapolis in Brown County.

Religion was a central force in the Coatses' life. Dan and Marsha had met at Wheaton College, an evangelical liberal arts college in Illinois, 50 years earlier. The Wheaton College motto is

"For Christ and His Kingdom." Evangelist Billy Graham was a dominant and abiding influence at the school.

In a lengthy prayer session, the four agreed they needed to make some decisions about their futures. Should Pence run for president or a second term as governor? Should Coats seek another term in the Senate?

"We talked about the future and where God might lead each of us," Coats later explained. "We prayed that God would be clear, and I think I raised the question that we should pray for clarity, not for what we want but clarity for what God would want."

Coats did not believe any of them had a special line to God. "It is just simply built into our faith that ultimately we are his children, and he has a plan for us. And we don't know what it is, and our job is to be obedient to ask for clarity, and then to fulfill it."

Pence recounted the Old Testament story of David, who was hiding from King Saul in a cave when God sent a spider to weave a web across the cave opening. On seeing the web, Saul did not enter the cave. The spider had concealed David's presence and saved his life. The story showed that even a spider might be an instrument of great salvation in the hand of God.

Marsha Coats, whose grandparents were ministers, had never heard a sermon as serious and deep. The story raised obvious questions. Could a spider, normally a cause for fear, bring salvation?

By the end of the dinner, two decisions emerged. Coats would not run for another Senate term after his term ended, and Pence would not run for president.

Pence's unexpected selection as Trump's running mate had taken them all by surprise.

In their post-election call, Pence proposed Coats come speak to Trump even if he did not want a job. He could describe how the Senate works.

Coats had been around long enough to know this was a recruitment tactic dressed up as a request for wise guidance. Coats bit anyway. In late November, he traveled to see the president-elect at Trump Tower in New York City. Coats was uneasy. When the *Access Hollywood* tape revealing Trump's lewd comments about women surfaced during the campaign, Coats had blasted his party's nominee on Twitter: "Donald Trump's vulgar comments are totally inappropriate and disgusting."

"So you want a job," said Trump, acting as if he was unaware of or didn't care about Coats's earlier comments.

"No, no, I don't want a job."

"How about becoming an ambassador?"

"I've been an ambassador," Coats said. He had served four years as ambassador to Germany for George W. Bush.

"How about Russia or China?" Trump asked, suggesting that would be a promotion.

Coats explained he had been banned from Russia several years earlier because of his vocal criticism of the Russian invasion of Crimea.

"That's great," Trump said, adding, "We'll send you to Russia and that'll really stick it to them!" Trump was clearly basking in his role as the future president.

Just then Trump was informed that Harold Hamm, a billionaire Oklahoma oilman and big Trump money man, had arrived.

"Bring him in," Trump said. The more people around the better, it seemed. "This guy, he sticks a straw in the ground and up comes fucking oil," Trump said. "Wherever he drills, he finds oil."

The discussion quickly turned away from Coats to Hamm. Almost as an afterthought, Trump said he would call Coats about a job.

Coats left Trump Tower and didn't hear anything for a few months. But a month after their meeting, Pence phoned again. "The president would like you to be director of national intelligence."

Coats paused. The role, often referred to in its abbreviation DNI or as the intelligence czar, had been created in the wake of the massive information and coordination failures before the 9/11 terrorist attacks. This was one of the biggest jobs the president could offer—the top position in the intelligence world overseeing 17 intelligence agencies including the CIA and the National Security Agency, which intercepted worldwide communications. As a member of the Senate Intelligence Committee, Coats knew the post of DNI would virtually guarantee him admission to the president's national security inner circle and the very center of the central nervous system of the American espionage establishment and its secrets.

Still, Coats was reluctant. Marsha urged him to take the job. "Such an awesome position, and powerful and kind of frightening," she said.

She understood her husband's uneasiness about Trump. He had split the Republican Party. Republican members of her own family had told her before the election they could not vote for Trump, even when he looked like the presumptive nominee. Marsha was the sole Republican committeewoman for Indiana, appointed by Pence three years earlier.

She asked her family members, who are you going to vote for, then?

We probably won't vote, they said.

That's not right, she said. They were Republicans. "As Americans, you need to vote. And that's part of what living in a democracy is all about."

One outspoken relative said of Trump, "He's not a Christian. He's not a nice person. He's not a moral man."

By then Marsha had sorted out her own position on Trump. Privately she knew he was, as she put it, "a philanderer and a womanizer, no doubt about that." Trump was pro-life, however, and he had promised to fund a stronger military.

The family would not budge. As committeewoman, she needed to deliver the state of Indiana to the Republicans. And after Trump won the Indiana primary, Marsha Coats weighed in with a stark declaration of her endorsement in a public letter to fellow Indiana Republicans.

"I fear if we do not unite to support Donald Trump, we will again open the door for at least another four years of Washington implementing a left-wing agenda," she wrote. "Conservatives stand to lose not only the White House and control of the executive agencies but also the Supreme Court.

"As a conservative, pro-life, evangelical, female Republican, I understand the conflict many in our party feel about supporting Donald Trump. Trump was not my first or even my second choice. He is not a humble man.

"I truly believe the office will change Donald Trump. I believe it will humble him. And I think even Donald will be impelled to turn to God for guidance."

Dan Coats had even handed a copy of his wife's open letter to Trump when the Republican nominee was in Indiana. Later Trump ran into Marsha Coats and promised, "I won't let you down." He put his arm round her and said to others there in a friendly, warm way, "She scolded me."

"Trump is so controversial," she later said to an associate. "He's the kind of person that would inspire crazy people."

Dan Coats accepted the DNI post. He concluded Pence was trying to seed the Trump cabinet with allies, people who shared his religious values, and he agreed to be nominated. As a former senator, he was easily confirmed in an 85 to 12 vote.

Real life set in immediately. Security personnel tore up the Coatses' Northern Virginia home to set up a Sensitive Compartmented Information Facility (SCIF) in the basement of their three-story house to handle the most important and highly classified information. Cameras and a sophisticated security system also were installed, and intelligence and security personnel began manning the basement SCIF around the clock. Outside, security teams in 12-hour shifts sat in a car in front of their house. Privacy no longer existed. With all the people and apparatuses, Coats and his wife even worried that they were being spied on.

Soon after starting the job and attending his third intelligence briefing to the president, the President's Daily Brief, Coats asked for some time alone with Trump.

"Mr. President," Coats said, "there will be times when I will be walking in here to brief you on intelligence, and you're not going to be happy with what I have to say." That was his job, and he wanted the president to know it was not personal. Coats felt the declaration sort of freed him up.

In his first three months as DNI, Coats felt utterly overwhelmed. The intelligence culture was radically different from his world. His liberal arts and law degree background had been just right for the Senate. But the intelligence community was dominated by scientists, engineers and mathematicians, all driving the extraordinary technology of modern intelligence collection. Everyone talked in acronyms, codewords and ever-increasing levels of classification and special compartments for sensitive programs. Intel was rolling in from outer space to the sea bottom and everywhere in between.

Adding to the disorientation, Coats never knew which Trump he'd find in residence when he walked into the Oval Office three times a week for the President's Daily Brief. The PDB was designed to give—and showcase—the most useful inside and high-level sensitive intelligence about national security issues. Some days, Trump would be in a fine mood, even good. Other days Trump would lash out abusively. "I don't trust the intelligence," he said, making it clear he saw the intelligence people as enemies.

To help reduce the stress, Marsha fixed nice dinners with wine, a special pleasure because they had once signed pledges at Wheaton College not to drink.

"Was it a good day or a bad day?" she would ask carefully, but with intense curiosity.

"It was a good meeting today," he said sometimes. The president listened, asked good questions. Trump was smart and could be engaging and even charming.

Then there were bad days. "The president didn't really want to hear the information, or if he heard it, he would disagree with it, say, I don't believe that."

Coats had hours of reading to finish at night, and the travel was nonstop. He'd regularly spend 23 or 24 hours on a plane to go to and get back from a conference in Singapore, for example.

The difference between his old friend Pence's relationship to the intelligence agencies and Trump's was stark. Pence visited all the U.S. intelligence agencies, spending two or three hours, wanting to learn, building up morale. Trump turned down Coats's invitations to tour the NSA or elsewhere. Determined to convince the president of the intelligence agencies' worth, Coats decided to bring the intelligence directors to the Oval Office. He asked each: What are your crown jewels of collection? He was looking for the incredible stuff that gave the United States a degree of security unimaginable to an outsider.

Trump responded best when Coats brought a Navy submarine captain to the Oval Office. The handsome, charismatic officer looked like a movie star. He described Top Secret programs that could track the submarines of Russia and China. In another program, United States submarines could pick up expended missiles off the bottom of the ocean that had been launched by adversaries.

Whoa! Trump said. That guy's really something.

But the bad days were more frequent. Coats began to think Trump was impervious to facts. Trump had his own facts: Nearly everyone was an idiot, and almost every country was ripping off the United States. The steady stream of ranting was debilitating. The tension never abated, and Coats would not bend facts to suit the president's preconceptions or desires. Coats was shocked. "Trump was on a different page than just about anything I believed in."

Trump's habit of tweeting at all hours of the day and night, including about important foreign policy matters, was personally disruptive for Coats. He found himself waking up in the middle of the night thinking, oh my God, what has he tweeted? Finally, Coats decided he would look at the tweets in the morning, concluding he could not let himself get in the habit of thinking he had to wake up at 2:00 or 3:00 a.m. just to see if there were any tweets. It was also clear to Coats that the tweeting meant Trump was not sleeping. What were the president's sleep hours? Coats heard the president was starting his work day later and later, now 11:30 a.m. Maybe that was a clue.

Marsha was stunned at her husband's reports about the president's arrogance. "Who could go into this office of being president and not realize how inadequate they are? Anybody would feel like they needed divine help in order to tackle that job and do it well."

Marsha, who had a degree in psychology and had once had a family-counseling practice, worried that her husband was dragging. He was losing weight. His shirts were hanging loosely on his body.

"Dan," she said one night, "you're going to be a failure at this job if you don't start eating and sleeping and believing in yourself.

"You are disrespecting God. God put you here." If you are not doing the job, she said, you are letting down not just the country or Trump. Being director of national intelligence was part of God's plan for him. He was letting God down.

Marsha was tired of his complaining. "You wouldn't be in this position if the Lord didn't believe you were the right man for the job."

FIVE

◆───◆

B radley Byers, 38, a former Marine F-18 fighter pilot who had flown combat missions in Afghanistan and Iraq, joined Mattis's office as a civilian liaison to the White House. He was part of a so-called "Beachhead Team" of three dozen Trump appointees at the Pentagon who did not have to be confirmed by the Senate. They were supposed to work in Mattis's suite of offices at the Pentagon and give the White House leverage in Mattis's operation.

The first week of the Trump administration, Trump was scheduled to come to the Pentagon on January 27 for a ceremonial swearing in of Mattis. The president also was in a dead sprint to sign as many executive orders as possible to demonstrate how he was changing government and overturning Obama's legacy. He planned to sign some at the Pentagon.

"Brad," Mattis said in the morning, "what executive orders does the president intend to sign?"

Byers did not know but promised to find out. He called and emailed the White House staff secretary's office and cabinet affairs. The orders for the day were still being edited. There had been no NSC or cabinet meetings. Eventually the executive orders were sent by email.

Trump was arriving. The orders were printed out and each put in a leather folder.

Byers finally looked at the second one, titled "Protecting the Nation from Foreign Terrorist Entry into the United States." It was a travel ban preventing people from seven majority-Muslim countries from entering the United States.

Six months earlier, as a civilian, Mattis had publicly criticized candidate Trump's proposed ban on Muslim immigrants. In the Middle East, Mattis had said, "they think we've completely lost it. This kind of thing is causing us great damage right now, and it's sending shock waves."

Mattis was ceremonially sworn in at the Pentagon's Hall of Heroes, which honored more than 3,000 service members who had received the Congressional Medal of Honor, the highest combat award. He thanked Trump and Pence and welcomed them to "the headquarters of your military, your always loyal military, where America's awesome determination to defend herself is on full display."

Trump, professing "total confidence" in Mattis, called him "a man of total action. He likes action."

As the ceremony came to a close, Trump signed the travel ban order and handed it to Mattis. Mattis was stunned.

As soon as the news broke, some veterans in the Congressional Medal of Honor Society immediately conveyed their fury that the hall had been used as a staging ground for the controversial travel ban. Their blunt message to Mattis: That's not what we fought for.

Mattis felt it was a gross process error. There was no process. Who was deciding these things?

The travel ban, which began as a campaign promise Trump made in December 2015 when he called for "a total and complete shutdown of Muslims entering the United States until our country's representatives can figure out what the hell is going on," became a symbol of Trump's anti-immigrant attitudes and policies.

On March 19, 2017, *The Washington Post* ran an article saying that many in the Pentagon privately called Byers "the commissar," a Soviet-era communist official who was supposed to monitor the loyalty of commanders.

Mattis saw the article and asked Byers to stick around after the morning meetings.

"I suppose you read the article," Mattis said. "If you're going to float around these circles, you better get used to it. They will either figure out the bad stuff about you, or they'll make it up." He told some funny stories about times he thought the press got it wrong about him when he was a general.

When Byers left the office, a large group was standing outside for another meeting.

"Hey, young man," Mattis said loudly, so everyone could hear, "you keep your sense of humor. And when all else fails, fuck 'em!"

"So the White House thinks you're their guy," Mattis later told Byers, "and I've got you." Mattis made it clear he did not want any daylight in public between himself and President Trump on any issue. That way Mattis could have influence. Any public daylight could be fatal.

In early April, Trump ordered a modest response of 59 Tomahawk missiles at Syria's Shayrat Airbase as punishment for Bashar al-Assad's use of chemical weapons.

The next morning, Trump phoned Mattis at the Pentagon in what was supposed to be a congratulatory call. Mattis put Trump on the speakerphone and some of the senior staff gathered around his desk to listen.

Trump had seen photos of the damage. "I can't believe you didn't destroy the runway!" the president shouted. He was in a rage and seemed beside himself.

"Mr. President," Mattis finally responded, "they would rebuild the runway in 24 hours and it would have little effect on their ability to deploy weapons. We destroyed the capability to deploy weapons" for months. That was the mission the president had approved, and they had succeeded.

In April, Byers carried a letter from Secretary of Commerce Wilbur Ross to Mattis about an investigation into steel and aluminum tariffs the president, a strong believer in tariffs, had ordered. The president believed domestic production of steel was in jeopardy because of cheaper foreign imported steel.

"Brad," Mattis said after reading the letter, "I've got North Korea, I've got Syria, I've got the Horn of Africa all on fire. I don't give a shit about steel." But he did care about the alliance with South Korea—a major exporter of steel. Any tariff could severely damage the critical relationship. "Deal with it," Mattis said.

Mattis sent a memo to the White House reporting that "U.S. military steel usage represents one-half percent of the total U.S. steel demand" and the military would be able "to acquire the steel necessary to meet national defense requirements."

Byers kept Mattis informed weekly, if not daily, about White House tariff discussions. Dealing with it meant that Byers literally took Mattis's place at the cabinet-level meetings.

At 10:00 a.m. on June 26, Byers sat at Mattis's placard in the Roosevelt Room for the cabinet-level meeting on steel tariffs. Byers took notes. The debate turned on how best to impose tariffs. Byers found the lack of context or definition of the problem rendered the talks aimless.

"The president is expecting to come in," said Reince Priebus, the chief of staff. "I'm going to advise him that we're not ready for him." He left for the Oval Office and came back in about two minutes. "Against my advice," the chief of staff said, visibly nervous, "the president wants to hear this debate."

Soon Trump walked in and everyone stood.

"We're going to put a tariff on all steel and aluminum, on everything coming in," the president said, "and see what happens."

This approach drove Gary Cohn, the chief White House economic adviser, crazy. He had argued passionately that the American economy was too important to haphazardly experiment with.

The president added that they should not worry about NAFTA, the North American Free Trade Agreement, which he was trying to renegotiate. Then he shifted to trade deficits, especially with South Korea.

"We are a consumer-driven economy," Cohn said, reminding the president of the consequences of imposing tariffs. "And the prices are going to go up. And that's going to have a significant impact on our gross domestic product"—overall economic growth.

"We need three percent gross domestic product growth," Mick Mulvaney, the director of the Office of Management and Budget, agreed, "or we are out of business."

"The world is taking advantage of us," Trump said, batting away their concerns, "and it's time for a change. I would love to leave South Korea." America was being taken advantage of. The United States was paying to keep 30,000 troops in South Korea to protect South Koreans. "We are the piggy bank that everyone wants to rob."

Trump was jovial and dropped several F-bombs. "Don't worry about everything."

Cohn offered one more argument against steel tariffs. "We're not a steel-producing nation. We're a goods-producing nation. If we increase the price of steel, our goods become overpriced and we can't compete."

The internal White House war for and against tariffs continued.

Byers was in the Oval Office, seated by the Resolute Desk, on July 21 as Trump signed an executive order to assess how to strengthen the manufacturing and defense industrial base.

"You were a wrestler?" Trump asked Byers.

"Yes, sir, I was," Byers replied. He had been the captain of the North Carolina wrestling team for two years and qualified three times for the NCAA championships. "Why would you ask?"

"Those ears," the president said. "You have wrestling ears." This was classic cauliflower ear, the buildup of fibrous tissue from repeated impacts. "Were you any good?"

"Yes, sir. I can hold my own."

"I bet you were good," Trump said. "You know what? I would've been a great wrestler. I never wrestled in my life, but I would've been a great wrestler. You know why?"

"No sir. Why?"

"Because I'm tough," Trump said. "And you've got to be tough to be a wrestler."

Trump had hosted several pro-wrestling events and even participated in a "Battle of the Billionaires" in 2007. He was inducted into the World Wrestling Entertainment Hall of Fame in 2013.

Trump signed the executive order and they all posed for a picture. The group included White House trade adviser Peter Navarro.

"Peter," Trump said, "I need you to take charge of negotiations on steel." Trump said that U.S. trade representative Robert Lighthizer and Commerce Secretary Wilbur Ross were weak negotiators and that Navarro needed to be tough, hard-line.

Trump added, "Not to mention my fucking generals are a bunch of pussies. They care more about their alliances than they do about trade deals."

Navarro appeared to be flattered by Trump's remark and said he would be happy to take over the negotiations.

Once Byers returned to the Pentagon, he asked Mattis for a private meeting. They met alone the next day.

"What's on your mind?" Mattis asked.

There was an interchange in the Oval Office involving the president that I should tell you about, and it's very uncomfortable, Byers said.

"Brad, don't you worry at all," Mattis said. "Just tell me what happened."

Byers explained the president had mentioned that generals weren't tough enough on steel and aluminum tariffs and were more worried about alliances.

"Tell me exactly what he said."

The president said, Byers recounted, "my fucking generals are a bunch of pussies. They care more about their alliances than they do about trade deals."

Byers could see the secretary's mind racing to assess the situation. For the president to speak that way in front of a subordinate like Byers and others was a gross violation of a basic Leadership 101 principle—praise in public, criticize in private.

"Brad," Mattis said, "I really appreciate your telling me that. Would you mind putting that in an email for me?"

Byers followed Mattis's order and wrote an email to document what had occurred.

SIX

On January 26, 2017, the sixth day of the Trump presidency, Matt Pottinger—then head of Asia policy for the National Security Council staff and not yet the deputy national security adviser—was summoned to a meeting with the new president.

Trump said that President Obama had told him that North Korea would be his biggest, most dangerous and most time-consuming problem. Kim Jong Un, the 32-year-old erratic leader, had nuclear weapons and could be well on his way to building an intercontinental ballistic missile that could reach the United States.

What should I do? Trump asked Pottinger.

Pottinger thought the Obama administration policy toward North Korea of "strategic patience" had been a disaster. As he saw it, the strategy had broadly been to hope the regime fell apart on its own and crawled to the negotiating table.

Within a month Pottinger had options for Trump—literally nine, but better understood as three big options with shades of difference. The range went from accepting North Korea as a nuclear power all the way to regime change either through CIA covert action or a military attack.

On March 17, two months after his inauguration, Trump decided on a policy of maximum pressure—ratcheting up economic, rhetorical, military, diplomatic pressure and, if necessary, covert action. The campaign was designed to show Kim he was in greater danger and would pay a bigger price with nuclear weapons than he would without them. The overall goal was denuclearization.

The economic pressure was set up to choke off North Korea's ability to make money in its overseas embassies and missions in 48 countries. Economic sanctions were imposed that banned 100 percent of North Korean coal exports. Nations that allowed North Koreans to work within them agreed to push them out. North Korean restaurants and other overseas businesses connected to the regime were shut down. North Korean seafood operations abroad, which were run by Kim's military to make money, were targeted. Oil imports were cut off.

One of Trump's first nominations just two weeks after being elected president had been Representative Mike Pompeo, who had served three terms in the House, as CIA director. An evangelical Tea Party Republican, Pompeo, 52, graduated from West Point in 1986 first in his class of 973. He also had a Harvard Law degree.

Around the beginning of March, Pompeo met at the CIA with Andy Kim, a legendary CIA operator who had just retired after 29 years running some of the agency's most successful intelligence operations against North Korea.

Born in South Korea, Andy Kim had come to the United States as a teenager with his immigrant parents. Fluent in Korean and educated at one of the elite high schools of South Korea, Kim was an ideal, sophisticated undercover operator. He fit in. He knew the language and culture and was well connected to the South Korean leadership class. He knew how to read between the lines of all the scary shibboleths about North Korea and could figure out which must be true or not.

A CIA case officer for decades, Andy Kim had recruited and built relationships with spies and assessed them and the quality of their information. He had operated undercover from U.S. embassies in Tokyo, then Beijing, Warsaw, Hong Kong, back to China, then Seoul, and finally Bangkok, Thailand.

Pompeo said that North Korea was at the top of President Trump's agenda. He wanted to eliminate the threat from North Korea to the United States homeland and rid North Korea of its nuclear weapons.

What would you do? Pompeo asked. How would you go about accomplishing this ambitious goal?

As Pompeo knew from his time on the House Intelligence Committee, the CIA collected intelligence mostly from human sources, analyzed that intelligence to describe what it might mean for U.S. national security, and also conducted covert action to change events abroad to further U.S. policy. Ideally covert action would be done without the United States' role being discovered or known.

You have talented people in the CIA, Kim told Pompeo. But those talents are spread around the agency in the different departments of collection, analysis and covert action. If you really want to change, you need to bring those people under one tent to create synergy. That would be challenging.

Kim said the culture in the agency wedded people to their departments. Departments protected their turf and didn't share the best information even when they should. One tent had been needed for a long time. The CIA had done this successfully for other geographic areas but not North Korea. Somebody new with new ideas was needed, he said.

Like Pottinger with Trump, Andy Kim told Pompeo that Obama's policy of strategic patience had not worked. In practice it had meant not engaging with North Korea, handicapping the CIA and the U.S. government. Not engaging meant not understanding. Kim Jong Un was new, having come to power only six years ago. "We are still trying to figure out who Kim Jong Un is and what makes him tick," he explained. There is an opportunity there to try something different.

Will you come back to create a North Korea mission center with control over all collection, analysis and covert action to engage? Pompeo finally asked.

Kim said he would need new resources. Covert action, especially if it was going to be planned and undertaken, would require lots of new money. But it was too late—the budget was set for the year.

Pompeo said he could get him the money he needed.

Kim said a fully enabled North Korea mission center would involve hundreds of people—some already there and some that would be new.

Pompeo promised. "I will support you."

After an hour, Kim accepted the job. He would return. As a case officer, his job had been to assess people. Pompeo was determined, mission-focused and no-nonsense. Pompeo might be the guy who had the clout and energy to follow through, Kim reasoned.

But then again Kim had seen enough of the government and the CIA to know people with the right ideas and right energy often got sucked into bureaucratic traditions and were never able to shake themselves loose and accomplish anything. Good people wanted to be the good guy in the system and the team, make no waves, get promoted to bigger and better jobs.

The recent CIA history on covert action was bleak as well. Prior to the 2003 military invasion of Iraq, the CIA had effectively washed its hands of any possible operation to overthrow Iraqi leader Saddam Hussein, saying it was too hard.

In the CIA's reexamination of its role following the spectacular failure of the Iraq War, the Iraq Operations Group was referred to as "The House of Broken Toys" and CIA leadership concluded it was an abdication of responsibility to not give a president covert action options. In retrospect, overthrowing Saddam through covert action, though difficult and risky in the extreme, would have been so much less costly in terms of lives and money.

Mattis planned military operations for North Korea, and Tillerson made the diplomatic efforts. Kim, in turn, planned for covert action to overthrow the North Korean leader in the event President Trump signed a formal order, called a finding, authorizing an operation.

SEVEN

R od Rosenstein, the deputy attorney general, was summoned to the White House on Monday, May 8, four months into the Trump presidency.

On the surface Rosenstein, 52, was one of the quietly powerful men of Washington, part of the unseen bureaucracy, often overlooked and seemingly just an anonymous cog in the wheels of government. Previously he had been relatively obscure as the U.S. attorney in Baltimore. But at this moment, Rosenstein was in the middle of everything.

Rosenstein had occupied the number-two spot at the Justice Department for just 12 days. Because his boss, Attorney General Jeff Sessions, had recused himself in March from the investigation of Russian interference in the 2016 presidential election, Rosenstein was now in charge of that probe.

Russia was the story of the day as the U.S. intelligence agencies had concluded that Vladimir Putin had personally directed organized interference in the U.S. election. Foreign interference in presidential politics was espionage at the highest level. The media was in a frenzy. Had Russia put Trump in the White House? Was this Watergate?

Sessions and White House counsel Don McGahn held regular weekly lunches. This week, Rosenstein had been asked to attend.

McGahn and Sessions were, by official title, the legal heavy-weights in the new administration. But now, as deputy, Rosenstein was in charge of the highest-profile investigation in the United States. By Justice Department tradition, the deputy attorney general also had day-to-day supervision of the FBI. He arrived at the White House early.

Rosenstein had a third advantage. Since Sessions had recused himself from the Russia inquiry two months earlier, President Trump had furiously and repeatedly raged against his attorney general for not protecting him. Trump was "steaming, raging mad," noted *The Washington Post* on March 5.

The disintegration of the Trump-Sessions relationship gave Rosenstein an opening to develop a rapport with the president. A Harvard Law graduate, Rosenstein had been a law-and-order, by-the-book career federal prosecutor for nearly 30 years. He considered himself a "pre–Fox News Republican" because he did not like the hyper-conservatism and what he considered the reflexive pro-Trump coverage.

When Rosenstein moved into the deputy's office, he noticed a new flat-screen TV. "My God," he said to himself, "I'm not watching television." He unplugged it. He also took the little TV that was in the outer office for his assistants and secretary and put it in a closet.

Aware of Trump's obsessive TV watching, he thought he would like to advise the president, "Turn off the TV and run the country."

Just days earlier, FBI director James Comey had briefed Rosenstein in the department command center on the Top Secret Russia investigation, codenamed Crossfire Hurricane. The FBI had four open cases on Trump campaign aides. The investigation was 10 months old and was moving too slowly, Comey had said.

"There's one more shoe to drop," Comey said, "and that is whether Attorney General Sessions made false statements." Sessions had met with the Russian ambassador despite having said at his confirmation hearing that he'd had no contact with Russians.

Rosenstein immediately pushed back and said he was not sure whether the legal standard applied here. Sessions's discussion with the ambassador was incidental and brief, not of substance, and he had plausibly claimed he did not remember the contact.

David Laufman, a senior offical in the National Security Division, who was also at the briefing, was astonished that Rosenstein defended Sessions so openly. Laufman noticed that others in the room visibly registered surprise.

Possibly more important, Rosenstein had concluded by the end of Comey's briefing that the Russia investigation so far did not seem to be about Trump personally, but about his aides. Comey had said the president was not technically under investigation.

As Rosenstein saw it, Crossfire Hurricane was instead focused on what Russia had done to meddle in the election—its actions, operations and purpose. The investigation's second focus was on those in Trump's circle who seemed to have lied about their contacts with Russian officials. The amount of lying was extensive. Comey—and now Rosenstein—were deeply suspicious. Why so many lies? Something or many somethings were being concealed. Rosenstein found all this sinister.

At the White House luncheon that May 8, McGahn told Rosenstein that Trump was planning to fire Comey.

Rosenstein was not surprised. On the last day of November 2016, Sessions, then still a senator from Alabama and Trump's pick for attorney general, had invited Rosenstein to his office. Sessions wanted to recruit Rosenstein. Sessions said the administration would need "a fresh start" at the FBI.

Now, six months later, Rosenstein, who at Harvard Law had been a member of the conservative Federalist Society, felt comfortable with Trump's apparent decision. In Rosenstein's strong view, the president had the power to fire anyone he wanted. Article II of the Constitution said unambiguously, "The executive power shall be vested in a President of the United States of America." Not the cabinet, not the White House staff, not the National Security Council, not the Justice Department.

Sessions arrived at the White House and the lunch with McGahn began. Comey was the main and only course, Rosenstein quickly saw. Sessions angrily alleged that the FBI director leaked derogatory information to the media about Sessions himself.

That was plausible, Rosenstein knew, because he had heard Comey say Sessions might have made a false statement.

White House chief of staff Reince Priebus ran into the room, seeming very jittery. He wanted to know how they could expedite the removal of Comey. "We've got to get this done," Priebus said. Clearly Trump was on the warpath. Comey had to be ousted now.

Nothing was resolved at the lunch. But the heat was on.

At 5:00 p.m. the same day, Rosenstein was again called to the White House, this time for a meeting with Trump and Sessions. Rosenstein could see firsthand how Trump was obsessed with Comey.

Trump said that Comey had privately told him three times that he was not personally under investigation in the Russia probe. Why would Comey not say this publicly? Trump asked. What was going on? How could this be happening?

Rosenstein thought the president had a point. If he was not under investigation—and Rosenstein knew from Comey that he wasn't at this point—then perhaps, given the president's unique status as head of the executive branch, a statement should be made.

But the FBI did not like to say publicly when someone was not under investigation, for technical, traditional and frankly ass-covering reasons. In part, this was because someone might come under investigation later on. Then how to correct the record?

This was more than a squirrelly bureaucratic dance. It gave

the FBI and prosecutors great leverage as they interviewed witnesses. These witnesses and their lawyers knew the tables could turn quickly if someone was not forthcoming.

In the May 8 meeting, Trump did most of the talking and would not take his laser focus off of Comey. Rosenstein saw no coherent train of thought, no logical or organized presentation of the issues, alternatives or possible consequences. No moment of concluding, here's how the decision will be made—let alone, here's the decision.

Rosenstein was new to White House meetings and the private Trump, so he kept quiet. He was astounded how the president's rambling monologue continued in every way but a straight line. He found it important, though, that Trump did not say he wanted to get rid of the Russia investigation—he wanted to get rid of Comey.

Should Comey be given a chance to resign voluntarily? asked a deputy White House counsel.

McGahn agreed he should.

Rosenstein thought that was reasonable, but stayed quiet.

Trump said he had been working for days on a termination letter to send to Comey, and had personally dictated it to his aide Stephen Miller. "Have you seen my letter?" the president asked Rosenstein.

No.

"Madeleine," Trump called out to his special assistant, Madeleine Westerhout, who sat right outside the Oval Office. "Bring in the letter."

Rosenstein started to read:

"Dear Director Comey, While I greatly appreciate your informing me, on three separate occasions, that I am not under investigation concerning the fabricated and politically-motivated allegations of a Trump-Russia relationship with respect to the 2016 Presidential Election, please be informed that I, along with members of both political parties and, most importantly, the American Public, have lost faith in you as the Director of the FBI and you are hereby terminated."

Trump continued talking nonstop—loud, emphatic and angry. Rosenstein struggled to read the letter and also pay attention. He looked down to read and then up to pay attention to the president, whose urgency only increased. Up, down, up, down.

The letter was four pages of stream-of-consciousness grievance—Comey's refusal just five days prior in public congressional testimony to say the president was not a target of the Russia investigation, his handling of the Hillary Clinton email investigation, and his alleged failure to hold leakers accountable.

"I don't think it is a good idea to send this letter," Rosenstein said. He didn't think the letter showed criminal intent on Trump's part to sidetrack the Russia investigation by firing the FBI director, but Comey's removal would no doubt trigger suspicions. He also thought the scattershot nature of Trump's draft letter showed a disturbed mind.

"Well," Trump asked, "what do you think?"

Firing Comey would be fully justified, Rosenstein said, on the single issue of his handling of the Clinton email investigation. In July 2016, Comey had usurped the Justice Department's role and declared the investigation over, then publicly and harshly condemned Clinton for "extremely careless" handling of "very sensitive, highly classified information." The FBI was not supposed to issue judgments.

This alone had undermined confidence in the FBI, Rosenstein said, and that could be restored by removing Comey.

Trump liked that. You write that in a memo to Jeff, who will send it to me with a recommendation, he said. "And then I'll fire Comey." Here was a path. Trump was suddenly organized, linear and decisive. "Put the Russia stuff in," he added, clearly meaning that Comey had three times said the president was not under investigation. Trump said he wanted the memo the next morning.

Rosenstein was back at Justice about 6:00 p.m.

"The president is going to fire Comey," he told his staff. He told them to assemble a critique of the FBI director.

Now he had to write a memo. "I'm a lawyer," Rosenstein said. "I can write." It was going to be a long night. Someone ordered pizza.

Comey's closing out the email investigation in public was unprecedented, Rosenstein wrote. "I do not understand his refusal to accept the nearly universal judgment that he was mistaken." Rosenstein cited the public condemnation of Comey by attorneys general and their deputies who had served in Republican and Democratic administrations.

"The director laid out his version of the facts for the news media as if it were a closing argument, but without a trial. It is a textbook example of what federal prosecutors and agents are taught not to do."

Rosenstein wrote until 3:00 a.m. He came back into the office at 7:30 a.m. the next day, May 9, and reviewed the memo with Scott Schools, associate deputy attorney general and ethics adviser. "I want you to flyspeck this," Rosenstein said. It had to be 100 percent accurate. Schools merely suggested a few edits and found a grammatical mistake.

"I'm not sure the White House is going to like this," Rosenstein said. The memo was very sympathetic to Clinton, painting her as a victim abused by Comey. Rosenstein believed he would have written the same memo if Clinton were president.

"Where's the memo?" McGahn asked in a 10:00 a.m. phone call to Rosenstein. The president was ready—and impatient—to act.

Still working on it. At noon, McGahn called again.

"I've sent it up to Sessions," Rosenstein said. He assumed that Trump knew how to fire someone.

At 1:00 p.m. Sessions had his chief of staff, Jody Hunt, send the Rosenstein memo, headed "Restoring Public confidence in the FBI," to the White House with Sessions's endorsing cover letter.

Comey was in Los Angeles speaking at a Diversity Agent Recruitment event.

"COMEY FIRED," he read on the TV screen along a back wall. He thought it was a well-designed joke at first, and then he understood it wasn't.

He reached Andrew McCabe, his deputy—now the acting director. I must have really hosed something up, Comey said.

McCabe, an intense 21-year FBI veteran, was floored. He revered Comey, though he thought the director had seriously overreached on the Clinton email investigation.

Soon McCabe got word that the president wanted to see him at 6:30 p.m.

Sitting behind the Resolute Desk in the Oval Office, Trump said that he had great hopes for McCabe as acting director. As for a permanent director, Trump said, we're going to get somebody great—it might even be you.

"FBI Director James Comey Is Fired by Trump," read one headline on the *New York Times* website that night. "In Trump's Firing of James Comey, Echoes of Watergate," read another. The news was splashed across the front pages in banner headlines the next morning.

Many legal scholars noted that while the president does have the power to fire any official, he may not do so for a corrupt or illegal purpose. To some, Comey's firing seemed to come close to the line.

The White House put out a statement saying the Comey firing was Rosenstein's idea.

Rosenstein could not believe the Comey firing was all being

put on him. About 8:00 p.m. he spoke with McGahn. "Don, it's not true. It's preposterous. I may have to testify. I may have to resign." He reminded McGahn that President George W. Bush had fired eight U.S. attorneys in December 2006 ostensibly for their performance but, as it turned out, for political reasons. Trump had "the authority to do this," Rosenstein said, "but you've got to tell the truth about the reasoning."

McGahn said he agreed.

Rosenstein made it clear he did not want to join in putting out a "false story."

Trump called Rosenstein. The president had been watching Fox News and the coverage had been great. Rosenstein ought to have a press conference.

No, Rosenstein said, he did not think that was a good idea. If asked, he would have to truthfully say the Comey firing was not his idea.

The next morning, Wednesday, May 10, at the FBI, McCabe convened a series of meetings designed to protect the Russia investigation and make sure it was on solid footing. Were there any individuals that the FBI had identified on whom they should consider opening new cases?

In the middle of this review, the president called McCabe. McCabe recounted the conversation in his 2019 book, *The Threat*:

It's Don Trump, he said.

Hello, Mr. President, how are you?

Boy, it's incredible, Trump said, how really happy people are that Comey had been ousted. I have received hundreds of messages from FBI people saying how delighted they are. Have you seen that? Are you seeing that too?

McCabe believed that Comey was a beloved and revered figure at the FBI, and people were upset, not delighted. He wrote that many at the FBI were in tears and compared the firing to "a death in the family. The death of a patriarch, a protector." But McCabe did not want to say any of this to the president and contradict him.

In a burst of emotional prose, McCabe wrote, "We felt as if we'd been cast onto the dustheap. We were laboring under the same dank, gray shadow of uncertainty and bleak anxiety that had been creeping over so much of Washington during the few months Donald Trump had been in office."

Still on the phone, Trump talked about how upset he was that Comey had flown home on his government plane from Los Angeles. How did that happen?

The FBI lawyers approved, McCabe said, and the plane had to come back with Comey's protection detail anyway. So McCabe had given the go-ahead.

Trump flew off the handle. That's not right! I don't approve of that! That's wrong! It seemed that the president repeated himself at least five times, perhaps seven.

I'm sorry you disagree, McCabe said, but that was my decision.

I want you to look into that! The president ordered. Will Comey be allowed in the FBI headquarters building to get his personal stuff?

His staff, McCabe said, would pack his personal belongings and take them to his home.

I don't want him in the building! Trump ordered. I'm banning him from the building. I don't want him in FBI buildings.

McCabe let Trump's ranting spiral on.

How is your wife? Trump asked. Jill McCabe, a pediatric physician, had run unsuccessfully for the state Senate in Virginia in 2015 as a Democrat. The Democratic governor Terry McAuliffe, a close friend and fundraiser for Bill and Hillary Clinton, had directed $467,500 from his political action committee to her campaign. The Virginia Democratic Party, effectively controlled by McAuliffe, gave her $207,788. That was a lot of money for a state

Senate campaign. Trump had previously tweeted about this and insinuated some conspiracy.

Jill was fine, McCabe said.

How did she handle losing? the president asked. Is it tough to lose?

It's tough to lose anything, McCabe answered. She had rededicated herself to taking care of kids in the emergency room.

That must've been really tough, Trump said in what sounded like a sneer. To be a loser. Shifting dramatically, the president said, You'll do a good job. He said he had a lot of faith in McCabe.

McCabe wrote a contemporaneous memo recounting the exchange with the president, filling three quarters of a page. McCabe knew Comey had written many contemporaneous memos to record his own meetings and calls with Trump. The memos clearly showed that Comey was convinced the president was dishonest, corrupt and possibly attempting to obstruct justice.

Neither Comey nor McCabe had told Rosenstein about the memos and their deep suspicions of Trump.

EIGHT

On May 11, two days after Comey was fired, Rosenstein was surprised to read a story on the *New York Times* website headlined, "In a Private Dinner, Trump Demanded Loyalty. Comey Demurred."

The remarkable story reported that Trump had a private one-on-one dinner with Comey on January 27, seven days into the Trump presidency. The president asked for a personal pledge of loyalty, the story said, attributing it to two people who had heard Comey's account of the dinner.

The White House denied the story but acknowledged there was such a one-on-one dinner.

Rosenstein saw more than a ring of truth in the story. Trump was known to demand loyalty of those in his circle. It was clearly an inside story and had specifics. Trump, according to the account, eventually asked for "honest loyalty." Comey answered, "You will have that."

Rosenstein could plainly see that Comey was fighting back, getting his version out. Rosenstein started asking around, trying to get to the bottom of what might have happened at the dinner.

McCabe knew about the conversation, and had seen a detailed three-and-a-half-page memo recounting the one-hour-and-20-minute dinner that Comey had prepared and shown him. Setting the scene, Comey wrote that he and Trump had sat at a small oval table in the middle of the White House Green Room.

The conversation was "chaotic," Comey had written, "conversation-as-jigsaw-puzzle in a way, with pieces picked up, then discarded, then returned to."

Comey said he told Trump that he realized he could be fired by Trump at any time but he wanted to stay. "I explained that he could count on me to always tell him the truth. I said I don't do sneaky things. I don't leak. I don't do weasel moves."

But McCabe was not forthcoming about the existence of the memo to Rosenstein.

What the hell is going on? Rosenstein asked, feeling alone and cut out. "I was on an island," he said later.

After a regular intelligence briefing the next day, Friday, May 12—McCabe's first as acting director—he asked Rosenstein if he would stay behind to talk. When they were alone, McCabe said the Senate Intelligence Committee was trying to interview people for their Russia investigation the FBI wanted to interview first. He wanted Rosenstein to protect the FBI process.

Rosenstein readily agreed. The more the Justice Department and the FBI had the upper hand in the investigation, the more they could control it. The congressional intelligence committees could be demanding and leaky.

Rosenstein confided to McCabe that he was shocked that the White House was trying to make it appear that firing Comey had been his idea, laying out a story line with him at the center. He had only written the memo at Trump's direction. In an interview with NBC television anchor Lester Holt the day before, Trump had said he was going to fire Comey no matter what Sessions and Rosenstein recommended—but Rosenstein still felt vulnerable and twisting in the wind, alone.

McCabe thought Rosenstein looked a little glassy-eyed. Are you sleeping at night? McCabe asked his nominal supervisor.

I'm working 16 to 18 hours a day and not getting enough sleep, Rosenstein said, and the news trucks were camped outside his home. It was nerve-racking, unpleasant and personal evidence of the media and political frenzy. There was no one at the department he felt he could trust except his own team, a small circle of career lawyers.

Then Rosenstein dropped the headline: I have been thinking about appointing a special counsel to oversee the Russia investigation.

That would help the credibility of the investigation, McCabe said, agreeing completely.

For Rosenstein, the question of a special counsel had been percolating for days. He saw pluses and minuses. Over the decades, independent investigations had operated with great latitude— Nixon's Watergate in the 1970s, Reagan's Iran-contra in the 1980s and Clinton's Whitewater and Monica Lewinsky in the 1990s. They did not report to the Justice Department and were not monitored. That was not the case now, Rosenstein knew. The law and the rules had changed significantly. Under the current regulations, a special counsel was just another employee of the Justice Department with no more authority than the 93 U.S. attorneys who were subject and accountable to the attorney general. Because Sessions was recused, a special counsel would be under Rosenstein's supervision.

A special counsel would have the aura of independence. But paradoxically, appointing a special counsel could give Rosenstein more control. The special counsel would report to him and he would monitor the office closely.

Rosenstein had been a young attorney working for Whitewater independent counsel Ken Starr in the 1990s. He had been appalled by how Starr had asked for and obtained authority to expand his mandate beyond his original authority to investigate the Clintons' property deals in the Whitewater Development Corporation. He was soon conducting a dragnet. Whitewater became a full, unlimited open-ended investigation of the Clintons. It led to the discovery of President Clinton's affair with White House intern Monica Lewinsky, and to Clinton's subsequent impeachment.

On May 16, McCabe called Rosenstein. "I think you should know that Comey wrote memos about his discussions with President Trump," McCabe said. "They are under lock and key."

Not entirely. About two hours later, *The New York Times* published a blockbuster story about the contents of one Comey memo. In an Oval Office meeting on February 14, Trump had said of the investigation into former national security adviser Michael Flynn: "I hope you can see your way clear to letting this go, to letting Flynn go. He is a good guy. I hope you can let this go."

Pretty unsavory of Trump, Rosenstein thought. Former prosecutors like Comey wrote such contemporaneous memos about people they suspected of possible crimes.

To Rosenstein, it was pretty clear that the FBI leadership thought a group of Russian sympathizers had taken over the United States government.

Rosenstein should have been told about the memos. The FBI clearly didn't trust the Justice Department, or him. He thought the bureau was operating like J. Edgar Hoover—a power unto itself.

"I don't understand why *The New York Times* has these," he said to McCabe, "and I don't have them, and my prosecutors don't have them."

Outraged, Rosenstein sent one of his deputies to the FBI to get copies of the Comey memos. He felt sandbagged. This was clearly bad faith. He had been set up.

Soon he also learned that McCabe and his staff were discussing whether the president was under investigation. But McCabe also did not include Rosenstein in these discussions. Clearly he should have been.

The topper came when Rosenstein learned that McCabe—on his own—had made President Trump himself a subject of the investigation. A subject is someone whose conduct is within the scope of a grand jury's investigation, but who is neither a target of the criminal investigation nor simply a witness.

Rosenstein was shocked and asked his deputies if McCabe had this power.

The answer was yes. What extraordinary power resided with the FBI.

Rosenstein felt caught between Trump and the FBI. He was suspicious of both. Was there a way to navigate between the two—to ensure an old-style, aggressive, nonpartisan investigation based only on credible evidence, but ensure the inquiry was not a broad, out-of-control fishing expedition like Ken Starr had conducted of Clinton?

He did not like the partisan atmosphere in Washington. The Fox News network, especially opinion broadcaster Sean Hannity, had a Svengali-like influence on Trump that Rosenstein privately labeled "malicious." Too many right-wing nuts had influence. He also found no comfort or credibility with mainstream media reporters, who he believed were prisoners of their partisan sources.

Rosenstein wanted to find a middle course. For practical purposes, appointing a special counsel would amount to a strategy of riding both horses—an intense, hands-off investigation, but one that was scrupulously fair. And appointing a special counsel under the new rules would give Rosenstein firm control of that investigation.

Rosenstein had met Robert Mueller, then the acting U.S. attorney for Massachusetts, in 1989 as a 24-year-old Harvard Law student working as an intern in Mueller's office.

Mueller's career had been exemplary, especially his 12-year tenure as FBI director. Rosenstein was struck by Mueller's rectitude.

After much debate and internal, personal turmoil, Rosenstein decided to pull the trigger and appoint a special counsel for the Russia investigation.

Mueller was literally the only person for the task. The Russia investigation was intelligence heavy. Mueller knew the intelligence world of the CIA and the National Security Agency as well as anyone. Mueller, a former Marine, would make the investigation better and faster, not worse and slower.

Rosenstein approached Mueller about the job, saying that he would have to give up his private law practice as a partner in the Washington law firm of WilmerHale. This has to be full-time. Ken Starr had not given up his position at Kirkland & Ellis, a private law firm, while serving as independent counsel.

Would you be available if I wanted a special counsel?

No, Mueller said.

If I decided we needed you, would you do it? Rosenstein asked, more directed.

No, Mueller said again.

But the next Monday, Mueller sent word through one of Rosenstein's deputies that he had changed his mind and would be willing to do it.

Rosenstein would monitor all Mueller's work, setting up some face-to-face meetings with the special counsel. He would arrange for his top Justice Department deputies to have biweekly meetings with Mueller or his top deputies.

"Let me know if you find anything that shows coordination or conspiracy with Russia," Rosenstein instructed. That was the core mission.

On May 17, 2017 in a one-page order, Rosenstein appointed Mueller as special counsel to investigate "Russian interference with the 2016 presidential election" and to "prosecute federal crimes arising from the investigation."

His personal assessment of his decision was that it would serve three purposes: restore public trust in the investigation, get McCabe out of the investigation, and put the investigation in the hands of someone trustworthy.

After appointing Mueller, Rosenstein spoke with McGahn at the White House. The president should be encouraged, he said. Mueller's going to expedite this. Rosenstein wanted to find out whether Trump aides had coordinated with Russia, not to get Trump. A special counsel investigation would be best for everyone.

When Trump was informed, he said, "This is the end of my presidency. I'm fucked!"

In line with Rosenstein's assurances, the official White House statement from Trump released at 7:30 p.m. that evening said: "As I have stated many times, a thorough investigation will confirm what we already know—there was no collusion between my campaign and any foreign entity. I look forward to this matter concluding quickly. In the meantime, I will never stop fighting for the people and the issues that matter most to the future of our country."

The conciliatory tone was the opposite of Trump's mood.

On Thursday morning shortly after 10:00 a.m., Trump tweeted angrily that he wondered why there had been no special counsel for "all of the illegal acts" of Hillary Clinton and the Obama administration. The Russia investigation is, he said, "the single greatest witch hunt of a politician in American history."

In some respects that day, May 18, was the worst day so far in the Oval Office. Trump's anger, more than any previously seen by his inner circle, was uncontrollable. He oscillated—stormed—between the Oval Office and his private dining room. "We barely got by," said Rob Porter, then the White House staff secretary.

Trump is a large man—around 6-foot-3 and about 240 pounds, almost the size of a football linebacker. On the move and in a rage, he is frightening. Why Mueller? "I didn't hire him for the FBI." Trump had interviewed Mueller for perhaps another tour as FBI director and rejected him. "Of course he's got an axe to grind. Everybody's trying to get me." Impeachment talk was on the TV.

What power does a special counsel have? Trump asked.

Virtually unlimited, Porter, a lawyer, explained.

"They're going to spend years digging through my whole life and finances," Trump said. "They're out to get me. It's all Jeff Sessions' fault. Rod Rosenstein doesn't know what the hell he is doing. He's a Democrat. He's from Maryland." Rosenstein was a lifelong Republican.

"Rosenstein was one of the people who said to fire Comey and wrote me this letter. How could he possibly be supervising this investigation?"

Trump stayed mostly on his feet, continuing to move between the Oval Office and the dining room. "I have to be fighting," he said in a frenzy. "I am the president. I can fire anybody I want. They can't be investigating me for firing Comey. And Comey deserved to be fired! Everybody hated him. He was awful."

The next Sunday, Rosenstein called both Mueller and McCabe in. "I don't want Andy participating in the investigation," Rosenstein said.

McCabe protested emphatically, saying, "I have no conflict."

Rosenstein said that for appearances' sake, McCabe should not be involved.

After McCabe left the room, Rosenstein worked out a chain of command on the Russia investigation with Mueller that would ensure that McCabe would not get information from it.

Later, during a House Judiciary Committee hearing on June 28, 2018, Republican representative from Florida Ron DeSantis, who would later become governor of that state, remarked to Rosenstein, "They talk about the Mueller investigation—it's really the Rosenstein investigation. You appointed Mueller. You're supervising Mueller."

NINE

◆———

In Trump's orbit, the president's 36-year-old son-in-law, Jared Kushner, occupied a unique, central role. He was officially listed on the White House roster as senior adviser, but acted as a de facto chief of staff—he would come to outstay three actual ones—and was deeply involved in presidential business. Kushner graduated from Harvard in 2003 and had a combined JD/MBA degree from New York University. Intelligent, organized, self-confident and arrogant, Kushner was often deployed personally by Trump as an out-of-channels special project officer.

In the first months of his administration in 2017, Trump asked Kushner to take on some of the most important and sensitive parts of the foreign policy portfolio, including acting as his liaison with Saudi Arabia and with both Mexico and China on trade issues. He also assigned Kushner the job of resolving the eternal conflict between the Israelis and Palestinians. This immediately sidelined Secretary of State Rex Tillerson, and interfered with his and Mattis's plans to guide—or control—Trump on foreign policy.

If Kushner could not find a Middle East peace plan, "nobody can," Trump said.

Kushner didn't. He presented four or five versions of his plans to Tillerson, who increasingly voiced skepticism.

On one version Kushner proposed Israel take the Jordan Valley, a 65-mile-long tract of land along the border between Jordan to the east and Israel—including much of the West Bank—to the west.

"That'll never fly," Tillerson told him.

So out it came, only to go back in the plan later.

Tillerson thought Kushner relied too much on economic development and ignored all the hard issues between Israel and Palestine.

"If you make the economic benefits big enough," Kushner argued, "people will say yes." Money was the key, just pump money. Trump talked that way also.

Tillerson told Kushner he did not understand the history. "These people are not going to care about your money," he said. "Or they'll take your money and five years from now, you'll be right back where you are today. That's not going to buy you peace."

Kushner strongly disputes this and believes he developed an original, balanced plan for peace between Israel and the Palestinians. He concluded Tillerson was not up to the job of being secretary of state and resented Kushner's 20-year relationship with Israeli prime minister Netanyahu.

For his part, Tillerson thought Kushner's dealings with Netanyahu were "nauseating to watch. It was stomach churning."

On Monday, May 22, 2017, Trump was in Tel Aviv, meeting with Netanyahu at the King David Hotel. It was the second stop, after Saudi Arabia, on Trump's first international trip as president. Jared Kushner ran out to grab Tillerson.

"You've got to go in there," an aide said. "They're showing the president this video. It's awful. The president's just exploding. You've got to go in there and calm the president down."

By this point there was enough distrust between Tillerson and the White House that Tillerson didn't know whether Kushner was playacting, or even setting him up. But he went into the Trump-Netanyahu meeting.

"Watch this," Trump said. "This is unbelievable! You've got to see this."

They played the video again for Tillerson. It showed a series of spliced-together comments from Palestinian Authority president Mahmoud Abbas, who was supposed to be Israel's partner in the peace deal that Kushner was trying to put together. It sounded like Abbas was ordering the murder of children. Tillerson believed it was faked or manipulated, taking words and sentences out of context and stringing them together.

"And that's the guy you want to help?" Netanyahu said.

Tillerson studied the video, a crude effort of short snippets that had no context.

After Netanyahu left, Tillerson said to Trump, "Mr. President, you realize that that whole thing was fabricated?"

"Well," Trump said, "it's not fabricated. They got the guy on tape saying it."

Trump had always supported Israel but had recently began expressing doubts about Netanyahu and wondering aloud if the Israeli prime minister might be the real problem. Trump had even earlier said to Netanyahu on a Washington visit that he believed he was the obstacle to peace, not Abbas.

It was Tillerson's view that Netanyahu had manufactured the tape to counter any pro-Palestinian sentiments that were surfacing.

The next morning Trump met privately with Abbas and his people in Bethlehem and unloaded in a tirade. "Murderer!" Trump said to Abbas. "Liar!" I thought you were this grandfatherly figure that I could trust. "Now, I realize you're nothing but a murderer. You tricked me!"

Kushner disputes all of this and recalled that the president's reaction to the tape was much calmer.

"Now," Trump said finally to Abbas, "we're going to go outside, because they've got all the press out there. I'm going to say some nice things about you, and you're going to say some nice things about me. But now you know how I feel."

Abbas went first before the press and played his part.

"Your Excellency, Mr. President and dear friend, Donald Trump," Abbas said, "it's my pleasure to welcome you here in Palestine and receive you as a great guest of our people here in Bethlehem, the birthplace of Jesus.

"I would like to reiterate, Your Excellency, Mr. President, our commitment to cooperate with you in order to make peace and forge a historic peace deal with the Israelis."

When his turn came, Trump said, "I want to offer my deep appreciation to the Palestinians and President Abbas for hosting me today."

Trump eventually ordered the closure of the Palestinian Liberation Organization office in Washington, D.C. in September 2018 and canceled nearly all U.S. aid to the West Bank and Gaza, as well as $360 million in annual aid previously given to the U.N. agency for Palestinian refugees.

TEN

◆

Dan Coats promised his wife, Marsha, he would reclaim control over his life. "I'll shape up," he promised her.

At DNI headquarters in Virginia, he called in his senior staff about three months into his tenure.

"I'm not going to be able to go the long haul here unless we can do three things," Coats said. "One, I've got to get a good night's sleep." Trump's tweeting was continuing to keep him up at night. The job was never leaving him. "Number two, I can't just scarf down a McDonald's at 3:00 in the afternoon because I'm scheduled to do stuff. I've got to have a time when I can have a decent meal. Third, I've got to have exercise." He knew it was a stress reliever. "You've got to build that into my schedule—45 minutes at least three times a week. I need a trainer, someone to really push me.

"Finally, it's an impossible job. One person cannot do all of this." Certainly he couldn't. He was going to hire a principal deputy to handle all the inside, technical and managerial nuts and bolts. He selected Sue Gordon, who had 37 years in the intelligence world as a former CIA analyst, cyber expert, and deputy director of the National Geospatial-Intelligence Agency.

"Sue, I can't handle all this. I give you the leash. You run this. I'll be Mr. Outside"—meaning he would deal with the White House, the National Security Council, State and Defense. He would be the man on the Hill, briefing and taking soundings in the House and Senate. And his number-one priority would be deepening relationships with the foreign intelligence services: the British, the Israelis, the Saudis, the Germans. The foreign services were great collectors of intelligence in their areas of the world, had some fantastic human sources and could put events in historical context.

"You're Mrs. Inside," he said to Sue Gordon.

Mattis hadn't known Coats but looked him up on Wikipedia to get some of the basics and asked a few people about him. The two had lunch. Mattis was immediately taken with Coats's gentlemanly demeanor, soft on the outside but with a spine of steel on the inside—what Mattis called "vertebrate." Mattis and Coats soon began lingering after NSC meetings when Trump had left.

"What the hell is going on?" Coats asked in a private sidebar conversation with Mattis after one session. In just one example, Trump wanted to withdraw U.S. troops from Afghanistan and South Korea. There was a rush. Instantly. "Get them out!" Trump had commanded.

"That's crazy," Mattis said to Coats. "That's dangerous."

Coats was troubled by the absence of a plan or a consideration of the human dimension—the impact on the troops, the allies, the world—or a sense of the weight of the office.

"The president has no moral compass," Mattis replied. The bluntness should have shocked Coats, but he'd arrived at his own hard truths about the most powerful man in the world.

"True," Coats agreed. "To him, a lie is not a lie. It's just what he thinks. He doesn't know the difference between the truth and a lie."

They found themselves often looking across the table at each other in the Situation Room with concern. They had to deal not only with America's adversaries but with the failure of the administration to work together and define its strategy.

Mattis concluded that Coats would not waver. Whenever the president would challenge the intelligence findings, Coats firmly stuck to the facts. Mattis knew that Coats was carrying a burden, but was sure he could stand the strain. Still waters ran deep in Dan Coats. He was cool and not defensive, unintimidated by complexity. Mattis found himself often thinking that Coats was a model of what was needed in government service—although maybe he was too decent.

As Coats's relationship with Mattis grew closer, his friendship with Pence grew more distant. "Once he became vice president," Coats said, "he built that kind of cocoon around him that basically said, this is the role of the vice president." In Coats's eyes, his old friend had become passive, subservient and obedient.

Marsha Coats was more charitable. "Mike Pence," she told others, "no doubt, he believes God put him where he is and his job is to be a good VP. A loyal and supportive—even though he doesn't agree with so much of it."

Of Pence, Marsha said, "One time, we had dinner with him. We didn't want to put him on the spot. Something outrageous had happened. We were at the White House, at some dinner. And he came over to say goodbye. And I just looked at him, like, how are you stomaching this?" Marsha Coats added, "I just looked at him like, this is horrible. I mean, we made eye contact. I think he understood.

"And he just whispered in my ear, '*Stay the course.*'"

At the same dinner, Dan Coats said that was exactly what Pence had said to him: "*Stay the course.*"

ELEVEN

———— ◆ ————

One day after work at the Pentagon in late 2017 Defense Secretary Mattis slipped quietly, unnoticed, into the cavernous National Cathedral in Washington.

Mattis directed his security detail to allow him to enter alone so he could pray and reflect. He was growing increasingly alarmed about the possibility of a war that could kill millions.

For the first year of the Trump presidency, Mattis had been living on permanent alert. North Korean chairman Kim Jong Un now had, for the first time, both nuclear weapons and intercontinental ballistic missiles (ICBMs) that could carry a nuclear warhead to the United States homeland.

Kim had been shooting off missiles at an alarming rate. Mattis had monitored these in real time about half a dozen times through a Top Secret National Event Conference, an emergency meeting of the military and national security team over secure voice communications. The conference put the senior leaders in direct communication so they were poised to respond immediately.

President Trump had delegated authority to Mattis to use a

conventional interceptor missile to shoot down any North Korean missile that might be headed for the United States.

"If the word had come that it was inbound for Seattle, we were already launching interceptors," Mattis privately told others.

If the North Koreans realized the United States had shot down their missile, or had even tried to, they would likely prepare to fire more missiles. "The potential we'd have to shoot to prevent a second launch was real," according to Mattis.

That would require approval from President Trump, and the United States and North Korea might soon be in the nightmare of nuclear war.

North Korea had several dozen nuclear weapons on Mobile Erector Launchers (MELs) so they could be moved around and hidden. Mattis was surprised that the North had done such a re-markable job of hardening, dispersing and concealing their nuclear weapons and missiles.

President Trump's detachment compounded the problem for Mattis. "I never cared much what Trump said," Mattis said privately, because Trump's orders were so random, impulsive and unthoughtful. "I ran the Department of Defense. I kept him informed in my private meetings. I wouldn't do it in public, because he would have to play a role then. But I didn't get any guidance from him, generally, other than an occasional tweet."

Only the president could authorize the use of nuclear weapons but Mattis believed the decision would rest on his recommendation.

"What do you do if you've got to do it?" Mattis asked himself. "You're going to incinerate a couple million people.

"No person has the right to kill a million people as far as I'm concerned, yet that's what I have to confront."

Trump's policy of maximum pressure on North Korea included not only draconian economic sanctions but also an unprecedented personal rhetorical assault on Kim, threatening "fire and fury" and nuclear obliteration in scores of tweets and public remarks. The third element was military pressure.

Here Mattis was walking a narrow line. He had wide latitude to pressure Kim militarily, though the defense secretary understood that one person's perceived pressure could be somebody else's provocation.

A longtime student of history, Mattis knew from memory one of President Abraham Lincoln's codes of war from the midst of the Civil War in 1863: "Men who take up arms against one another in public war do not cease on this account to be moral beings responsible to one another and to God."

War could not be divorced from moral responsibility. Mattis often said he had seen too many boys die in his 40 years in the Marines.

President Lincoln also had said, Mattis knew, "I have been driven many times upon my knees by the overwhelming conviction that I had nowhere else to go."

The majestic, gray-stone cathedral, with its 300-foot tower, is a spiritual home of the nation and slows time for anyone who enters. It seemed the right place for Mattis to go. He felt a solemn hush and walked the several hundred feet to the small War Memorial Chapel hidden from view at the rear of the cathedral.

A few rows of chairs faced a modest altar and an oversized sculpture of the head of the crucified Jesus Christ, crowned by a halo of brass meant to suggest cannon shells. To Mattis, it looked like a bursting bomb.

Inside the War Memorial Chapel stood a screen given by the 28th Marine Regiment on the 20th anniversary of Iwo Jima, the bloodiest and most vicious World War II battle, where the Corps had 26,000 casualties, including 6,800 dead.

Mattis sat quietly in the candle-lit War Memorial alcove. He had been in enough fights to know what one on the Korean Peninsula would entail. Chaos, blood, death, uncertainty, the drive to live on. Yet the question he needed to ask himself was how to carry out his assigned role knowing his decisions might have epic consequences? If the country were in peril, he would have to stop an escalation by Kim. Nuclear weapons existed as a deterrent, not to be used. Use would be madness, he knew, but he really had to think the unthinkable to defend the United States.

These awful thoughts had been in the back of his mind for months, and it was now time to bring them out front.

He did not think that President Trump would launch a preemptive strike on North Korea, although plans for such a war were on the shelf. The Strategic Command in Omaha had carefully reviewed and studied OPLAN 5027 for regime change in North Korea—the U.S. response to an attack that could include the use of 80 nuclear weapons. A plan for a leadership strike, OPLAN 5015, had also been updated.

Mattis stayed in the chapel for ten minutes, unburdening himself as much as possible.

He returned to the National Cathedral several more times that year around the close of business, when few people were there. No one ever seemed to recognize him. Sometimes on these other visits he walked across the nave through tall iron gates to the Holy Spirit Chapel, a small, wood-paneled alcove with depictions of the Holy Spirit as a dove.

A small sign said: Quiet Please.

He considered his reflections and prayer deeply personal. With each visit, he'd spend just enough time to feel a little stronger. There was never a point of complete comfort.

"This weighed heavily on me every day. I had to consider every day this could happen. This was not a theoretical concern."

Should there be a sudden military confrontation requiring a decision, he did not want, as he often said, to be Hamlet debating with himself, wringing his hands, indecisive and melancholic. He did not want to discover a hollow pit in his stomach saying, "Oh, my God, I'm not ready!" He had to find peace before the moment came.

"I was focused completely on how to prevent this or stop it as quickly as possible. Recognizing that the worst possible situation might dictate the use of nuclear weapons, with all that means in terms—not just that war, but the way it would change the shape of the world. That now nuclear weapons can be used again." He could not shake the moral or strategic implications. "And there just comes a point where you have to settle that in your own mind with your own conscience."

For months Mattis had witnessed a maddening whirlwind of uncertainty, provocations, pressures and the search for a diplomatic solution with North Korea, all the while carrying out the policy of maximum military pressure.

After months of apprehension, on July 3, 2017, North Korea had launched its first ICBM capable of reaching the United States. On a trajectory to maximize distance, the Hwasong-14 could have traveled between 4,000 and 5,000 miles to Alaska, Hawaii and perhaps even the West Coast. This was a genuine crisis. President Trump had publicly promised North Korea would not achieve this capability.

With approval from Mattis, General Vincent Brooks, the commander of the U.S. and South Korean alliance, ordered a U.S. Army tactical missile fired as a demonstration and warning. The missile was launched from the beach along a path running parallel to the North-South border and traveled 186 miles into the East Sea. That was the exact distance between the launching point of the U.S. missile and the North Korean missile test site, as well as a tent where satellite photos showed Kim Jong Un was watching the missile launch.

The meaning was meant to be clear: Kim Jong Un needed to worry about his personal safety. But no intelligence was picked up that indicated the North Koreans realized the U.S. missile could have easily been aimed north at the test site or at Kim.

Western news coverage of the U.S. and South Korean demonstration was sparse.

General Brooks said in a provocative public statement, "Self-restraint, which is a choice, is all that separates armistice and war."

The South Korean military conducted its own live-fire exercise missile into the East Sea and said, "We may make resolute decisions any time."

Three weeks later, on July 28, North Korea fired a more powerful ICBM. It could have traveled 6,200 miles and hit much of the continental United States. General Brooks ordered more demonstration missiles. In case anyone missed the message, he said in a statement that the alliance tactical missile test "provides deep-strike precision capability, enabling the Republic of Korea/United States alliance to engage a full array of time-critical targets under all weather conditions."

Again, there was no evidence in public or in the intelligence that North Korea understood. This demonstrated the limitations of trying to send messages with missile tests.

At 5:57 a.m. on Tuesday, August 29, sensitive intelligence showed North Korea was about to launch another missile. Mattis signed on to the Top Secret National Event Conference.

He could join in from the SCIF in his residence on Potomac Hill, a government-owned compound near the State Department. The Pentagon had also created the capability for Mattis to sign on from anywhere in the world. When he was out of Washington in the United States or overseas, a communications team would be in an adjacent hotel or embassy room where they erected a secure SCIF in a tentlike structure. He could vividly remember an aide desperately shaking him awake from restless sleep for a conference. Wherever he was, he regularly slept in his gym clothes so he could get to the National Event Conference as fast as possible.

Even if he was being driven down a street, a second vehicle always accompanied his car. That was the communications team, not security.

His communications equipment included a geospatial map with a small icon that would track the missile's anticipated flight path.

From his location Mattis could issue an order to shoot if the missile appeared to threaten South Korea, Japan or the United States.

Mattis had a light in his bathroom at his quarters in Washington that would flash if he was in the shower when the National Event Conference alert came.

A bell would also ring in the bathroom, bedroom and kitchen announcing that the conference was standing up because a North Korean missile had been launched or was ready on the launching pad.

It was a nonstop crucible, personal and hellish. There were no holidays or weekends off, no dead time.

On this Tuesday morning, U.S. military bases and ships with interceptor missiles had checked into the National Event Conference. Alaska was up and ready to shoot, Vandenberg Air Force Base in California was up, the Navy Seventh Fleet. SBX—short for the sea-based X-band, self-propelled mobile radar floats that formed part of the U.S. ballistic missile defense system—signed on.

Mattis watched silently as information came in rapidly. Uncertainty and dread mounted. Was this it?

NorthCom, the Defense Department regional command covering North America, quickly assessed that the missile was medium range and not a threat to the United States. But Mattis watched the icon for the North Korean missile arc up and out, over the Home Islands, a World War II era term for the Japanese archipelago, and drop into the sea. If North Korea had a malfunction or a miscalculation, the missile could have dropped on the Japanese homeland, triggering a major international crisis. Flying directly over Japan was a clear escalation, and changed the character of the threat.

Secretary of State Tillerson was on the National Event Conference and declared, "North Korea is out of control."

South Korea wanted to respond with at least a visible bombing training exercise within their borders. The next day, the South Koreans flew a unilateral F-15 bombing training mission delivering munitions on a South Korea bombing range about 20 kilometers from the North Korean border.

Mattis could see the maximum military pressure was not being felt or seen by the North. He began looking for more aggressive response options and wondered if they should take some actual bombing action in a North Korean port to send the message.

One of Mattis's favorite books was historian Barbara Tuchman's *The Guns of August* on the causes of World War I. Nations in Europe had all made elaborate plans for war, but none had actively sought war. In 1914 the assassination of the Archduke Franz Ferdinand in Sarajevo, Bosnia, set off the chain of events that triggered the war. By its end in 1918 more than 16 million soldiers and civilians had been killed.

What chain of events with the North might trigger war? Mattis pondered.

The intelligence gathering leading to the alerts was no less than spectacular, in a special category called "exquisite collection." Mattis often knew within seconds of a launch. Computers would quickly determine where the missile would land. It took time to answer some of the key questions. Did the missile have a warhead? Was it a test? An attack?

The National Event Conferences became smoother and more orderly. The training was paying off—no U.S. military radar failure, no failure of other equipment. "Ready to fire," Mattis heard each time. It was click, click, click, click, click, click. Then they would all stand by and wait. Is this what the edge of Armageddon might be like?

If there was a warning of a missile about to be fired, Mattis would often sign on to the National Event Conference early. Even if the trajectory indicated it was not coming toward the United States or was short-range, he would stay on the network to listen anyway. It became his own drill, what he called "anticipatory planning," for his role as sentinel, perhaps as decision maker to shoot down the missile. What would he say or order—if?

"Don't think that you can deal with this when the time comes," he told himself. "Sort it out now. Worst-case scenario. And now it's time to go to church. Now, go back, dust off the war plans and study it. Are we missing something? Is there something else we can do?"

On September 4, North Korea conducted its sixth nuclear test. It was estimated to have 17 times the power of the Hiroshima bomb, and many scientists concluded it was a hydrogen bomb.

Five days later, September 9, Chairman of the Joint Chiefs Joseph Dunford summoned the senior military leaders to the Tank, their conference room in the Pentagon. Dunford told General Brooks that they were looking for military options to ratchet up pressure and were worried that the United States was heading straight into war with North Korea.

On September 22, Trump tweeted: "Kim Jong Un of North Korea, who is obviously a madman who doesn't mind starving or killing his people, will be tested like never before!"

The following day, North Korean foreign minister Ri Yong Ho called Trump "Mr. Evil President" in a speech at the United Nations General Assembly and said a strike on the U.S. mainland was inevitable. Trump responded later that day with another tweet: "Just heard Foreign Minister of North Korea speak at U.N. If he echoes thoughts of Little Rocket Man, they won't be around much longer!"

The rhetorical overkill seemed mindless to Mattis. He believed that ridicule and taunting was unproductive, childish and dangerous.

"I got over enjoying public humiliation by second grade," Mattis once told the president.

Trump did not respond, but continued the tweeting.

On issue after issue, policy after policy, Mattis believed there were ways for a president to be tough and keep the peace. "But not with the current occupant. Because he doesn't understand. He has no mental framework or mode for these things. He hasn't read, you know," he told an associate.

Reading, listening, debating and having a process for weighing alternatives and determining policy were essential, Mattis believed. "I was often trying to impose reason over impulse. And you see where I wasn't able to, because the tweets would get out there."

On September 25, the U.S. command flew a simulated air attack, sending B-1 bombers and some 20 other planes, including cyber-capable aircraft, to cross the Northern Limit Line that separated South and North Korea in the sea. The planes stopped short of entering into North Korean territorial airspace or over North Korea itself, but it was an extremely provocative action. The South Korean National Security Council met with President Moon Jae In and sent word that the United States may have gone too far with North Korea.

Details of these provocative actions were not explained publicly, and the American people had little idea that July through September of 2017 had been so dangerous.

One day in his Pentagon office, Mattis addressed his senior staff sitting around the table head-on. "It can seem like routine here, gentlemen. And if you're not concerned about war, well, war is very concerned about you. And if you're not attentive to this, no one is."

Mattis believed there had been significant accomplishments at the Pentagon under Trump: dramatic increases in military budgets, readiness, training, discipline and new weapons.

But he had a central, running argument with Trump concerning allies. Mattis saw that the Europeans in NATO, the Middle East, South Korea and Japan were essential. The relationships needed to be nurtured and protected.

"All the victories," he said, "were becoming just submerged by this mercurial, capricious tweeting form of decision making."

What, Mattis wondered, made Trump think anyone could make it alone in the world? What reading of history, what intellectual thought could give a person any confidence in that? A country always needed allies, he was sure. A person always needed allies. And this was the tragedy of Trump's leadership and the bottom line: "It was inexplicable to think otherwise. It was indefensible. It was jingoism. It was a misguided form of nationalism. It was not patriotism."

Trump's impact on the country would be lasting. "This degradation of the American experiment is real. This is tangible. Truth is no longer governing the White House statements. Nobody believes—even the people who believe in him somehow believe in him without believing what he says."

When he walked out of his last visit to the cathedral, Mattis had cleared the decks. "I'm ready to go to work. I'm not going to think any more about the human tragedy." If he were alive after such a war, he would sort it out in retirement at his boyhood home in Richland, Washington, on the banks of the Columbia River.

President Trump said many times in public that he averted war with North Korea by meeting with Kim. He told me that Kim anticipated such a war with the United States.

"He was totally prepared," Trump told me on December 13, 2019.

"Did he tell you that?" I asked.

"Ah, yes, he did," Trump said.

"He did?"

"He was totally prepared to go," Trump replied. "And he expected to go. But we met."

In our December 30, 2019, interview, Trump again claimed credit. "If I weren't president, we would have—perhaps it would be over by now, and perhaps it wouldn't—we would've been in a major war," he said.

But in February 2020, the thought apparently still gave him pause. "It would've been a bad war, too," he told me. "It would've been a rough war."

DNI Dan Coats, who oversaw the 17 U.S. intelligence agencies, said, "We all knew we were on the road to conflict."

Kim told CIA director Pompeo the same in their first meeting—that he was ready to go to war. "We were very close," Kim told Pompeo.

"We never knew whether it was real," Pompeo later told an associate, "or whether it was a bluff." Whatever the case, the U.S. had to be ready.

TWELVE

◆

General Vincent Brooks, the U.S.-South Korea commander, met with Rex Tillerson in South Korea on November 7. The secretary of state had flown in in advance of Trump's first visit to South Korea.

Brooks knew that Tillerson had zero credibility with North Korea. Trump had undermined his secretary of state with a tweet a month earlier, writing that Tillerson was "wasting his time trying to negotiate with Little Rocket Man. Save your energy Rex." Intelligence picked up from the North was clear: If this person isn't speaking for the president, we don't need to waste our time with him.

Mattis and Tillerson had failed to convince Trump that South Korea was making a significant contribution to its own defense. The president wouldn't budge. Brooks was going to try illustrating the point by taking Trump to Camp Humphreys, the massive base the South Koreans had built for the joint American and South Korean forces.

After Trump landed around 12:30 p.m. and had lunch with

troops at Osan Air Base, Brooks joined him in Marine One and they took off for Camp Humphreys. As they flew, Brooks pulled out a map of the base, showing Trump how it had tripled in size from the old base and could house 46,000 military and civilians. He had superimposed the base map over a map of Washington to give Trump a sense of scale. The base stretched from Key Bridge to Nationals Park, about four miles.

South Korea had spent about $10 billion of their own money on the base, Brooks said.

"Hmm," Trump said, "that's a lot of money."

Brooks said the South Koreans had covered 92 percent of the cost.

"Why didn't they pay for all of it?"

U.S. law required that the United States control and pay for all the sensitive communications equipment and for the SCIFs, Brooks said. The work had to be done by U.S.-cleared contractors and through a U.S.-controlled procurement process. Without those legal restrictions, South Korea probably would have paid 100 percent.

Brooks took the president on an aerial tour of the giant base, pointing to the map of D.C. for references as Marine One swung from points corresponding with Arlington Cemetery, to Key Bridge, around toward the White House, down to the Capitol and Nationals Park and back to the Jefferson Memorial before landing.

Trump and Brooks moved from the helicopter to the Beast, the presidential limousine.

Trump noticed some AH-64 Apache combat helicopters. "Are those ours?"

"Yes, Mr. President. That's a battalion of about 18." South Korea had just purchased two battalions' worth and the U.S. had added a second battalion of its own. A year ago there had only been one battalion of Apache helicopters in South Korea, and now there were four.

"Are they any good?"

"There's no greater killer," Brooks said.

Trump indicated his approval.

After meeting with President Moon and some U.S. and South Korean troops, Brooks guided Trump to Eighth Army headquarters, where he hauled out some charts illustrated with candy gumballs to show the composition of the force.

Each gumball represented 10,000 troops, he said. Under current conditions, the United States had three gumballs, and South Korea had 62. In a time of war, after 200 days to fully mobilize, the United States would have a force of 720,000, according to the war plans, and the South Koreans 3.37 million.

Brooks hoped the stark difference in gumballs would show South Korea was carrying more than its share of the load.

Hmm, Trump said.

Brooks said that South Korea had spent $460 billion in its own defense in the last 15 years, and would soon spend $13.5 billion more on additional arms such as unmanned aerial systems missiles and fighter aircraft from U.S. defense industries.

"We will find out how serious North Korea is," Trump said to Brooks. "We're playing about five different games simultaneously. If we can't make a deal, we have to be ready."

They flew to Seoul with Tillerson, White House chief of staff John Kelly and National Security Adviser General H. R. McMaster, passing over a large campus with three tall glass buildings.

"What's that?" Trump asked.

"Samsung," Brooks said. The electronics and cell phone manufacturing giant accounted for about 15 percent of the South Korean economy. The campus was so big it was actually known as Samsung Town in Seoul.

"That's what I'm talking about." Trump said. "This is a rich country. Look at these high-rises. Look at the highway infrastructure." A train passed underneath. "Look at that train! Look at all of this. We're paying for all of this. They should be paying for everything."

It's our presence that led to that wealth, Brooks said, trying to push back. The South Koreans bear our DNA in the way they operate as a capitalistic democracy and in their military doctrine, customs and protocols. This economy, and South Korea itself, is an example of what can happen with a determined relationship and alliance over time. The connection went deeper than any individual military, diplomatic or economic transaction.

On the flight Trump asked Brooks, Should I go to Panmunjom? He was referring to the Joint Security Area (JSA) at the former village of Panmunjom at the DMZ that marks the border between South and North Korea.

Yes, Brooks said, making an on-the-spot call. You should go.

Before Trump's trip, Mattis had warned Brooks not to do anything to endanger the president. "Do not take him to the JSA," Mattis had ordered. Brooks hoped Mattis would understand he was acting in the tradition of the commander on the scene overriding orders. Trump should see what the South Koreans needed the U.S. to help defend, and Brooks thought he could keep the president safe by keeping the plan as secret as possible.

Why should I go? the president asked.

You would look weak if you didn't, Brooks answered. The trip would add weight to his speech the next day before the National Assembly of South Korea.

The White House sent word to Brooks that night that the president wanted to go to the DMZ early the next morning before his speech. Brooks sent an ALERT—a header Mattis had asked his commanders to use for an immediate operational matter—to the secretary of defense: "ALERT: POTUS team notified us today POTUS decided to visit the DMZ."

The next morning, Trump boarded Marine One. The fog was heavy but the pilots thought the route was navigable. The riskiest part was the landing area at Panmunjom, which involves a sharp 90-degree turn in the DMZ. Getting it wrong would mean the president could be in North Korea.

About 20 minutes into the flight, the pilots were taking it slow at about 3,000 to 4,000 feet. It was pea soup outside. The president had already had two Diet Cokes.

"They know I'm coming, don't they?" Trump asked.

Mr. President, we don't have any intelligence that would indicate that the North Koreans know you're coming, Brooks said.

"I got up this morning," Trump said, "and told Melania, kissed her goodbye, and said, 'I might not see you again.' It's not that I'm worried about myself," Trump added. "If something were to happen to the president of the United States, it would be the worst thing that could happen to us as a country."

Suddenly Marine One made a hard left bank and went into a loiter, holding in place. After a few minutes, the military aide slid his hand abruptly across his throat.

"We're turning around," John Kelly said. "We can't get in. It's too thick."

"This is terrible," Trump said. "I've got to get in. But I know I can't. I know you guys have got to make the decision. You've got to make a safety decision. I got it. This is horrible. This is going to be terrible." He worried that the news coverage would be about him turning back and not making it to the DMZ. "This is going to make us look weak."

Marine One landed safely and Trump went into the Beast. They waited a while to see if there would be a break in the weather so they could try again. Others could see Trump through the Beast's windows. There was an obvious rant happening inside the vehicle.

Brooks had a chance to speak briefly with McMaster while they waited. As senior Army officers, they had known each other a long time.

How are you? Brooks asked.

"I got to get a new flak vest," McMaster joked.

What do you mean?

"This one's got so many holes in it just from my day-to-day activities that I'm going to have to get a new flak vest."

The weather never cleared, and the trip was called off.

Trump later gave a rousing 35-minute speech to the South Korean National Assembly. Matt Pottinger, then serving as the National Security Council's senior director for Asian Affairs, was elated. There's never been a speech like that, he believed, though it was also reminiscent of a speech Reagan had once given in Korea. It was Trump's Morning in South Korea. He called the economic, cultural and political awakening there "the Korean Miracle"—an economy 40 times that of North Korea.

Trump could not resist, "Since my election exactly one year ago today, I celebrate with you. The United States is going through something of a miracle itself. Our stock market is at an all-time high." He cited low unemployment and a new "brilliant Supreme Court Justice," referring to Neil Gorsuch, whom he had nominated January 31.

He waved the big stick at North Korea. "Currently stationed in the vicinity of this peninsula are the three largest aircraft carriers in the world, loaded to the maximum."

He added, "We have nuclear submarines appropriately positioned."

The obsessive golfer said, "The Women's U.S. Open was held this year at Trump National Golf in Bedminster, New Jersey, and it just happened to be won by a great Korean golfer."

Twenty-four miles to the north, he said, is where "the prison state of North Korea sadly begins." Forced labor, famine, malnutrition, gulags, torture, rape, murder, Kim's cult of personal repressive leadership—"the horror of life in North Korea."

"America does not seek conflict or confrontation, but we will never run from it. We will not allow American cities to be threatened with destruction."

Addressing Kim, he said, "the weight of this crisis is on your conscience. . . . The weapons you are acquiring are not making you safer. They are putting your regime in grave danger. Every step you take down this dark path increases the peril you face."

THIRTEEN

————— ◆ —————

Meanwhile, one of Andy Kim's first actions had been to reach out to an old back-channel contact in the North Korean intelligence service he'd developed 20 years earlier. The White House sanctioned a meeting, and he arranged to meet his contact in a third country. His instructions were to find out what North Korea wanted.

North Korea was continuing its nuclear and missile testing, and making provocative public statements attacking the U.S. But Andy Kim sensed that was for domestic consumption in the North. The contact could not give Andy Kim authoritative information about the real goals because in North Korea only one person, the leader, has any significant control.

Andy Kim had no idea what might follow the meeting, where it might lead or in what direction. His only assessment was that North Korea also wanted to engaged. How and when were unclear.

Some clues soon began to emerge shortly after Trump's visit to South Korea. One of the first was Kim Jong Un's statements following a November 29 ICBM missile test, a huge milestone for North Korea. Instead of sounding bellicose, however, Kim Jong

Un gave a January 2018 speech effectively announcing he was done with military preparations and escalations. He now had his "mighty sword"—the powerful ICBM that could carry a nuclear weapon—to protect his country. His intention was to turn his focus to improving the North Korean economy.

There were also signs of a thaw in the usually tense relationship between South and North Korea. The newly elected South Korean president, the left-leaning Moon Jae In, had signaled he wanted closer relations with his Northern counterpart, hinting even possible reunification with the North. With the Winter Olympics scheduled to begin in early February in Pyeongchang, South Korea, an open question was North Korea. Would it participate? Would it cause trouble?

In January, Moon formally invited North Korea to talks about the Olympics, the first time in two years the two countries had talked formally, and North Korea announced it would send a delegation of athletes to participate in the games. A military hotline, disconnected for two years, also was reconnected.

Sensing an opportunity, Trump sent Vice President Pence on a tour of Asian countries, with the real purpose being a secret meeting with the North Koreans. Pence, however, denounced North Korea's nuclear intentions during his trip and the meeting was canceled two hours before its scheduled start time.

Less than a week after the end of the Olympics, however, President Moon, who was eager to deescalate tensions and engage the U.S. directly in talks, sent his national security adviser Chung Eui Yong, on March 5 to meet with the North Korean leader. Three days later, Chung visited the White House to brief key Trump cabinet members on what Kim Jong Un had promised.

Chung also had a meeting scheduled the next day with Trump. But Trump got word that the South Koreans were at the White

House meeting with McMaster and cabinet members. Why don't I just see them now? Trump said, jumping the gun and inviting Chung to the Oval Office.

Chung explained that Kim had made four explicit promises. He was committed to denuclearization; North Korea would refrain from any further nuclear or missile tests; routine joint military exercises between South Korea and the United States could continue. And lastly, Kim was eager to meet with Trump.

McMaster reminded the president that Kim had been willing to have his own uncle killed, and Trump should be careful about believing his promises.

"I'm willing to meet with Kim," Trump said, dismissing McMaster's caution. "Why don't you"—and he pointed to Chung— "go announce it."

It was unprecedented for such an important presidential announcement to be made by a foreign official at the White House. Trump wanted Chung to go before the cameras outside the West Wing and announce the four ideas. He directed McMaster to work with Chung on the statement.

McMaster and Pottinger sat down with Chung to make sure Trump's comments and intention were not misrepresented. It was a negotiation that took almost an hour.

Standing outside the West Wing with two other South Korean officials and no American ones, Chung made the announcement after dark. He faced the Sticks, so-called because of the array of microphones from TV news crews. He summarized the four ideas and Trump's agreement to meet.

"Along with President Trump," Chung said in the carefully hedged agreed-upon language, "we are optimistic about continuing a diplomatic process to test the *possibility* of a peaceful resolution."

The announcement was big news. No sitting American president had ever met with a North Korean leader.

Trump loved the American news coverage of the forthcoming

meeting—"audacious," "a breathtaking gamble," "dramatic," a reflection of Trump's "improvisational style," leaving "dazed White House aides" with "another day of swirling drama" that "upended" previous plans, "head-spinning."

But many from the foreign policy establishment criticized Trump for agreeing to meet without locking down some commitments from the North Korean leader. The piling on was intense. In this view Trump had instantly given the North Korean leadership the international standing and legitimacy it had long sought.

Evan S. Medeiros, an Asia expert and adviser to former President Obama, said at the time, "We got nothing for it. And Kim will never give up his nukes. Kim played Moon and is now playing Trump." The drumbeat continued. Dozens of articles and opinion pieces in the major media explored the downside of such a meeting, often harshly.

Nearly two years later—after the president had held three meetings with Kim Jong Un—I asked Trump if he had given too much power to Kim by agreeing to meet.

"You know what I did?" Trump said. "One thing. I met. Big fucking deal. It takes me two days. I met. I gave up nothing. I didn't give up sanctions. I didn't give him anything. Okay? Didn't give him anything."

I mentioned what President George W. Bush had once said to me about Kim's father, Kim Jong Il. "I loathe Kim Jong Il," Bush had said, because he starved his people and kept tens of thousands in deplorable, hard-labor prison camps.

"And you know what? That attitude got him nothing," Trump said. "In the meantime, they built a huge nuclear force during the last two administrations." So Trump said he agreed to meet. "What the fuck? It's a meeting. I agreed to meet. What? You mean instead of sitting home reading your book, I met?"

———

Before Trump's sudden announcement that he was willing to meet with Kim, Tillerson had been working the traditional State Department channel to North Korea through Sweden. Andy Kim didn't think Tillerson was fully utilizing the talents at the State Department. He was trying with just a few people on his own staff. Many veteran diplomats felt his management at State was heavy handed and some had resigned.

Tillerson often seemed at odds with the White House position. He'd twice before made public statements in support of talks, only to be contradicted by the White House. Trump wanted any talks to be between him and Kim.

The most recent episode had occurred in December 2017, when Tillerson said, "We've said from the diplomatic side we're ready to talk anytime North Korea would like to talk, and we're ready to have the first meeting without precondition." He added, "Let's just meet and let's—we can talk about the weather if you want." A White House spokesman pushed back, saying, "The administration is united in insisting that any negotiations with North Korea must wait until the regime fundamentally improves its behavior. As the secretary of state himself has said, this must include, but is not limited to, no further nuclear or missile tests."

Tillerson, whose relationship with Trump seemed to be badly fraying, began to hear chatter that something else was going on that he did not know about. He approached CIA director Pompeo.

You know, Pompeo said, we've got this channel. We keep it open all the time, but we're not doing anything.

Tillerson could tell Pompeo was not being honest with him. He was being shut out. That frustrated him. But he also thought the approach was wrong. The CIA seemed to be exactly the wrong route if they were to build some foundation to go forward with North Korea. Not only was it clandestine, but it excluded China.

Tillerson saw China, a critically important trading partner with North Korea, as central to North Korean policy. He told

President Xi in an earlier meeting, I have to know that you're standing behind Kim with your hand around his neck. And every time he misbehaves, you just give him a gentle squeeze so he knows you're there.

All Xi did was smile.

Tillerson was in Ethiopia, not at the White House, on March 8 when Trump had the South Koreans announce that he would meet with the North Korean leader. In fact, the day before the surprise announcement Tillerson had publicly revealed how far he was out of the loop, saying "We're a long way from negotiations."

CIA director Pompeo had also missed the announcement. He was on his plane coming back for the meeting scheduled the next day when Trump called the audible. Pompeo huddled with his deputy, Gina Haspel, and Andy Kim.

Haspel recounted what had happened.

What was the president's motive? Pompeo asked. Putting the South Koreans out there to make the announcement? Was it designed to distance Trump from the summit? That was unlikely since Trump would be out front personally with the North Korean leader. Or was it just one of Trump's impulsive, spur-of-the-moment decisions?

None of the three had an answer.

Andy Kim said the South Koreans had suggested to him that the North was hung up on a statement Trump had made during the 2016 campaign: "If he came here, I'd accept him," candidate Trump said of Kim Jong Un, "but I wouldn't give him a state dinner like we do for China and all these other people that rip us off." Trump had continued to rail against state dinners in general, adding that instead, "We should be eating a hamburger on a conference table."

North Korea had its own Lessons Learned from dealing with the United States, Andy Kim said. His North Korean counterparts had this explanation: Back in December 2000 President Clinton had intended to go to North Korea, but Republican George W. Bush had won the election instead of Clinton's vice president, Al Gore. As president-elect, Bush didn't want Clinton to make the trip. Clinton, now a lame duck, felt he had to honor the request and he canceled.

So what was the lesson? The North knew negotiations took a long time. The United States had elections every four years and plans could easily be derailed and everything could blow up. The best course was to start dealing with a new American administration early so there was time. So, that is one of the reasons the North wanted to deal with Trump early, Andy Kim said.

A few days later Tillerson was in Kenya, halfway through his trip to visit five African nations, when he received a call from chief of staff John Kelly at about 2:00 a.m. local time.

"Hey, you need to get back right away," Kelly said.

"What's going on?" Tillerson asked.

"The president's going to fire you," Kelly said. "I told him he can't do that while you're gone."

"Well, John, okay," Tillerson said. "What's going on?"

"I don't know. I don't know what happened." Kelly said he was in his office and one of his staffers told him that H. R. McMaster and U.N. ambassador Nikki Haley were in the Oval Office meeting with the president. "I rushed down the hall just in time to see them coming out. I walked in. All I know is the president's just ranting and raving about you. He said, 'It's time for Tillerson to go. Never did like him.'"

"Was there a specific issue?" Tillerson asked.

"I don't know," Kelly said. "I don't know what they said to him, but they got him all spun up."

"I'll have to see what the fastest I can get back is, but obviously I'll have to cancel a lot of head-of-state meetings and this is going to raise a lot of questions, and so we need to think about how you want me to respond to those," Tillerson said. "Because people are going to wonder, has something bad happened back in Washington?"

Kelly called Tillerson back about an hour later. The president had agreed not to do anything until Tillerson returned. "But I still think you ought to try to get back as soon as you can," Kelly said.

Tillerson truncated his trip by one day without canceling any of his head-of-state visits, and landed at Andrews Air Force base at 4:00 a.m. on March 13. He called Kelly. The secretary of state had been up for nearly 72 hours straight.

"I'm on the ground," Tillerson said. "I'm going to run to the house. I'm going to take a shower. I'm going to get about two hours of sleep. And I'll be in the office between 9:00 and 10:00."

Shortly before 9:00 a.m., Tillerson was getting dressed when he got a call from his own chief of staff.

"Have you seen it?" she asked.

"No." Tillerson did not have a Twitter account, so anytime the president tweeted something, somebody had to tell him.

The staffer read Tillerson the president's tweet, posted at 8:44 a.m., firing the nation's chief diplomat.

"Mike Pompeo, Director of the CIA, will become our new Secretary of State," Trump wrote in the tweet. "He will do a fantastic job! Thank you to Rex Tillerson for his service! Gina Haspel will become the new Director of the CIA, and the first woman so chosen. Congratulations to all!"

Tillerson was never told why he was fired. The president did not give him a reason. It had earlier leaked out that Tillerson had called Trump a "fucking moron" at a July 20, 2017, Tank meeting. Probably nothing could have triggered Trump's insecurities more.

After the news broke, Tillerson got a call from Mattis.

"Mr. Secretary, I don't know what to say," Mattis said.

"Jim, you don't have to say anything," Tillerson said. "But I want to say something: Thank you. I couldn't have had a better partner."

They had stopped or slowed some of Trump's intentions in Afghanistan and South Korea, but their ambitious goal of directing foreign policy had largely failed.

Speaking to reporters on the South Lawn of the White House that morning, Trump thanked Tillerson for his service and said he was "a good man." But he was hardly effusive in his praise.

"Rex and I have been talking about this for a long time," Trump said. "We get along, actually, quite well, but we disagreed on things."

Around noon, Tillerson got a call from the president, who was traveling to California for a fundraiser and to inspect border wall prototypes.

"Hey Rex, how you doing?" Trump said.

"I'm fine, Mr. President."

"Well, I hope you saw all those nice things I said about you," Trump said. "You know, you're going to be fine. I know you never wanted to do this job. You can go back home to your ranch now, where you really wanted to go."

Trump invited Tillerson to come visit him in the Oval Office when he returned from California. "We'll get a nice picture of us shaking hands."

"Okay," Tillerson said, and hung up the phone. At 2:00 p.m., he gave a five-minute farewell address at the State Department in which he didn't mention Trump by name.

"This can be a very mean-spirited town," he said. "But you don't have to choose to participate in that. Each of us gets to choose the person we want to be, and the way we want to be treated, and the way we treat others."

The betrayal was deep for Tillerson. In his view, the president had broken two of the three promises he had asked for before taking the job: Trump had agreed to let Tillerson pick his own senior staff, but Trump or the White House had continually meddled with or vetoed Tillerson's picks. And the president had pledged they would never have a dispute in public, but he had been summarily fired, without discussion and by tweet. The only promise Trump had kept was not to pull Tillerson's nomination.

"Tillerson Ousted as Trump Silences Dissent in Cabinet," read the headline across the front page of the next day's *New York Times*.

Trump questioned Mattis when they met for lunch not long after Tillerson's firing.

"Aren't you friends with him?" Trump asked.

"No, no, we weren't friends," Mattis said. "We're best of friends. But I'll work with whoever you put in, because you're the president. You're the one who was elected, not me."

As a first step Trump wanted Pompeo to go to North Korea to meet Kim Jong Un on his behalf.

Andy Kim described for Pompeo what it would be like to meet with the North Koreans. They will start with the party line that the United States created the hostility and was exclusively responsible for the bad relations. Then they'll repeat and repeat. You're going to be just sick of hearing the same thing. Don't object or try to argue with them. They were told to make that statement. You are going to have to let them finish. So you're going to stay there for a long time. They've been practicing this for a long time. Relax. But you'll never enjoy it.

On Easter weekend 2018, Pompeo flew to North Korea. He was still CIA director, not yet confirmed as secretary of state. Andy Kim and a few staff accompanied him to Pyongyang. After they arrived, they were escorted to a room in a government guesthouse. Kim Yong Chol, the vice chairman of the Central

Committee and former general and former head of the North Korean intelligence service, greeted Pompeo. Kim Yong Chol was generally thought to be the number two, but with such a dominant number one, it was hard to tell for sure.

You have come a long way, but we have had these hostilities for 70 years, Kim Yong Chol said. Yet Kim Jong Un has made four promises. He is willing to meet with President Trump. He intends to denuclearize. The leader will accept joint United States–South Korean military exercises. And he will abstain from testing.

South Korea, our ally, told us that was what Kim Jong Un had said, Pompeo acknowledged. We trust our ally but we need to verify. Without verification, we have a problem. Our mission is to hear from Kim Jong Un directly.

Why don't you rest, Kim Yong Chol said, and I'll let you know when and if Kim Jong Un will see you.

The tentativeness was maddening, but Andy Kim knew it was inevitable.

Kim Yong Chol left and came back quickly.

I think the chairman is ready to meet you so let's go, he said.

Only two people could attend—no staff. Pompeo and Andy Kim went. After driving 15 minutes, they approached a regular-looking office building, and drove inside. Immediately they saw it was a fortress concealed inside what looked like an office building. There was a large wall with lots of guards and defenses.

In a conference room, Kim sat on one side of a table, and Pompeo took a seat on the other. Kim wore his trademark black suit and seemed a little nervous at first. He did not speak from any notes or talking points. That was when Kim told Pompeo, "We were very close" to war.

The South Koreans told us that you have intent to denuclearize, Pompeo said. Is that true?

I'm a father, the leader said. I don't want my kids to carry nuclear weapons on their backs the rest of their lives. So, yes.

Pompeo and the leader quickly agreed they did not want the tensions to escalate. That was good for no one. So let's come up with solutions.

You told the South Koreans that you're willing to meet with President Trump, Pompeo said, and you saw the president openly say he accepts the idea. So can we talk about how to set up a working-level meeting to come up with the right agenda for the summit?

Kim seemed to agree.

Andy Kim thought that Kim quickly relaxed and seemed very natural.

The rest of the discussion focused on the four promises.

Trump and the North Korean leader exchanged short letters coinciding with Pompeo's trip.

"Dear Chairman Kim," Trump wrote in three paragraphs, "Thank you for extending an invitation for us to meet. I would be glad to meet with you.

"I would like to convey my thanks as well for hosting Director Pompeo in Pyongyang. He has my total confidence.

"I look forward to working with you toward greater improvement in our relations and to mutually creating a better and safer future."

Kim's letter was more enthusiastic.

"Dear Excellency," Kim began. Trump later told me with pride that Kim addressed him as "Excellency."

"I'm prepared to cooperate with you in sincerity and dedication," the North Korean leader said, "to accomplish a great feat that no one in the past has been able to achieve and that is unexpected by the whole world."

Pompeo traveled to North Korea a second time on May 8 and 9, just weeks after the Senate confirmed him as secretary of state in a 57 to 42 vote.

A key question was who really had influence with Kim Jong Un. At dinner, his sister Kim Yo Jong was deferential, calling him "Great Leader" and "Supreme Leader, never "My Brother." That could reflect her discipline, Andy Kim reasoned. She was clearly devoted to him and a behind-the-scenes player, handling protocol, coordination of events. Often she was the key emissary. At the dinner she didn't cross the line to demonstrate familiarity with her brother.

The contrast with Ri Sol Ju, Kim Jong Un's wife, was stunning. Ri was in her early 30s with long dark hair. She was the mother of Kim's children and as a teenager had reportedly been a member of a North Korean cheerleading team. At one point the Great Leader lit a cigarette.

That's not good for your health, Andy Kim said matter-of-factly. He hoped it would be taken as just a friendly aside.

Kim Yong Chol and the sister froze up and seemed almost paralyzed, waiting for Kim's reaction. No one spoke to the leader that way.

Yes, that's right, said his wife, Ri. I've told my husband about the dangers of smoking.

At the dinner, course after course was served. The North Koreans wanted Secretary of State Pompeo to stay the night. We came at sunup and we have to leave at sundown, Pompeo said.

The dinner was dragging on. Finally Pompeo said, We're not getting anywhere. We need you to give us a list of sites for developing and testing nuclear weapons. He did not make much headway and announced he was going to leave.

The North Koreans held up his plane for several hours but finally let him depart.

Following Pompeo's departure, three Americans who were

being held prisoner in North Korea—Tony Kim, Kim Hak Song and Kim Dong Chul—were released and safely returned to the United States.

Early on the morning of May 10, Trump greeted the freed detainees when they arrived at Joint Base Andrews in Maryland.

"We want to thank Kim Jong Un, who really was excellent to these three incredible people," Trump said. "We're starting off on a new footing."

FOURTEEN

———◆———

After former FBI director Robert Mueller was appointed special counsel to investigate Russia-Trump 2016 campaign links, Trump began a drumbeat of attacks. But Senator Lindsey Graham, Republican from South Carolina and Trump's closest friend in the Senate, took a different tack.

"I respect the decision," Graham said on Fox News. "He's a good choice in terms of respect among members of both parties. He's a seasoned former FBI director."

The two friends continued to disagree in public and in private.

In April 2018, Graham cosponsored a bill to protect Mueller and his work. Cosponsored as well by a bipartisan group of moderates—Thom Tillis, a North Carolina Republican, and Democrats Cory Booker of New Jersey and Chris Coons of Delaware—the bill was approved by the Senate Judiciary Committee 14 to 7. But Senate Majority Leader Mitch McConnell said it was unnecessary, and Graham knew he would not bring it to the floor.

Trump's opposition to the probe went beyond Twitter outbursts. The president called White House counsel Don McGahn at home twice on June 17, 2017, and ordered him to have Mueller removed by Deputy Attorney General Rod Rosenstein. "Call Rod, tell Rod that Mueller has conflicts and can't be the special counsel," Trump said in the second call. "Call me back when you do it." McGahn did not follow through on the president's orders.

Graham didn't buy Trump's attacks on Mueller and the Russia investigation. Over the years, Graham had watched Mueller as FBI director and concluded he was independent and fair-minded.

If Trump had colluded or coordinated with the Russian government in 2016, it would be a disaster for Trump and the Republican Party.

"Listen," Graham told Trump, "if you actually did this, even though it was before you were president, you cannot serve."

"I didn't do it," Trump told Graham. "I've done a lot of bad things, but I didn't do this."

"I believe you on both counts," Graham said. The denial, in his view, had the ring of truth.

In private conversation with the president, Graham repeatedly urged Trump to let Mueller's investigation take its course. If Trump was being honest with the country and had done nothing wrong, Graham argued, he should let the investigation go forward.

There's only one man in the country with the ability to clear you of working with the Russians, Graham told Trump in early 2019. "I can't clear you of working with the Russians. You can't clear you of working with the Russians. If you didn't work with the Russians, there's one of two things going to happen. He's going to make shit up to prove that you did when you didn't," which was Trump's fear. Or he's going to tell the truth.

Graham continued to see Mueller as a straight shooter.

"If you're being honest with me and I'm right about Mueller, you'll be fine," he told the president. "Now, if I'm wrong about Mueller, then I'll be the first to say it. If you're not honest with me, I'll be the first to say that."

"I didn't make phone calls," Trump told Graham. The president was insistent: "I didn't work with Russians!"

"Mr. President, there's only one thing that would turn me against you, and that is if you actually worked with the Russians."

"I didn't," Trump said.

"I believe you," Graham replied. "Because you can't work with your own government. Why should you be working with the Russian government?"

Trump laughed. "Yeah, that's true," he said.

But there was nothing funny about the Mueller investigation. In the media, as well as among Democrats and many Trump critics, the Mueller probe was widely held out as Trump's Watergate.

"You can see evidence in plain sight on the issue of collusion, pretty compelling evidence," House Intelligence Committee chairman Adam Schiff said in a February 2019 interview on CNN.

In Washington there was an expectation that Mueller's report was the other shoe to drop and could potentially lead to Trump's impeachment.

Mueller's team supposedly did not leak, which only increased expectations that he had something big.

The Washington Post and *The New York Times* continued the media investigation, publishing dozens of front-page stories about many of the same questions Mueller was investigating.

FIFTEEN

—◆—◆—

Pompeo returned from Pyongyang in April with a letter from Kim expressing an openness to meet, and passed it to Trump. The president wasted no time writing back.

"I agree with everything you said," Trump wrote in a letter to Kim dated April 3, "and have very little doubt that our meeting will be a momentous one for both our countries and for the rest of the world."

Plans for their meeting got under way. It was a remarkable pivot in relations between the chairman and the president, who just months earlier had been exchanging insults that were unusually personal.

The diplomatic courtship between Trump and Kim in 2018 and 2019 is captured in 27 letters that I obtained and 25 are reported here for the first time. Florid and grandiloquent, they trace how the two forged a personal and emotional bond.

Trump has personally said they are "love letters." They are more than that—they reveal a decision by both to become friends. Whether genuine or not, probably only history will tell.

The language is not out of the traditional diplomatic playbook. They resemble declarations of personal fealty that might be uttered by the Knights of the Round Table, or perhaps suitors.

A first meeting was nearly scuttled after Trump was quoted suggesting in a May 17, 2018, meeting that if Kim didn't make a deal with Trump, he could meet a fate similar to slain Libyan leader Muammar al-Qaddafi, who was overthrown in 2011.

"The model, if you look at that model with Qaddafi, that was a total decimation," Trump said publicly. "We went in there to beat him. Now that model would take place if we don't make a deal, most likely. But if we make a deal, I think Kim Jong Un is going to be very, very happy."

North Korea's vice foreign minister, Choe Son Hui, responded: "Whether the U.S. will meet us at a meeting room or encounter us at a nuclear-to-nuclear showdown is entirely dependent upon the decision and behavior of the United States."

On May 24, Trump wrote Kim a letter canceling the summit.

"Sadly, based on the tremendous anger and open hostility displayed in your most recent statement, I feel it is inappropriate, at this time, to have this long-planned meeting," Trump wrote. He tweeted out a copy of the letter.

But the dispute was short-lived. South Korean president Moon Jae In helped arrange talks between American and North Korean diplomats on the North Korean side of the border on May 27, and the summit was back on schedule just days after Trump had canceled it.

Kim wrote to Trump on May 29 that he had "great expectations" for the summit, "an event the entire world is focusing on." He added: "I sincerely hope that our first meeting, about to happen at no small pains, will lead to more wonderful and meaningful meetings."

On June 12, 2018, Trump and Kim finally met at the Capella Hotel in Singapore, beginning their summit at 9:05 a.m. local time.

The two shook hands before the news media for about 12 seconds before turning to the cameras.

"Holy shit," the president later told me he said to himself. The moment made a memorable impression on him. He claimed the wall of news cameras was among the largest he had ever seen in his life, even more than he had seen in Hollywood at the Academy Awards.

After shaking hands, the two retreated to a one-on-one meeting. Trump later said he found Kim to be "far beyond smart."

In their initial meeting, Trump said, the two leaders talked about "the tremendous potential" North Korea had. Trump said he told Kim he didn't want to remove him, alluding to the Qaddafi threat, and he wanted him to lead the country to greatness. "It could be one of the great economic powers of the world," Trump recalled saying. "It's locationally situated between China, Russia and South Korea."

By end of the meeting, Trump and Kim signed a short, four-point agreement. The most consequential part of the agreement said that North Korea, reaffirming its earlier agreement with South Korea, "commits to work toward complete denuclearization of the Korean Peninsula."

Kim did not return from the summit empty-handed. Trump said he would guarantee North Korea's security. In a news conference after the meeting, Trump made a surprise announcement: The United States would be ending joint military exercises with South Korea. The North Korean regime had long seen the joint exercises as a threat.

"We will be stopping the war games, which will save us a tremendous amount of money, unless and until we see the future negotiation is not going along like it should," Trump said. "But we'll be saving a tremendous amount of money. Plus, I think it's very provocative."

While the détente with North Korea was far from complete, Trump was quick to declare the trip a success.

"Just landed—a long trip, but everybody can now feel much safer than the day I took office," Trump wrote in a tweet the morning of June 13. "There is no longer a Nuclear Threat from North Korea."

In a second tweet, Trump added: "Before taking office people were assuming that we were going to War with North Korea. President Obama said that North Korea was our biggest and most dangerous problem. No longer—sleep well tonight!"

Trump's 391-word agreement with Kim did not end the nuclear threat from North Korea—it simply reaffirmed a loosely worded declaration that Kim had signed with South Korea in April 2018. The agreement was less specific regarding denuclearization than prior agreements Kim's predecessors had signed in 1992 and 2005 during the Clinton and Bush administrations.

"Saying it doesn't make it so," Senator Chuck Schumer of New York, the Democratic minority leader, said in remarks on the Senate floor on June 13. "North Korea still has nuclear weapons. It still has ICBMs. It still has the United States in danger. Somehow President Trump thinks when he says something it becomes reality."

Mattis was taken completely by surprise that Trump had canceled the training exercises with South Korea.

In accordance with Trump's announcement, Mattis suspended major military exercises such as Ulchi-Freedom Guardian, an annual exercise which involved 18,000 U.S. troops and up to 50,000 South Korean troops.

Smaller units, however, needed to train, Mattis told Trump. "We're not going to have the troops sitting in the barracks. That's no good. The troops are worthless to you as president, they're worthless to me as secretary of defense if they are not out there training." He reminded the president that these troops in South Korea rotated to and from Iraq and Afghanistan. They needed to be battle-ready.

There is too much emphasis on terrorism and fighting the old Bush wars, Trump said.

That is so the terrorists can't come after the United States here, Mattis replied, as happened with the 9/11 attacks.

"I always hear that," Trump complained. "That means we've got to fight everywhere in the world."

"No, it doesn't, sir."

Back at the Pentagon, Mattis ordered a workaround. "All platoon, company, battalion, brigade level exercises, regimental exercises continue," he said. "Air group continues. Naval exercises continue. The president doesn't mean we're all going to sit in the barracks now and look at the walls, okay guys. So let's not everybody suck their thumbs."

Smaller exercises with regiment-sized units made up of several thousand troops didn't have to be briefed back to Washington. Only the high-level exercises were in the president's crosshairs. Mattis reduced those to command post and communication network exercises. "They won't have troops in the field." No field maneuvers, nothing that could be called a war game.

In South Korea, the U.S. and South Korea commander General Brooks quickly worked to reduce the visibility of the exercises. He immediately scaled back the size of units, changed the timing and lowered the volume of communications so there was less public news about the training and less in view of Kim and Trump.

Mattis was frustrated with the message being sent to China, Russia and North Korea. "What we're doing is we're actually showing how to destroy America," he said later. "That's what we're showing them. How to isolate us from all of our allies. How to take us down. And it's working very well. We are declaring war on one another inside America. It's actually working against us right now."

SIXTEEN

On February 13, 2018, Dan Coats and the other top intelligence chiefs gave public testimony before the Senate Intelligence Committee about global security threats.

Senator Mark Warner of Virginia, the senior Democrat on the committee and thus its vice chairman, took a slight detour. "With a simple yes or no, do you agree with Director Pompeo that we haven't seen a significant decrease in the Russian activity" to interfere in the upcoming 2018 and 2020 U.S. elections?

All agreed with Pompeo, then still head of the CIA, who said to laughter, "I agree with Director Pompeo."

Under the headline "Russia Is Targeting 2018, Top Spies Warn," *The Washington Post* reported the assessment of the intelligence chiefs "stands in contrast to President Trump." In its front-page story, *The New York Times* reported, "The warnings were striking in their contrast to President Trump's public comments."

The next day at the PDB, Trump was upset. Why did that have to go public? Why wasn't their testimony behind closed doors in a secure room?

Coats knew this was a sore point with the president and he wanted to be accommodating since the intelligence chiefs had made their point. The Senate Intelligence Committee had insisted on a public hearing, Coats told Trump. "We don't like it. We protested. We would prefer to do this in a secure environment."

After a summit meeting with Putin in Helsinki, Finland, on July 16, 2018, Trump stood next to the Russian leader at a press conference and openly questioned the conclusion of the U.S. intelligence agencies that Russia had interfered in the 2016 presidential election.

"They said they think it's Russia," Trump said. "I have President Putin. He just said it's not Russia." He added, "I don't see any reason why it would be. . . . President Putin was extremely strong and powerful in his denial."

Trump had met with Putin for over two hours alone without any other U.S. official present other than the translator.

Former Republican House Speaker Newt Gingrich, who normally supported Trump, tweeted: "It is the most serious mistake of his presidency and must be corrected—immediately."

John O. Brennan, the former CIA director for President Obama and a persistent Trump critic, went further, tweeting, "Donald Trump's press conference performance in Helsinki rises to & exceeds the threshold of 'high crimes and misdemeanors.'" He called Trump "treasonous," adding, "Not only were Trump's comments imbecilic, he is wholly in the pocket of Putin."

Coats, some 16 months into the job, was beside himself and released his own rebuke: "We have been clear in our assessments of Russian meddling in the 2016 election and their ongoing, pervasive efforts to undermine our democracy, and we will continue to provide unvarnished and objective intelligence in support of our national security."

As DNI, Coats had access to the most sensitive intelligence—intercepts and the best deep-cover human CIA sources in Russia. He suspected the worst but found nothing that would show Trump was indeed in Putin's pocket. He and key staff members examined the intelligence as carefully as possible. There was no proof, period. But Coats's doubts continued, never fully dissipating.

Coats knew that Russia had a "demographic crisis," with a predicted 7 percent population drop in the next 30 years. But he also knew Putin was playing his weak hand very well. Trump's affinity for Putin was never fully explained to Coats. Whenever he would question something about Russia or Putin, the president would say, but they have nukes. They've got nukes. Coats must have heard it dozens of times. Once the president put it this way: "Russia has 1,243 fucking nuclear weapons." Actually, Russia had about 1,600 actively deployed large nuclear warheads and 6,500 overall. Trump believed such a large nuclear arsenal changed the strategic calculus.

July 19, 2018, was a turning point for Coats. He was attending a public security forum in Aspen, Colorado—an annual gathering in an informal atmosphere. The forum included discussion panels, interviews and long dinners in the cool mountains far from the hot Washington summer. Sitting tieless and relaxed in an afternoon session, Coats was interviewed onstage by NBC foreign affairs correspondent Andrea Mitchell. Just before opening a question-and-answer session, Mitchell reported the breaking news that the White House had announced Putin would be visiting the White House in the fall.

"Okaaaaay," Coats said, laughing it up. "That's going to be special."

The Aspen audience of foreign, defense and intelligence policy experts immediately joined the laughter. Coats had made it clear, not very subtly, that he did not know what was going on between Trump and Putin.

Back in Washington, Trump was furious. The director of national intelligence seemed to be making fun of the president. Coats made a public apology, and later went to see the president to try to explain.

"The last thing I wanted to do, Mr. President, was embarrass you. That was not my intent. I was so taken by surprise. I just didn't handle it the way I should have, and I want to apologize to you for that."

Trump knew how to shatter someone with pure, conspicuous silence. There was no outburst. He just listened and said absolutely nothing. He was as brutally nonresponsive as a person could be; the art of the cold, silent rebuke.

Coats realized the trust between them, never solid, had evaporated, blown away in a cool July breeze.

A week later at the opening of a White House meeting, Trump said scathingly, "Dan has become a celebrity."

The greatest threat to the national security apparatus, Coats believed, was that Trump wanted to ignore any kind of process that went through experts—people steeped in certain issues or certain parts of the world, often for their whole careers. In effect, and often literally, the president said, I don't need that to be done. I don't need these people. I don't need a National Security Council. I just need myself, and perhaps three or four people I trust and work with. Trump didn't care for assessments or options. It was just whatever Trump wanted to do.

"Oh, Mr. President," Coats said more than once, "it's a little more complicated than that."

Trump would get upset as if he was being undermined and thwarted. The president believed he could pick up the phone and call anybody he wanted. Trump's attitude was: "I can solve all these problems." He thought he could get better intelligence on his own. Coats knew that key leaders such as Putin, Xi of China and Erdogan of Turkey would lie to Trump. They played Trump skillfully. They would roll out the red carpet for him, flatter him, then do what they wanted.

Coats felt like he had never cracked the code with Trump.

"I can't believe what he said," Coats often exclaimed to his staff, wife or Mattis, reacting to some Trumpian declaration. And then the next day, Trump would say the opposite. Coats's head was often spinning.

In late July 2018, just weeks after the Trump-Putin meeting, Coats gathered the intelligence chiefs—FBI director Christopher Wray, NSA director General Paul Nakasone, CIA director Gina Haspel—in the Situation Room for a classified briefing to President Trump on election security and foreign power interference in the upcoming 2018 midterm elections. Haspel had replaced Pompeo at the CIA in May.

Though Coats knew Russian interference was a sore subject with the president, he charged ahead with the briefing. We continue to see a pervasive messaging campaign by Russia to try to weaken and divide the United States, he said. Russia is the chief culprit, but other countries are potentially involved—China, Iran. We will assure the American people that their vote will be counted accurately and won't be manipulated.

I like that, Trump said.

The NSA and CIA had evidence, highly classified, that the Russians had placed malware in the election registration system in at least two counties in Florida—St. Lucie County and Washington

County. There was no evidence yet that the malware had been activated. It was sitting there to be used.

The voting system vendor used by Florida was used by state election registration systems all around the country.

The Russian malware was sophisticated and could be activated in counties with particular demographics. For instance, in areas with higher percentages of Black residents, the malware could erase every tenth voter, almost certainly reducing the total vote count for Democrats. The same could potentially be activated to reduce Trump votes in Republican districts.

The bottom line: The Russians are here.

CIA director Haspel was among the most vocal about the possibly catastrophic impact. This could be potentially more damaging than prior Russian meddling.

Coats said his office was leading an interagency working group that met weekly to integrate their efforts to insure election security.

FBI director Wray said he had a Foreign Influence Task Force working with all of his 56 FBI field offices to deal with the threat that was both broad and deep in scope. The Russian 2016 interference could be duplicated and intensified.

Other than the highly classified information about the malware, Trump said he wanted the intelligence leaders to tell the public.

"You should do this," Trump said pointing to Coats. "Go public. Dan, take that to the press corps here in the White House." He wanted it done right away. "That's great."

Coats was surprised. It was the only time Trump had asked Coats to convert an intelligence briefing into a presentation for the public.

So on August 2, Coats and most of the intelligence chiefs appeared together in the White House press briefing room. Haspel was unable to make it because of some previous commitment.

Coats later chuckled, marveling at her good tradecraft. She knew when to be present and when not to be—particularly when not to be out front publicly.

"The president has specifically directed us to make the matter of election meddling and securing our election process a top priority," Coats told the press corps. Coats mentioned Russia many times, the other intelligence chiefs just a few times.

Coats couldn't help himself. "It goes beyond the elections, it goes to Russia's intent to undermine our democratic values, drive a wedge between our allies, and do a number of nefarious things," he said.

Asked by a reporter if he would support more sanctions on Russia, Coats stepped out of his intelligence role and went further about the policy of relations with Russia. "I would support any efforts that we can collectively put together to send a signal to Russia that there is a cost—a price to pay for what they're doing, and if we want to have any kind of relationship whatsoever in dealing with things of mutual interest, the Russians have to stop doing what they're doing, or it's simply not going to happen."

Almost the minute the words came out of his mouth, Coats realized he had overreached by suggesting that the entire U.S.-Russia relationship might be in jeopardy. It was an answer better suited to his former role as senator than his current one as DNI.

At the next intelligence briefing, Trump blew up in a rage and began to chew them all out. What was that briefing? he asked, apparently upset about all the focus on Russia. "Why'd you do that?"

"Because we were told to do that by you," Coats said.

Mr. President, Haspel said, defending her colleagues though she had not been part of the press conference, that's exactly what you told us to do. We did that because you said do it. We didn't say anything more than what you said to go out and do.

Coats's mind whirled. The incidents of discord kept piling up.

In one meeting, Trump handed Coats an article on his wife, Marsha, dated September 14, 2018. It was a nice light article, filled with pictures, on her educational, family and evangelical past and what it was like to be the wife of Trump's top intelligence man.

"Show that to your wife!" Trump said to Coats, almost throwing it in his face. "Give that to your wife." It almost seemed to be an echo of Trump's comment about Coats being a celebrity.

At this point, Coats had become so flummoxed by Trump and the tense, almost nonexistent relationship that he interpreted the president's comment to mean that his wife was more on Trump's side than Coats.

Representative Devin Nunes, the Republican chairman of the House Intelligence Committee, publicly alleged in early 2018 that on numerous occasions the intelligence community had collected information about U.S. citizens involved in the Trump transition. Nunes said that the Obama administration had improperly "unmasked" sensitive intelligence reports so that they could identify who, precisely, was speaking with foreign intelligence targets.

Normally, if a target of U.S. foreign intelligence is under surveillance while speaking with an American citizen, the citizen's identity is "masked" in the intelligence report with a placeholder such as "US Person 1." Unmasking was routine when an intelligence or other official needed to know the identity of the U.S. citizen in order to understand the report. For example, if a foreign ambassador were to speak to a U.S. citizen while under surveillance, it would be routine for an intelligence official reviewing the report to request the unmasking of the name of the citizen.

Trump thought Nunes was exposing the spying that he contended had been directed at his campaign. He thought it was great.

After one briefing Coats took the president aside.

"Mr. President," Coats said, trying to figure out a way to be tactful. Unmasking happens routinely thousands of times a year, he explained. "I know Devin Nunes is trying to be doing everything he can to support you. But he passes information to you that turns out to be false. In the end, it hurts you. Devin has told you something that is not true. If you would contact us first so we can verify that, whether it's true or not, it puts you in a better position. We could assess whether or not what has been said is backed up by the evidence, or factual, before you go public."

Trump did not agree at all. "Devin Nunes is the most courageous person in town." To others, Trump said that Nunes should get the Congressional Medal of Honor.

Coats knew President Dwight Eisenhower had said that the White House is "the loneliest house I've ever been in." It seemed to Coats that Trump was alone a lot in an empty house, particularly on weekends. And that, Coats believed, had to have an impact, increasing Trump's sense of isolation. Coats found that Trump was becoming more and more paranoid and lonely.

The president's phone habits were also troubling to Coats, especially at night. At one point after about nine months in office, Coats had stopped getting transcripts or readouts of the president's conversations with foreign leaders. He had his staff inquire with the NSC staff. Why? He never got an explanation after several tries. But he never asked the president directly. Coats finally concluded that the mad and maddening phone calls reflected Trump's style, who he is. And it wasn't going to be fixed.

One response was to let the disarray flow over him, but Marsha could see her husband internalized the turmoil.

Coats knew that Pompeo was better at managing the president than the rest of them. He had the president's confidence. A number of times when Pompeo had still been CIA director, Coats and the other intelligence chiefs would turn to him and say, you're the best person to present this to the president, because we don't think he's going to like it. But if you present it, he may go along. Pompeo was successful in showing that withdrawing all U.S. troops from Afghanistan—one of the president's longtime goals, even obsessions—would risk another 9/11 style attack.

Pompeo, the West Point graduate and former Army officer, knew not to challenge Trump openly. When Trump wanted to withdraw from the Iran nuclear deal, Pompeo only argued that Iran was in technical compliance.

Ted Gistaro, an up-and-coming CIA officer with two decades' experience, was Trump's principal briefer at the PDB sessions until 2019, when he was replaced by Beth Sanner. Gistaro, who had started before the election, pulled all the intelligence together and interacted with the president more than anyone else from the intelligence world. He took copious notes during every Oval Office briefing. Gistaro had a day-to-day compilation of all the formal intelligence presentations and discussions in the Oval Office. Trump trusted him and the two had a good relationship.

But one day the president impatiently lashed out at Gistaro. Coats had never seen Trump target Gistaro, who seemed shocked.

Coats walked out with Gistaro. "Ted, how are you? I'm sorry you had to take that hit."

"I'm not working for this president," Gistaro replied sharply. "I'm working for the integrity of the intelligence community."

Coats's relations with Trump soured quickly as the president persisted in asking Coats to stop or get control of the FBI's Russian investigation. Trump wanted Coats to say there was no evidence of coordination or conspiracy with Russia in the 2016 presidential campaign.

Coats repeatedly tried to point out that the FBI had a criminal side and an intelligence side. He had oversight and a role in the intelligence side. But he had no role, zero, in the criminal investigations—including the Mueller probe of Russian interference.

Trump disagreed, or did not understand, and acted as if Coats was insubordinate.

SEVENTEEN

— ◆ —

Mattis and his counterpart, Chinese defense minister Wei Fenghe, boarded a helicopter at the Pentagon on November 8, 2018, for a 10-minute flight south over the Potomac River. Washington glistened on the other side of the tree-lined, meandering river. It was a postcard picture, and the world seemed calm and at peace. It wasn't, Mattis knew.

Their destination was Mount Vernon, the historic estate of George Washington. After landing, the leaders of two of the world's most powerful militaries stepped into the crisp fall air.

Mattis was on a mission both personal and professional. As the civilian head of the United States armed forces, he was sure that his job was, if possible, not simply to avoid war but to prevent war.

China was building up a nuclear strike force—not just a few nukes intended for deterrence, or what the French call a *force de frappe*, but a significant nuclear force.

Mattis knew he had to proceed carefully—firmly, but gently. Early in his career, he had been a Marine recruiter and had often been sent into schools where his presence was not welcome. The experience had taught him the value of persuasion when you could not order someone to comply.

Wei, a former member of China's governing Politburo and a former artillery and rocket force officer, had not seen combat. Mattis had, in the deserts of the Middle East—Kuwait, Afghanistan, Iraq. Mattis believed a lack of wartime experience often lured people into taking risks they otherwise might not.

Actors playing George and Martha Washington escorted Mattis and Wei around the 500-acre estate. In the 21-room main house, Mattis intentionally stopped and pointed out the key to the Bastille, prominently displayed in Mount Vernon's central hall. The key had been a gift to George Washington from the Marquis de Lafayette, who had received it after angry French citizens had stormed the Bastille, a symbol of royal repression, near the start of the French Revolution.

"You see, in true revolutionary societies, you let political prisoners *out* of jail," Mattis said. It could not be lost on Wei that Mattis knew China was now considered the global leader in the number of political prisoners.

At the end of the tour, the actors retreated to the estate's greenhouse. Mattis and Wei, accompanied by only an interpreter, continued their walk along a path. Mattis carried a lantern to light the way.

Mattis reminded Wei, "We weren't part of the 100 years of humiliation," a reference to a time of international subjugation of China when many countries extracted huge financial concessions. Except for a brief time spanning from the beginning of the Cold War in 1949 to 1972 with Nixon's opening of China, "we haven't been adversaries. The American people actually have an affection for China."

Now Mattis pushed closer to the bone. "Are you aware that it was the Americans that created the world that allowed the hard-working Chinese people to advantage themselves and move out of poverty?" Mattis asked, turning to look at Wei. Trade with America had helped propel the dramatic modernization of China.

Wei looked intently at Mattis and pulled him close, an apparent gesture of unusual affection.

"Yes," Wei said. "And we know we owe the Americans most of the thanks for this." No ambiguity. "Absolutely," he said. "We owe the Americans most."

"Well, that's good to hear," Mattis said. "So I hope we can figure out how to make things work."

Mattis had been trying for months to develop a strong relationship with his Chinese counterpart. While his earlier personal meetings had been cordial, there were underlying tensions stemming from the trade war and China's expansion in the South China Sea, where they built artificial islands and installed missile systems and landing strips for jet fighters and bombers on the contested Spratly Islands.

The U.S. Navy was apoplectic over the Chinese expansion into what was internationally considered free and open seas, and where it regularly conducted freedom of navigation exercises.

Mattis and Wei's first meeting at a June 2018 conference for Asian defense ministers in Singapore had been followed by Mattis's visit to Beijing's Forbidden City later that month, where he was greeted with a night he thought made *The Great Gatsby* look like a cheap date. Now, six months later, Mattis decided it was time for a more candid discussion with his counterpart.

As they continued down the path at Mount Vernon, Wei told Mattis he was disappointed China had been disinvited in May from RIMPAC, a massive international naval military exercise held biannually in Hawaii, after China placed weapons in the Spratly Islands.

"What do you expect me to do?" Mattis asked. "Two months before the biggest naval exercise in the world, you violate President Xi's words to President Obama in the Rose Garden that you would not militarize the Spratlys. We remember words around here."

In September 2015, Xi had said "China does not intend to pursue militarization" of the Spratlys. China's continued militarization of the islands was considered a violation of the Law of the Sea treaty, which China had signed, and a U.N. tribunal in 2016 ruled China had no evidence for its claim to "historic rights" over large areas of the South China Sea.

"Either your president lied to our president and actually intended to militarize the Spratlys," Mattis said, "or your military's not obedient to civilian control. And either one of those worries me."

"Well, but General, they were defensive weapons," Wei replied.

"General—General, come on. I may be wearing this"—Mattis pointed to his civilian suit—"but we're both generals," Mattis said. "I've been shot at by defensive weapons and offensive. I can't tell the difference, okay?"

Wei smiled slightly as the translator's words sank in.

The bottom line, Mattis said, is "I want to cooperate with you. I'm looking for ways to cooperate. But we're going to confront you when you decide to screw with us."

In Mattis's view, the island military installations were part of a bigger Chinese plan: Shanghai would replace New York City as the center of world finance by 2030. Taiwan would be reincorporated as part of China. The only way for China to do that would be with intimidation or force.

The two walked further into the woods, Mattis's lantern illuminating the path. They had walked for half an hour.

Mattis and Wei returned to Mount Vernon's greenhouse for dinner. As they ate, the West Point choir sang. The cadets were in dress uniform with Mount Vernon arrayed behind them. Each song was introduced by a different cadet speaking Mandarin, which they were all studying.

Mattis hoped the show would be a personal memory for Wei.

Next the Marine Corps silent drill team carried out marches and a perfect rifle drill with no sound or oral cadence. The message was one of lethal coordination.

Mattis and Wei resumed their walk after dinner.

"Those last guys," Wei asked. "Who were they?"

"They're Marines."

"They look very fit."

"They run three miles in 18 minutes. And they're all at over 21 pull-ups."

Mattis reminded Wei of the history the two nations shared.

"Remember, the Americans have never tried to contain you," he said. "We want you to play by the rules. But the bottom line is: How are we going to manage our differences when two nuclear-armed superpowers step on each other's toes? That is the fundamental question of this age. And the whole world is watching." He referenced the two world wars fought in the previous century: "Are we going to be as stupid as the Europeans, and twice in the 20th century light the world on fire? Or are we not going to do that?"

Mattis noted how the nations of the Pacific region had stood up to various forces over the past 200 years. "No one country is going to dominate the Pacific," he said. "History is very 100 percent compelling on it. If you think you're going to take over the Pacific, you'll just be the fourth who thought so," he said, referring to the European colonialists, fascist and militarist powers, and Soviet communists who had made attempts. The United States is not afraid to fight when necessary, he said.

"Look if you want to fight, I'll fight. I'll fight anybody. I'll fight frigging Canada, okay," Mattis said. "But I've had enough of fighting. I've written enough letters to mothers. I don't need to write any more. And you don't need to write them, either."

Mattis knew that like Wei, most of China's military officers had perhaps never experienced armed combat—and certainly had not in any major conflicts since China's short-lived invasion of Vietnam in 1979.

Mattis wanted Wei to know that war would be extraordinarily tough on the Chinese.

"I'll just tell you," Mattis said, "the country I would most be willing to fight would be one whose entire officer corps had never heard a shot fired at them. War is so different from training that a shock wave will go through them. I've got—probably 80 percent of my officers have been shot at in one form or another. But I'd prefer not to put them through another war."

EIGHTEEN

I n late 2018, it was time for Mattis to fill several important four-star jobs in the military—a complicated minuet of recommending the right general or admiral for the job best suited to their strengths and particular responsibilities. It had to be elegantly orchestrated. Mattis had one focus: Who best to lead if there was a war?

Mattis probably knew more about actual fighting of wars— about life in the infantry with bullets flying, on ships at sea for months at a time, and planes loaded with bombs and missiles— than any recent secretary of defense.

General Joe Dunford was retiring as chairman of the Joint Chiefs of Staff, and Mattis had the perfect candidate to replace him as the number-one military man and chief military adviser to the president. The chairman could be a potent force in a time of war, as General Colin Powell had demonstrated when he served as chairman during the First Gulf War in 1991—one of the most sensible, short and relatively low-casualty wars of all time. Powell, a Vietnam veteran, had pushed for an overwhelming force of

500,000 U.S. military personnel in the operation in order to get in, get out, and protect as many soldiers as possible.

Mattis had been a 41-year-old lieutenant colonel then, commanding a battalion of 1,250 in the blistering heat of the Saudi desert. They spent five months preparing for the mission to eject Saddam Hussein's Republican Guard from Kuwait. Mattis lost 20 pounds. His superiors estimated that half of his troops would be either killed or wounded while breaching the Iraqi lines—a staggering prospect. Mattis rehearsed his troops nonstop, teaching them to maintain momentum at all costs and to improvise. No days off, no television, no phones. During the training, the fastest breach had taken 21 minutes. In actual combat, it took 11 minutes. Extraordinarily, none of his Marines were killed in the fight.

Without reservation, Mattis wanted "Fingers"—Air Force Chief of Staff David L. Goldfein—to be the new chairman. "Fingers" was Goldfein's call sign because of the mastery of cockpit controls he'd developed over 4,200 flying hours across six types of aircraft. At 58, he was skilled, young, vigorous, humble and the most proven strategic thinker. He would bring a level of intellectualism to the job that the president had resisted.

When Mattis had been CentCom commander in the Middle East, Fingers had been the Air Force component commander for two years. He had performed brilliantly and was probably the most "joint" Air Force general Mattis had ever seen—meaning he demonstrated an ability to look beyond the capabilities of his own service and find ways to integrate with and complement others.

For example, when Fingers arrived in 2011, U.S. aircraft carriers would sail through the dangerous, Iran-controlled Strait of Hormuz with their only air cover provided by Navy planes—standard service-on-service parochialism. Fingers soon had Air Force F-15s and F-16s escorting the carriers and teed up helicopters and F-18s on the carrier deck, ready to launch. Between the constant fighters overhead and the F-18s on the carrier, the Iranian

Republican Guard soon began to fade away. It was a classic case of flooding the zone—the airspace—as well as increased readiness and training.

Mattis also knew he could work well with Fingers. When Mattis had tasked him with reorganizing the war plan for the Gulf and Iran, Fingers took Mattis's guidance and cited Eisenhower's advice: If a problem can't be solved easily, make it bigger. As Mattis put it, if the Iranians had a 29-inch reach, he wanted a 30-inch reach. And Fingers had given it to him, expanding the airspace so the American air power had a greater reach than the Iranians'. Fingers was cunning, accepted guidance and had well prepared CentCom for possible war.

Just as meaningful to Mattis, Fingers had been shot down in an F-16 over Bosnia in 1999. He knew that coming face-to-face with your own mortality changed the way you look at the world, at war and at yourself.

Mattis also had to find a new NATO commander. Given Trump's ceaseless criticism of NATO, he thought Army Chief of Staff Mark Milley would be the best. Mattis considered him a loud optimist. *The New York Times* would later call him "a general who mixes bluntness and banter." In June 2018, Trump had praised Milley for being "good at pricing" bombs as well as "throwing them." Mattis thought Milley would both appeal to Trump and infuse NATO with the needed self-confidence, bolstering the alliance.

Under Mattis, the Army had many changes to make and needed to gut many now irrelevant programs. Milley oversaw a methodical improvement in Army brigade readiness, bringing the number deemed immediately combat ready up from three to 30, a remarkable improvement.

Milley also improved the physical fitness of the Army, an issue of immense importance to Mattis. "It was humiliating to watch the U.S. Army march in a parade and then go watch the Mexican army or the Ukrainian army or the Norwegians," Mattis said. The armies of other nations were so much more fit. He concluded that a third of the Army was overweight or obese. It was appalling. Milley had aggressively raised Army physical fitness.

Mattis recommended Fingers to Trump to be the next chairman of the Joint Chiefs of Staff and Army Chief Milley to take over the NATO command. The defense secretary's recommendations for these top military posts were almost always accepted by the president.

But David Urban, a lawyer-lobbyist and early Trump supporter who had helped Trump win the crucial state of Pennsylvania in 2016, weighed in with the president directly. Urban, a West Point graduate, advocated that Milley, instead of Goldfein, be made chairman. Pompeo, another West Pointer, also recommended Milley.

Trump quickly offered the top job to Milley, who accepted. Questions would linger on how Milley earned the chairmanship and whether he was too accommodating to Trump. Mattis thought it hurt Milley's reputation because it looked too much like raw politics.

Mattis was sure Milley's fellow Joint Chiefs would not have chosen him as chairman. His style was too brash. But the other chiefs, of course, did not have a vote.

Mattis did not protest Trump's decision. "I wasn't paid to express my exasperation," Mattis told an associate. The damage was done. Mattis believed he had not really been given a shot because of the president's preemptive, impetuous decision making. The military and the country would lose Goldfein's leadership, although he stayed on as Air Force chief of staff. Milley was more than acceptable. Having a bond with the president might help. It also, though, might make it harder for Milley to stand up to the president—increasingly a central part of the job of chairman.

Mattis realized that, more than ever, he and Trump were not

hitting it off. But Mattis felt he was still winning more than he was losing. Behind the scenes, he continued to make gains on military readiness, budget and training. He was focused inwardly on his relationships with Pompeo, Coats and CIA director Haspel.

Trump's problem extended further, to the president's failure to build a smooth working team—to listen, gather various informed opinions, debate, identify options, debate some more and bring everyone on board with a decision.

"I consider myself the most reluctant person on earth to go to war," Mattis wrote in his 2019 book on leadership. But it had to be asked: What might it mean if a war came and the best person was not in the chairmanship? Suppose the great military leaders of World War II had been cast aside on the impulse of the commander in chief? In that environment, would there have been an Eisenhower or Marshall or MacArthur or Nimitz or Halsey? And what would have been the price paid for not having them there?

The answer, of course, was unknowable. But it was important to address the issue of succession. Every large organization or business had a responsibility to make sure there was a process for finding the very best. And in 2018, Mattis believed, the commander in chief had failed and let the country down.

Mattis had long detested and distrusted Iran. In 1983 Lebanese terrorists, later determined to be acting at the direction of Iran, drove two truck bombs into the Marine Barracks in Beirut, Lebanon. Those killed included 220 Marines and 21 other military personnel. Mattis, at the time a major assigned as the executive officer at the Naval Academy Preparatory School in Rhode Island, was tasked with making casualty calls in Rhode Island. First he visited seven families to tell them their sons were missing. Then he returned several days later. Your son has been found, he had to report. He's dead. And no, you can't have an open casket.

In 2013, after being fired by Obama, Mattis returned to Richland, Washington, a civilian for the first time in over four decades.

Over the years, he had written more than 800 letters to the families of those who had died under his command. These were the Gold Star families. He would often get replies from the families asking him to come see them. Or someone in the fallen Marine's unit would forward a copy of a handwritten note or letter. Mattis would have someone investigate to make sure it was authentic, and if so, would forward it to the family with a note from him: Here's what we found out about your son or husband. Often the family would then say, please come see us.

Then, with time on his hands, Mattis hit the road in his light brown 1998 Lexus sedan. He would stop to speak at organized groups of veterans or Gold Star families, or to an individual family. He would pull into a town, get a hotel room, read the folder about the fallen Marine or soldier, put on a suit and go pay his respects. Sometimes this led him to a mobile home, sometimes to the home of a very wealthy family.

He especially remembered a visit to a family in Utah with a large, beautiful home. He drove up a winding hill. Inside, he took a seat.

Tall windows fronted the house. The father, a doctor, was home early. The mother, a professor at a local college, had perfectly painted nails and every hair just right. They were stoic.

Their son had a four-year college football scholarship but had joined the Marines instead. He had died in combat years earlier. The mother talked about their deceased son, the mountains he had climbed. They took Mattis to a boy's bedroom still fully intact, preserved almost as a museum. They showed Mattis all the pictures—their son as a baby, grammar school, high school, the prom. The full American story. Mattis could only listen so long. There was only so much to say. After an hour, the visit was petering out.

The mother said General Stanley McChrystal, the commander in Afghanistan, had asked for 40,000 more troops in 2009, and President Obama had given 30,000. She had her history correct. If there were more, a million troops available, she asked, why didn't McChrystal get 80,000?

Mattis mumbled something about how the president had to weigh options. Finally, Mattis said, "You know, I can't give you a good answer other than we thought that was probably sufficient."

"Were you trying to make it fair for the enemy?" she asked. There was no anger in her voice, just sorrow, as if the wounds of the loss would never heal. All of a sudden the father became engaged and looked directly at Mattis—an unforgettable look.

"We certainly weren't trying to do that," Mattis answered defensively.

"We've studied you," said the mother. "We've read all the things you've done." Mattis was not the problem. "We know you're trying to be loyal."

The father stood and shook Mattis's hand, holding it for what seemed like 30 seconds, straining for some connection. The mother—cultured, refined, proper, educated—had one final thought about Washington: *"General, no one in that town back there gives a fuck what our family lost."*

NINETEEN

Mattis later described for others what it was like to attend meetings with Trump: "It is very difficult to have a discussion with the president. If an intel briefer was going to start a discussion with the president, they were only a couple sentences in and it could go off on what I kind of irreverently call those Seattle freeway off-ramps to nowhere. Shoot off onto another subject. So it was not where you could take him to 30,000 feet. You could try, but then something that had been said on Fox News or something was more salient to him.

"So you just had to deal with it. He'd been voted in. And our job was not to take a political or partisan position. It was, how do you govern this country and try to keep this experiment alive for one more year?"

Mattis frequently used a phrase coined by George Kennan, the father of the doctrine to contain the Soviet Union: "the treacherous curtain of deference" that comes down when someone is around high-level officials, especially presidents.

In Trump's case, there were additional impediments to connecting and communicating with the president. Mattis said beyond that sense of "Oh my gosh, I'm in the Oval Office," advisers had to push past "the additional curtains of Fox News, of his formative years. Those are long-held beliefs. So those were the real curtains. Because I saw Rex Tillerson and Dan Coats and Mike Pompeo at CIA and certainly Gina Haspel, myself, quite willing to come up with the facts. Joe Dunford never hesitated on it." Neither did H. R. McMaster or Treasury Secretary Steve Mnuchin.

"But the facts would be dismissed, and we'd be off on one of those ramps that circled around and started going. And then you're sitting there, and it's not deference at that point. It's grasping for a way to get it back on subject. And it was just very hard. And there wasn't a lot of time for it."

Mattis had repeatedly reminded the president that 77 nations and international organizations were fighting ISIS, the Islamic state, primarily in Syria. "Thirteen of those nations have military troops," Mattis noted.

What about the other nations? Trump asked. Who was ripping him off?

"The others are giving money, intelligence," Mattis said. "They're supporting programs, all sorts of things. Remember for every one of our troops that died in Syria, 1,000 Kurds have died in Syria." Actually it was more. "It is in our interest to keep fighting." Trump had promised to defeat ISIS in the presidential campaign, and Mattis had urged a war of no less than "annihilation"—a concept Trump loved and vigorously approved.

On December 6, 2018, Mattis was in Ottawa for a meeting of the 13 defense ministers of the nations contributing troops to the ISIS fight. His chief talking point: They needed to stay in the fight. Every country needs to stay.

"We meet at a great time," Canadian defense minister Harjit Sajjan started off at the closed-door meeting. "We can say how great this alliance has been. We've broken ISIS's back. But it isn't over."

Mattis was sitting next to him, quite happy to be indoors with the temperature outside hovering around freezing.

"We must not declare victory," said France's Minister of the Armed Forces Florence Parly, leaning forward, "and walk away and wonder why it comes right back at it." On the verge of victory was the time to stay the course and avoid the temptation of a premature withdrawal.

Everyone seemed to be nodding.

"It is critical at this point that we not take our eye off the ball," said the British minister.

Perfect, thought Mattis. Everyone was on board. He could ignore his written talking points. He wouldn't have to say a word. The sale was made.

Finally the meeting was turned over to him as the representative of the lead nation.

Mattis summarized the others' points and said he couldn't agree more strongly.

They then all discussed how they would keep their troops there, the exact words to explain the essential rationale underlying their plans: They had to persist because the fight against ISIS was not over.

My God, this is great, Mattis thought. He called White House chief of staff John Kelly. "John, the nations are with us. They're not pulling. They're going to stay on the ground. It's time to force it into the Geneva peace process"—to support the Kurds, who had done most of the fighting. "I'll talk to Mike Pompeo."

Back in Washington on Wednesday, December 19, Mattis saw a tweet pop up from the president: "We have defeated ISIS in Syria, my only reason for being there during the Trump Presidency."

Later that day, Trump released a one-minute video and tweet underscoring his earlier message: "After historic victories against ISIS, it's time to bring our great young people home!" The United States was withdrawing from Syria.

The brief video, complete with title cards and high production values, showed Trump standing outside the White House discussing the "heartbreaking" task of writing letters to the families of the fallen.

"We won," Trump said in the video. "And that's the way we want it, and that's the way they"—he pointed to the heavens—"want it."

Mattis was shocked. Once again Trump had not consulted his secretary of defense and made a major announcement with no warning.

His first thought: How could we break with our allies? His second was the timing: It was just two weeks after the Ottawa meeting with all the commitments and pledges. He sat there and thought, my God, they're going to think I lied to them. They won't believe that I had no idea about this. And now we're going to leave them high and dry. We're going to do what Obama did when he said we're going after the Syrians for the chemical weapons use and the French planes were armed, they were ready to go when he walked. And the Kurds were going to be left unprotected and possibly slaughtered by Turkey.

"John," Mattis said in a call to John Kelly, "I need an hour with the boss."

"You got it," said Kelly.

Mattis figured that Kelly knew what it was about, but the chief of staff, who had been blindsided by the president so many times and announced ten days earlier that he would soon be leaving, did not ask. Nine months earlier, Mattis had watched Rex Tillerson be fired by tweet.

The decision announcements by tweet were all wrong, in Mattis's view. Trump lived in his own head and if he wanted, out came an idea or a decision. It did not matter what anybody else thought.

Mattis once said, "In any organization you become complicit with what the organization is doing." For nearly two years Mattis had gone along. As the commander in chief, Trump called the shots. Mattis decided he was no longer going to be complicit.

He went to his Pentagon office and began writing his resignation letter. Just in case he was successful in rolling back the president's announced decision, he didn't want anyone to have a copy of the letter. He had successfully changed the president's mind at least temporarily on Afghanistan and some other matters. It had never been pretty, but he knew he was not paid for pretty. He thought there was a chance he would come back from a meeting with Trump and still be secretary of defense. He asked a trusted senior member of his staff to type the resignation letter. There were only two copies. One went with him, and one stayed in his desk.

At the White House, Mattis found the president in a good mood. They walked into the Oval Office and sat down.

"Mr. President, we've got to come to an understanding here. This enemy is not going away." He noted that he had been through this before, when Obama walked away from Iraq. "These terrorist groups regenerate." The U.S. military had to win not just the fighting but the peace. "Our allies are there, and we can force this thing to closure now if we still have traction, if we still have our troops there."

Mattis was like a broken record, repeating that the strongest military presence gave the diplomats the leverage to speak with authority—work with the diplomats, avoid the use of additional military force.

"You guys will have us fighting forever," Trump said.

"No," Mattis said. "The Kurds have done the fighting. Let's be right up front."

"It's cost us billions."

"Well, a lot of other nations too—77 nations plus Interpol, Arab League, NATO."

Trump was not moving, Mattis could see. There was no give.

He had decided, and that was it. Mattis had seen it before. Nothing. It was over.

"We beat them," Trump said. "There's no need."

"We're not taking casualties," Mattis said. "But we haven't beaten them. We've done the military part. Now we have to win the part that's going to make sure we don't have to go back in, like your predecessor who pulled out of Iraq too early and we have to go back in."

Trump did not agree.

Mattis knew he could only quit once. "Mr. President, it's probably best you read this."

He handed the letter to the president, who read:

"One core belief I have always held is that our strength as a nation is inextricably linked to the strength of our unique and comprehensive system of alliances and partnerships. While the US remains the indispensable nation in the free world, we cannot protect our interests or serve that role effectively without maintaining strong alliances and showing respect to those allies. . . .

"Because you have the right to have a Secretary of Defense whose views are better aligned with yours on these and other subjects, I believe it is right for me to step down from my position."

"It's not a real nice letter," the president said.

"Mr. President, if you and I don't agree that we're parting over the allies—the way we look at allies—then the press is going to come up, rightly, with a hundred different reasons why I'm leaving."

"That's fair," Trump replied.

Then Mattis delivered his central message: "You're going to have to get the next secretary of defense to lose to ISIS. I'm not going to do it."

Is the letter going to be public? the president asked.

"It's got to be public," Mattis replied. "Number one, it'll leak if we don't do it. Just put the thing out there and say, 'This is all it is.'"

Yeah, okay, Trump agreed.

But they both knew it was a lot more.

Trump walked Mattis to the door. They parted with what Mattis later called a "nonadversarial handshake"—no fireworks.

In his car, Mattis called his chief of staff, retired Rear Admiral Kevin Sweeney. "There's a letter in my top desk drawer." Have it released to the press. "Tell all the senior staff I want to see them, the political staff" and the senior civilians. "I need to see them in the conference room in the next 20 minutes."

When they gathered in the conference room, Mattis said, "It's crucial that none of you quit. Steady, steady, steady. Every enemy is looking at us now. We'll get through this. The deputy is sitting beside me." Deputy Secretary Patrick Shanahan had been in the job for more than a year. "It's going to be a smooth turnover.

"I've offered to be here all the way through February," he said. That was almost two months away and would get them through the upcoming NATO meeting.

"You have to steady everyone now. And if someone wants to bring it up say, yeah, that's interesting, but where are we on the budget? Oh yeah, that's interesting, but what about the deploying Army unit? Just force them to focus."

Soon calls started flooding in from about four dozen senators and members of Congress. It was about 50/50 Republicans and Democrats. Very bipartisan. Defense was largely bipartisan.

Mattis believed he had good relations with most. He had attended the Senate lunches—the Republicans-only lunches, and the Democrats-only lunches—trying to answer their questions. He'd been given a standing ovation at one of the Democrats' lunches.

Sorry you are leaving, was the common message.

Mattis tried to say the same thing to each congressional caller, sometimes rather harshly: "It's time for you to decide if you're a coequal branch of government or if you're just going to talk like you're one."

Mattis found that most acknowledged his observation and didn't fight it.

"I'm not here to tell you where to stand on an issue," Mattis said. "But you seem to be awfully angry at times, and you have the power of the purse. So what are you doing about it? I've done everything I can."

At 5:21 p.m. Trump tweeted: "General Jim Mattis will be retiring, with distinction, at the end of February . . . General Mattis was a great help to me in getting allies and other countries to pay their share of military obligations . . . I greatly thank Jim for his service!"

But three days later, Trump said that Mattis would be leaving early, on January 1. At a cabinet meeting the next day, Trump said, "What's he done for me? How has he done in Afghanistan? Not so good. I'm not happy with what he's done in Afghanistan and I shouldn't be happy."

Trump continued, "As you know, President Obama fired him, and essentially so did I." Later he called Mattis "the world's most overrated general."

When I asked Trump about Mattis a year later, the president said Mattis was "just a PR guy."

Mattis summarized, "When I was basically directed to do something that I thought went beyond stupid to felony stupid, strategically jeopardizing our place in the world and everything else, that's when I quit."

TWENTY

———— ◆ ————

Jared Kushner's unorthodox ties to foreign leaders and regular conversations with them outside secure channels raised suspicions among the intelligence agencies.

His interim Top Secret security clearance was downgraded and ultimately denied. The rejection meant Kushner could not have access to sensitive intelligence, impeding his ability to work.

White House chief of staff John Kelly wanted Kushner's security clearance handled by the book, but the president personally ordered that Kushner be granted the highest security clearance. This gave him access to Top Secret intelligence classified as Sensitive Compartmented Information (SCI) and fed a constant tension between Kushner and Kelly.

Kelly was rankled by the off-line style Kushner had adopted in general that allowed him to dip in and out of presidential business at will. It undermined the chief of staff's attempts to channel the workflow of Trump's chaotic Oval Office through him.

Kushner and Kelly both maneuvered to be first among equals with Trump. "Kelly was killing me in a million ways," Kushner said. To Kushner's relief, his rival finally left in early 2019.

His departure cleared the way for both Trump and Kushner to turn to what was foremost in both their minds: reelection. The vote was nearly two years off, but the campaigning was permanent.

"There are basically three things that need to happen to really give you a super-strong chance at winning reelection," Kushner told the president.

"Number one, build the wall and get the immigration numbers down. That's a promise that's not being kept." Trump's border wall between the U.S. and Mexico had been "the signature campaign issue" of 2016.

"Number two, get the Mexico-Canada deal done because that is 34 percent of our exports, and a huge amount of our trading volume that we can get certainty on.

"Number three, if we can get to a deal with China, that's like a cherry on top. And it will also give a huge amount of rocket fuel to the economy."

Kushner was also working on criminal justice reform, which was personally important to him. His father had been convicted of illegal campaign contributions, tax evasion and witness tampering and spent 14 months in prison.

Kushner brought in Republican Senators Mike Lee, Tim Scott, and Chuck Grassley to meet with Trump. The senators were arguing in favor of relaxing and reducing mandatory minimum drug sentencing and disparities between sentences handed down for crack and powder cocaine offenses. Kushner wanted to try to get Trump on board with the sentencing reform provisions. They made their pitch.

"Okay," Trump said, "I like it. This makes sense. Let's do it."

Kushner walked out with Mike Lee, who seemed surprised and delighted. "So he said yes!"

"No, no, no, no," said Kushner. "That's a soft yes."

"What do you mean?" Lee asked.

"Well," Kushner said, "now I have to bring in the people who totally disagree with this and who are going to tell him this is a bad idea. He's going to side with them. And then we're going to have a debate on both of them."

Kushner said he had developed this conclusion about Trump's famously frequent reversals and changes of mind: "With the president, there's a hundred different shades of gray. And if people try to get a quick answer out of him, it's easy. You can get him to decide in your favor by limiting his information. But you better be sure as hell that people with competing views aren't going to find their way to him. And when that happens, he's going undo his decision."

This was an asset, as Kushner saw it: "He almost uses his ability to read people and keep people off balance as his best filter to determine when somebody is trying to pull something on him. He knows that he's kind of the final funnel before a decision. He's very good at kind of knowing when somebody is bullshitting him."

In 2018, Senate Majority Leader Mitch McConnell and Speaker of the House Paul Ryan had a simple question: How do we get the president not to change his mind again?

Guys, Kushner said to the Republican leaders, shifting blame away from Trump, "it's not that he changes his mind. It's that he wasn't staffed correctly. People weren't giving him all the facts and so he found out different facts. So you can't try to trick him into making a decision and then expect that he'll hold to that decision."

Kushner believed Trump's mindset from his years in real estate was: "You make a deal. There's still a lot of details to work out. So you could always change your mind if the details don't fall into place."

His solution: "Make sure that the president has all the information on the front end so that he doesn't change his mind later."

Where others saw fickleness or even lies, Kushner saw Trump's constant, shifting inconsistency as a challenge to be met with an ever-adapting form of managing up. Incomplete information, inadequate staffing—the appearance of impulsive decision making was all someone else's fault, according to Kushner.

John Kelly had a less flattering assessment. "Crazytown," Kelly said.

TWENTY-ONE

D an Coats launched the new year, 2019, with an updated National Intelligence Strategy and an old proposition: "This strategy is based on the core principle of seeking the truth and speaking the truth to our policymakers."

The strategy warned about "weakening of the post-WWII international order and dominance of Western democratic ideals, increasingly isolationist tendencies in the West and shifts in the global economy." It also decried "Russian efforts to increase its influence and authority" that "are likely to continue and may conflict with US goals and priorities in multiple regions."

Coats's "truths" were built on many of the old themes that Trump rejected.

A week after releasing the strategy, Coats gave his Worldwide Threat Assessment publicly before the Senate Intelligence Committee on January 29. He identified climate change as a security threat. Russia's relationship with China was "closer than it has been in many decades." North Korea was "unlikely to completely give up its nuclear weapons and production capabilities."

Coats said intelligence officials didn't believe Iran was developing a nuclear weapon—a direct contradiction of one of Trump's core national security arguments.

Everything he said was based fully on intelligence, but Coats could not have more conspicuously stuck his finger in the president's eye.

Fred Fleitz, president of the Center for Security Policy, a right-leaning Washington think tank, appeared on Fox Business and suggested that Coats ought to be fired, saying the intelligence service "has simply evolved into a monster that is basically second-guessing the president all the time." Lou Dobbs, host of the show Fleitz appeared on and Trump's friend and supporter, tweeted Fleitz's quote and suggestion.

The next day the White House canceled the daily intelligence briefing, the PDB. Trump tweeted:

"The Intelligence people seem to be extremely passive and naive when it comes to the dangers of Iran. They are wrong!" He added, "Perhaps Intelligence should go back to school!"

On February 7, Senate Intelligence Committee chairman Richard Burr said that after a two-year investigation, his committee had found no evidence of Trump-Russia collusion. "If we write a report based upon the facts that we have," Burr said, "then we don't have anything that would suggest there was collusion by the Trump campaign and Russia."

Trump celebrated on Twitter, and he asked Coats to help. "Richard Burr said that he hasn't seen any evidence of that. Is this something you can do? You're head of intelligence. It would have a major impact. Others have said it. Why can't you say it?"

"Mr. President," Coats replied, "that's not something I can do. It's not part of my job." His connection to the FBI was the intelligence-gathering side. He had nothing to do with the side of the FBI that did criminal investigations, he repeated once again.

Chris Ruddy, the CEO of Newsmax and one of Trump's closest confidants, said in a February 18 interview on CNN: "I'm hearing from sources around the White House there's just general disappointment of the president with Director Coats. There's a feeling that maybe there needs to be a change of leadership in that position coming up."

A front-page story in *The Washington Post* on February 20, citing sources familiar with the matter, reported that Trump was "frustrated," "enraged" and "increasingly disenchanted" with Coats and was considering removing him.

After several days of reading about himself in the news, Coats came home and told Marsha, "I'm going to write my resignation letter and take it to Trump and say, 'I quit.'"

"I think you ought to give it to him, and let him make the decision," she advised.

Coats wrote out a letter, brief and to the point, saying, I cannot do this job effectively without your confidence and support. I am offering my resignation so that you can find someone who will better be able to serve you. He tried to strike the same tone that his friend Mattis had adopted two months earlier.

Coats offered no warning to Trump he was submitting a resignation letter. He did not want to be another Jeff Sessions, the attorney general Trump had regularly and publicly trashed, who had left in the fall of 2018. Sessions had been just one of many hounded out of high administration positions by Trump's vicious tweets. Coats wanted out on his own terms.

Coats went to the Oval Office to see Trump alone and handed the president his resignation letter.

I keep reading senior White House officials have said that I am not loyal and not a team player, Coats said.

No, no, Trump said.

Coats mentioned someone who had been quoted in the media.

I don't even know that guy, Trump said.

Coats tried another name.

I hardly know the guy, the president insisted.

I'm not going to go through this, Coats said. It could be a thousand cuts. Most of the published reports come from anonymous sources only cited as senior White House officials or Trump friends. He had seen this before. When Trump was unhappy with someone, out came the endless undermining and criticism.

Trump dismissed this. The White House sources were fake, he said. "I didn't say that." Coats did not believe the president's denials for a minute.

Trump took Coats's letter, seemed to read it carefully, and handed it back.

Suppose I don't accept this? Trump asked. Can I not accept this?

Clearly that was possible. Giving Trump a choice had been Marsha's point.

"Would you be willing to stay on?" Trump finally said. "I'm asking you. This is a tough time for you to announce your resignation." The Mueller report into Russian election interference was reported to be coming out soon. If Coats left, his departure would be misinterpreted. "It's the wrong timing for this."

Coats paused. Okay, he finally said. But I can't keep having this chatter coming out of the White House and your friends that you don't have confidence in me. "I can't do my job effectively if I have all these leaks and all these things coming about what you think of me and the intelligence community."

No, no, Trump said. You're doing a good job. Let's work this out. We'll go forward.

At some point in the future, Coats said, he would want to step down.

Don't you want to do it the right way? Trump asked, apparently implying there was a way to resign so it would not appear that Trump had fired him. Don't you want to leave in a more positive way? Let's work it out.

Coats finally agreed. After about ten minutes he left with his unaccepted resignation letter in hand.

Paradoxically, he felt relief. He had effectively put conditions on staying. And at least they had had a talk—not laying all the cards on the table, but more intimate than ever before. Trump had been the one who asked him to stay. Coats could see how his resignation could be misused as the Mueller investigation was supposedly winding down. The interpretation would be that Coats knew something and he wanted to get out before the big expected revelations from Mueller. It would be unfair to create that perception, since Coats knew nothing about the coming Mueller report.

But Coats continued to harbor the secret belief, one that had grown rather than lessened, although unsupported by intelligence proof, that Putin had something on Trump. How else to explain the president's behavior? Coats could see no other explanation. He was sure that Trump had chosen to play on the dark side—the moneyed interests in the New York real estate culture, and international finance with its corrupt, anything-to-make-a-buck deal making. Anything to get ahead, anything to make a deal.

Coats realized that Trump had been able to make a deal with him, a raw political deal—hold that resignation for now, we'll do it later, soon, but without a tweetstorm against you. He had played into Trump's protection racket.

Coats saw how extraordinary it was for the president's top intelligence official to harbor such deep suspicions about the president's relationship with Putin. But he could not shake them.

Pence did not want to hear talk about Coats resigning. "Look, we need to support the president," Pence told Coats. "Let's look on the positive side of things that he's done. More attention on that. You can't go."

Coats saw Pence was on a mission—stay the course.

TWENTY-TWO

Deputy Attorney General Rod Rosenstein kept tight control over Robert Mueller's Russia investigation. He aggressively wielded Justice Department regulations giving him authority to overrule Mueller on any "investigative or prosecutorial step" to maintain leverage over the investigation. The existence of that authority was sufficient; he never formally had to exercise it.

The general public perception continued to be that Mueller was on to another Watergate that could end the Trump presidency. "It's Mueller Time" was a rallying cry so popular it became a T-shirt slogan.

In reality, however, it was Rosenstein time. He oversaw the investigation with diligence and an iron hand, continuing to send a deputy for biweekly meetings with Mueller and his team.

Mueller's prosecutors were mindful that Trump could order Rosenstein to fire Mueller. If Rosenstein refused, Trump could fire Rosenstein and find someone who would get rid of Mueller.

The president's campaign of public intimidation, tweets and claims the investigation was a "witch hunt" rattled many on Mueller's staff. The whole investigative atmosphere was stay in your lane, no mission creep. After Trump's controversial 2017 meeting with Putin in Hamburg where he confiscated the translator's notes, they debated—but only in jest—about subpoenaing the translator's notes. They knew if they dared, they would be fired.

After a long internal debate, Mueller decided not to issue a formal subpoena to Trump to compel his testimony. There was a belief that if they asked for the subpoena, the legal battle in the courts would take months, even a year. Or Trump could fire Mueller in response.

Mueller told his prosecutors they should not stretch themselves too thin. If they tried to get it all, they could wind up getting nothing.

Aaron Zebley, Mueller's deputy, told the prosecutors he had the "pen," on the final report, meaning he had Mueller's authority as final editor. One overriding consideration, Zebley said, was to make sure the report was a definitive account so no conspiracy theories, no "grassy knoll" theories, would emerge as had happened after the 1963 assassination of President Kennedy. But it was a last-minute rush and debate among the senior prosecutors. The result was a compromise that is one of the most confusing lines in the history of high-profile investigations: "While this report does not conclude that the president committed a crime, it also does not exonerate him."

Trump and Senator Lindsey Graham played a round of golf at Trump's West Palm Beach, Florida, club on the morning of Sunday, March 24. Trump was worried because Attorney General Bill Barr, who had replaced Sessions in early 2019, was expected to release a letter summarizing the Mueller report. Barr had served as attorney general for President George H. W. Bush and held a strong, sweeping view of presidential power.

Before releasing the letter, the attorney general called Graham to give him a heads-up. Mueller's investigation had been historic and lengthy—19 lawyers, some 40 FBI agents and other professionals, 2,800 subpoenas, 500 search warrants, 500 witnesses.

"You're not going to believe this," Barr said.

"What?" Graham asked.

"After two fucking years he says, 'Well, I don't know, you decide,'" Barr said.

"What do you mean?" Graham asked.

"Well, there's no collusion," Barr said. Mueller had found no evidence that Trump or his aides had worked illegally with Russia to interfere in the 2016 election. That was great news.

But Barr said Mueller's report was "convoluted" on the critical question of whether Trump had obstructed justice. He had not reached a conclusion.

Barr sent a copy of the letter to Graham's Senate office and one of his staffers called Graham with a more complete summary of the findings. The letter was addressed to Graham as chairman of the Senate Judiciary Committee, and three other congressional leaders.

The core finding of the Mueller report, according to Barr's letter, was that ". . . the investigation did not establish that members of the Trump Campaign conspired or coordinated with the Russian government in its election interference activities."

For the president and his allies, this was cause for serious celebration—no evidence of working with the Russians.

The second conclusion on obstruction of justice was less sweeping but still legally exculpatory, Graham saw. After all, Mueller's report stated that while it did not "conclude that the President committed a crime, it also does not exonerate him."

Graham had served six years as an Air Force lawyer and several as the chief Air Force prosecutor in Europe. Although Mueller was operating under a long-standing Department of Justice policy that a sitting president could not be charged with a federal crime,

Graham felt the phrase "does not exonerate" was gratuitous. It was not the job of prosecutors to exonerate. They had to decide whether to charge or not to charge. Mueller's language smacked of then–FBI director James Comey's 2016 announcement in the Hillary Clinton email investigation that he would not recommend charges, but that her conduct was "extremely careless."

Mueller wrote in his report that "fairness concerns" prevented him from even reaching a judgment that the president committed crimes when no charges could be brought. Ordinarily, a person accused of a crime has a right to a fair, public trial and can use that process to clear his or her name. However, Mueller wrote, "a prosecutor's judgment that crimes were committed, but that no charges will be brought, affords no such adversarial opportunity for public name-clearing before an impartial adjudicator.

"The concerns about the fairness of such a determination would be heightened in the case of a sitting President, where a federal prosecutor's accusation of a crime, even in an internal report, could carry consequences that extend beyond the realm of criminal justice."

Mueller concluded he had the option to state in his report that he was confident, after a thorough investigation, that Trump clearly did not commit obstruction of justice. "Based on the facts and the applicable legal standards, however, we are unable to reach that judgment," the Mueller report states.

Barr said in his letter that while Mueller had not reached legal conclusions about alleged obstruction, he and Deputy Attorney General Rosenstein "have concluded that the evidence developed during the Special Counsel's investigation is not sufficient to establish that the President committed an obstruction-of-justice offense."

The full report with grand jury redactions would be released later, Barr said.

For practical purposes, the Mueller investigation was over, Graham believed. There would be sniping, criticism and second-guessing. The full report undoubtedly would dwell on incidents that were not pretty and would show Trump scheming and teetering on the edge of misconduct. But even if Mueller's report itself did not exonerate Trump, the essentials of exoneration were there in Barr's letter: no further indictments, no criminal charges of the president, no continuing investigation.

The question at the end of these long, seemingly endless investigations was always: What's next? There was no what's next. What happens tomorrow? The answer so far: No official action. Trump's opponents and the Democrats would beat the Russian interference drum whenever possible. But it would sound hollow and be yesterday's stale news, Graham believed.

Graham gave a summary of the good news to Trump.

At 4:46 p.m. that afternoon, Trump stepped before reporters on the tarmac at Palm Beach International Airport and spoke for the first time about Barr's version of the Mueller report's conclusions.

"So after a long look," Trump said, "after a long investigation, after so many people have been so badly hurt, after not looking at the other side where a lot of bad things happened, a lot of horrible things happened, a lot of very bad things happened for our country—it was just announced that there was no collusion with Russia.

"It's complete exoneration," Trump added—directly contradicting the Barr letter, which quoted the Mueller report's statement that it "does not exonerate him."

"What do you think?" Trump asked Graham after he boarded Air Force One.

"Well, Mr. President, very few presidents get two terms in their first term, but you just have," Graham said. "This is the first day of a new presidency."

"Yeah, that's a good way to look at it," Trump replied.

"Mr. President, this cloud has been removed," Graham said.

Trump seemed contemplative—probably the least demonstrative of anybody on the plane. It was out of character for him.

Trump, his staffers and Graham deplaned from Air Force One at Joint Base Andrews outside Washington to board Marine One and fly back to the White House.

Graham and Trump sat across from each other. It was a beautiful early spring evening.

"Isn't that great?" Trump said, now in a good mood. "Can you believe we're doing this shit? Can you believe I'm here, president of the United States, and you're here? Can you believe this shit? Isn't it the greatest thing in the world?"

It was apparently his way of absorbing the reality that, after two years of Mueller, it seemed over.

Marine One flew so close to the Washington Monument it felt as though they could almost touch it.

As the helicopter approached the White House grounds, a throng of journalists waited.

"There are the animals," Trump said. "They're the most heartbroken people in America."

"Yeah, be easy on them," Graham replied. "This is a bad day for them." Graham recommended Trump be brief in his comments to the reporters. "Here's my two cents," Graham said. Say something like, "America's the greatest country on earth. Good night." He added, "If you'll say that and nothing else, they'll all fall over dead."

Marine One landed at 7:04 p.m. Trump walked onto the South Lawn, looked directly at the cameras and said: "I just want to tell you that America is the greatest place on earth. The greatest place on earth. Thank you very much. Thank you." And he walked away.

When Graham got home, his phone was ringing.

"Did you see them?" Trump said.

"Who?" Graham replied.

"The animals," Trump said.

"No."

"When I said that, they all were stunned. They were speechless. The first time in my life nobody asked me 120 questions," Trump said. "That was the perfect thing to say."

Years of countless headlines detailing possible ties or flirtations among Trump people and others connected to the Russian government were replaced by a new story.

"Mueller Finds No Conspiracy" was the next morning's banner headline in *The Washington Post*. In *The New York Times*, the banner headline read: "Mueller Finds No Trump-Russia Conspiracy." A news analysis in the *Times* was headlined "Burden Lifts, Leaving President Fortified for Battles to Come."

The Barr letter likely did more to shape public perception of the special counsel's investigation than the 448-page Mueller report itself, which was released in redacted form to the public nearly four weeks later.

On March 27, Mueller wrote to Barr complaining that his widely publicized four-page summary letter "did not fully capture the context, nature, and substance of this Office's work and conclusions." He wrote, "There is now public confusion about critical aspects of the results of our investigation."

The basis for Mueller's criticism became evident once the report was made public in April 2019 and could be compared to Barr's four-page summary. But Mueller took no steps to change the outcome, nor could he in a practical sense. His work was within the Justice Department, which Barr controlled.

On April 29, 2019, Rosenstein submitted his one-page resignation letter to the president. In what was almost a fan letter, Rosenstein raised the American flag and Trump's campaign motto.

"We staffed the Department of Justice and the U.S. Attorneys' Offices with skilled and principled leaders devoted to the values that make America great," Rosenstein wrote.

"I am grateful to you for the opportunity to serve; for the courtesy and humor you often display in our personal conversations; and for the goals you set in your inaugural address: patriotism, unity, safety, education, and prosperity."

Trump's inaugural address would probably not be remembered for those themes but for his invocation of "American carnage."

The central flaw in the Mueller investigation was that the prosecutors never found an inside witness who could tell a story of corrupt, illegal conduct. There was no comparable figure to John Dean, Nixon's White House counsel, who testified in 1973 to both his own illegal actions and Nixon's. There was no Linda Tripp or Monica Lewinsky to testify that President Clinton had lied in public statements and in a civil suit about Lewinsky's affair with Clinton.

The investigation would not hang over Trump into the 2020 election. Rosenstein felt that on the Mueller investigation he had made Trump bulletproof for the election and had done him a favor.

The president was not guilty of obstruction of justice in Rosenstein's view. "I knew there was no basis to indict the president," Rosenstein told an associate. "I knew months before."

When Barr appeared before the Senate Judiciary Committee on May 1, Democrats pelted him with accusations that he acted politically in his handling of the Mueller report—more as Trump's defense attorney than as the head of the Justice Department.

"You put the power and authority of the office of the attorney general and the Department of Justice behind a public relations effort to help Donald Trump protect himself," Senator Mazie Hirono of Hawaii said.

Several days later, more than 700 former federal prosecutors released a statement arguing that Trump's conduct described in the Mueller report "would, in the case of any other person not covered by the [Department of Justice] Office of Legal Counsel policy against indicting a sitting president, result in multiple felony charges for obstruction of justice."

But after 22 months of investigation without the bombshell findings anticipated by some of Trump's opponents and critics, Mueller and his report faded from the headlines. In an April 2019 column, "Public Has Mueller-Report Fatigue and Wants to Move On," *San Diego Union-Tribune* political columnist Michael Smolens wrote that the Mueller report had become "white noise."

In a March 2020 opinion issued in a Freedom of Information Act lawsuit seeking the lifting of redactions in the Mueller report, Senior U.S. District Court Judge Reggie B. Walton, an appointee of George W. Bush, wrote that Barr "distorted the findings in the Mueller Report."

Walton wrote that Barr failed to note in his letter that Mueller's probe "identified multiple contacts . . . between Trump campaign officials and individuals with ties to the Russian government." On the obstruction issue, Walton wrote, Barr "failed to disclose to the American public" that the reason Mueller determined not to make a traditional prosecutorial judgment was because of the Justice Department's policy against charging a sitting president with a federal crime.

"The inconsistencies between Attorney General Barr's statements," Walton wrote in his opinion, "made at a time when the public did not have access to the redacted version of the Mueller Report to assess the veracity of his statements, and portions of the redacted version of the Mueller Report that conflict with those statements cause the Court to seriously question whether

Attorney General Barr made a calculated attempt to influence public discourse about the Mueller Report in favor of President Trump despite certain findings in the redacted version of the Mueller Report to the contrary."

Walton's opinion did not address the substance of the investigation or whether Mueller or Barr should have reached different legal conclusions regarding the president's actions. The legal case in which he issued the opinion focused on whether the Justice Department properly redacted the report, or whether some redactions should be removed under the Freedom of Information Act. It was a public relations critique accusing Barr of carrying water for Trump.

Trump never let up on his attacks on the Mueller investigation into Russia's role in his 2016 victory. On May 23, 2019, Barr announced a new investigation into alleged spying on the Trump campaign, potentially by law enforcement and intelligence agency officials. The Justice Department was turning the tables.

Dan Coats and CIA director Gina Haspel made an appointment to see Barr.

The Mueller investigation had already torn inconclusively through the intelligence agencies, they said. Why did this need to be done? It will be very disruptive to the agencies.

Barr said he thought there was more out there that had not been investigated.

Haspel said the investigation could have a negative impact on morale at the CIA. Her people were spooked by the new investigation, and some wondered if they would need to get an attorney.

No, Barr said, he did not think so. He tried to be reassuring. It's not going to have that much of an impact.

Haspel disagreed. It was like Mueller Two. It would be a "nightmare" for the agency.

Coats suspected Barr had former CIA director Brennan in his sights but did not say so. He asked if John Durham, the U.S. attorney appointed to oversee the case, would be looking at Coats's own people at the office of DNI.

Potentially, Barr said.

Coats was worried about the GS-14 employee who had just done his or her job and passed along intelligence and seemingly routine reports. He also thought that Durham would be looking at Obama's former DNI James Clapper, who was one of the persistent public critics of President Trump.

Coats and Haspel said they would give the Justice Department any documents they requested because the president had so ordered. They had no choice.

But hopefully you will do this in the right way, Coats said.

"I hope you can do this in a way that it's not going to cause a lot of problems," Haspel said. "And can we stay informed in terms of what you plan to do and make sure we know what's happening?"

"Don't worry," Barr said. "We will. We will. Your people won't need to be concerned."

Barr said he would let them know what he had learned and if there was anything they should do. Before anything was released, he said, they would have an opportunity to respond. Presumably they could make their case. But there was a lawyerly caution, though he was obviously trying to calm them down.

"Don't worry, don't worry," Barr said. "This is not a witch hunt. There's more out there and we just need to know what it is."

Mueller testified before the House Judiciary Committee on July 24, 2019, giving an uneven performance that frustrated Republicans and Democrats alike with fumbling, incomplete answers. He appeared, at times, to lack familiarity with his own report. He did little to help the public understand the dense legal document his office had produced.

Barr and Trump had defined the report, and Trump continued to publicly assail the Mueller investigation as a "witch hunt" and a "hoax."

Ultimately, Mueller's investigation led to 34 indictments, including Trump's personal attorney Michael Cohen, campaign chairman Paul Manafort, deputy campaign chairman Rick Gates, national security adviser Michael Flynn, political confidant Roger Stone and a number of Russian nationals. But Trump emerged relatively unscathed, and in doing so had dealt a blow to his political enemies.

Trump later told me, "The beautiful thing is, it all evaporated. It ended in a whimper. It was pretty amazing. It ended in dust."

He had weathered the greatest threat to his presidency to that point, and perhaps come out politically stronger but no doubt more emboldened than before.

TWENTY-THREE

————◆————

The three months since Coats had withdrawn his resignation letter at the president's request had not been good. Coats's insistence he would not get involved in the Russia probe had only further isolated him. When they met, the president's body language not only radiated distrust, but contempt. Coats knew there was no way to survive such a personal rift, and as the animus grew, so too did Coats's despondency.

On Saturday, May 25, 2019, of Memorial Day weekend, at his grandson Jack's soccer game in the Maryland suburbs, Coats felt as low as he ever had.

"Hey, I need to make a phone call," he announced to his family. He walked off into the wooded park alone and dialed his friend Mattis, who had been out of office for five months.

"I'm really having a hard time here," Coats confided. It was a cry from the heart. "I just need to talk to somebody who kind of knows what I'm going through. You do."

Coats said he needed some guidance. He did not have to tell Mattis that the current situation was untenable. This is not at all what I came here to do, Coats said. He felt depleted.

"I haven't spoken out," Mattis commiserated. He had maintained his silence since his resignation in December. "I've made my case before the president. He listened. In the end he just didn't agree with me." Trump's disdain for the allies and decision to pull out of Syria with no warning, no consultation, had been Mattis's red line. "I've buried too many boys. That was a terrible decision."

Coats said the mounting personal tensions between him and Trump and their fundamental differences on the nature of the security threats were debilitating.

"This is not good," Mattis said. "Maybe at some point we're going to have to stand up and speak out. There may be a time when we have to take collective action."

"Well, possibly," Coats said. "Yeah, there may."

"He's dangerous," Mattis said. "He's unfit."

Speaking out didn't seem to work, Coats said. Admiral Bill McRaven, who had led Operation Neptune Spear, the raid that killed Osama bin Laden in Pakistan in 2011, had continuously mounted an aggressive, personal and public criticism of Trump. In an open letter to Trump published in *The Washington Post* in August 2018 after Trump revoked John Brennan's security clearance, McRaven had written that the president had "embarrassed us in the eyes of our children, humiliated us on the world stage and, worst of all, divided us as a nation." He challenged Trump to revoke his security clearance: "I would consider it an honor."

McRaven, a Navy SEAL, was one of the most celebrated military figures, a warrior scholar, bestselling author and now chancellor of the University of Texas system.

Trump had blasted back, calling McRaven "a Hillary Clinton fan" and suggested he should have captured bin Laden earlier. As best Coats could tell, McRaven's gutsy stand seemed to have had no impact.

Mattis said they still had to consider stepping forward.

"Jim, what would that be?" Coats asked.

"I don't know," Mattis replied, "but we can't let the country keep going" on this course. He repeated, "This is dangerous."

"Look," Coats said, "others have tried and it's had no impact whatsoever. They get tarred and feathered."

"What would make a difference?" Mattis asked.

"If the Senate stood up," Coats said. He knew the Senate intimately, especially the Republicans. He had served 16 years as a Republican senator. And he kept in touch with half a dozen Republican senators who were friends. None were bailing on Trump—not out of conviction, but for political survival. "The Senate's not going to stand up."

But Coats pursued the question with some of his old friends from the Senate.

"I bet you have some interesting conversations in closed session," Coats said to one senator.

"Yes, we sure do," said the senator.

Others expressed the same view, and Coats realized nobody in the Senate needed to be told what was happening. They knew. The senators just desperately wanted to get past the November 3 election. If he was still in the Senate, Coats believed the worst course of action would be not to speak up, lose the Senate majority and lose your reputation. He believed the Senate had not fulfilled its obligation under the Constitution to be a check and balance. There should be a moment to demand accountability from Trump.

Should Trump be reelected, Coats hoped one Republican senator would lead the charge and insist on a change in the way decisions were made in the interactions with the president.

TWENTY-FOUR

———◆———

Trump began following a series of op-eds written by John Solomon in *The Hill* newspaper alleging that former vice president Joe Biden had interfered in a corruption investigation in Ukraine, the second-largest country in Europe and a former member of the Soviet Union. The unproven allegation was that Biden, who had the Ukraine account for the Obama administration, worked to block the investigation of Burisma, a large Ukrainian gas company. Biden's son Hunter was a member of Burisma's board and was reportedly paid $50,000 a month.

Congress had initially appropriated $250 million for the Pentagon to provide security assistance to Ukraine, which was in a border dispute with Russia over the annexation of Crimea. On June 19, Trump personally asked about plans for the assistance—a highly unusual request from Trump, who rarely paid attention to such small details. On July 12, Trump directed a hold on the military support funding. And on July 25, a formal hold was placed on the funds.

Earlier that day, Trump had spoken by phone with recently elected Ukrainian president Volodymyr Zelensky.

In the call, a transcript of which Trump later ordered released, he asked Zelensky to talk with Attorney General Barr and the president's personal attorney, Rudy Giuliani, about an investigation of the Bidens.

Three days after the call, Sunday, July 28, was golf day. Trump played 18 holes in the morning at his Trump National Club in Northern Virginia. It was a sweltering midsummer day.

After playing, he stopped in the clubhouse and ran into Dan Coats and his wife, Marsha. Members of the club, they were having lunch before a scheduled tee time later in the afternoon.

Trump seemed taken aback, although he knew they were members. Marsha, a trained psychologist, had a feeling something was going on. The look on Trump's face was one of guilt and dismay, she thought.

Surprise, thought Dan Coats.

About an hour later, the Coatses were playing the long, straight 508-yard, par-four fourth hole, when a member of Coats's security team came running up. Your chief of staff, Viraj Mirani, wants to talk to you.

The New York Times just released a story saying that Trump has replaced you, Mirani told Coats.

On the sixth hole—a 583-yard, par-five—Coats read Trump's 4:45 p.m. tweet: "I am pleased to announce that highly respected Congressman John Ratcliffe of Texas will be nominated by me to be the Director of National Intelligence . . . Dan Coats, the current director, will be leaving office on August 15th. I would like to thank Dan for his great service to our Country."

Coats and Trump had never set a date for his departure. Coats had hoped to stay until September to wrap up some pending decisions. Where did August 15 come from, he wondered.

Later, when it became public that a whistleblower in the intelligence community was alleging improper conduct by Trump,

Marsha Coats concluded that Trump or someone around him didn't want her husband to be the one to receive the report. She believed Trump wanted Coats out because he would have turned the whistleblower report over to Congress rather than protect the president.

Ratcliffe was an ardent Trump supporter, but was forced to drop out following news reports that he had exaggerated his role prosecuting terrorism cases as a U.S. attorney. Trump eventually renominated Ratcliffe, who was confirmed and assumed office in 2020. The whistleblower report was eventually made public.

The linkage between the withheld aid, which in the end totaled about $400 million, and Trump's request for an investigation into the Bidens ultimately led the House of Representatives to impeach Trump.

TWENTY-FIVE

—————◆————

Following their June 2018 Singapore summit, the correspondence between Kim and Trump increased in both frequency and affection.

"I just have arrived back in America, and the media for North Korea and you has been fantastic," Trump wrote to Kim on June 15. "They have great respect for you and your country."

Trump followed with a letter on July 3 urging Kim to work with Pompeo, who would visit North Korea to make progress on three objectives: First, returning prisoner-of-war remains. Second, allowing technical experts to visit a missile test site Kim agreed to shut down.

"Third and most importantly," Trump wrote, "Secretary Pompeo is under my instructions to find agreement with you on taking the first major steps toward the final, fully verified denuclearization of the Korean Peninsula and toward a more peaceful future between us."

Kim did not discuss specifics when he wrote back on July 6.

"The significant first meeting with Your Excellency and the

joint statement that we signed together in Singapore 24 days ago was indeed the start of a meaningful journey," Kim wrote. "Wishing that the invariable trust and confidence in Your Excellency Mr. President will be further strengthened in the future process of taking practical actions, I extend my conviction with the epochal progress in promoting the DPRK-US relations will bring our next meeting forward." DPRK stood for the Democratic People's Republic of Korea, the formal name of North Korea.

In letters over the months that followed, Kim and Trump heaped praise upon one another while gently underscoring the demands each had made in the Singapore negotiations.

Both leaders said they hoped to broker an official end to the Korean War because hostilities only ceased under the terms of the 1953 armistice. Technically, they were still at war.

On July 30, Kim wrote: "I feel pleased to have formed good ties with such a powerful and preeminent statesman as Your Excellency, though there is a sense of regret for the lack of anticipated declaration on the termination of war."

Trump replied on August 2: "It is now time to make progress on the other commitments we made, including complete denuclearization."

"If our historic meeting two months ago signaled a new beginning to the DPRK-US relationship," Kim replied August 12, "my next meeting with you will be an opportunity to plan for a safe and solid future. I'm sure that the effort you and I are putting forth will continue to bring about satisfactory results."

On September 6, Kim wrote Trump his longest and most specific letter yet and started to put conditions on denuclearization. Historically the U.S. had rejected conditions outright.

"We are willing to take further meaningful steps one at a time in a phased manner, such as the complete shutdown of the Nuclear Weapons Institute or the Satellite Launch District and the irreversible closure of the nuclear materials production facility,"

Kim wrote in the September 6 correspondence. "I am deeply convinced that the many miraculous changes that we have brought about this year beyond the imagination of everyone will lead to many more in the future on the basis of the excellent relationship that exists between Your Excellency and myself."

The two leaders made clear their mutual desire to meet again, often portraying their diplomatic relations as an us-against-the-world effort.

"As I wrote in my previous letter," Kim wrote on September 21, "my confidence and respect for Your Excellency will never change, though many people are skeptical about the current status and the prospects of the relations between our countries about our ideas of resolving the issue of denuclearization in the future. I, together with Your Excellency, will definitely prove them wrong."

Trump wrote back in a five-sentence letter on December 24: "I look forward to our next summit and to making real progress on denuclearization and a really bright future for your people under your leadership in the year ahead."

Then the next day, Christmas, Kim wrote Trump a much longer letter describing their Singapore meeting in almost romantic prose.

"It has been 200 days since the historic DPRK-US summit in Singapore this past June, and the year is now almost coming to an end. Even now I cannot forget that moment of history when I firmly held Your Excellency's hand at the beautiful and sacred location as the whole world watched with great interest and hope to relive the honor of that day. As I mentioned at that time, I feel very honored to have established an excellent relationship with a person such as Your Excellency.

"As the new year 2019 approaches, critical issues that require endless effort toward even higher ideals and goals still await us. Just as Your Excellency frankly noted, as we enter the new year the whole world will certainly once again come to see, not so far in the future, another historic meeting between myself and Your Excellency reminiscent of a scene from a fantasy film."

When I first read that Kim saw this as "reminiscent of a scene from a fantasy film," I was shocked.

Trump replied on December 28: "I just received your letter and very much appreciate your warm feelings and thoughts. Like you, I have no doubt that a great result will be accomplished between our two countries, and that the only two leaders who can do it are you and me." Trump added that Hanoi or Bangkok would be acceptable locations for their next summit.

Trump wrote again on January 8 to wish Kim a happy birthday. "You will have many great years of celebration and success," he wrote. "Your country will soon be on a historic and prosperous path."

On January 17, Kim wrote to introduce a special envoy he was sending to Washington to arrange the next summit. "I would like to believe that while last year was a meaningful one in which we put an end to the longstanding hostile relations between the DPRK and the US and made a commitment to a new future, this will be a more significant year that will see our bilateral relations develop into a new higher stage," he wrote.

Following envoy Kim Yong Chol's visit to Washington, the two nations agreed to a second summit between the two leaders in February in Hanoi.

"We are together doing something very historic," Trump wrote to Kim January 18. "I will see you soon." Unlike the other letters, which were typed and signed "Sincerely," this was handwritten in Trump's black magic marker and signed: "Your friend, Donald J. Trump."

Trump wrote Kim once more before their Hanoi summit, sending a short note on February 19 along with four pictures of their earlier meeting. "I look forward to seeing you next week," Trump wrote. "It will be great."

On February 27 and 28, 2019, the North Korea–United States summit was held in Hanoi, Vietnam.

The two sides had intended to hold a signing ceremony on the last day, but the meeting fell apart.

Trump and Kim spent two hours together with their respective staffs.

News reports following the abrupt ending said Kim had offered to dismantle the Yongbyon Nuclear Scientific Research Center—the nation's major nuclear weapons facility, located in the far north—but he would not go far enough in offering to dismantle other, more active facilities as well. And while Trump was prepared to undo some economic sanctions, the reports said, he was not prepared to fully lift five rounds of sanctions that had been devastating for the North Korean economy.

Trump had his own version of events in Hanoi, as he related to me: Almost from the start, Trump said, he instinctively knew Kim wasn't ready to get where he needed him to go.

Kim was ready to give up one of his nuclear sites, but he had five.

"Listen, one doesn't help and two doesn't help and three doesn't help and four doesn't help," Trump said. "Five does help."

"But it's our biggest," Kim said, referring to the Yongbyon center.

"Yeah, it's also your oldest," Trump said. "Because I know every one of the sites. I know all of them, better than any of my people I know them. You understand that."

Kim would not budge from his position.

"Do you ever do anything other than send rockets up to the air?" Trump asked Kim. "Let's go to a movie together. Let's go play a round of golf."

Finally, the reality set in.

"You're not ready to make a deal," Trump said to Kim. "You're not there."

"What do you mean?" The look on Kim's face was utter shock.

"You're not ready to make a deal," Trump said. "I've got to leave. You're my friend. I think you're a wonderful guy. But we've got to leave, because you're not ready to make a deal."

Trump's implied message, Pompeo thought, was: Don't shoot. We're friends. We can trust each other. We will work it out.

The summit was reported as a failure.

Letters between Trump and Kim following the Hanoi summit were cordial but infrequent. Their relationship got more attention than progress on denuclearization.

Trump did not write again until three weeks later, on March 22, in a letter in which he pledged permanent friendship. "Thank you again for making this long journey to Hanoi," he wrote. "As I said to you when we parted ways, you are my friend and always will be."

On June 10, Kim wrote Trump another letter of verbose flattery.

"Like the brief time we had together a year ago in Singapore, every minute we shared 103 days ago in Hanoi was also a moment of glory that remains a precious memory," Kim wrote. "Such a precious memory that I have in my unwavering respect for you will provide an impetus for me to take my steps when we walk toward each other again someday in the future.

"I also believe that the deep and special friendship between us will work as a magical force. . .

"Your Excellency Mr. President, I still respect and lay my hopes on the will and determination that you showed in our first meeting to resolve the issue of our unique style that nobody had ever tried, and to write a new history. Today's reality is that without a new approach and the courage it takes, the prospects for resolution of the issue will only be bleak.

"I believe the one day will come sooner or later when we sit down together to make great things happen, with the will to give another chance to our mutual trust. Such a day should come again. It may well be recorded as yet another fantastic moment in history."

Two days later, on June 12, Trump wrote back to say he would like to meet again.

"It is hard to believe that a full year has passed since our historic first meeting in Singapore," Trump wrote. "It was on that day, one year ago, that you and I made a number of extraordinary commitments to one another—you committed to completely denuclearize, and I committed to provide security guarantees. We both committed to establish new relations for our two countries and to build a lasting and stable peace regime on the Korean peninsula.

"I completely agree with you. You and I have a unique style and a special friendship. Only you and I, working together, can resolve the issues between our two countries and end nearly 70 years of hostility, bringing an era of prosperity to the Korean peninsula that will exceed all our greatest expectations—and you will be the one to lead. It will be historic!"

Using Twitter, Trump proposed the next meeting between the two leaders as spontaneous. While in Japan on June 29 for the G20 summit, Trump tweeted: "If Chairman Kim of North Korea sees this, I would meet him at the Border/DMZ just to shake his hand and say Hello(?)!"

The June 29 tweet was followed by a more formal letter later that same day.

"As you may have seen," Trump wrote, "I am traveling today from Osaka, Japan to the Republic of Korea, and since I will be so close to you, I would like to invite you to meet me at the border tomorrow afternoon. I will be near the DMZ in the afternoon and propose a meeting at 3:30 at the Peace House on the southern side of the military demarcation line. I have no specific agenda for our meeting, but think it would be great to see you again since we will be so close to each other. Hope to see you tomorrow!"

Kim accepted Trump's invitation.

On June 30, 2019, Trump and Kim met at the Joint Security Area, a zone of distinctive blue buildings on the border of North Korea and South Korea.

The two leaders faced each other, Trump standing in the gravel on the South Korean side and Kim on the other side of a short concrete slab marking the actual border.

"Would you like me to come in?" Trump asked.

"Yes, I would like you to come in," Kim replied.

Trump walked over the border of the two countries, marking the first time a U.S. president entered North Korea, and the two leaders walked a few steps into North Korean territory.

After the crossing, the two leaders spoke to each other briefly through interpreters.

"I want to thank you," Trump said, according to the official White House transcript of the exchange. "Look, I mean, the world is watching, and it's very important for the world."

Kim told Trump that he had been surprised by the president's letter the day before proposing a meeting at the border.

"Meeting at such a place shows that we are willing to put an end to the unfortunate past and also open a new future and provide positive opportunities in the future," Kim said. "If it was not for our excellent relation between the two of us, it would not have been possible to have this kind of opportunity."

"It was an honor that you asked me to step over that line," Trump said. "And I was proud to step over the line."

The event was an international media spectacle, but it achieved no immediate substantive diplomatic outcome. "A Ratings-Minded President Gets the Shot He Wanted," read a headline in the next day's *Washington Post*.

"Being with you today was truly amazing," Trump wrote to Kim on June 30. "Even the media, which always likes to say that everything is bad, is giving you accolades for inviting me into your country. They said you demonstrated great foresight and courage in accepting a meeting on such short notice and very public notice. Most importantly I thought our meeting went very well. The potential of your country is truly limitless, and I am confident that incredible prosperity awaits you and your people in the future as we continue to work together."

Attached to Trump's June 30 letter was a copy of *The New York Times* front page, which featured a four-column picture of Trump and Kim. "Chairman, great picture of you, big time," Trump added in a marker.

Trump wrote again July 2, sending 22 photographs along with his letter. "It was an honor to cross into your country and to resume our important discussion," Trump wrote. "I have tremendous confidence in our ability to strike a big deal that leads to immense prosperity for you and your people, sheds you of your nuclear burden, and inspires generations to come. These images are great memories for me and capture the unique friendship that you and I have developed."

More than a month later, August 5, Kim wrote Trump the longest letter exchanged between the two.

The tone was polite. But the message was that relations between Kim and Trump may have cooled off for good. It sounded like a disappointed friend or lover.

Kim thanked Trump for the pictures of their meeting at the border. "I'm delighted to receive each and every single picture you specifically chose from that day, which holds special meaning and will remain an eternal memory from that momentous and historic day," he wrote. "Those photographs now hang in my office. I express my appreciation to you, and I will remember that moment forever."

But Kim was upset, he said, because military exercises by the U.S.–South Korea alliance had not fully stopped.

"My belief was that the provocative combined military exercises would either be cancelled or postponed ahead of our two countries' working-level negotiations where we would continue to discuss important matters," Kim wrote. "Against whom is the combined military exercises taking place in the southern part of the Korean Peninsula, who are they trying to block, and who are they intended to defeat and attack?"

He continued: "Conceptually and hypothetically, the main target of the war preparatory exercises is our own military. This is not our misunderstanding . . .

"As if to support our view, a few days ago the person who they call the minister of national defense of South Korea said that the modernization of our conventional commercial weapons was deemed a 'provocation' and a 'threat' and that if we continue to 'provoke' and 'threaten' they will classify my administration and military as an 'enemy.' Now and in the future, South Korean military cannot be my enemy. As you mentioned at some point, we have a strong military without the need of special means, and the truth is that South Korean military is no match against my military."

Kim said he did not like the U.S. military's role. "The thing I like even less is that the US military is engaged in these paranoid and hypersensitive actions with the South Korean people.

"I am clearly offended and I do not want to hide this feeling from you. I am really, very offended," the letter continued. "Your Excellency, I am immensely proud and honored that we have a relationship where I can send and receive such candid thoughts with you."

In remarks on the South Lawn of the White House on August 9, Trump spontaneously brought up Kim's latest letter when answering a reporter's question on a different topic. While Kim's letter warned Trump had offended him, the president turned it on its head.

"I got a very beautiful letter from Kim Jong Un yesterday," Trump said. "It was a very positive letter."

"What did it say?" a reporter asked.

"I'd love to give it to you," Trump said. "I really would. Maybe—maybe sometime I will."

The CIA never figured out conclusively who wrote and crafted Kim's letters to Trump. They were masterpieces. The analysts marveled at the skill someone brought to finding the exact mixture of flattery while appealing to Trump's sense of grandiosity and being center stage in history.

TWENTY-SIX

◆ ◆

I brought something that I've never shown to anybody. I'm going to show it to you," Trump told me on December 5, 2019. "I'll get you something that's sort of cool." He picked up the phone on the Resolute Desk in the Oval Office. "Bring me some pictures with Kim Jong Un and myself, crossing the line. Those nice color ones that I just saw."

The 74-minute interview that afternoon was three months before the coronavirus pandemic consumed the United States and the world. It would be my first of 17 interviews with him for this book.

"This is on the record for the book," I said. "I really am here to listen to your case. And I want to do policy. Because having done nine presidents, the policy is what matters. It's the spine and definition."

"I agree," Trump said. "I agree. Policy can change, also, though, you know? I like flexibility. Some people say I change. I do. I like flexibility, not somebody that has a policy and will go through a brick wall for that policy when you can change it very easily and not have to go through the wall."

As we waited for his staff to bring the photos, I mentioned the CIA had concluded that Kim is "cunning, crafty, but ultimately stupid."

"I hope you write that," Trump said, "And I hope you write my answer. I disagree. He's cunning. He's crafty. And he's very smart. And he's very tough. You know—"

"Why does the CIA say that?"

"Because they don't know," Trump said. "Okay? Because they don't know. They have no idea. I'm the only one that knows. I'm the only one he deals with. He won't deal with anybody else."

Trump had had three meetings with Kim at that point.

Later, based on more in-depth reporting, I learned that the top CIA expert on North Korea agreed with the president that Kim was clever, manipulative but also quite smart.

An aide brought in pictures that show Trump and Kim. All of these shots were photos that had already been released and widely circulated at the time of the event.

"This is me and him," Trump said. "That's the line, right? Then I walked over the line. Pretty cool. You know? Pretty cool. Right? That's the line between North and South Korea. That's the line. That's North and South Korea. That's the line. That line is a big deal. Nobody has ever stepped across that line. Ever." Many others had crossed the border into North Korea, but Trump was the first sitting U.S. president to do so.

Trump continued, "I said, would you like me to come in? He said, yes, I would like you to come in. Nobody's ever done that. I mean, they're cool pictures when you—you know, when you talk about iconic pictures, how about that?"

"But it's still a dangerous relationship," I said. "Would you agree?"

"Yeah," Trump said, "but it's less dangerous than it was. Because he likes me. I like him. We get along. That doesn't mean I'm naive. That doesn't mean that I think, oh, it's going to be wonderful. He's a very tough cookie. And he is smart, very smart."

"You're convinced he's smart?"

"Beyond smart. Look, he took over, when he was 27 years old, a volatile place where the people are very smart. Same as South Korea. They're the same. Okay? Same people. Very smart."

Trump did not dispute that Kim was also violent and vicious. He said that Kim "tells me everything. Told me everything. I know everything about him. He killed his uncle and he put the body right in the steps where the senators walked out. And the head was cut, sitting on the chest. Think that's tough? You know, they think politics in this country's tough."

The president continued, "Nancy Pelosi said, oh, let's impeach him. You think that's tough? This is tough. These are great pictures." He pointed at one of the pictures. "Look, did you ever see him smile? Did you ever see him smile before?"

North Korean state media regularly releases photos of Kim smiling at various events. The president said he could give me copies of some of the pictures.

"The NorthCom commander in Colorado Springs is presidentially designated to shoot down a missile that might hit the United States homeland from North Korea," I said. This would only be the case if the secretary of defense was not available.

"That's correct," the president said. "Yeah, we're all set. Because you have to be set."

"So you're comfortable with that delegation of authority to NorthCom?"

"Sure. Well, you have to be prepared. I don't wait for anything. I don't wait for anything. Nothing bothers me. I don't wait for anything. If I did, I would've been not here a year ago. They've been trying to impeach me now for three years. No, more. They've been trying to impeach me from the day I came down the escalator, okay, you want to know the truth," he said, referring to the launch of his campaign. "They've been trying to get me from that time."

He showed me a photo. "Look, nice picture. But—no, the relationship is good."

"So, hard question, President Trump," I said. "I understand we really came close to war with North Korea."

"Right. Much closer than anyone would know. Much closer. You know. He knows it better than anybody," he said, referring to Kim.

"Did you tell him?"

"I don't want to tell you that. But he knows. I have a great relationship, let me just put it that way. But we'll see what happens." He noted that for two years North Korea had not conducted nuclear or intercontinental ballistic missile tests. The last ICBM test by North Korea had been in November 2017.

"I can't tell you what the end is going to be yet, how it's going to end," Trump said. "He's tested short-range missiles. Which, by the way, every country has short-range missiles. There's no country that doesn't have them. Okay? It's not a big deal. That doesn't mean after January he's not going to be doing some things. We'll see what it is. But I have a great relationship."

Many foreign policy figures had said that Trump gave Kim too much by agreeing to meet without formal, written conditions. "So have you given Kim too much power?" I asked. Kim had said he wouldn't shoot more ICBMs. "Because if he's defiant, if he shoots one of those ICBMs, what are you going to do, sir?"

"If he shoots, he shoots," Trump said. "And then he's got big problems, let me put it that way. Big, big problems. Bigger than anybody's ever had before."

Then Trump digressed to reveal something extraordinary—a secret new weapons system. "I have built a nuclear—a weapons system that nobody's ever had in this country before. We have stuff that you haven't even seen or heard about. We have stuff that Putin and Xi have never heard about before. There's nobody—what we have is incredible."

Later I found sources who confirmed the U.S. military had a secret new weapons system but no one wanted to provide details and were surprised Trump had disclosed it. Trump had asked for and received massive funding increases for the National Nuclear Security Administration, which maintains the nuclear weapons stockpile, since taking office.

Trump told me all he gave Kim was a meeting. "You look, look at the good picture. He's having a good time. You know? Nobody's ever seen him smile. Look. Look at him smiling. He's happy. He feels happy."

"Did you think it's kind of Nixon to China," I asked, referring to President Nixon's opening to China in 1972.

"No, I don't want to even talk about Nixon to China. I think Nixon to China—I think China's been a horrible thing for this country. Horrible because we've allowed them" to become an economic powerhouse.

The military always tells you the alliances with NATO and South Korea are the best bargain the United States makes, I noted, a great investment in joint defense.

"The military people are wrong," Trump said. "I wouldn't say they were stupid, because I would never say that about our military people. But if they said that, they—whoever said that was stupid. It's a horrible bargain. We're protecting South Korea from North Korea, and they're making a fortune with televisions and ships and everything else. Right? They make so much money. Costs us $10 billion. We're suckers."

It costs the United States approximately $4.5 billion annually to station troops in South Korea, $920 million of which is paid by the South Korean government.

"There is anger out there" in the country, I said. "And the question is, you're sitting here in the Oval Office. Why? Why all that anger?"

"Okay," the president said, "I think it's for a number of reasons. But before I agree to even answer that question, okay? I have to say this: There's also many Democrats that silently will vote for me. And it happened last time. The Obama Democrats that came out—I was going to say Barack Hussein, but I figured I wouldn't say that today, because I want to keep this very nice. The Obama Democrats who came out and they voted for me, and it was a tremendous percentage. And the Bernie Sanders Democrats, they voted for me."

Exit polls showed about 9 percent of those who identified as Democrats voted for Trump in 2016, and about 7 percent of those who identified as Republicans voted for Clinton.

I raised former President Obama and said that many thought he was smart.

"I don't know. I don't think Obama's smart," Trump said. "See? I think he's highly overrated. And I don't think he's a great speaker. Oh, he's so—hey look. I went to the best schools. I did great. I had an uncle who was a professor at MIT for 40 years, one of the most respected in the history of the school. For 40 years. My father's brother. And my father was smarter than he was. It's good stock. You know they talk about the elite. Really, the elite. Ah, they have nice houses. No. I have much better than them. I have better everything than them, including education."

"This is an important moment in history," I said, "where they're going to impeach you, the House is going to impeach you."

"Yeah."

"And we're sitting in the Oval Office here. And you are content, happy, proud."

"Yeah."

"Any angst?"

"No."

The deputy press secretary interrupted, saying, "We've got about five minutes, gentlemen." The treasury secretary was waiting.

"Oh, that's okay," Trump said. "Go ahead. I find it interesting. I love this guy. Even though he writes shit about me. That's okay."

"What's the Trump-Pence strategy to win over, in the next 11 months, the persuadable voter?" I asked.

"I don't know," Trump said. "You know what? I'll tell you what the Trump-Pence strategy is: To do a good job. That's all it is. It's very simple. It's not a—I don't have a strategy. I do a good job."

"Why don't you give me your taxes?" I asked. "No, seriously."

He cited his standard argument that his tax returns were being audited by the IRS, although I knew that would not stop him from releasing his taxes if he wanted.

"Do you know what I made last year?" Trump asked. "Four hundred and eighty-eight million or something like that. I made four hundred and eighty-eight—and that's because I'm not there. Meaning I would have done much better. Four eighty-eight."

Trump reported at least $434 million in income in 2018, according to his financial disclosure form filed with the Office of Government Ethics in May 2019.

I noted the split-screen effect of the impeachment debate in the House and this discussion in the Oval Office. I knew it was a big show. He had all his props on the Resolute Desk: the parchment appointment orders of the judges stacked in the middle of the desk, the large rolls of pictures of him and Kim, and a binder with letters from Kim. I had interviewed Presidents Carter, Clinton, George W. Bush and Obama in the Oval Office. All sat in the standard presidential seat by the fireplace and did not have props.

"It's as if you had won the biggest lottery ever," I said.

"I did. Every day I won it. Nancy Pelosi has driven my poll numbers through the roof. And she comes out with, I pray for our president. She never prayed for me in her life."

"Okay. In a sentence, what's the job of the president? What is your job as you see it?

"I have many jobs."

I offered my standard definition. "I think it's figuring out what the next stage of good is for a majority of people in the country—"

"That's good," Trump said.

"—and then saying," I continued, "this is where we're going, and this is the plan to get there."

"Correct," Trump said. "But sometimes that road changes. You know, a lot of people are inflexible. Sometimes a road has to change, you know? You have a wall in front and you have to go around it instead of trying to go through it—it's much easier. But really the job of a president is to keep our country safe, to keep it prosperous. Okay? Prosperous is a big thing. But sometimes you have so much prosperity that people want to use that in a bad way, and you have to be careful with it."

As I listened, I was struck by the vague, directionless nature of Trump's comments. He had been president for just under three years, but couldn't seem to articulate a strategy or plan for the country. I was surprised he would go into 2020, the year he hoped to win reelection, without more clarity to his message.

"By the way, could I ask you a question?" Trump inquired. He wanted to know who I thought would get the Democratic nomination for president.

I had a terrible track record on such predictions and took a pass. "Who do you think is going to be your opponent?" I asked.

"I'll be honest with you, I think it's a terrible group of candidates," Trump said. "It's an embarrassment. I'm embarrassed by the Democrat candidates. I may have to run against one, and who knows? It's an election. And I'm looking pretty good right now."

TWENTY-SEVEN

◆

S hortly before my second interview with President Trump on the afternoon of Friday, December 13, the House Judiciary Committee had voted to send two impeachment articles against the president to the full House of Representatives.

Trump was charged with pressuring Ukrainian president Volodymyr Zelensky in the phone call to investigate former Vice President Joseph R. Biden and Biden's son while leveraging some $400 million in security assistance to Ukraine in its fight with Russia. The second article charged him with obstructing Congress' investigation by ordering administration officials to ignore subpoenas. The vote to impeach was 23 to 17 along strictly partisan lines.

I wanted to see how Trump was handling impeachment.

The president seemed unbothered, even cheery, and had time for a one-and-a-half-hour interview in the Oval Office. He asked his photographer to take our picture. While we did, he explained he liked long neckties so the back could be tucked in the label. "Don't you hate it when it flies?"

He took me on a tour of his hideaway office, the spot where

President Clinton had secretly met with White House intern Monica Lewinsky. The "Monica Room," Trump called it, and gave a knowing smirk. We returned to the Oval Office for the interview.

"What's your relationship with Mitch McConnell?" I asked.

"Very good," he said, but provided no details when I pressed. "You know what Mitch's biggest thing is in the whole world?" Trump asked. "His judges. He will absolutely ask me, please let's get the judge approved instead of 10 ambassadors." Trump agreed judicial appointments were the right priority. "We don't need thousands of people going to the State Department. We've got thousands and thousands of people. It's so ridiculous. I don't want them."

We turned to North Korea, which had recently threatened to send a "Christmas gift" to the United States, with a spokesman saying, "The dialogue touted by the US is, in essence, nothing but a foolish trick."

Of Kim, Trump said, "He didn't respect Obama. Didn't like him. Thought he was an asshole."

I asked why Trump had pivoted to meet with Kim after aiming harsh, warlike rhetoric at him for more than a year.

"It's very complicated," Trump said. "I always ask the one question, why are we defending South Korea?" The United States had 30,000 troops stationed in South Korea. "We're losing a fortune. It's a rich country. I say, so we're defending you, we're allowing you to exist."

I was surprised that he would make such an extreme statement—that South Korea's very existence depended on the United States "allowing" it.

"Why are we doing that?" Trump continued. "Why do we care? We're 8,500 miles away." Seoul, South Korea is about 5,100 miles from Seattle and 7,000 miles from the East Coast of the United States. "Why do we care? Why do we have our 32,000 soldiers over there, willing to fight for you?"

The U.S. military leadership believed that stationing U.S. troops in South Korea had maintained the peace in Asia for decades, and the long and successful alliance with South Korea was a bargain.

Trump said he asked the same question of Japanese prime minister Shinzo Abe. "I ask Abe. He's a friend of mine. I say, why are we defending Japan? You're a rich country. Why are we defending you and you're paying us a tiny fraction of the cost? The establishment hates that question, which shows you how stupid the establishment is."

I tried to bring the conversation back to Kim Jong Un. What happened at your first meeting with Kim in Singapore, I asked.

"You know, it was the most cameras. I think I've seen more cameras than any human being in history. There's like hundreds of them. It's free. I get it for free. It costs me nothing. It's called earned media. And you do earn it. They say I spent 25 percent what Hillary did but I got $6 billion worth of earned media." It was actually 50 percent, according to analysis firm media-Quant.

"Tell me as best you can recall what happened in Singapore?"

"The Singapore event was a monster," Trump said. "They had a thing set up for the media the likes of which you have never seen. I've never seen a thing like it. Thousands. Thousands. Do we have any pictures of that?"

"But I want to see what you think of this man," I said, trying to bring his focus away from the PR extravaganza to the substance of the meeting. An aide brought in a large 16-by-20-inch photo of Trump and Kim seated and smiling.

Kim, Trump said, had pledged to work toward the denuclearization of the Korean Peninsula. "He has a hard time with the word 'denuclearization.' He signed an agreement. He promised me. But he has a real hard time. He backs up." He found a real estate metaphor for Kim's reluctance to give up nuclear weapons:

"It's really like, you know, somebody that's in love with a house and they just can't sell it."

The Singapore meeting was crucial, Trump said. "We really got along. It was a great chemistry."

Trump had privately described meeting Kim this way: "You meet a woman. In one second, you know whether or not it's all going to happen. It doesn't take you 10 minutes, and it doesn't take you six weeks. It's like, whoa. Okay. You know? It takes somewhat less than a second."

Trump continued recounting. "We then had a lunch. I've never seen anything like it. Every single person was sitting up. A general stood up to make a statement. He snapped to attention. There was no carpet, it was like a nice, beautiful wooden floor. His chair snapped back 20 feet. Hit the wall behind him. I said, holy shit. And I joked, I said, I want you people to act like these people. You know, kidding to all my people."

"Kidding, but not kidding," I said. I tried to verify the story in my subsequent reporting but couldn't find anyone who remembered it.

Trump said he told Kim when it came to denuclearization, "I know every one of your sites better than any of my people." He reminded me again of his late uncle, Dr. John Trump, a physicist who taught electrical engineering at the Massachusetts Institute of Technology and was awarded the National Medal of Science in 1983. "He was at MIT for 42 years or something. He was a great—so I understand that stuff. You know, genetically."

Trump continued, "The top person at MIT came to the office about a year ago. Brought me a whole package on Dr. John Trump. He said he was one of the greatest men. He was brilliant. I get that stuff."

"Did Kim Jong Un—if I may ask this—did he say anything that was threatening?"

"Not even a little bit. No."

Trump veered to a new subject. This was when he told me, "I'm breaking China's ass on trade. China's gone to a negative GDP."

Apparently only one prominent economist, Xiang Songzuo of Renmin University in China, agreed with this.

Trump veered again, turning this time to Russia. "We could do such great things with Russia, but because of the phony Russia investigation—started falsely and corruptly and illegally now as it turns out—but because of that, you know, we're held back. And he knows that too. Putin said to me in a meeting, he said, it's a shame, because I know it's very hard for you to make a deal with us. I said, you're right."

We ping-ponged between a few more subjects and landed on Afghanistan. Trump's generals had resisted his desire to withdraw U.S. troops from the 19-year war. "So the first thing the generals tell you when you want to pull out, they say, Sir, I'd rather fight them over there than fight them over here. And if you're sitting behind this beautiful desk, the Resolute Desk, and you have four guys that look like they're right out of Hollywood saying, yes, sir—they'll do whatever you say. I say, what's your opinion, General? Sir, I'd rather fight them over there than fight them over here. I've had four generals say almost the exact same words. That's a hard line if you're sitting here and you have to make that decision, when you have guys that you respect making that statement."

Trump continued, "But I then say, well, does this mean we're going to be there for the next 100 years?"

At the end, he gave me the large, poster-size picture of himself with Kim. He asked one of his aides, "Do you have a round thing for this so he can take it? Or even a rubber band or something. Because you can't fold it, you'll ruin it. I don't even know why I'm giving it to you. That's my only one."

As he had in our earlier interview, Trump told me, "He never smiled before. I'm the only one he smiles with."

TWENTY-EIGHT

—————◆—————

"**I**'m thinking of hitting Soleimani," President Trump said, pulling his golfing partner Senator Lindsey Graham aside on the afternoon of Monday, December 30, 2019.

They were on the front nine of Trump International Golf Club in West Palm Beach, Florida, four and a half miles from Trump's Mar-a-Lago estate and club. Iranian General Qasem Soleimani was the head of the Revolutionary Guard's violent and covert special operations division known as the Quds Force. He was widely considered the most powerful man in Iran after Ayatollah Khamenei, and the driving force behind Iran's terrorist acts overseas. One of Soleimani's militias had just killed a U.S. contractor in a missile attack in Iraq; the next day, the situation would escalate into a siege of the American embassy in Baghdad.

"Oh, boy, that's a giant step!" said Graham, unnerved. Killing Soleimani would be an unexpected play, and a potentially dangerous one.

Soleimani had menaced the United States for decades. Since 2007, he had been under surveillance by a specially formed U.S.

intelligence cell created to target and stop the Quds Force from providing material and training to Iraqis fighting against U.S. forces. Over time, Soleimani became known as one of the most dangerous people in the Middle East, more in control of Iran's foreign policy than its minister of foreign affairs.

Soleimani had been in Trump's sights ever since retired general and former vice chief of staff of the Army Jack Keane told him while he was still president-elect that Soleimani had given Shia militias in Iraq "an advanced IED developed by his engineers and scientists that could penetrate any known equipment on the battlefield," even a tank. Hundreds of American soldiers had been killed and wounded by the devices.

Keane told Trump that President George W. Bush's national security team had asked Bush to authorize the destruction of two bases in Iran where Soleimani's forces were training foreign fighters. But Bush had refused, Keane said. Bush said he thought he would be impeached if he struck inside Iran.

Graham, who had become a sort of First Friend to the president, said that if Trump killed Soleimani, he would have to think about what other steps to take to deter Iran from further escalation. "If they retaliate in some way, which they will, you've got to be willing to take out the oil refineries." Graham had reminded Trump for years that oil was the lifeblood of Iran's economy, the real soft spot. Threaten to take them out of the oil business, Graham urged. But, he cautioned, if you do, "this will be almost total war!"

The stakes would go up, Graham said. "You kill him, new game. You go from playing $10 blackjack to $10,000-a-hand blackjack."

"He deserves it," Trump said. "We have all these intercepts showing that Soleimani is planning attacks."

"Yeah, he's always been doing that," Graham replied. "This is what he does. With the election coming, you've got to think about how you respond and how you expect Iran to respond."

Threatening military action would have to mean a strike in Iran if Trump wanted to be credible. "That risks major war."

Graham had told Trump earlier in his presidency that Iran's theocratic rulers "would eat grass before they would give up." But they could be influenced by economics in addition to ideology. Financial pressure and sanctions might cause the people to turn on their leaders.

Iran was behind both the missile strikes that had killed an American and the militias that had stormed the embassy. "We're not going to let them get away with this," Trump said.

"Mr. President," Graham said, "this is over the top. How about hitting someone a level below Soleimani, which would be much easier for everyone to absorb?" This was a role reversal for Graham. He was usually the hawk trying to convince a reluctant Trump to take military action. But a strike on Soleimani could mean the president was rushing the country into dangerous, uncharted territory.

On the golf course, Trump tended to focus on the golf. He would drop out of the world, enjoying the endless tinkering with his swing. This week he was changing his grip on his clubs, strengthening it by turning his hands away from the target. He was pleased with the result. His drives landed 10 to 15 yards further, beyond 250 yards.

Later Mick Mulvaney, Trump's acting chief of staff, made an urgent request of Graham. Graham and Mulvaney had both served in South Carolina's congressional delegation and knew each other well.

You've got to find a way to stop this talk of hitting Soleimani, Mulvaney almost begged. Perhaps he'll listen to you.

Four days later, Trump ordered the drone strike which killed Soleimani.

———

Several hours after Trump and Graham's golf game, I was sitting in the reception area of Mar-a-Lago waiting to interview Trump—our third interview that month. I had no clue about a potential strike on Soleimani. I wanted to review with him Mueller's Russia investigation and Trump's impeachment by the Democratic House of Representatives just 12 days earlier. The news, the daily story, was impeachment. Or so it seemed as I watched Mar-a-Lago club members stream in for dinner at what a Secret Service agent called "the regular evening soiree."

The club, originally built as a private home in 1927, was opulent and luxurious in an Old World way, like a gilded, candle-lit version of the Wizard of Oz's castle. A 16-inch plaque stood prominently on the receptionist's table. It read: "Donald J. Trump. The Mar-a-Lago Club. The only six-star private club in the world."

Suddenly, Trump in suit and tie, appeared with billionaire Nelson Peltz in tow. Peltz is the 77-year-old founding partner of Trian Fund Management, an investing firm whose portfolio includes holdings in Wendy's and other prominent brands. Prompted by Trump, Peltz said, "Oh, he's doing great things for the economy. It's all him!"

Peltz has a $123 million estate near Mar-a-Lago and saw his net worth increase from $1.4 billion in 2016 to $1.6 billion in 2019—a paper gain of $200 million. He kept pointing at Trump, repeating, "It's all him! It's all him! He did it!"

At one point Trump pointed to the gold leaf on the 20-foot-high ceiling. "Look at that," he said. "See that? See that?"

Trump then escorted me back to a private conference room. We sat next to each other at a large table. Hogan Gidley, his deputy press secretary, sat more than six feet away on the other side of the table, recording the interview on his mobile phone.

We addressed impeachment. Trump told me he considered himself "a student of history," adding, "I like learning from the past. Much better than learning from yourself and mistakes."

Despite being impeached, Trump looked well rested and relaxed.

This contrasted with other recent presidents who'd been in trouble, Trump said. "Nixon was in a corner with his thumb in his mouth. Bill Clinton took it very, very hard. I don't."

Early in the interview I mentioned Nixon's famous quote to David Frost in 1977 after he had resigned the presidency: Of his opponents, Nixon had said, "I gave them a sword. And they stuck it in. And they twisted it with relish. And, I guess, if I'd been in their position I'd have done the same thing."

In the rough transcript of the July 25 call with the Ukrainian president that the White House had released, Trump says, "There's a lot of talk about Biden's son, that Biden stopped the prosecution and a lot of people want to find out about that so whatever you can do with the Attorney General would be great. Biden went around bragging that he stopped the prosecution so if you can look into it. . . . It sounds horrible to me."

I asked Trump whether, looking back, he felt he "gave them a sword" by releasing the transcript of the call with President Zelensky.

"It's a perfect phone call," Trump said, repeating his public line of defense. "No. I don't. I didn't give them a sword."

Trump continued, "They never in a million years thought I was going to release the call, number one. Number two, they never in a million years thought that we had it transcribed." Trump insisted he should be given "great credit" for having the transcript of the call released.

"It's the transcript that's the sword for them," I said.

"Let's assume I didn't have a transcription," Trump said. "Then I would've lived with a false report by a whistleblower saying that it was a terrible call."

But the transcript proved that the whistleblower, despite not personally witnessing the call, had given an accurate summary in his report.

"Can I ask you this, President Trump? As a matter of policy, would you want the president of the United States to be talking to foreign leaders about investigating anyone? That's just bad policy, isn't it?"

"Let me explain. Let me explain. No, let me explain," Trump insisted. Biden was "corrupt."

"You understand what I'm—as a matter of policy, do you want the president of the United States—" I started to ask, but the president cut me off.

"I think it's fine. But there's no—Well, let me tell you—"

"You do?"

"When we're giving vast amounts of money to a country, I think you have to say if they're corrupt. Why is it that there's such corruption when we're giving it? And you know, there's another thing that I also talk about. And I talk about why isn't Germany, France, the European nations who are much more affected by Ukraine than us" paying more, he asked. "Because Ukraine is like a massive wall. Think of it as a wall between Russia and Europe, okay?"

"Understand," I said, but didn't want him to change the subject. "Will you allow me to persist with, I think, this is the important, core question in this?"

"There wasn't a thing—excuse me, Bob, there wasn't a thing wrong with that call."

I did persist. "Do you want the policy of the United States to be that the president of the United States can talk to foreign leaders and say, investigate? I want you to talk to the attorney general about investigating somebody who's a political opponent?"

"No. No. No. I want them to investigate corruption. What he did was corrupt. I want them to investigate corruption. And I didn't say, call my campaign manager. I said, the attorney general of the United States—"

"I understand the defense. I'm asking the policy question," I said.

"And you have to say one thing: no, I want corruption investigated. And how can we investigate corruption in a foreign country? How can we do that? We can't do that. We can't do it because we're not—you know, we don't have access. We're giving billions of dollars away to a foreign country. Yes, we should have the right to investigate corruption. I believe that strongly."

"I understand the points you're making. I'm asking the policy question. Is this a good policy for the president of the United States, to be talking to foreign leaders about investigating anyone—"

"Corruption. Yes, corruption."

"Well, but naming a political opponent."

"If the political opponent is corrupt, they can let us know. Look, his son—"

"Do you think that's the president's job?"

"His son—" Trump tried to go on.

"Is that the president's job? I'm sorry to persist on this, but—"

"The president's job is to investigate corruption. If there was corruption, we're giving billions of dollars to a country, that country should let us know if there's corruption."

"You don't see the other side on this at all?"

"I don't see it at all, no."

"Zero?"

"No. If there was no corruption—but there was corruption. And when you look at that tape of Joe Biden—Quid Pro Joe, they call him. Quid. Pro. Joe," he said, enunciating each word carefully. "When you look at that tape, Bob, that's—that's the ultimate quid pro quo. Okay? It's the ultimate."

Trump was referring to Biden's January 23, 2018, appearance at the Council on Foreign Relations, where he talked about helping force Ukrainian prosecutor General Viktor Shokin from office. Shokin's ouster had been sought by the United States and other Western countries for failing to pursue corruption cases—including an investigation into Burisma, the Ukrainian gas company.

The president continued, "I'm only saying this. Look, I'm only saying this. That conversation I had with [Zelensky] was perfect. But here's what happened. You had an informer who now disappeared. You had a second whistleblower who now disappeared. You had the first whistleblower who reported the call. He reported it totally different than—there were eight quid pro quos."

Trump's facts were muddled. The whistleblowers remained masked under federal law. Several times in late 2019 the president said, without basis, that he had been accused of "eight quid pro quos," an exaggerated misstatement of the allegations against him. Trump then tried to shift the subject to chairman of the House Intelligence Committee Adam Schiff.

"I'm just asking the policy question," I said. "Would you want the next president of the United States to be talking to foreign leaders about investigating political opponents?"

"I would want the next president of the United States to investigate corruption. And in fact, we have a treaty signed with Ukraine, because it is a very corrupt country in the past—hopefully the new president will do something about it—but we have a treaty that we actually have to do it."

The Mutual Legal Assistance Treaty between the United States and Ukraine allows the Justice Department to investigate corruption in Ukraine but doesn't obligate it.

"You see why I'm asking these questions?"

"Look, look, what happened here is very interesting."

"Indeed it is," I said.

"They made up a phony conversation," Trump said, "and it sounded terrible." Trump was referring to a dramatized summary of the call that Adam Schiff had given in a House Intelligence committee hearing on the whistleblower report on September 26. Schiff led into his heavily paraphrased account by saying, "It reads like a classic organized crime shakedown. Shorn of its rambling character and in not so many words, this is the essence of what the president communicates." Schiff went on to parody the call in the style of a mafia boss, wrapping up by saying, "It would be funny if it wasn't such a graphic betrayal of the president's oath of office." It was clear Schiff was dramatizing, but he had given Trump a big opening to criticize him.

"When you released that transcript," I said, "you gave them a sword, President Trump."

"No, the opposite."

"Yes, you did. Well, I know you say you—"

"Look, let me ask you a question," Trump said.

"Sure, of course."

"You ready? If I didn't have that transcript, I would have a very big problem right now."

"No sir. You would not."

"Excuse me. I had a whistleblower—"

"There's a kind of clarity in a transcript," I said. What's more, it contained the truth, released and validated by Trump. "I know this going back to the Nixon tapes. As soon as you have a transcript, even though it's not entirely perfect, verbatim, as soon as you have that, that's what everyone focuses on."

"Here's my problem," Trump said later, summarizing, "the whistleblower report was a fraud."

I had not yet read the public whistleblower report, but I knew the whistleblower had written that he was not a witness to most of the events, including the phone call. I also knew the report had largely been proven accurate.

"If I didn't have a transcript," Trump said, "I would've had a big problem."

"But it just would've been a whistleblower report," I said. "It has very fuzzy status, because it's just a whistleblower report."

"I think you're wrong," Trump said.

"It doesn't have any standing," I said. Unlike the transcript of the call he released, the report had not been hard evidence. "It's not proof."

Trump went on to attack the report and the whistleblower's lawyer as "a real scumbag."

"Okay," I said. "You're willing to have this conversation, and you know me well enough, I'm—I really want to understand in a comprehensive way." I added, referring to the whistleblower report, "It's not evidence." But the transcript was evidence—it was proof of what had been said.

Trump looked across the table to deputy press secretary Gidley for backup.

"Mr. President," Gidley said, "all I was getting was questions about this report. All I was getting. For days."

"And by the way," Trump said, "I got approval from Ukraine before I released it. Because I was very—I said, jeez. It's a terrible thing to do. A terrible thing to do. So we called Ukraine. We said, do you mind if we release this conversation? And we got approval. Otherwise I wouldn't have been able to release it."

Our conversation had gone from interview to confrontation. He did not seem to understand or accept my central point—the president of the United States had no business asking for a criminal investigation of his political opponent. It was clear we were not going to agree, so I decided to move on.

"I'm going to tell you something from my experience," I said.

"Go ahead," Trump said. "Nobody more experienced."

"Well," I continued, "you're willing to have this—as you know in the Nixon case, I always said afterwards, as soon as the Watergate burglars were caught, if Richard Nixon had gone on television and said, you know, 'I'm the man at the top. I'm indirectly responsible for this. I'm sorry. I apologize,' it would've gone away."

"I would never have done it here," Trump said. "Yeah, Nixon should've done that. But I shouldn't have done, because I did nothing wrong. I did nothing wrong."

"Have you ever found that you did nothing wrong, but apology is the path to ending the issue?" I asked.

"I wouldn't apologize if I did nothing," Trump said. "Can't do it. If I did something wrong I could apologize."

I said, "I'm telling you, from too many decades of experience in cases like this, if you apologized it would go away."

"I think if I apologized," Trump explained, "it would be a disaster. Because that would be admitting I did something wrong, and I didn't."

The House Democrats who voted for impeachment centered their claims on the transcript of the phone call. "You clearly wanted the Bidens investigated," I said, trying again.

"No. No," Trump said. "I want corruption investigated." He repeated that he wanted to know why Germany and France were not putting up money for Ukraine. "Why is it always the foolish United States?"

"I know it wouldn't fit with your persona to apologize," I said.

"I would totally apologize if I did something wrong."

I shifted ground. "Who's the person you trust most in the world?"

Trump paused for several seconds. Then he chuckled and said, "That's an interesting question. I don't know. I don't want to get into it, because I have so many people—I have great family. I trust my family members."

"Okay," I said. "Ask them if you should apologize."

"Bob, I think you have to look at the whistleblower report."

"I will," I promised. I indicated I realized he was allowing me to push him. "I appreciate your indulgence. I am telling you my experience, and my conviction, my reportorial belief, you gave them a sword when you released that transcript."

Trying to get the Bidens investigated was improper, or as many Republicans would later say, "inappropriate."

"I so disagree with you," he said, laughing. "If I didn't have a transcription, they would have made up a story that was so phony, and I would've had no defense."

"I met Ivanka coming in," I said, referring to his daughter. "Take her for a walk around this lovely place."

"I'll ask her," Trump said.

"And say, should—would an apology, carefully phrased, end this or put it in a context?"

"It would be a disaster," Trump said. "In my opinion."

Again from across the table, Gidley jumped in. "Disaster. You're right. You're 100 percent correct. The media would not give him—no way they'd—they would destroy him for that."

"I have this reputation of not being willing to apologize," Trump said. "It's wrong. I will apologize, if I'm wrong."

"When's the last time you apologized?"

"Oh, I don't know, but I think over a period—I would apologize. Here's the thing: I'm never wrong. Okay. No, if I'm wrong—if I'm wrong—I believe in apologizing. This was a totally appropriate conversation. It was perfect. And again, if I did something wrong, I would apologize. Okay?"

Trump's best-known recent apology followed the release of the *Access Hollywood* tape in October 2016.

Late in the interview I asked again if Trump would take that walk with Ivanka.

"I will, but I disagree with you so much," Trump said. "It wouldn't matter what she said."

I pressed one last time. What would he do if Ivanka thought he should apologize?

"It wouldn't matter what she said," he repeated.

Dan Scavino, Trump's social media director, had walked in. Trump pulled him into the debate. "He thinks I should apologize," Trump said. "I think if I apologized, it would be a disaster. I don't know."

"A hundred percent," Scavino said. "The media would kill" Trump.

Scavino, one of Trump's closest aides, had his laptop open at the table.

"Show him this thing," Trump said.

"You won't even believe this," Trump said. "Watch this."

Scavino played a 90-second clip which was a spliced-together selection of stumbles, hesitations, pauses and confusions from Mueller's testimony before Congress on July 24. Interspersed were shots of members of the committee looking on in wonder, indifference and surprise. It was funny in an unkind way. Mueller was visibly unsteady. Trump stood over my shoulder and watched. He laughed and chuckled, delighted, as if this was payback for the two years of Mueller.

Next up on Scavino's laptop was a clip of Trump's February 2019 State of the Union speech before Congress 11 months prior. Instead of his words, hyped-up elevator music played as the camera panned over extended shots of senators and members of Congress watching from their seats. One of the first shots was of Bernie Sanders, who looked bored.

Trump had a different interpretation. "They hate me," the president said. "You're seeing hate!"

A shot of Elizabeth Warren was next. She was paying attention but had a bland, unemotional look on her face.

"Hate!" Trump said.

A shot of an expressionless Alexandria Ocasio-Cortez. Trump pointed at her.

"Hate! See the hate!" he said.

The camera lingered a particularly long time on Kamala Harris, who had a straight, even polite look on her face as the dubbed-in music played in the background.

"Hate!" Trump said. "See the hate! See the hate!"

TWENTY-NINE

───────◆───────

I n January 2020, Senator Lindsey Graham was basking in his role as chairman of the Senate Judiciary Committee, one of the most powerful roles in the Senate. All nominees for federal judgeships came through his committee.

Trump was pushing hard to appoint a slew of federal judges. There was a steady and seemingly unrelenting flow of names. The Senate had confirmed 187 of Trump's judicial appointments by December 2019.

On the evening of January 7, Graham reflected on the key pillar of the Trump revolution.

"I didn't know we had so many fucking judges," Graham said. "I think every town's got a judge. Some are a little wacky. Most of them are really good. But a few outliers. The problem is when you only need a simple majority, you don't need to go outside your own party."

In 2005, under President George W. Bush, Graham, John McCain and a bipartisan group of 12 other senators had held firm to resist a proposal to eliminate the use of a filibuster in the Senate for judicial appointments. A filibuster effectively allowed one senator to block the appointment of a judge. Senate rules required 60 votes to overcome a filibuster, meaning in effect each nominee needed the support of at least 60 senators.

But in 2013, under Obama, Senate Majority Leader Harry Reid, infuriated by Republicans' use of the filibuster, pushed the elimination through.

"I don't think I've ever seen John McCain more upset," Graham recalled. "Because that's the beginning of the end."

The result was making the judiciary more ideological, Graham realized. The rule change had removed the need to strive for compromise. "If you've got to reach across the aisle and pick up 10 votes, you're going to have a different judge than if you don't."

When the Democrats got back in power with a Senate majority they would do the same thing, he predicted.

Now with Trump's appointments "there's some wacky ones, but there's some that didn't make it. I said no. No, we're not going there.

"But we have weeded out some really wackos. It's only going to get worse over time, though. The judiciary is going to get far more ideological. It changes the Senate. It's just a matter of time until the Senate becomes the House"—more ideological, more partisan and focused on the short term rather than able to take a long view.

The filibuster on legislation would be next to go, Graham worried. "If Trump wins reelection and we take back the House and we've got a small majority in the Senate, they'll be so much pressure on all of us to change the rules."

If he had anything to do with it, Graham said, he would work not to change the rules any further.

In the meantime, he said, "the judiciary's going to fundamentally change in our lifetime." The nominees will have to be approved by outspoken ideologues in the party "because you don't need any support from the other side."

Graham spoke to Chief Justice John Roberts frequently. "John Roberts is very much worried about this drift. He's an institutionalist at heart. He's joined several 5 to 4 decisions because he doesn't want the Court, I think, labeled as a political party."

THIRTY

———— ◆ ————

At the very end of December, a 79-year-old physician, 5-foot-7, grandfatherly and calm, was sorting through emails, notes and phone messages from a worldwide network he had developed over 35 years.

Beep! His internal radar went off. "China. New virus. Wet market. Wow."

Dr. Anthony Fauci, the government's top infectious disease expert, was seeing the first reports of a new mysterious pneumonia outbreak at a seafood and live-animal market, known as a wet market, in China.

Fauci had been director of the National Institute of Allergy and Infectious Diseases for 36 years, a nearly unheard of longevity in a top government post, and oversaw a vast research effort to detect, treat and prevent a wide array of infections and immunological diseases.

He had been at the forefront of most of the most severe global outbreaks in the last four decades, including the emerging HIV/AIDS crisis in the 1980s, anthrax, SARS, swine flu, and Ebola. As late as fall 2019 he was working on the hunt for a universal flu vaccine and an HIV vaccine, two Holy Grails of infectious disease research.

He worried that a catastrophic pandemic lurked around the corner with the potential to alter civilization. "My concern is that there are always emerging infections," Fauci said at his Jesuit high school alma mater in June 2019. "The ones that are the most devastating are ones that spread rapidly—respiratory illnesses. . . . I worry about a pandemic."

Reports of a new infectious disease from China scared the hell out of him. China had been a threatening source of some of the most virulent and deadly virus outbreaks for years, including SARS, H5N1 and H7N9 bird flus.

Was this new illness similar to the 2003 SARS outbreak? he wondered. The SARS virus was believed to have started in a bat, then jumped to a civet cat who was sold in a Chinese wet market to be sacrificed for a feast. SARS was deadly to its victims, but people with SARS generally were not infectious until the fifth or sixth day of their illness, when they showed serious symptoms, so the disease was considered to have inefficient human-to-human spread. People who were ill were easy to identify and isolate before infecting others. SARS had infected over 8,000 people worldwide and killed nearly 800 before it was contained. But it could have been much worse. No SARS deaths were recorded in the United States.

The new outbreak, later labeled Covid-19, had apparently begun in Wuhan, China.

On New Year's Eve, December 31, 2019, Dr. Robert Redfield also saw the first report of an unexplained pneumonia in a large city in China and immediately went on alert.

Redfield, 68, an expert virologist and the director of the Centers for Disease Control and Prevention (CDC), the public health agency charged with protecting Americans' health, read an "urgent notice on the treatment of pneumonia of unknown cause" released online by the Wuhan Municipal Health Committee in China. One of the CDC's major responsibilities was to monitor global health threats to try to stop them before they reached the United States.

Redfield had 23,000 people, including contractors, working for him all over the world, compared to Fauci's 2,000. Redfield, with his distinctive gray chin curtain beard, liked to keep a low public profile. The CDC considers itself "the nation's health protection agency." As director, Redfield's immediate focus is on the cause of the disease, or what is called the etiology.

A devout Catholic, Redfield had gone through a religious awakening during a private 10-minute conversation with Pope John Paul II in 1989 and believed in the redemptive power of suffering. Redfield prayed every day, including a prayer for President Trump.

He treated the information out of China with urgency.

The CDC's first formal report, filed the next day despite the federal holiday, is a remarkably detailed three-page document (see photo insert). Titled "China Pneumonia of Unknown Etiology Situational Report," it is dated January 1, 2020, and marked "For Internal Use Only/Not for Distribution." The report was disseminated to other top health officials, including Health and Human Services secretary Alex Azar.

In a section headlined "Topline Messages," the report stated:

1. The current situation relates to an epidemic of pneumonia of unknown etiology centralizing on a local seafood market, Hua Nan Seafood Market in Wuhan, China

2. Despite news reports mentioning the possibility of SARS, there is no actual evidence implicating SARS

3. 27 cases reported to date . . .

4. The clinical syndrome includes fever, few with difficult breathing, and with bilateral lung infiltrates on
chest x-ray

5. The seafood market has been closed for disinfection
since they also sell wild animals.

In other sections, the report said:

- There has been no obvious transmission among people
to date

- There has been no hospital staff who have been infected to date

- The Wuhan Municipal Health Commissioner released
an announcement just before 2PM December 31

- Laboratory testing is underway for respiratory pathogens to include SARS

- The cases so far have been limited to Wuhan.

The report included a map showing Wuhan's location in China,
and three pictures of the market.

On January 2, the second CDC Situational Report was updated
to include the significant information that the Hua Nan market
was said to sell bats, a known reservoir of diseases that are transmissible and deadly to humans, and other wild animals. "The seafood market has been closed for disinfection since they also sell
animals including chicken, cat, dog, bat, marmot, snake, seafood
and other animals." The report also noted, "Two media reports of
illness outside of Wuhan were published today."

Redfield worried about the possible emergence of a pandemic

bird flu coming out of China yet again—H5N1 and H7N9 had killed an extraordinary 60 percent and 40 percent respectively of people infected.

On January 2, Redfield shared his concerns with the National Security Council's biodefense directorate, which reported to Pottinger and O'Brien.

Redfield and Fauci conferred about what China was reporting. In each of the 27 cases, the illness had allegedly jumped from an animal to a human.

Fauci and Redfield thought that seemed like a stretch. All 27 people were infected from animals in the same market? Did all those people actually go to that market or eat animals and get it from animals? Or was it likely there was human-to-human spread, which could vastly increase the likelihood of a major outbreak?

Significantly, the CDC's January 3 Situational Report noted there were now 44 cases. Lab testing had ruled out seasonal and avian influenza and some other common respiratory pathogens, although SARS was still a possibility. "Hong Kong, Taiwan, Singapore and the Amur Region in Russia have implemented border screening of people traveling from Wuhan," it reported. This level of caution was relatively rare.

Redfield sent an email to George Gao, the head of the Chinese CDC, who has an Oxford PhD in biochemistry and is an expert in coronaviruses, on the afternoon of Friday, January 3, to set up a private phone call. Redfield knew Gao well and had worked with him over the years.

Are you certain that it's not human-to-human spread? Redfield asked. Some of those infected were from the same family and lived together, Redfield noted, increasing the chances of human-to-human spread.

They had been at the same market, Gao said.

Redfield was skeptical.

Why don't we send our disease detectives, Redfield said to Fauci, from their Epidemic Intelligence Service, to Wuhan to see what was going on?

Fauci said if the disease was really only traveling from animals to humans, the spread would likely be inefficient, and a massive outbreak was unlikely.

Redfield wanted to get his experts to the scene in Wuhan. The proven way to contain the spread of an infectious disease was to first have an understanding of its scale and characteristics. The way to do that was to have his medical experts—epidemiologists, virologists, CDC doctors, but no political people—on the ground at the earliest stages of an outbreak to see for themselves. Time was critical. If the CDC team could get into Wuhan, they would be able to give him an assessment and also help the Chinese. Perhaps that assessment would be the difference between containment and disaster. Redfield sent Gao another email the next day.

"CDC has substantive experience," he wrote, "in identifying the etiology of pneumonia outbreaks caused by novel pathogens. CDC also has a long history of working collaboratively with the government of China on pneumonia and respiratory infectious diseases."

He continued, "I would like to offer CDC technical experts in laboratory and epidemiology of respiratory infectious disease to assist you and China CDC in identification of this unknown and possibly novel pathogen."

At this point, Fauci thought, they would have to just count on the Chinese being honest and see what happened.

Redfield again spoke with Gao. He reported to O'Brien and Pottinger. The call was both troubling and bizarre. China was stonewalling.

He filled Pottinger in on the details. Gao was not forthcoming at all. Redfield was deeply concerned by Gao's tone, which was different from his previous experiences with him. Gao sounded like a hostage and expressed serious anxiety. When pressed, he offered nothing about possible human-to-human spread. In an unexpected turn Gao wanted the United States to send their experts but he said he couldn't issue the invitation. Instead could Redfield request the Chinese ask for U.S. experts?

Redfield was beyond frustration. Each day counted. On January 6 he converted his January 4 email word-for-word to a formal letter to Gao on the U.S. Department of Health and Human Services letterhead. Redfield figured the formal letter would give Gao some ammunition with his superiors. The Chinese sat on it.

Redfield pinged Gao through the U.S. embassy in Beijing asking if there was a response. Can we come to China? The answer came back: Thanks again for the offer.

What's going on? Redfield complained to Fauci. They weren't getting a yes and they weren't getting a no. From his past relationship with Gao, he did not expect this. He tried everything to get an affirmative invitation. Nothing.

They were at the most critical stage. He needed on-the-ground data.

One explanation, Redfield and Fauci agreed, was that the Chinese are proud, with sophisticated medical doctors and equipment, and probably felt they didn't need help from anybody else. Fauci threw up his hands. Here we go again. China being China—remote, aloof and secretive. Since they knew of no cases of the strange pneumonia in the United States, it would be hard to press much harder.

By January 5, according to the CDC Situational Report #5, there were 59 cases in Wuhan, more than double in four days. SARS and MERS (Middle East Respiratory Syndrome) had been ruled out. Local health experts were recommending wearing masks and avoiding closed and airless public places and crowded places. Media speculation about SARS continued to swirl.

The CDC posted a Level 1 travel notice for Wuhan on January 6. Level 1 was the lowest, which served to simply alert travelers of the presence of a health problem in the area and urged them to "practice usual precautions" and "avoid living or dead animals, animal markets, and contact with sick people."

The Situational Report for January 6 noted the sprawling seafood market was located next to a train station "which serves as a transportation hub at the center of China's domestic train routes and will soon be especially congested as we enter Chinese New Year."

The Chinese New Year celebration would begin on January 24 and span 16 days. One *Bloomberg News* story, dubbing it the "World's Biggest Human Migration," reported that three billion trips would be taken within China and to other countries for the holiday.

The CDC report also noted that "viral pneumonia in Wuhan has been a hot topic on Chinese social media for the past week." According to the CDC, a hashtag, translated as #WuhanReportedMysteriousPneumonia, was being actively censored on Chinese social media.

Redfield grew increasingly worried as reported cases increased. On January 7, he stood up his Incident Management Structure, a process reserved only for serious health matters. In two years as CDC director, he had only done this twice before. It was first dubbed "2020 China Pneumonia Response," then almost immediately renamed "2020 Pneumonia of Unknown Etiology Response." The initiative was launched with the main objectives "to prepare for potential domestic cases and to support the investigation in China or other countries if requested."

The CDC Situational Report said there was no specific screening at train stations or airports in Wuhan. "Media has begun to report high demand of N95 respirators in China," it noted. The N95 was a sophisticated mask used by health care workers.

Redfield called and suggested to Gao that the Chinese go out

CENTERS FOR DISEASE
CONTROL AND PREVENTION

China Pneumonia of Unknown Etiology
Situational Report
January 1, 2020
EPI Week 1

Topline Messages

1. The current situation relates to an epidemic of pneumonia of unknown etiology centralizing on a local seafood market, Hua Nan Seafood Market in Wuhan, China.
2. Despite news reports mentioning the possibility of SARS, there is no actual evidence implicating SARS
3. 27 cases reported to date, 7 were severe, and others are stable and under control; 2 cases have recovered and are ready to be discharged from the hospital
4. The clinical syndrome includes fever, few with difficult breathing, and with bilateral lung infiltrates on chest x-ray
5. The seafood market has been closed for disinfection since they also sell wild animals

China CDC Actions

Responses in outbreak-affected areas

- China National Health Commission has sent an expert team to Wuhan (Lab and Epi)
- China CDC has conducted a field investigation
- Testing for respiratory pathogens as well as SARS is currently underway
- All cases are undergoing treatment
- Close contacts to the cases are being tracked
- Sanitary treatment of the seafood market is underway as well as a hygiene study
- After preliminary investigation and analysis, the reported cases are considered viral pneumonia
- There has been no obvious transmission among people to date
- There has been no hospital staff who have been infected to date
- The investigation about the cause of epidemic is still ongoing and awaiting laboratory identification

Communications and Policy Outreach

- The Wuhan Municipal Health Commissioner released an announcement just before 2PM December 31
- U.S. CDC has worked closely with the U.S. Consulate in Wuhan and the U.S. Embassy to develop appropriate messaging to include prevention messages
- Hospitals were urged to offer treatment and report cases in a timely manner
- Official information and updates will be shared on:
  http://wjw.wuhan.gov.cn/front/web/showDetail/2019123108989 (per China CDC)

On January 1, 2020, New Year's Day, the Centers for Disease Control and Prevention began producing a series of detailed daily reports about the spread of an epidemic through Wuhan, China, and beyond. "The current situation relates to an epidemic of pneumonia of unknown etiology [cause] centralizing on a local seafood market, Hua Nan Seafood Market in Wuhan, China," the first report states. "There has been no obvious transmission among people to date."

Novel Coronavirus (nCoV) 2019
Situational Report
January 13, 2020
Report Day 13 (new information in blue)

Topline Messages

- On January 10, 2020, Chinese health authorities have preliminarily identified a novel (new) coronavirus as the cause of an outbreak of pneumonia in Wuhan City, Hubei Province, China. To date, a 41 cases of novel coronavirus (nCoV) 2019 have officially been reported; 7 patients had severe illness; one death in a patient with serious underlying medical conditions, and 6 patients had been discharged.
- Cases in this outbreak were identified between December 8, 2019 and January 2, 2020.
- Most patient cases in China had some link to a large local seafood and animal market, suggesting a possible zoonotic origin to the outbreak.
    - Influenza, avian influenza, adenovirus, SARS-CoV, and MERS have been ruled out for all cases.
    - There is no confirmed human-to-human transmission and no reported transmission to health care providers.
- Chinese investigators were able to fully sequence the virus genome. China publicly posted the genetic sequence of the novel coronavirus 2019 (nCoV-2019) on January 12. This will facilitate further diagnosis and development of specific diagnostic tests for this virus in other countries.
- With the release of the sequence, CDC laboratories now have the capacity to detect nCoV-2019 by sequencing virus isolates and comparing the sequences against the genetic sequence released by China.
- CDC has begun work on a diagnostic test that will allow laboratory detection.
- On January 13, 2020 Thailand reported a confirmed case of nCoV in a traveler from Wuhan City to Thailand. This is the first infection with novel coronavirus 2019 detected outside of China.
- On January 6, 2020, CDC released a level 1 travel health notice ("practice usual precautions") for this destination. Updates to this notice were posted on January 11, 2020. https://wwwnc.cdc.gov/travel/notices/watch/novel-coronavirus-china .
- On January 8, 2020, CDC issued a HAN and partner notification to inform clinical providers and public health officials about the outbreak and related guidance. Guidance is being updated this week to inform this evolving outbreak.
- On January 10, CDC launched a dedicated webpage for this outbreak where updates and information will be posted as the situation evolves: https://www.cdc.gov/coronavirus/novel-coronavirus-2019.html. The website was updated on January 11 and subsequently on January 13, 2020.
- On January 11, information about the outbreak was added to an online feature on Lunar New Year: https://wwwnc.cdc.gov/travel/page/lunar-new-year-2020
- On January 11, CDC shared a "muster" (situational awareness briefing) on the outbreak with Customs and Border Protection (CBP) to inform CBP officers at US ports of entry and provide recommendations for detecting and responding to sick travelers from Wuhan.
- CDC developed messaging for posting on CDC monitors at US airports with the highest volumes of travelers from Wuhan.

The CDC Situational Report for January 13 alerted officials that "Thailand reported a confirmed case of nCoV in a traveler from Wuhan City to Thailand. This is the first infection with novel coronavirus 2019 detected outside China."

President Donald J. Trump, in a February 7, 2020, interview with the author, reflected on the presidency. "Look, when you're running a country it's full of surprises," Trump said. "There's dynamite behind every door."

Robert O'Brien, pictured right, is Trump's fourth national security adviser. Matthew Pottinger, pictured left, is a former *Wall Street Journal* reporter and Marine, and is O'Brien's deputy. During a Top Secret President's Daily Brief on January 28, 2020, on the coronavirus, O'Brien told Trump: "This will be the biggest national security threat you face in your presidency." Pottinger said, "I agree with that conclusion," and urged Trump to cut off travel from China to the United States.

Retired General James Mattis, Trump's first defense secretary, clashed with the president over staying the course in the war against ISIS and resigned in December 2018. "When I was basically directed to do something that I thought went beyond stupid to felony stupid," Mattis said, "strategically jeopardizing our place in the world and everything else, that's when I quit."

In late 2017, Mattis several times slipped quietly, unnoticed, into the National Cathedral in Washington to pray. Mattis sat quietly in the chapel's candle-lit War Memorial alcove, pictured. "What do you do if you've got to do it?" Mattis asked himself, contemplating the prospect of nuclear conflict with North Korea. "You're going to incinerate a couple million people."

Rex Tillerson, the former CEO of ExxonMobil, told Trump in 2016 he would accept his nomination as secretary of state, but "I want you to promise me that we are never going to have a public dispute. If you're unhappy with me, call me and ream my ass out. It's all behind closed doors." Trump fired Tillerson by tweet and later publicly called him "dumb as a rock and totally ill prepared and ill equipped to be Secretary of State."

President Trump asked Dan Coats, who had served 16 years as a Republican senator from Indiana, to be his first director of national intelligence. "Mr. President," Coats said, "there will be times when I will be walking in here to brief you on intelligence, and you're not going to be happy with what I have to say." That turned out to be the case numerous times.

Secretary of State Mike Pompeo visited North Korean leader Kim Jong Un in April 2018 while he was still CIA director. The South Koreans told us that you have intent to denuclearize, Pompeo said to Kim. Is that true? I'm a father, Kim replied. I don't want my kids to carry nuclear weapons on their backs the rest of their lives.

Republican senator Lindsey Graham of South Carolina became a First Friend to Trump and advised him in endless phone conversations and golf outings. "If you try to be the law-and-order president alone," Graham told Trump in June 2020, "you're going to lose."

Special Counsel Robert Mueller completed his 22-month investigation into Russia–Trump 2016 campaign coordination in spring 2019. A summary in his long-anticipated report was unclear and confusing, seeming to reach two contradictory conclusions: "While this report does not conclude that the president committed a crime, it also does not exonerate him."

Deputy Attorney General Rod Rosenstein oversaw the Mueller investigation with an iron hand. Rosenstein felt on the Mueller investigation he had made Trump bullet-proof for the 2020 election. The president was not guilty of obstruction of justice in Rosenstein's view. "I knew there was no basis to indict the president," Rosenstein told an associate after the investigation.

Attorney General William Barr assumed office in February 2019. "You're not going to believe this," Barr said before releasing a four-page letter summarizing his conclusions about the Mueller report. "After two f—ing years he says, 'Well, I don't know, you decide.'" Barr did in his March 24, 2019, letter about Mueller's findings.

Jared Kushner, the president's son-in-law, was often deployed personally by Trump as an out-of-channels special project officer. Kushner said, "One of his greatest strengths is that he somehow manages to have his enemies self-destruct and make stupid mistakes. He's just able to play the media like a fiddle, and the Democrats too. They run like dogs after a fire truck, chasing whatever he throws out there. And then he solves the problem and does the next—then they go on to the next thing."

Beep! went Dr. Anthony Fauci's internal radar when he saw early reports of the new coronavirus. Fauci, the nation's top infectious disease expert, thought, "China. New virus. Wet market. Wow." On briefing Trump, Fauci told an associate, "His attention span is like a minus number. His sole purpose is to get reelected."

Dr. Robert Redfield, director of the CDC, saw the first report of an unexplained pneumonia in China on New Year's Eve, December 31, 2019, and immediately went on alert. As the virus spread in 2020, he privately told others of his deepest fears. "We were now in a race," Redfield said. "I think we all understood now we were in a race. We're in a marathon. We're in a two-year, three-year race. Not a one-year, not a six-month race."

Dr. Deborah Birx, pictured second from right, was the response coordinator for the White House Coronavirus Task Force, led by Vice President Mike Pence, pictured right. When Treasury Secretary Steve Mnuchin was opposed to shutting down travel from Europe to the U.S., he said it would bankrupt everyone and destroy the economy. "What data are you relying on for that?" asked Birx. "You've been asking me for my data. What data do you have?"

"I get along very well with Erdogan, even though you're not supposed to because everyone says 'What a horrible guy,'" Trump said about Turkish president Recep Erdogan in a January 22, 2020, interview. "But for me it works out good. It's funny, the relationships I have, the tougher and meaner they are, the better I get along with them. You know? Explain that to me someday, okay? But maybe it's not a bad thing. The easy ones are the ones I maybe don't like as much or don't get along with as much."

President Trump and North Korean Leader Kim Jong Un exchanged a series of at least 27 private letters in 2018 and 2019, reviewed by the author. After meeting in Singapore, Kim wrote Trump they would have "another historic meeting between myself and Your Excellency reminiscent of a scene from a fantasy film."

"I didn't do it," Trump said of accusations his 2016 campaign had worked with Russians. "I've done a lot of bad things, but I didn't do this." Despite the criticism of his relationship with Putin, the president said he had support. "I have Russia and Sean Hannity with me," Trump said during a January 20, 2020, interview with the author.

In a February 6, 2020, phone call, Chinese president Xi Jinping rebuffed Trump's multiple offers to send public health officials into the country to investigate the new virus. Trump told the author he thought Xi may have intentionally let the virus spread: "I think what could've happened, is it got away from them and he didn't want to contain it from the rest of the world because it would've put him at a big disadvantage."

The author conducted an hour-and-14-minute interview with President Donald Trump in the Oval Office on December 5, 2019. It was the first of Woodward's 17 interviews with Trump, totaling more than nine hours, from December 2019 to July 2020. Also pictured, from left to right, are Acting Chief of Staff Mick Mulvaney, Counselor to the President Kellyanne Conway, Principal Deputy Press Secretary Hogan Gidley, Woodward, and Vice President Mike Pence. "I have built a nuclear—a weapons system that nobody's ever had in this country before," Trump said in this interview. "We have stuff that you haven't even seen or heard about. We have stuff that Putin and Xi have never heard about before. There's nobody—what we have is incredible."

and test people who had not been to the market. Soon Gao reported that they had identified cases not associated with the market. The January 8 Situational Report noted that now there were only "some epidemiologic links" to the market.

Thailand and Vietnam had been added to the list of countries conducting border screening of people from Wuhan, and the CDC was engaging with "personal protective equipment supply chain partners" to "increase awareness of supply chain status." The report noted that *The Wall Street Journal* was reporting China had discovered a new strain of coronavirus, and a Wikipedia article had been established for the outbreak.

On January 10, Chinese scientists published the genome of the virus online, giving international scientists their first glimpse of the new coronavirus.

Fauci called his team from the Vaccine Research Center together. Let's start making a vaccine, Fauci directed. Who the hell knows where this is going? So the center began work right away and launched the vaccine project Moderna later bought that was a positive prospect for a vaccine.

Fauci was intensely focused on the efficiency of transmission question. Just how infectious was the new virus? The feedback he got from China was happy talk. The official Chinese line continued to be that the virus was not a big deal. It is not that efficient. It is less deadly than SARS. We have it under control.

The CDC Situational Report for January 13 alerted readers that "Thailand reported a confirmed case of nCoV in a traveler from Wuhan City to Thailand. This is the first infection with novel coronavirus 2019 detected outside China."

That report hit Redfield hard. It told him, almost for sure, that there was human-to-human spread and the disease was being carried outside China.

Meanwhile, Redfield had another phone conversation with Gao. You can't believe what's going on over here, Gao said. It's much, much worse than you're hearing.

Holy shit, Fauci said. They haven't been telling us the truth. It is really transmitting efficiently.

The CDC began developing a diagnostic test and issuing warnings for airports and ports of entry to the U.S. about travelers from Wuhan. It held a call with over 300 attendees from state and local health departments in the U.S.

On January 15, the CDC Situational Report hedged, saying: "Some limited human-to-human spread may have occurred. . . . The possibility of limited human-to-human transmission cannot be ruled out, but the risk of sustained human-to-human transmission is low."

Pottinger, who had begun making his own calls to sources from his days as a *Wall Street Journal* reporter on SARS, told Redfield he was gathering evidence not only of human-to-human spread but also asymptomatic spread, meaning a person without symptoms could be a carrier and infect others. Was it possible that a former journalist would get to the bottom of the new virus faster than the doctors? Redfield wondered. They would have to wait and see.

On January 17, Redfield activated the entire CDC and assigned thousands of his staff to work on the new virus. Screening of travelers from Wuhan began at airports in New York, San Francisco and Los Angeles. He feared the greatest health crisis since 1918 might be upon them.

Pottinger also calculated the death rate for Hubei province, whose capital was Wuhan, could be six times normal. He based his estimate not on information from the intel community or reported death rates out of China, but from Chinese social media and phone conversations with people on the ground. He determined this could translate into thousands more deaths in Wuhan in one month.

THIRTY-ONE

◆—◆

Trump surprised me at home with a call about 1:30 p.m. on Monday, January 20, Martin Luther King Jr. Day. I literally had just walked in and did not have my tape recorder. So the account of this call is based on my handwritten notes.

A Very Stable Genius, a book by my two *Washington Post* colleagues Philip Rucker and Carol Leonnig, was being released. The book was highly critical of him. "It won't do well," Trump told me.

The book went on to became a number-one national and *New York Times* bestseller.

I asked Trump if he had read it.

"No, I just read a review," he said. He disputed a scene in the book which suggested he did not seem to know much about Pearl Harbor during a private tour of the USS *Arizona* Memorial, which rests above the sunken hull of the battleship bombed by the Japanese in 1941. Rucker and Leonnig reported that chief of staff John Kelly was stunned that Trump did not know the history of Pearl Harbor and needed it explained to him.

"I know everything about Pearl Harbor," Trump said to me. "How can they say I don't know?" He then accurately recited some of the history. "This is all made up."

I said that they were excellent reporters who had sources. "This is a good faith effort," I said.

"Well," he said, "70 percent of it's made up."

"They have sources," I repeated. I said I thought he was misguided in his blanket criticism of the media as "fake news." Yes, everyone got things wrong sometimes. But he ought to understand the common denominator was the "good faith effort" with real sources.

"Well," he joked, "I have Russia and Sean Hannity with me."

Trump cited a Rasmussen poll showing he had a 51 percent approval rating among likely voters as of January 16. He said it was wonderful.

"You don't believe polls, do you?" I asked.

"Well, no," Trump said, "I don't. I don't believe them." Polling had widely predicted a Hillary Clinton victory in 2016.

What do you think of *The New York Times* editorial page, which just endorsed Amy Klobuchar and Elizabeth Warren for the Democratic nomination for president? I asked.

"I so dream about running against Elizabeth Warren," Trump said, loudly and with apparent sincerity.

Trump said that Henry Kissinger had been in the Oval Office recently and told him how great he looked, given the impeachment. "During all of Watergate and Nixon's impeachment investigation, he was a basket case."

I had the letters that Kim Jong Un had written to Trump. I said I wanted to get the other side—the letters Trump had written to Kim.

"Those are so Top Secret," Trump said. He did not want me to have them. "You can't mock Kim. I don't want to get in a fucking nuclear war because you mocked him."

I said I would be careful and stick to what was in the letters. "I'm not going to mock him."

Later in the interview, we returned to the Trump-Kim letters. "Don't mock Kim," Trump repeated. "I don't want a fucking nuclear war," he said again. He returned to the new nuclear weapons he had. "I have such powerful weapons. They're so powerful you wouldn't believe it. You wouldn't even put them in your book."

About two minutes after our call ended, at 1:53 p.m., Trump retweeted the tweet he had originally sent on January 16 publicizing the Rasmussen poll. Adding to his earlier tweet, Trump wrote, "And they say you can add 7% to 10% to all Trump numbers! Who knows?"

Rasmussen polls have consistently shown higher results for Trump than those conducted by other firms. The national average of presidential job approval polls that day showed he had an approval rating of about 44 percent. Rasmussen was called one of the most accurate of all major pollsters in 2016, showing Clinton up two points on the day before the election. Most other polls had Clinton leading by three to six points.

Trump attended the World Economic Forum in Davos, Switzerland in late January, an exclusive gathering of world and financial leaders. The first reported coronavirus case in the U.S. had just been identified. "It's one person coming in from China. We have it under control. It's going to be just fine," Trump said, making his first public comment on the coronavirus during an interview in Davos. "We think it is going to be handled very well," he said during a separate interview. "We've already handled it very well."

Trump called me January 22, just after 9:00 p.m.

"I just got back" from Davos, he said. "I literally just landed." Trump's voice boomed over the speakerphone.

I asked about his strategy for dealing with Chinese president Xi Jinping. He had signed a trade deal with China a week earlier.

"Well, first of all, his personality is incredible," Trump said. "His strength, his mental and physical strength, is great. He's very, very smart. He's very cunning. I get along with him fantastically well." He said they'd had some "rough patches" during the trade talks. "Outside of religion, trade is the most dangerous thing there is." Interesting sociology, I thought.

Trump believed China had originally planned to wait until after the November 2020 election to agree to a trade deal. "China went out, hired the best pollsters in the country, and they said Trump's going to win in a landslide," he claimed. "They said, might as well get it over with."

He thought his relationship with Xi had been "strained very much during the deal. We heard China—you know, China's had the worst year they've had in 67 years." He indicated that businesses had shifted away from China during the trade war. "I had all the cards," he said. The United States' growth had gone up and China's had gone down. "So we're now the number-one country by far." After the trade deal, Trump said, "our country is rocking now like it hasn't rocked."

I asked Trump about his decision making in foreign policy. He told me he was working with the Turkish leader on the war in Syria.

"I get along very well with Erdogan, even though you're not supposed to because everyone says 'What a horrible guy,'" Trump said. President Recep Tayyip Erdogan is a repressive leader with a terrible record on human rights. "But for me it works out good. It's funny, the relationships I have, the tougher and meaner they are, the better I get along with them. You know? Explain that to me someday, okay?"

That might not be difficult, I thought, but I didn't say anything.

"But maybe it's not a bad thing," he continued. "The easy ones are the ones I maybe don't like as much or don't get along with as much."

Trump told me he had recently called Roberto Azevêdo, the head of the World Trade Organization, which Trump believed had been "ripping us off like crazy for 25, 30 years." In early

December, the United States had blocked the appointment of judges to an appeals panel and hobbled the WTO's ability to resolve trade disputes between nations.

On the call Trump said, "Roberto, you treat us very badly. The United States is considered this very wealthy place, and China is considered a developing nation, and India's a developing nation. If you're a developing nation, you get things that nobody else will get. We're going to be a developing nation." When Azevêdo protested, Trump said, "Here's what I'm doing: I'm pulling out of the World Trade Organization."

Azevêdo announced his early resignation from the WTO in May amid the ongoing dispute and the coronavirus pandemic.

The president brought up the European Union, which he felt had also been "ripping us off for years" and been "formed to screw the United States." Trump said he had been waiting to take on the European Union until his trade deals with China, Mexico and Canada were done. "I don't want to be fighting every country in the world at the same time."

Trump grew exercised when I tried to break up his litany of trade achievements and grievances—which we covered nearly every time we spoke—with more questions about foreign policy.

"No, no, I made all these deals but nobody wants to talk about them!" he exclaimed. He said the media preferred to focus on "the impeachment horseshit." Then he said he hoped my wife Elsa wasn't listening, "because I don't want to have her hear. Because I know her ears must be very beautiful and very—she doesn't hear bad language."

Trump said the news covered "the impeachment thing 95, 96 percent of the time. They talk about the economy less than one percent, and it's the greatest economy in the history of the country. So I have to talk about them myself, Bob."

While the economy was doing very well, it was not the greatest in the history of the country.

Trump told me about a dinner he'd hosted. Jeff Bezos, the CEO of Amazon who purchased *The Washington Post* in 2013, had attended. He said he'd pulled Bezos aside, or possibly called him the next day, and said, "Jeff, you don't have to treat me good. But just treat me fairly. When I do something great, say it's great. When I do something good, say it's good. And when I do something bad, knock the hell out of me."

Oh, I never get involved, Bezos had said, according to Trump. He played no role in *The Washington Post*'s news coverage of Trump or anything else.

"What do you mean you don't get involved?" Trump said. You're losing millions a year on the newspaper. "Of course you get involved."

The *Post* was not losing money and has apparently been a profitable business under Bezos's ownership.

Bezos had insisted he never got involved.

I had known Bezos for more than 20 years and worked at the *Post* for 49 years. I told Trump that I believed that was true. There was an iron curtain between the newsroom and ownership.

"Hard to believe," Trump said. "If I really knew it was true, I'd treat him much differently. Because I haven't been very nice to him, you know." *The Washington Post*'s strong independence from Bezos seemed to genuinely strain credulity for Trump. "It's just hard for me. Maybe it's a different personality. But it's hard for me to believe."

After a few minutes, we returned to the subject of the newspaper. "The people at the *Post* are upset about the Khashoggi killing," I said, referring to Jamal Khashoggi, a *Washington Post* contributing columnist who had been critical of the Saudi royal family and was murdered and dismembered in Istanbul in 2018. Saudi Crown Prince Mohammad bin Salman, known colloquially as MBS, was widely and credibly believed to have ordered the killing. "That is one of the most gruesome things," I said. "You yourself have said."

"Yeah, but Iran is killing 36 people a day, so—" Trump said.

I pressed him on MBS's role in the Khashoggi killing. My reporting showed that Trump had told others about the crown prince. "I saved his ass," Trump had said after the U.S. outcry over Khashoggi's murder, and "I was able to get Congress to leave him alone. I was able to get them to stop." He'd sarcastically told members of Congress, "Let them trade with Russia instead. Let them buy a thousand planes from Russia instead of the United States. Let them go to China and buy all of their military equipment instead of the United States. Fellas, you've got to be smart."

In May 2019, Trump had used his emergency authority to bypass the objections of Congress and sell the Saudis $8 billion in arms.

Now, Trump said, "Well, I understand what you're saying, and I've gotten involved very much. I know everything about the whole situation." He said Saudi Arabia spent hundreds of billions in the United States and was responsible for millions of jobs. Of MBS, Trump said, "He will always say that he didn't do it. He says that to everybody, and frankly I'm happy that he says that. But he will say that to you, he will say that to Congress, and he will say that to everybody. He's never said he did it."

"Do you believe that he did it?" I asked.

"No, he says that he didn't do it."

"I know, but do you really believe—"

"He says very strongly that he didn't do it," Trump said. "Bob, they spent $400 billion over a fairly short period of time."

Trump was referring, as he often did, to the deals struck in advance of his trip to Saudi Arabia in 2017. In a fact-check, the Associated Press wrote, "Actual orders under the arms deal are far smaller, and neither country has announced nor substantiated Trump's repeated assertion that the Saudis are poised to inject $450 billion overall into the U.S. economy."

"And you know, they're in the Middle East," Trump went on. Saudi Arabia was an important ally. "You know, they're big.

Because of their religious monuments, you know, they have the real power. They have the oil, but they also have the great monuments for religion. You know that, right? For that religion."

"Yes," I said. "All those countries are vulnerable unless we provide protection."

"They wouldn't last a week if we're not there, and they know it."

Later in the interview Trump again returned to *The Washington Post*. "If you look at all the things we've got completed now, it's incredible," Trump said, "including, by the way, making *The New York Times* and *Washington Post* and cable television successful. Because they were all going down the tubes. But they'll be gone. When I leave, they're all going down. They're going to be gone."

"I hope that's not the case," I said. Then Trump and I spoke at the same time. "Because I think it's really important that we have the First Amendment," I said. "You know that."

"Well, I hope so, but it's going to be the case," Trump said. He wondered aloud which paper was "more dishonest," *The Washington Post* or *The New York Times*. "Hard to believe that Jeff Bezos is not controlling what's happening." It was clear that if Trump had owned a newspaper, he would be actively involved.

Trump said he had just "signed my 187th federal judge," and reminded me of his two Supreme Court appointments. "When I get out, I'll probably have more than 50 percent of the federal judges in the country appointed under Trump," he bragged. "The only one that has a better percentage is George Washington, because he appointed 100 percent."

Although Trump has repeated this claim often, it is not factual. Among recent presidents, Clinton, Carter and Nixon had each filled a greater percentage of federal judgeships by late January of the fourth year of their first term. He was also not alone in appointing two Supreme Court justices in his first term—Presidents Obama, Clinton and George H. W. Bush had also done so.

I said my reporting showed that Trump had nominated some judges that Lindsey Graham, chairman of the Senate Judiciary Committee, and other Republicans had rejected.

"Yeah," Trump said. "When they don't like them, I don't put them in." He added, "In some cases they're not conservative or they don't believe or they came out with a couple of bad decisions or something."

"Graham is worried that the judiciary is going to become too partisan," I said. "Do you worry about that?"

"Well, it depends," Trump said. "Yeah, it's very partisan right now, basically. It's always a party vote. I mean, look, the whole country right now is a partisan vote."

Toward the end of the interview, Trump seized on an offhand mention I'd made of President Obama. "Ninety percent of the things he's done, I've taken apart," Trump said.

According to a tally kept by *The Washington Post*, by January 20, 2018, Trump had issued 17 executive actions and the administration had made 96 cabinet-level agency decisions that would "review, revoke and overwrite key parts of his predecessor's domestic legacy." Obama issued 276 executive orders over his eight years in office.

Our interview had lasted a little over half an hour, a freewheeling, late-night tour of the world according to Trump. The president wanted to project high spirits. He believed he had won his trade war with China and proclaimed victory for the American economy in Davos. He told me to come in for another interview soon.

"We'll see if we can actually get a fair book," he said.

The next day, January 23, in the midst of Trump's impeachment, Chinese health authorities locked down Wuhan and several nearby cities, suspending outbound flights, trains and buses and locking down more than 35 million people.

At the White House that day, halfway through the Top Secret President's Daily Brief in the Oval Office, chief briefer Beth Sanner told President Trump at that point the intelligence community had a pretty benign take on the coronavirus.

"Just like the flu," Sanner said in terms of severity. "We don't think it's as deadly as SARS." We do not believe this is going to be a global pandemic, she said.

The PDB was supposed to contain not only the most classified and sensitive intelligence but the most relevant so the president would be tipped off to a pending crisis. O'Brien and Pottinger were disappointed in the intelligence community, and the presentation only reinforced their determination to penetrate what they were sure was a Chinese cover-up.

Though there would later be news reports that the written version of the PDB contained warnings about the virus, these stories did not cite specifics. It was also well established by this time that Trump did not read the PDB but relied on oral presentations.

When Pottinger saw the news reports he scratched his head and went back and reviewed all the intelligence reports, finding nothing. "Complete fucking bullshit," he said. "What intel? There was none."

The virus now appeared to be spreading like crazy. On January 24, Chinese scientists finally published a report in *The Lancet*, perhaps the world's most respected medical journal, stating "evidence so far indicates human transmission" of the coronavirus.

Alex Azar, the secretary of Health and Human Services, called his counterpart, Ma Xiaowei, the Chinese health minister the morning of January 27. Pottinger was on the call. Nearly a month had passed since the first reports from China.

Can we send our guys in? Azar asked. Let us do it. We've got experts. We can provide support. We can help. Let's share samples.

World Health Organization rules required that samples be shared. Just you say it, they're ready to go. Their bags are packed.

Thank you very much, said Ma. It's great to hear from you. We'll look at it.

No answer followed. Azar was angry, but avoided any open disagreement and tweeted that he "conveyed our appreciation for China's efforts."

A new impeachment sensation appeared that day with a report in *The New York Times* about former national security adviser John Bolton's unpublished book manuscript, *The Room Where It Happened*. Bolton, in what the *Times* described an "explosive account," wrote that Trump told him that he wanted $391 million in security aid to Ukraine frozen until the Bidens were investigated—the subject of the impeachment.

While the media was riveted by the Bolton bombshell, the virus alarm bells were going off more intensely than ever for Pottinger, who had stepped up his efforts to gather information from his own medical and political sources in China.

The Chinese were effectively saying we don't want our people getting together with yours. We want to keep them separate. We do not want collaboration. As the case numbers escalated in Wuhan, Pottinger noted the Chinese were increasing information barriers and trying to keep U.S. reporters out of Wuhan. The few who slipped in were put in hotel rooms and told not to leave. Others were later expelled. Pottinger concluded the Chinese were more aggressive with expulsions than the Soviet Union at the height of the Cold War. All signs were pointing to an effort to hide something.

Even before the virus crisis, O'Brien and Pottinger believed China represented the greatest and most fundamental existential national security threat to the United States.

"They would love world domination," O'Brien said during a

private, closed-door West Wing briefing December 20, 2019. "Be the premier power in the world. There's no question about it."

"No doubt about it," Pottinger said. Under President Xi "the ideology is now front and center again in a way it hasn't been since Mao."

Earlier O'Brien and Pottinger had aggressively argued against allowing the Chinese firm Huawei, the largest telecommunications equipment manufacturer in the world, into U.S. markets. O'Brien was convinced that Huawei wanted to use its fifth generation (5G) wireless network eventually to monitor every citizen in the world. It was another major national security threat to the United States. O'Brien said, "Backdoor your medical records, your social media posts, your emails, your financial records. Personal, private data on every American. Micro-target you based on your deepest fears."

"Every member of Congress," Pottinger said.

With the ground reports out of Wuhan showing the new virus spreading quickly, O'Brien knew the Chinese were going to try to get out of Dodge. The mayor of Wuhan had acknowledged as much on January 26, saying five million people had left the city in the week before the Chinese government locked it down.

The Chinese were wealthier than they had been 10 or 20 years ago in prior pandemics, O'Brien knew, but their health care system was still weak and overburdened. It was inevitable they would try to flee to the West, to the United States or Europe, to avoid the virus or find better treatment and hospitals.

Already, all across China, streets and highways were empty, shops and schools closed. Public transit was shut. An increasing number of countries had closed their borders to visitors who had been to China.

The United States, however, was still open to Chinese travel.

Something awful and dangerous was happening before their eyes, Pottinger insisted to O'Brien.

So at Trump's next PDB, January 28, O'Brien issued his declaration that the virus would be "the biggest national security threat you face in your presidency," and Pottinger backed him up.*

The next day, the White House announced the creation of a Coronavirus Task Force. Press secretary Stephanie Grisham said in a written statement: "The risk of infection for all Americans remains low, and all agencies are working aggressively to monitor this continuously evolving situation and to keep the public informed."

In a Michigan speech January 30 Trump said, "We have very little problem in this country at this moment—five. And those people are all recuperating successfully. But we're working very closely with China and other countries, and we think it's going to have a very good ending for it, so that I can assure you."

On Friday, January 31, about 3:00 p.m. Fauci, Azar and Redfield were hovering outside the Oval Office waiting to go in and make a presentation to Trump and Pence. They had been discussing the next steps. "They're shutting down Wuhan," Fauci said to the others. We better take them seriously. "We'd better shut them down." They all knew the first rule of epidemiology: Time would govern how an outbreak could build with exponential growth and surprise and explode. Or be contained. That day three major airlines—American, Delta and United—had announced the suspension of flights between the U.S. and China for the next several months.

Eventually they were shown in and took chairs around the front of the Resolute Desk awaiting the president. O'Brien and Pottinger sat further away, near the couches. The door from Trump's inner private office swung open and he walked in.

How's everybody? he asked in a friendly collegial tone. How's everything?

"Mr. President," Vice President Pence said, "Secretary Azar's

* See prologue.

going to introduce something and then we're going to hand it over to see if you have any questions of Tony and Bob."

"Mr. President," Azar said, "we have a lot of activity in China. They clearly have a major outbreak. They are shutting down major parts of the country including, essentially, the whole city of Wuhan, and we think that there's a considerable danger of there being a large influx of people coming in from China."

One calculation was that 22,000 people a day came into the United States from China. At the end of the week over 100,000 people were coming from a country that had already shut themselves down because of the coronavirus.

"So it looks like we really need to shut ourselves down," Azar said. Travel from China into the United States needed to be dramatically restricted.

Trump turned to Fauci, the face of reasonable, authoritative, white-coat advice. What do you think, Tony? Trump asked.

"You just heard it, Mr. President," Fauci answered. He sat right across from the president at his desk. "It's pretty clear that we have a big infection concentrated in China, and we have thousands of Chinese coming in every day. So it really looks like we're really got to shut it down." There were six cases in the U.S.

"Do you think it's the right thing to do?" Trump asked. "What is that going to mean?"

There was some discussion that trade and commerce could probably continue. Products from China could continue to be imported.

Americans would be allowed back but only if they quarantined themselves for 14 days, which is the incubation period for the virus. "We've got to let Americans come back, because part of the tradition of our country is that you don't strand Americans outside the country," Fauci said.

They told Trump that it would be the first mandatory federal quarantine in 50 years. The last had been the smallpox scare of 1969.

How is this virus different from the flu? Trump asked. In a bad season like 2017–18 some 60,000 people died from the flu in the United States.

We don't know anything about this virus, Fauci answered. "We don't know where it's going. We don't know what its potential is. And as bad as flu is, we have so many decades of experience with seasonal flu. Even though there are a certain number of hospitalizations and deaths each year, we kind of have a pretty good idea of what the endgame is with flu. We know what a good season is. We know what a bad season is. With this, it's all uncharted waters. That's why we're reacting. Because of what we're seeing is happening in China. It's devastating the place. So whatever the hell is going on in China right now is a hell of a lot different than a regular flu season."

"Is this a brand-new virus?" Trump asked.

"You bet it's brand-new," Fauci said.

Azar and Redfield seconded this.

There were two apparent differences, Fauci said, from earlier viruses like SARS. First it apparently transmits human-to-human more easily and apparently faster. Second, people who do not have symptoms, called asymptomatic, can transmit this virus. That was not the case with SARS or most earlier viruses. But there were one or two cases of clear asymptomatic spread in China. "We don't know the extent of what this is going to be, but clearly it is happening."

Fauci knew from a report from Germany that asymptomatic spread "is absolutely the case." The German report, printed as a letter to the editor on the *New England Journal of Medicine*'s website on January 30, stated, "The fact that asymptomatic persons are potential sources of 2019-NCoV infection may warrant a reassessment of transmission dynamics of the current outbreak." The language was technical and understated, but the message about the dangers posed by asymptomatic spread was clear.

Azar, Redfield and Fauci were recommending strong travel restrictions on China.

Mick Mulvaney, a 52-year-old conservative former congressman with a gentle style who had been acting White House chief of staff for a year, said he thought they might consider some unintended consequences.

What's going to happen to the stock market? Mulvaney asked. What's going to happen with the tenuous trade relationship? The overall relationship with China? Would the Chinese retaliate? There would be things that might happen that we are not anticipating.

The consensus from the three health officials was that if there was an outbreak in the United States, the consequences of not restricting travel from China might be worse.

"Are you guys comfortable with this?" Trump asked.

They were.

Do you feel confident that this is the way to go?

Yes.

"Tony, are you sure, now?" he asked of Fauci.

"Yes, Mr. President," Fauci said. "I think this is the only way we've got to go right now."

Almost speaking in one voice the three reiterated that we have to prevent American citizens returning from China from causing infections here. So the Americans would have to be quarantined for 14 days so if they are infected they would pass the incubation period.

"Okay," Trump said. "That's fine." He looked at O'Brien and Pottinger, who were in the back in the Oval Office away from the desk. "Are you guys okay with this?"

O'Brien said he was.

"Absolutely," said Pottinger, the hawk. "This is the only way to go."

Trump gave his final approval, and Azar, Redfield and Fauci

went out to announce the Chinese travel restrictions in the White House press room.

Redfield spoke first. "This is a serious health situation in China, but I want to emphasize that the risk to the American public currently is low." He repeated himself for emphasis. "We have confirmed six cases of this novel virus in the United States. The most recent case had no travel history to China."

China was reporting 9,700 cases and more than 200 deaths.

Fauci twice said there were lots of unknowns. "We still have a low risk to the American public."

Finally, Azar spoke. "Today President Trump took decisive action to minimize the risk of the spread of novel coronavirus in the United States," he announced. "I have today declared that the coronavirus presents a public health emergency in the United States." He said that U.S. citizens returning from China would undergo 14 days of mandatory quarantine, and that Trump had signed a presidential proclamation "temporarily suspending the entry into the United States of foreign nationals who pose a risk of transmitting the 2019 novel coronavirus"—namely foreign nationals who had traveled in China within the last 14 days. Azar called the measure "prudent, targeted and temporary" and stressed once more that "the risk of infection for Americans remains low."

"Administration Elevates Response to Coronavirus, Quarantines, Travel Restrictions" ran the headline of the lead story in *The Washington Post* the next day, pushing impeachment aside. In *The New York Times* the news appeared below the fold, headlined, "Declaring Health Emergency, U.S. Restricts Travel from China."

Despite the conclusive evidence that at least five people wanted the restrictions—Fauci, Azar, Redfield, O'Brien and Pottinger—in an interview March 19, President Trump told me he deserved exclusive credit for the travel restrictions from China. "I had 21 people in my office, in the Oval Office, and of the 21 there was one person that said we have to close it down. That was me. Nobody wanted to because it was too early."

On May 6, he told me, "And let me tell you, I had a room of 20 to 21 people and everyone in that room except me did not want to have that ban."

At least seven times, including a press briefing, a televised town hall, interviews on Fox News and ABC and in meetings with industry executives and Republican lawmakers, he has repeated versions of this story.

Even when he made what appears to have been a tough and sound decision on the advice of his top national security and medical experts, he wanted—and took—all the credit for himself.

THIRTY-TWO

Trump's State of the Union address, February 4, was a rousing, self-confident one-hour, 18 minutes that will likely be remembered most for its theatrical tribute to Rush Limbaugh. The conservative and controversial radio host had revealed the day before he had been diagnosed with advanced lung cancer. Trump announced he was awarding the Presidential Medal of Freedom, the nation's highest civilian honor, to a visibly stunned Limbaugh. Just as theatrically, Speaker Nancy Pelosi ripped up a copy of Trump's speech on camera.

The next day, February 5, 2020, the Senate acquitted Trump on the two articles of impeachment, with a vote of 52 to 48 on abuse of power and 53 to 47 on obstruction of Congress. Senator Mitt Romney of Utah was the sole Republican who voted to convict the president along with all the Democrats, and did so only on the abuse of power count.

"What he did was not perfect," Romney said in an impassioned speech before the vote. "No, it was a flagrant assault on our electoral rights, our national security and our fundamental values. Corrupting an election to keep oneself in office is perhaps the most abusive and destructive violation of one's oath of office I can imagine."

Just eight years earlier, Romney had been the Republican party's presidential nominee—a split he spoke of in near-biblical terms.

"I'm sure to hear abuse from the president and his supporters," he said. "Does anyone seriously believe that I would consent to these consequences other than from an inescapable conviction that my oath before God demanded it of me?"

Even for many of the GOP senators who voted to acquit Trump on both charges, it was hardly a day of celebration.

Senator Lamar Alexander—at age 79, an old-school establishment Republican and two-time presidential candidate who was not running for reelection to the Senate—acted, for many, as the conscience of the Senate majority. While he said Trump's behavior did not meet "the Constitution's high bar for an impeachable offense," he conceded Trump had acted improperly. Questions about whether Trump deserved to remain in the presidency, he said, should be left to voters in the 2020 election, now only nine months away.

"It was inappropriate for the president to ask a foreign leader to investigate his political opponent and to withhold United States aid to encourage that investigation," Alexander said. "When elected officials inappropriately interfere with such investigations, it undermines the principle of equal justice under the law."

In total, 10 Republican senators who voted to acquit said in statements or interviews Trump's actions were wrong, improper or inappropriate. "Let me be clear, Lamar speaks for lots and lots of us," Senator Ben Sasse, Republican of Nebraska, said. "I believe that delaying the aid was inappropriate and wrong."

The president had won the votes of these Republicans, but not their approval.

Former DNI and senator Dan Coats, out of the administration for five months, watched Trump's impeachment with few illusions. He felt he understood the Senate far better than the intelligence world or the White House. He was sure every senator up there, including the Republicans, knew what had transpired. Trump obviously had pushed for an investigation of the Bidens and had delayed or stymied the aid to Ukraine. Was this sufficient to remove Trump from office? It was possible to argue either way. But to remove a president with a such a strong base in their party was pretty much unthinkable. A shrinking minority of Republicans genuinely supported Trump. The others had made a political survival decision.

With all the "formers" attached to his name, Coats did not want to be the person to speak out and say, "Hey, you guys got to stand up." So he remained silent.

After the travel restrictions were imposed, China was still not allowing American government health officials in, O'Brien and Pottinger reported to the president in an update.

Should I talk to President Xi? Trump asked. Should I make a call? Do you think Xi would call us if he was ready? Could this be embarrassing for Xi? Let's offer a call, Trump finally decided.

The Chinese never accepted a proposed call on the spot. In the meantime, Trump had calls with other heads of state. His common refrain: Can you believe this happened? Things were going incredibly well, Trump said, and this came out of the blue.

Listening on the calls, O'Brien thought, Well it actually didn't come out of the blue. It came out of China. It's derailed us.

The call with Xi was finally arranged for Thursday, February 6, at 9:00 p.m. Washington time. The Senate had acquitted Trump in his impeachment trial the day before.

Trump took the call in the White House residence. Though

he had a reputation for bravado and harshness, he began with his trademark personal greeting—pleasant and collegial, just a few sentences. He had a tendency in calls like this to be sympathetic. Pottinger was on the call and considered it "very Trumpian."

Trump got down to business quickly, for him. I just wanted to call and say that we will help 100 percent on the Covid-19, Trump said. We have tremendous health officials. And while I know you can do it, we have great experts who are willing to help.

We have the Centers for Disease Control, Trump continued. They handled the Ebola crisis in Africa. We would love to help you and wipe this out. We want to eradicate this virus and the people at CDC are ready to, but they need visas.

It was unusual for the president to discuss routine logistics like visas.

Xi thanked Trump for the offer but was noncommittal, side-stepping the request. But he didn't say no outright. Xi noted China was working with the World Health Organization to coordinate for outside experts to come in, and suggested the U.S. could participate in a WHO delegation.

Xi said he was personally overseeing China's effort and had made major progress. He gave the general impression that everything was under control.

For a second time, Trump pressed in a nonconfrontational way for Xi to allow American health officials in. Help from the U.S. would arrive if President Xi asked for it, he said.

Xi said China was being open and transparent, and said that China's actions were safeguarding not just China, but the world. Then, Xi mentioned that the WHO was calling on countries to refrain from excessive reactions. "I ask the United States and your officials not take excessive actions that would create further panic."

"Panic" was an unusually strong word. It was clear Xi was obliquely criticizing the United States for restricting travel from

China, but he did not go further other than to indicate that he would like the international flights restored.

Trump expressed hope that warmer weather might play a role in minimizing the threat of the virus, and Xi suggested it was possible. Temperature plays a big role, he said. Once it gets into the 50s Fahrenheit, the virus does not really hold up well. China did not have anything definitive on treatments that might work, he said. He compared it to the 2003 SARS outbreak.

Trump, taken aback that he'd been rebuffed twice, shifted to mention in hopeful terms the trade deal the two countries had signed two weeks earlier. Xi seemed to have no more to say, so Trump shifted again.

The state visit to China that he and Melania had made in 2017 was the most impressive foreign visit they had experienced, Trump said.

You and the first lady come again once the situation permits, Xi said.

Trump had persisted in making multiple offers to send U.S. health officials, but had gotten nowhere with Xi.

The call had lasted 30 minutes but only had about 15 minutes of substance because of delays for translation.*

That weekend, on February 9, Fauci, Redfield and other members of the Coronavirus Task Force took their seats at a table in a large conference room in Washington. Over 25 state governors, in town for a National Governors Association meeting and scheduled to attend a black-tie dinner with Trump later that night, had asked for a briefing on the coronavirus. Sitting at three long tables in a U-shaped layout, the governors wanted guidance and seemed to be looking for the inside story.

---

* The next day, February 7, 2020, I talked with Trump. He knew a surprising amount about the virus and said in the presidency "there's dynamite behind every door." See prologue.

The coronavirus outbreak is going to get much, much worse before it gets better, Redfield warned.

We have not even seen the beginning of the worst, Redfield said, letting his words sink in. There is no reason to believe that what's happening in China is not going to happen here, he said. There were nearly 40,000 cases in China then, with more than 800 deaths, barely five weeks after announcing the first cases.

I agree completely, Fauci told the governors. This is very serious business. You need to be prepared for problems in your cities and your states. Fauci could see the alarm on the governors' faces.

"I think we scared the shit out of them," Fauci said after the meeting.

The official press release from the Department of Health and Human Services describing the meeting read: "The panel reiterated that while this is a serious public health matter, the risk to the American public remains low at this time, and that the federal government will continue working in close coordination with state and local governments to keep it that way."

The next day, President Trump said publicly three times—once at the White House, once on TV and once at a New Hampshire rally—that the virus would go away on its own. "When it gets a little warmer, it miraculously goes away," he said at the packed rally. "I think it's going to work out good. We only have 11 cases and they're all getting better."

Fauci attended a public conference in Aspen, Colorado, on February 11. The moderator, Helen Branswell of *STAT News*, a well-respected science news outlet, said, "You've been quite vocal about wanting more information out of China. What would you like to get your hands on?"

"We really need to know the scope of this," Fauci said. "The degree of asymptomatic transmission" would be the crucial piece of information. "That has a real impact on how you make certain policy decisions." If people who didn't show symptoms were giving others the disease, it would be much harder to contain.

Fauci repeated several times that the virus was low-risk. Clearly skeptical, Branswell said, "Explain to me why the risk is low. Because to me, when I look at this virus, it's spreading very efficiently."

"It's the message," Fauci said frankly. Americans didn't need to be frightened. "Right now we have 13 people." But again he hedged: "Is there a risk that this is going to turn into a global pandemic? Absolutely, yes."

Branswell asked about the danger of possibly downplaying the risk the virus posed to the U.S.

Fauci said, "The risk is really relatively low." He posed a hypothetical: How would it be, he asked, if he got up and said, " 'I'm telling you we've really, really got a big risk of getting completely wiped out,' and then nothing happens?" Then, he said, "your credibility is gone."

Fauci knew he was walking the finest of lines. The U.S. would never shut down with so few cases. If he proposed extreme remedies too soon, not only would he lose his credibility, but no one would listen or take action.

He didn't say it, but he thought, "Take a look at what's happening in China." The outbreak was severe.

During this period, from February 11 to 14, Trump repeatedly said the U.S. had only about 12 cases.

At an event a week later at the Council on Foreign Relations, Fauci was again the voice of reassurance. "To our knowledge, there aren't individuals in society in the United States that are infected" who aren't travel-related, he said. "We don't think so." But he added, "We don't know 100 percent, because they could have kind of come in under the radar screen."

Asked by another panel member to reiterate that the public

should not be buying respirator masks needed by health care workers, Fauci laughed. "I don't want to denigrate people who walk around wearing masks" but masks, he said, should be worn by sick people. "Put a mask on them, not yourself." He later added, to laughter from the audience, "I don't want to be pejorative against cruise ships, but if there's one thing you don't want to do right now, it's to take a cruise in Asia."

In a meeting at the White House on February 18, Pottinger cast the virus in geopolitical terms. North Korea had shut its border to China, cutting off its most crucial trading partner to keep out infection.

"The coronavirus is probably doing more to advance our maximum pressure campaign than anything at the moment," Pottinger said.

I reached President Trump by phone at 1:45 p.m. on Wednesday, February 19, 2020. He was on Air Force One, flying to Arizona for a rally. The coronavirus was not yet a focus.

What I wanted from the president, I said, "is what was going through your mind as you said what you said or made whatever decision it was on a range of issues in foreign policy, China, North Korea, Russia—"

"Soleimani was a very big event," Trump said, referring to his decision to have the head of the Iranian Quds Force killed in a drone strike on January 3. "The head of Pakistan, the prime minister of Pakistan, Khan, said *the* biggest event of his lifetime. I had no idea. Other people have said the same thing: it was an earth-shattering event." Trump and Pakistani prime minister Imran Khan had met privately in Davos on January 21, but I was not able to confirm if Kahn had said what Trump claimed.

Six days earlier, Attorney General Bill Barr had blasted Trump in a remarkable television interview, saying that Trump's tweets were making it "impossible for me to do my job."

Barr made the comments after Trump posted a tweet around 2:00 a.m. on February 11 protesting the Justice Department's sentencing recommendation of up to nine years for his political associate Roger Stone. The afternoon of February 11, the Justice Department filed a revised sentencing recommendation suggesting a sentence for Stone of three to four years. All four prosecutors withdrew from the case, one resigning from the Justice Department entirely.

"So what's this with Attorney General Barr going on now?" I asked Trump.

Anyone who has watched Trump's press conferences knows how he avoids issues, splits hairs and won't deal with hard questions. This is only amplified in a one-on-one setting—that maddening, convoluted dodging that drove Mattis, Tillerson, Coats and others crazy.

"It's a false statement," Trump answered. "Well, he made the statement about Twitter. I don't call it Twitter, I call it social media," as if that would make a difference. Barr had been explicit, and his public challenge to Trump was big news. Trump had continued to tweet complaints about the Justice Department, but hadn't targeted or responded to Barr directly.

Trump's mention of social media set him off. "Without social media, number one, I wouldn't have won, and number two, you know, I'm number one on Facebook. Zuckerberg," the CEO of Facebook, "came to the White House two weeks ago."

In early 2020, with 80 million followers, Trump had the ninth-most followed Twitter account, behind former president Barack Obama and several celebrities. In terms of likes and followers, his Facebook page ranks below dozens of others.

"So what's going on between you and the attorney general, sir?" I tried to persist.

Trump was still on Mark Zuckerberg. "Said, congratulations, you're number one on Facebook."

"This is all for the history," I said, trying to get some explanation about Barr.

"And I'm number one on Twitter," Trump said. "When you're number one and when you have hundreds of millions of people, whether they're against you or not they still read what you say. I don't need commercials. When you're number one, you don't need commercials. And number two is Modi, but he's got 1.5 billion people. I have 350. You know? So it's a little different." Trump and Prime Minister Narendra Modi, who has over 50 million followers, are the two highest-ranking current world leaders on Twitter.

"So tell me about the—this is all for the serious history, Mr. President."

"Social media," Trump said. He was on his track and would stay there. "I wouldn't probably be talking to you right now if it weren't for social media. At least not in this capacity. In Air Force One, beautifully riding to the great state of Arizona. You know? I wouldn't be talking to you probably. So it's very important."

"Sir, what did Barr say to you? This, again, is for serious history. You know, it's got a lot of people all in a twitter about it, to use that term."

"Good, that's what I like. I like that everybody's in a twitter. That's okay with me. Keep them that way."

"Well, it's working," I said.

He shifted the conversation to polling. "I put out a statement on that today, I don't know if you saw."

Earlier that day he had tweeted "Internal REAL Polls show I am beating all of the Dem candidates. The Fake News Polls (here we go again, just like 2016) show losing or tied. Their polls will be proven corrupt on November 3rd, just like the Fake News is corrupt!"

"The internal polls, we're beating everybody," he said. "But the fake news is at it again. They like to put in polls where I'm not" winning.

"Okay, now sir," I said, "anyone who knows the Constitution realizes you as president have authority over every department, including the Justice Department."

"Yep. That's right. Total. And I haven't exercised that authority. I've let people run it."

I noted that lots of people thought he shouldn't intervene, repeating the assertion I had made to him at Mar-a-Lago.

"This was the greatest crime, political crime in the history of our country," Trump said, referring to the investigation into his 2016 campaign, completed almost a year earlier. "They spied on this campaign. The opposite party, in control of the nation, spied on their opponent and their opponent's political campaign. They caused tremendous injustice. They caused tremendous damage. And they destroyed many lives."

"I'm looking at that really closely," I said.

"They got caught," the president said. "People that vote for me" know this, he said. "This was a treasonous act. This was a terrible act. These people would've been in jail. For 50 years they would've gone to jail. They would've spent 50 years in jail, meaning they would've died in jail. One of the most important things I did was firing the sleazebag named Comey."

He would not let go of these issues, and returned to them at every opportunity. But he seemed to provide just a recitation, without apparent emotion.

When I was able to take a turn to speak again, I laughed and said, "I've heard your views on that six times, sir." I suggested he ask his friend and adviser Lindsey Graham whether he thought it was a good idea for Trump to get in a public fight with the attorney general about his authority. "Is that a good thing for you to do?"

"I do want everyone to know that I do have the authority," Trump said, "but I've decided not to use it." He blamed the media. "They cut it up and they slice it up. You don't see the real deal.

"There has been no president even close that has done what I've done in three years," Trump said. "You know it and so does everybody else." He added in a challenging tone, "Let's see whether or not you're willing to write it."

In late February, China finally allowed World Health Organization scientists to enter the country to investigate. Redfield had wanted to send his team of investigators but only one CDC official was allowed in the group. Fauci's deputy director, Dr. Clifford Lane, was the only other American allowed to join the delegation to China from February 16 to February 24. The report released by the group indicated that asymptomatic infection was "relatively rare and does not appear to be a major driver of transmission" and praised China for "perhaps the most ambitious, agile and aggressive disease containment effort in history."

Lane, who had never before been to China and had no experience with Chinese handlers, reported personally to Fauci that there was a lot of disease there and it was spreading rapidly. But he said the Chinese seemed to be doing everything they could to contain the virus. Everything was locked down. No one was allowed out of their apartment except for food. Sick and healthy people alike were locked in their homes. If they decided to go out for something other than food, their neighbors would report them to the police, who would then come and question them. It was absolute, with almost no concern for human rights.

Lane also said he'd been impressed with the high-tech capabilities of the hospitals in Beijing. But neither American on the delegation had been allowed into Wuhan, the epicenter of the disease.

The WHO report contained a stark warning: "Much of the

global community is not yet ready, in mindset and materially, to implement the measures that have been employed to contain Covid-19 in China. These are the only measures that are currently proven to interrupt or minimize" the spread of the coronavirus. Those measures included surveillance, public engagement, cancellation of mass gatherings, traffic controls, rapid diagnosis, immediate case isolation, and "rigorous tracking and quarantine of close contacts."

As February drew to a close, the virus spread through Europe, most prominently in Italy, Asia and the Middle East. Global markets dipped.

The upbeat messages from the administration continued. "We have it very much under control," Trump told reporters on February 23. "Very interestingly, we've had no deaths." The next day he tweeted, "The Coronavirus is very much under control in the USA," and added, "Stock Market starting to look very good to me!"

But on February 25, as Trump boarded Air Force One to return from a state visit to India, the director of the National Center for Immunization and Respiratory Diseases at the CDC, Dr. Nancy Messonnier, issued a stark public warning. Schools might have to close, conferences might be curtailed, and businesses may have to have employees work from home. "The disruption to everyday life may be severe," she told reporters. "It's not so much a question of if this will happen anymore, but rather more a question of when this will happen, and how many people in this country will have severe illness."

Some conservatives, including Rush Limbaugh, immediately jumped on Messonnier as part of a deep state conspiracy to use the virus to undermine Trump. They pointed out that Messonnier was the sister of Rod Rosenstein, the former deputy attorney general, who had overseen the Mueller investigation and resigned in spring 2019.

Redfield knew Messonnier well and had a lot of respect for her. Their careers had been intertwined at federal public health agencies since the 1990s. Sometimes, he thought, you just have to say it the way you see it. She had given her honest assessment and tried to get people to prepare for what could happen.

The headlines echoed her warnings: "Viral Crisis in U.S. Is Deemed Likely," *The New York Times* said. "Threat to Americans called 'inevitable,'" *The Washington Post* reported. The S&P 500 fell more than 3 percent for the second day in a row. Trump, on his way back to the U.S. from India, called Azar and threatened to fire Messonnier.

On February 26, Trump announced at a news conference that Vice President Pence would replace Azar as the head of the Coronavirus Task Force. "When you have 15 people—and the 15 within a couple of days is going to be down to close to zero— that's a pretty good job we've done," the president said. "This is a flu. This is like a flu."

Asked whether schools should prepare for the coronavirus spreading, Trump said, "I think every aspect of our society should be prepared," but added, "I don't think it's going to come to that, especially with the fact that we're going down, not up. We're going very substantially down, not up."

Redfield continued urgently monitoring the summary of all the data coming into the CDC. His job was to keep America safe 24/7 from disease.

She was called Case #15. On February 15, an otherwise healthy woman in her 40s was hospitalized in Vacaville, California, with a severe respiratory illness. Intubated and on a ventilator, her condition worsened and she was transferred to University of California Davis Medical Center in Sacramento on February 19. The UC Davis staff requested a Covid test, but since she didn't fit the CDC criteria—virus symptoms and recent travel to China, or known contact with someone who had the virus—the test was not immediately administered. The CDC finally approved a Covid test days later when she continued to deteriorate.

Ten CDC staffers sent to California started tracing her contacts. None with a connection to China or other places with the virus could be found.

For Redfield she was a tipping point. Community spread, a public health term for an infection where the source is unknown, would open a new front in the battle against Covid in the U.S.

Then Case #16 came in, also from California, with no traceable source of infection. Redfield called it "non-linked transmission."

"There's evidence, now, that this virus has established community transmission in the country," he told others. "We are going to be in a fight."

The evidence of community spread gave Fauci his own sinking feeling. All of a sudden it was a case here and a case there. "Holy shit!" he said to himself. "Here we go."

Then, a few days later, Redfield saw an increase in influenza-like illness in New York. But the CDC's flu surveillance showed cases way, way down. It was not flu. He called Howard Zucker, the New York State health commissioner.

"Howard," Redfield said, "we've got a big problem in New York."

A couple of additional Covid cases in New York were diagnosed in people who had not come into the United States from China. They came from Italy. The light bulb went off and remained glowing.

Redfield didn't know where the virus was coming from, and didn't feel he had his hands around it.

In testimony before the House on the 27th, Azar said, "The immediate risk to the public remains low." He added, "It will look and feel to the American people more like a severe flu season."

The coronavirus finally began to enter the consciousness of Trump's reelection campaign. On the morning of February 28, Jared Kushner spoke by phone with Brad Parscale, Trump's campaign manager.

"We need more visuals," Parscale told Kushner. Trump should be "standing in front of amazing things. Put the white coat on. Look at the vaccine being made. Show America we're doing stuff."

That day the stock market fell for the seventh day in a row, reaching its worst week since 2008.

Later that day at a rally in South Carolina, Trump said, "The Democrats are politicizing the coronavirus, you know that, right? Coronavirus, they're politicizing it." He called Democrats' criticism of his handling of the virus "their new hoax," after the Russian investigation and impeachment, and their "single talking point."

Fauci, who was fast becoming the most recognizable face of U.S. government's coronavirus response, appeared on the *Today* show on February 29.

NBC reporter Peter Alexander asked the question on many people's minds: "So, Dr. Fauci, it's Saturday morning in America. People are waking up right now with real concerns about this. They want to go to malls and movies, maybe the gym as well. Should we be changing our habits and, if so, how?"

"No," Fauci said. "Right now, at this moment, there's no need to change anything that you're doing on a day-by-day basis. Right now the risk is still low, but this could change."

He was later glad he had added "but this could change." Yet as a practical matter, America's Doctor had given the green light to proceed with the weekend routine.

That same day, health officials announced the first U.S. death from Covid-19 had occurred overnight in Washington State. At the Coronavirus Task Force briefing at the White House that afternoon, Redfield said of the deceased, "The investigation at this time shows no evidence of link to travel or a known contact."

Asked by a reporter whether Americans should change their routines or daily lives, Trump said, "Well, I hope they don't change their routine. But maybe, Anthony," he said to Fauci, "I'll let you—I'll let you answer that. Or Bob?" he asked Redfield. "Do you want to answer that? Please."

"The American public needs to go on with their normal lives," Redfield said. "The risk is low. We need to go on with our normal lives."

THIRTY-THREE

—————◆—————

While in college more than 55 years ago, I knew an English professor who understood how elusive biography can be. The biographer, he argued, must find the true "reflectors" of a subject, the people who know the person as well as anyone. The ideal reflector enjoys a unique closeness personally and professionally with the subject, has vast experience with them, and can make a character assessment.

When I first heard about Jared Kushner, he seemed to worship his father-in-law, acting as an ever-loyal cheerleader and true believer. He once told associates, "When I disagree with the president, I always say, okay, what am I missing? Because he's proven time and time again to have good instincts."

He expressed awe at Trump's dominance of the media. "If the president didn't tweet it, it didn't happen. You send out a press release and it goes into the ether and nobody cares. He puts out a tweet and it's on CNN one and a half minutes later."

Initially I thought all of this meant Kushner would not be able to come close to sharing an honest character assessment of Trump.

Then on February 8, 2020, Kushner advised others on the four texts that he said someone in a quest to understand Trump needed to absorb.

First, Kushner advised, go back and read a 2018 opinion column by *The Wall Street Journal*'s Pulitzer Prize–winning columnist Peggy Noonan. Her column on Trump said: "He's crazy . . . and it's kind of working."

Kushner made it clear that his endorsement of the column was not an aside or stray comment, but was central to understanding Trump.

The son-in-law had to know that Noonan's column, dated March 8, 2018, and titled "Over Trump, We're As Divided As Ever," was not positive. Rather it was quite devastating. In it she called Trump a "circus act" and "a living insult."

"What you feel is disquiet," she wrote, "and you know what it's about: the worrying nature of Mr. Trump himself . . . epic instability, mismanagement and confusion."

A conservative speechwriter for President Ronald Reagan, Noonan wrote that with Trump, "We are not talking about being colorfully, craftily unpredictable, as political masters like FDR and Reagan sometimes were, but something more unfortunate, an unhinged or not-fully-hinged quality that feels like screwball tragedy."

Warming to her theme, Noonan wrote, "Crazy doesn't last. Crazy doesn't go the distance. Crazy is an unstable element that, when let loose in an unstable environment, explodes. And so your disquiet. Sooner or later something bad will happen. . . . It all feels so dangerous.

"Expecting more from the president of the United States springs from respect for the country, its institutions and the White House itself. It springs from standards, the falling of which concerns natural conservatives. It isn't snobbery. The people trying to wrap their heads around this presidency are patriots too. That's one of the hellish things about this era."

Kushner's second recommendation for understanding Trump was, surprisingly, the Cheshire Cat in *Alice in Wonderland*. He paraphrased the cat: "If you don't know where you're going, any path will get you there." The Cheshire Cat's strategy was one of endurance and persistence, not direction.

Kushner was explicitly saying *Alice in Wonderland* was a guiding text for the Trump presidency. Did Kushner understand how negative this was? Was it possible the best roadmap for the administration was a novel about a young girl who falls through a rabbit hole, and Kushner was willing to acknowledge that Trump's presidency was on shaky, directionless ground?

The third text Kushner recommended for understanding the Trump presidency was Chris Whipple's book *The Gatekeepers: How the White House Chiefs of Staff Define Every Presidency*. In the book, Whipple concluded that, after the president, the chiefs of staff held the fate of the country in their hands.

In a chapter on the Trump presidency added in March 2018, Whipple wrote that Trump "clearly had no idea how to govern" in his first year in office, yet was reluctant to follow the advice of his first two chiefs of staff, Reince Priebus and John Kelly. "What seems clear, as of this writing and almost a year into his presidency, is that Trump will be Trump, no matter his chief of staff," Whipple concluded.

A fourth text Kushner advised was necessary to understand Trump was Scott Adams's book *Win Bigly: Persuasion in a World Where Facts Don't Matter*. Adams, the creator of the *Dilbert* comic strip, explains in *Win Bigly* that Trump's misstatements of fact are not regrettable errors or ethical lapses, but part of a technique called "intentional wrongness persuasion." Adams argues Trump "can invent any reality" for most voters on most issues, and "all you will remember is that he provided his reasons, he didn't apologize, and his opponents called him a liar like they always do."

Kushner said that Scott Adams's approach could be applied to

Trump's recent February 4 State of the Union speech when he had claimed, "Our economy is the best it has ever been." The economy was indeed in excellent shape then, but not the best in history, Kushner acknowledged.

"Controversy elevates message," Kushner said. This was his core understanding of communication strategy in the age of the internet and Trump. A controversy over the economy, Kushner argued—and how good it is—only helps Trump because it reminds voters that the economy is good. A hair-splitting, fact-checking debate in the media about whether the numbers were technically better decades ago or in the 1950s is irrelevant, he said.

When combined, Kushner's four texts painted President Trump as crazy, aimless, stubborn and manipulative. I could hardly believe anyone would recommend these as ways to understand their father-in-law, much less the president they believed in and served.

Kushner had no official title during Trump's 2016 presidential campaign but had made many operational decisions—especially on costs, which he knew Trump constantly monitored. Now Kushner played a major role in the 2020 reelection campaign, one he called "a perfect, well-oiled machine" in contrast to the "experimental" 2016 run.

For 2020, Kushner said in February to others, "I set up three polling operations." They are independent of each other, he added. "The polling just shows time and time again, the president's doing great. We have the ability for a big blowout in 2020."

The House impeachment vote by Democrats, which Kushner called "so unfair," had been a bonanza for Trump's job approval ratings.

"We picked up eight points. We pounded the shit out of them," Kushner said of the Democrats. Eight points could be debated, but it did seem clear that the impeachment had given Trump a boost. A Gallup poll released on February 4 showed Trump's job approval rating had reached 49 percent, the highest of his presidency.

The real story of Trump's presidency, in Kushner's stated view, was the perception of Trump versus the reality. "You should see him in meetings. He interrogates people, keeps them off balance, but he will bend.

"The media is hysterical about Trump—so hysterical they can't be a check on him," Kushner argued. "Reporters are afraid to break the line on Trump's dysfunction. And if they do, they will be ostracized."

Earlier in February, the president had told me "there's dynamite behind every door." Trump, of course, had his worries, but Kushner dismissed to others the idea that trouble loomed. He would not even acknowledge this possibility. He had boundless confidence and was upbeat.

Trouble always loomed in the presidency. Wasn't surprise everywhere? The unexpected lurked around any corner, any day, every day. Wasn't it right and wise for any president to think defensively that there was dynamite behind every door?

For example, President George W. Bush's Top Secret President's Daily Brief on August 6, 2001, had included the memorable headline: "Bin Laden Determined to Strike in US." Not much or enough had been done. Thirty-six days later, Osama bin Laden's terrorist group had struck in New York City and Washington, killing 3,000 people and changing the course of history.

But Kushner was an optimist. Trump, he said, "has walked through many doors with dynamite" and survived. "He has mastered the presidency like never before."

He summarized, "The president has pushed the boundaries, yes. He's not done the normal thing. But it was the right thing for people. Everything is on track for the big blowout."

THIRTY-FOUR

◆

Kushner was by turns frustrated and bemused by other people's confusion about Trump. "He's unpredictable, which is a great strength. Nobody knows where that line is" that Trump won't cross. According to Kushner, Trump himself does not know. "This is the difference between a businessperson and politician, in the sense that every day the facts change. And so the line changes too."

This was often underscored by a cynical cost-benefit analysis. For instance, in December 2016, prior to taking office, Trump had questioned whether his administration would continue the "One China" policy that the U.S. has held since the Carter administration. Under the policy, the United States does not recognize the island of Taiwan as an independent nation and instead acknowledges only "One China" that includes Taiwan. Trump's decision to cast doubt on the policy angered China, and in a February 9, 2017, phone call with Chinese president Xi Jinping, Trump said he would honor it. Two months later, he welcomed Xi to Mar-a-Lago for a summit.

Kushner cast the "One China" decision as one of cynical pragmatism. "President Trump would say that he was going to respect the One China policy," Kushner said. "That wasn't that big of a give, because you could always say you wouldn't respect it a day later."

Kushner had additional explanations for Trump's fluctuations. "The hardest thing that people have in understanding him is they see him as fixed, where he's actually, he's not a solid, he's fluid in the sense that—and that's a strength." Trump's background in business had taught him "there's no deal until you sign on the line. Right? You can make a deal and then you go through it. But until the paper is signed, it's not a deal. And that's how he is. And so he'll always be flexible."

Of course flexibility can be a strength, in business and politics. But Trump's staff and cabinet rarely got a clear definition of direction or policy from the president until he decided or tweeted. Believing that "every day the facts change" is simply another version of Kellyanne Conway's 2017 statement that there are "alternative facts."

"He's not afraid to step into a controversial situation," Kushner said. "I think he's shown over time he's built up his courage to do it. Because he's stepped into a lot of situations where people said if you do this the world's going to end, and then the next morning the sun rises, the next evening the sun sets."

By early 2020, Kushner thought Trump had assembled a better and more dedicated White House team than they'd had before.

"In the beginning," Kushner told others, referring to the first years of the administration, "20 percent of the people we had thought Trump was saving the world, and 80 percent thought they were saving the world from Trump.

"Now, I think we have the inverse. I think 80 of the people

working for him think that he's saving the world, and 20 per-cent—maybe less now—think they're saving the world from Trump."

Let that analysis sink in: Twenty percent of the president's staff think they are "saving the world" from the president.

Kushner suggested that Trump had developed a new appreciation for some of the people who had been with him since the beginning of his administration. As the economic tasks of 2020 grew and Treasury Secretary Steve Mnuchin played a larger and larger role, Kushner told the president, "This is when you'll really appreciate having the neurotic New York Jews around."

Kushner said one of Trump's greatest strengths was "he somehow manages to have his enemies self-destruct and make stupid mistakes. He's just able to play the media like a fiddle, and the Democrats too. They run like dogs after a fire truck, chasing whatever he throws out there. And then he solves the problem and does the next—then they go on to the next thing."

The question was, he said, "What is the media obsessed with at a different moment? Because they've been melting down about something every day for as long as I've been in this politics business, for a couple of years. And then what's really happening? It's like a buffet where they'll always eat the worst thing you give them."

In meetings, Kushner said, Trump was "an expert at cross-examination. He's an expert at reading people's tells. He won't say, let me go with a nuanced position. He'll, in a meeting, say, well, what if we do 100? They'll say, oh, you can't do that. And then, he'll say, well, what if we do zero? It's like, holy shit. It's whiplash. So that's his way of reading people, is to see how certain are they of their position: Do they hold their ground? Do they buckle? So that's just his style.

"And by the way," Kushner added, "that's why the most dangerous people around the president are overconfident idiots." It was apparently a reference to Mattis, Tillerson and former White House economic adviser Gary Cohn. All had left. "If you look at the evolution over time, we've gotten rid of a lot of the overconfident idiots. And now he's got a lot more thoughtful people who kind of know their place and know what to do."

According to Kushner, one of Trump's greatest impacts was on the Republican Party. "Neither party is really a party. They're collections of tribes," he observed at one White House meeting. "The Republican Party was a collection of a bunch of tribes. Look at the Republican Party platform. It's a document meant to piss people off, basically, because it's done by activists." Kushner's theory was there was a "disproportionality between what issues people are vocal on and what the people, the voters, really care about."

Trump had united the Republican Party behind himself. "I don't think it's even about the issues," Kushner said. "I think it's about the attitude." He said Trump "did a full hostile takeover of the Republican Party."

Construction of the wall along the Mexico-U.S. border, paid for by the government of Mexico, was a central tenet of Trump's 2016 campaign and first on Kushner's list of things Trump needed to accomplish to win reelection in 2020. Mexico refused to pay, and five days after his inauguration, Trump had signed an executive order directing the Department of Homeland Security to identify and allocate all possible sources of federal funding. A DHS report said the wall would cost over $20 billion.

In the fall of 2019, Trump made Kushner the boss of the border wall. Kushner's approach was straight out of business school, with meticulous files and charts and review meetings every two weeks.

At one meeting on February 14, 2020, Kushner gathered 15 people and walked through a series of questions: Do we have the contracts for each section of the wall? Were they on time? What decisions needed to be made? Where were the bottlenecks? How to get costs down? Where was the money coming from—which Pentagon account? What's the feedback from the people on the ground?

By Kushner's calculations, they had built 121.4 miles of wall. But Customs and Border Protection (CBP) said 99 miles of that was "new border wall system constructed in place of dilapidated and/or outdated designs"—in other words, replacement or repair. Ten miles were "secondary border wall." One mile was of new wall "in locations where no wall previously existed." Kushner's goal was to build, replace or repair seven to eight miles a week and reach 400 miles by the end of the year. It wouldn't be complete yet, so they would be building the wall into 2021—presuming Trump was reelected. The hardest part was buying land.

"It's more complicated than I thought," Kushner told others.

Obtaining the funding had proved difficult. Trump worked every lever of the federal government. He got into a standoff with Congress, leading to a 35-day government shutdown in December 2018 and January 2019—the country's longest. He declared a national emergency in February 2019 to force a release of funds from the Department of Defense, fighting legal battles at every stage and ultimately winning a 5 to 4 Supreme Court case in July 2019.

They had muscled the system and busted through it, Kushner said. "The system's designed to do nothing."

Liberated from constraints, they moved money from Pentagon budgets for construction and antidrug programs to pay for the wall. "We looked under every seat cushion and found all the money we needed," Kushner said.

The wall was also not being built exactly where Trump had

wanted. Instead, it was being built in what the CBP had identified for Trump and Kushner as high-traffic areas. "It is a smart wall," Kushner said. CBP had drones, sensors and cameras, so they covered more ground with fewer people. Illegal border crossings were down. Drug seizures were up. Kushner hoped the return on investment might mean the wall would pay for itself.

Every two weeks, Kushner gave Trump an update on wall construction. The president was not interested in incremental progress.

"Get the fucking thing done," Trump said.

Kushner considered one of Trump's greatest skills "figuring out how to trigger the other side by picking fights with them where he makes them take stupid positions."

He recalled Trump's July 27, 2019, tweets about the district represented by the late Black Democratic congressman Elijah Cummings, which included Baltimore. "Cumming District is a disgusting, rat and rodent infested mess," Trump had tweeted. "No human being would want to live there."

Kushner saw this as baiting the Democrats. "When he did the tweet on Elijah Cummings, the president was saying, this is great, let them defend Baltimore," Kushner told an associate. "The Democrats are getting so crazy, they're basically defending Baltimore. When you get to the next election, he's tied them to all these stupid positions because they'd rather attack him than actually be rational."

Cummings's former district is in the top half of congressional districts in median household income, home prices and education levels. It has the second-highest income of any majority-Black congressional district in the country.

Chris Wallace had Mick Mulvaney, then the acting White House chief of staff, on his Sunday show the next day. "This seems, Mick," Wallace said, "to be the worst kind of racial stereotype—"

Mulvaney tried to interrupt.

"Let me finish," Wallace said, "Racial stereotyping. Black congressman, majority-Black district—I mean, 'No human being would want to live there'? Is he saying people that live in Baltimore are not human beings?"

"I think you're spending way too much time reading between the lines," Mulvaney said.

"I'm not reading between the lines," Wallace replied. "I'm reading the lines."

THIRTY-FIVE

O n the morning of Friday, February 28, eight months before
election day 2020, Trump's longtime campaign manager
Brad Parscale was feeling confident. At times, he was exuberant.
With a bushy, honey-red beard, a full 6-foot-8, he sat comfort-
ably in his 14th-floor office at Trump campaign headquarters in
Virginia. The backdrop was a sweeping, panoramic view of the
Potomac River.

"I'm a master brander," Parscale told several staff members and
visitors that day. He said Trump set the themes of campaigning
and governing, and Parscale's operation converted those themes,
along with Trump's tweets, into a massive, unmatched media blitz
of messaging and fundraising.

Put another way, Parscale said, "The president is the radio and
the music. We're the amplifier." Once in a while, Parscale said, his
job for Trump would make him what he called "the songwriter."
He would say, "Hey, here are a few things you should look at."

The campaign was rolling on at a feverish pace. Using artificial
intelligence, Pascale's operation would test up to 100,000 message

variables in a single day. For example, they tested whether a red or green press-to-donate button raised more money in fundraising. In ten seconds, the AI models could tell them how a particular ad performed compared to the last four million that had been run before it.

They had almost twenty $1 million fundraising days in a row lately. Trump's State of the Union address, held on February 4, had been the biggest day of the year so far, with $5.3 million raised.

Parscale, now 44, was one of the 2016 campaign's first hires and had stayed, working on media, as Trump hired and fired campaign managers.

"A blessing in disguise was his daughter's marriage to Jared," Parscale said. "I think Jared Kushner was the operator that he needed—the yin to his yang. A detail guy. Jared's meticulous."

Trump needed two important personality types, in Parscale's estimation. "Somebody to be meticulous with the details to make sure the organization's right." That was Kushner. "Number two, someone to understand his brand and marketing and sell his vision. That's me." There was a clear division of labor.

"I run everything political outside the White House. Ronna McDaniel, the RNC chairwoman, runs everything for the party and then Jared runs everything inside the White House."

Parscale knew the connection between Trump's tweets and the ads. "Think of Trump's head more like a starting point of every root narrative we have. In 2016 I made 5.9 million ads on Facebook. It was only about 35 root narratives. That's what the media's never gotten wrapped around their head."

Parscale was so proud of the campaign he was managing that he said, "They'll make movies about us someday."

He said Trump's impeachment in the House of Representatives and Senate acquittal led to a million new donors. The reward was "money and data." The average donation to the Trump campaign in the fourth quarter of 2019 was $40.87. Kushner calls this a "data-palooza," a term Parscale embraces.

Three years earlier Parscale had urged Trump to get organized. "Sir, get out there and get out there early. Being president is an advantage, but it's how soon you do it that's the advantage." Trump filed FEC documents on inauguration day and quickly followed up with a February 2017 rally in Florida.

"I do a lot of things that people in politics think are counterintuitive but they've worked really well. Become campaign manager 1,400 days before it starts. I'm the longest campaign manager in history."

The ability to contact voters, even low-propensity voters, had increased over the years. Previously the campaigns had to send someone to knock on a door or send mail, which was expensive. Parscale said now he could contact someone on their phone a hundred times for about 11 cents.

Which Democrats caused Trump the most trouble? "The more mainstream. The more they appeal to moderates. Look, this election is about moderates. That's who determines elections."

At this point he said he thought there would be three main issues in the campaign—the economy, immigration and health care.

Parscale conducted focus groups in 12 different cities in eight states all over the country with over 1,000 people about the presidential race.

One question was: Would you vote for someone you like but don't agree with his policies, or would you vote for someone you don't like but you like his policies?

"One hundred percent said, I'll vote for the guy I don't like, but like his policies. One thousand to zero."

Whether true or not, it seemed to be his strong view. Here was the paradox, according to Parscale. Trump believed "presence is so important. He'd say it's probably more important how I look when I give a speech than the speech I give."

Parscale added a corollary: "You get a picture with the president of China. It's more important than whatever you did there" in the meeting. The average voter would think, "Oh, the president's in China. I feel safe. We're not going to war with them."

As Parscale described it, Trump had a power to persuade that is almost mystical.

"Now I've finally known him so long, I come back and I say, you did that. I know what you did to me." Trump had made him see what he wanted him to see—such as toughness, but no war with China, Russia or North Korea. "He's like, I was right though. And I was like, yeah, you were right."

On election night, Trump told him, "Don't stand next to me." Trump was supposedly 6-foot-3, and Parscale was five inches taller. Appearance mattered. Appearance defined. There were few photos of the two together.

After the 2020 election, Parscale said, "My guess is there will be a huge rush of people wanting to befriend me. A lot of people think he's going to win. And in theory I have the key to the biggest data trove that's ever existed."

He added, "They'd have to offer me a lot of money though. I'm not doing this for free."

A visitor asked Parscale where the hole in reelection might be. "The coronavirus," he said emphatically. The main headline in *The New York Times* that day was "Coronavirus Fears Drive Stocks Down for 6th Day."

Sixty-four cases had been confirmed in the United States. The day before, Trump had said during remarks in the Cabinet Room, "It's going to disappear. One day—it's like a miracle—it will disappear."

To Parscale, the worry was jobs, not the influence the virus had on the stock market. "We never gained any votes from the stock market," he said. "If the stock market affects jobs, then we lose. Votes are for jobs and personal incomes."

Parscale stuck to his main worry. "The coronavirus. The thing you never see. The president kind of said this before: It's a long hallway and every day I open new doors. And one day I'm going to open a door and there's going to be a piece of dynamite behind it."

THIRTY-SIX

◆

Two days after giving a green light to a weekend movie and a workout at the gym, Fauci appeared on MSNBC on March 2 sounding subdued and wearing a white coat.

"We're dealing with an evolving situation," he said. The disease had "now reached outbreak proportions and likely pandemic proportions, if you look at multiple definitions of what a pandemic is. The fact is, this is multiple sustained transmissions of a highly infectious agent in multiple regions of the globe."

Redfield monitored the CDC's influenza-like illness surveillance network, which took in daily reports from health institutions across the country, tracking influenza types A and B. This would let epidemiologists anticipate when the flu was coming. Redfield looked at the beautiful curves it produced: influenza B peaked, and then fell. Influenza A peaked, and then fell. Now, in March, it was on its way down as flu season ended. But then a third peak appeared. Redfield had never seen a third peak before.

On March 3, Trump visited the National Institutes of Health in Maryland, where he was photographed speaking with doctors wearing white coats in a room bristling with scientific equipment—just as campaign manager Brad Parscale had advised. Three days later Trump toured the CDC in Atlanta, Georgia, in a red "Keep America Great" campaign hat, khaki pants and an open-necked shirt under a bomber jacket.

Speaking at the CDC, Trump promised, "Anybody that needs a test can have a test," seeming to contradict widespread reporting about the difficulty of being tested. Administration officials later worked to clarify that people need to go through their doctors or public health officials to access testing.

"We're not blind where this virus is right now in the United States," Redfield told reporters as he stood beside Trump. "I tell people, every time we see a new confirmed case, they should think of that as a success, because they know their public health community is out doing their job."

Chief among the lessons Redfield had learned from his days researching HIV was not to get ahead of the data. HIV was initially thought to only be transmitted by homosexual sex. Early on he questioned this and coauthored studies demonstrating it could be transmitted heterosexually as well. As important as it was to let people know what kind of road a disease would take them down, to prepare them, the moment he got ahead of the data, he would lose his credibility. When the CDC spoke, he wanted people to listen. He told people he was a data guy, not an opinion guy.

Brazilian president Jair Bolsonaro, a brash Twitter-using nationalist whom Trump had labeled the "Trump of the Tropics," was in Florida in early March and wanted to come to Mar-a-Lago to see Trump. National Security Adviser O'Brien was cutting back on foreign visits for the president because it looked like the virus was becoming a concern in the United States.

An exception was made for Bolsonaro. A photo opportunity was arranged, but it morphed into a dinner for Saturday night, March 7.

Trump and Bolsonaro sat at a table with O'Brien, Ivanka, Kushner and some of the other Brazilians traveling with Bolsonaro. O'Brien was later notified that three of the Brazilians at the table, but not Bolsonaro, tested positive for Covid-19.

After this became public, Bolsonaro downplayed the virus as part of a "fantasy."

O'Brien had an entirely different reaction. He worried he might be a historical footnote as the person responsible for exposing Trump to the virus or passing it directly to him. He spent a lot of time with Trump. There was not lots of testing available then, but he arranged to be tested. He was negative. Later, Bolsonaro tested positive. The virus was starting to feel real.

On March 9, with the stock market reeling, Trump tweeted, "Last year 37,000 Americans died from the common Flu. It averages between 27,000 and 70,000 per year. Nothing is shut down, life & the economy go on. At this moment there are 546 confirmed cases of CoronaVirus, with 22 deaths. Think about that!"

The New York Times headline the morning of Tuesday, March 10: "Markets Spiral as Globe Shudders Over Virus." The markets had plunged the day before. The *Times* wrote it was "their sharpest drop in more than a decade."

In remarks to reporters following a meeting with Republican senators, Trump said, "We're doing a great job with it. And it will go away. Just stay calm. It will go away." Virus cases in the United States were up by more than 200 from the day before.

O'Brien watched TV in his office, flipping between the cable networks. Italy was getting worse. There were images of people bleeding out and dying in the parking lots of Italian hospitals, not able to get in. This, in a major Western country with relatively good health care.

As the virus was spreading rapidly across Europe, O'Brien called several of his counterparts there—national security advisers or equivalents. The Chinese travel restrictions were having significant impact. In January before the restrictions, some 500,000 travelers had come from China to the U.S. In February there was an 86 percent reduction to 70,000.

We've stopped most travel from China, O'Brien told his counterparts. You should do the same.

The response was that this was an issue for the European Union in Brussels. Europe had to respond collectively.

Italy was being hit hard and had on March 9 imposed restrictions nationwide on domestic travel. Nearly 140,000 had come from Italy to the United States the previous month. Another 1.74 million had come from the other European countries such as France and Germany.

O'Brien was worried there was a hole in the original travel restrictions from China. Many of the Chinese who would have come to the United States were it not for the travel restrictions had instead traveled to Europe.

The other key player recently appointed to the team was Dr. Deborah Birx, whose decorated career as a physician, HIV/AIDS researcher and diplomat in federal government spanned more than 40 years. She was named the response coordinator for the White House Coronavirus Task Force. Birx had spent most of her career in the search for a vaccine for HIV, and in 2003 had helped lead the clinical trial that produced the first evidence of any vaccine to be effective in lowering the risk of HIV. Also the U.S. global AIDS coordinator at the State Department, she had worked closely with Fauci and Redfield throughout her career.

Birx reported that 35 states had Covid-19 cases now and 30 of those had been traced to travelers that had come from Europe, primarily through John F. Kennedy Airport.

O'Brien, Pottinger, Fauci and Redfield thought it was well past time to restrict travel from Europe.

A meeting was scheduled with Trump for the morning of March 11.

At the time, Kushner was intensely focused on an initiative to plant one trillion trees. Marc Benioff, the CEO of Salesforce, had brought the idea to Kushner, who brought it to Trump. "Everyone is pro-tree," Benioff said. Trump had made it one of the endless stream of tasks he had assigned to Kushner who was throwing himself into it with typical business-school efficiency.

But now the word came from his father-in-law that he needed immediate help on the mounting Covid-19 crisis.

In the Oval Office that morning, there was a consensus among the national security and health officials that they needed to act immediately to close down travel from Europe.

Treasury Secretary Mnuchin was opposed. Travel from Europe was about five times that from China. "This is going to bankrupt everyone," he said dramatically. "It's going to destroy the economy."

"What data are you relying on for that?" asked Birx. "You've been asking me for my data. What data do you have?"

Mnuchin said that was how the economy and markets worked.

Trump eventually approved the travel restrictions. They would be consistent with his decision on China.

Kushner assisted with drafting the prime-time television address that Trump had decided to give that night from the Oval Office. It was only the second of his presidency. A nationally televised evening address gave the speech the stamp of important business.

That afternoon, the World Health Organization officially declared Covid-19 a pandemic.

"This is the most aggressive and comprehensive effort to confront a foreign virus in modern history," Trump said at 9:00 that evening. "From the beginning of time, nations and people have faced unforeseen challenges, including large-scale and very dangerous health threats," Trump read. "This is the way it always was and always will be. It only matters how you respond."

The president announced he was halting travelers from most European countries for the next 30 days.

"Last week, I signed into law an $8.3 billion funding bill," he said. Several hundred times that would soon be required.

"The vast majority of Americans: The risk is very, very low," Trump said. "Wash your hands, clean often-used surfaces, cover your face and mouth if you sneeze or cough, and most of all, if you are sick or not feeling well, stay home." He made no mention of social distancing—staying six feet apart from others—and urged only those who were sick or not feeling well to stay at home.

"This is not a financial crisis, this is just a temporary moment of time," he said reaching to calm the markets. "The virus will not have a chance against us. . . . Our future remains brighter than anyone can imagine."

The speech received poor reviews. Trump seemed depleted on air, not in command of the material. He displayed none of the verve of the spontaneous, engaged true believer of his political rallies.

Peggy Noonan wrote the next day in *The Wall Street Journal*, "The president gave a major Oval Office address Wednesday night aimed at quelling fears; it was generally labeled 'unsettling.' "

That day, March 11, marked the beginning of a new consciousness in the country. There were over 1,000 cases and 37 deaths in the country. Colleges across the U.S. announced they were suspending classes. The actor Tom Hanks said that he and his wife, Rita Wilson, had tested positive for Covid-19 and would quarantine.

More dominoes fell. The next day, the NCAA announced it was canceling basketball tournaments and suspending all remaining games for the season. Trump acknowledged he would likely have to cancel his upcoming rallies. Broadway theaters closed.

Testifying before Congress, Fauci said that testing for the virus was "failing. I mean, let's admit it." The distribution of faulty test kits had prevented officials and scientists from getting a clear picture of the number of infections in the crucial early days of the virus's spread across the U.S. By the beginning of March, fewer than 500 tests had been conducted.

The Dow Jones fell 10 percent on March 12, prompting *The New York Times* banner headline: "WORST ROUT FOR WALL STREET SINCE 1987 CRASH." A giant chart on the front page of *The Wall Street Journal* showed the surging growth in the Dow from the early days of Obama's eight-year presidency and the first three years of Trump's. Then it fell off the cliff, down 20 percent since 2009.

On March 13, Trump declared a national emergency, the sixth of his presidency. He also announced the launch of a Google-related website that could "determine whether a test is warranted and to facilitate testing at a nearby convenient location." This would "cover the country in large part." Shortly after, Google tweeted that the tool in one of its small subsidiaries was still in development and was only intended to cover the Bay Area.

For two days straight that weekend, every story on the front page of *The Washington Post* was Covid-related. Americans cleared store shelves of hand sanitizer and toilet paper. The White House began instituting temperature checks. New York City announced the closure of its schools.

Matt Pottinger moved out of his small office in the national security adviser's West Wing suite to an office in the Eisenhower Executive Office Building. This would keep him and O'Brien separate, so one would be able to run the NSC if either got sick. Pottinger began wearing a mask and handed them out to the NSC staff working in the Situation Room. He couldn't require the staff to wear masks, but he urged them to. He and O'Brien had been using hand sanitizer for weeks.

Birx, Fauci and Kushner had privately been exchanging drafts of guidelines that would ask Americans to take "15 Days to Slow the Spread" of the coronavirus and effectively shut down the country. They'd sent them back and forth a few times, and Jared Kushner had looked at a draft and made some comments. Kushner's team worked on it for almost 24 hours straight, wrote it up with Derek Lyons, the staff secretary, then sent it to Fauci.

When Kushner got involved, it seemed to Fauci that meant the president would know more detail. No doubt Kushner would explain everything to him. That's good, Fauci thought, because that gave them a direct line to the president.

When Senator Lindsey Graham first heard early discussion about shutting down the country, he thought it was crazy. Then he saw projections of possible 2.2 million dead.

"I'm no expert here," Graham told Trump, "but if these projections are anywhere near right and you ignore them, you're going to have a unique place in history. Mr. President, if these things are remotely right and you don't act, it would be devastating to your presidency."

Trump gathered his team in the Oval Office that Sunday, March 15. Pence, Mnuchin, Fauci and Birx crowded around the Resolute Desk.

Fauci and Birx unrolled the guidelines to Trump. Physical separation is the key, they said. We should close down for at least 15 days to see what happens. They wanted to ask all Americans to work and attend school from home; to avoid gatherings of more than 10 people; to stay away from restaurants and bars; and to avoid traveling, shopping and visiting loved ones at nursing homes. They would recite the now familiar public health litany: wash your hands, don't touch your face, sneeze into a tissue, and disinfect surfaces.

The final draft shows the weakness of having too many hands on the drafting process. Nowhere do the guidelines urge social distancing—staying six feet away from others—one of the most effective universal mitigations.

If we can follow the guidelines for 15 days, they said, and close everything down, perhaps we can start to "flatten the curve"—in other words, to spread out the number of infections over time to avoid overwhelming the health care system all at once.

As Trump listened, Fauci and Birx went back and forth with a skeptical Mnuchin.

I'm concerned about what's going to happen economically, Mnuchin said.

Well, you know, Trump finally said, let's try it for 15 days. Maybe we'll be able to open up for Easter.

I don't think we should guarantee that, Fauci said. We won't be able to see the effect yet after 15 days.

Okay, let's give it a shot, Trump said.

I'm worried, Mnuchin said. But he didn't fight the decision.

That day at the briefing, Trump said, "This is a very contagious virus. It's incredible. But it's something that we have tremendous control over."

That same day, Kushner got another grim wake-up call. He was working on ramping up more testing sites and went to a briefing at the Health and Human Services offices. We've got bad news, he was told. There are only 1.2 million swabs available for administering tests in the country.

It was a brutal realization. After being involved for four days, the scope of the problem was becoming clear. What good were tests if you didn't have the swabs to administer them?

THIRTY-SEVEN

◆

Trump announced the "15 Days to Slow the Spread" guidelines the next day, March 16, at the coronavirus task force briefing. Asked about his frequent assertion that the situation was under control, Trump acknowledged, "The virus, no, that's not under control for anyplace in the world." He added, "I was talking about what we're doing is under control, but I'm not talking about the virus."

Kushner told others the guidelines were "very thoughtful, very well-received and acclaimed by D's and R's."

Graham believed Trump's decision to shut down for 15 days was probably the first time in Trump's life when he had to make a decision that was not in his best interest politically or financially. Graham was convinced Trump did it because he believed he had the power to save people's lives. He had chosen the road that would be the most detrimental to his number-one issue—the economy.

For Redfield it was one of the most difficult times of his four-decade professional life. "15 Days to Slow the Spread" was important, but not enough.

In private he told others of his deepest fears. "It's not to stop the spread," Redfield said. "We were now in a race. I think we all understood now we were in a race. We're in a marathon. We're in a two-year, three-year race. Not a one-year, not a six-month race. The race is to slow and contain this virus as much as humanly possible, with all our efforts, till we can get a highly efficacious vaccine deployed for all the American people and then beyond that to the rest of the world."

All the talk about the virus going away or disappearing was medically false.

In his agony, he recalled a parallel situation. Years ago when he had opened the Institute of Human Virology at the University of Maryland School of Medicine they brought in a group of scientists from around the world. One from Princeton posed a question: Suppose we knew that 15 years out a meteor was hurtling to the earth and going to run smack-dab in the middle and destroy the planet and blow everyone to bits. The question was how do you change that? How do we change the center of gravity, presumably of the meteor or even earth? The current race again the virus was the same.

His worry could not be deeper. "This virus will stop when it basically infects more than 70 percent of the world, or 80 percent of the world," Redfield told others. "Or the world develops a biological countermeasure that stops it," he added, referring to a vaccine. The meteor was heading to earth.

As states, cities, businesses and individuals began to implement the guidelines, the country effectively began to shut down.

In a tweet on March 16, Trump wrote, "The United States will be powerfully supporting those industries, like Airlines and others, that are particularly affected by the Chinese Virus. We will be stronger than ever before!" This appears to be the first time Trump publicly referred to Covid as the "Chinese virus."

Three days after Trump announced "15 Days to Slow the Spread," I conducted my eighth interview with him.

"This thing is a nasty—it's a nasty situation," Trump told me about the coronavirus on March 19, 2020.

Earlier that day, California governor Gavin Newsom had become the first governor to order residents to stay home except for essential needs—the first of a wave of shutdown orders across all 50 states that would eventually lead to tens of millions of unemployment claims and the nation's greatest economic downturn since the Great Depression.

The nation's death toll from coronavirus was still less than 200.

In our interview, the president spoke with pride about his leadership. He blamed China and President Obama and continued to accept no responsibility.

"I think we're doing very well," the president said. "We have to see what happens. We have it very well shut down. The American people are terrific. You know, what they're putting up with."

In the course of the 40-minute phone call, Trump at three separate points brought up the story of his January 31 decision to bar foreigners coming from China to enter the United States. The decision had averted "tremendous death," he said.

"Had I not done that, there would've been massive numbers of deaths by now," Trump said. "It was a big move. Because you know, we take in thousands of people a day from China. And China was heavily infected."

According to Trump, he made the decision in the face of great resistance from within and outside his administration.

I asked about his 13-year-old son, Barron. What did you tell him? I asked. The president told me about a moment days earlier when Barron had asked him about the coronavirus.

"He said Dad, what's going on? What's going on?" Trump told me. "I said, it's a very bad thing, but we're going to straighten it out.

"He said, how did it happen?" Trump continued. "I said, it came out of China, Barron, pure and simple. It came out of China. It should've been stopped. And to be honest with you, Barron, they should've let it be known it was a problem two months earlier. And the world would not—we have 141 countries have it now. And I said, the world wouldn't have a problem. We could've stopped it easily. And they didn't want to do the—they waited and waited. Kept it secret, secret. Then we started hearing things coming out. I told him how it was working. And I said, and now the whole world is infected and inflicted with this."

It was apparent the president was aware of the criticism he was receiving about his handling of the coronavirus. After surviving the 22-month-long Mueller investigation and the third impeachment trial in United States history, the real dynamite behind the door was the virus. The lives and livelihoods of tens of millions of Americans hung in the balance with every decision he made in dealing with the coronavirus.

In our interview, he seemed to understand the deadly severity of the disease.

"Part of it is the mystery," Trump said. "Part of it's the viciousness. You know when it attacks, it attacks the lungs. And I don't know—when people get hit, when they get hit, and now it's turning out it's not just old people, Bob. Just today and yesterday, some startling facts came out. It's not just old, older. Young people too, plenty of young people."

I asked Trump what had caused the shift in his thinking about the virus. "It's clear just from what's on the public record that you went through a pivot on this," I said, "to, oh my God, the gravity is almost inexplicable and unexplainable."

Just two days before, at the task force briefing, Trump had gone so far as to claim, "I've always known this is a—this is a real—this is a pandemic. I've felt it was a pandemic long before it was called a pandemic."

The president maintained his upbeat rhetoric in the early weeks of the virus had been deliberate.

"I wanted to always play it down," Trump told me, as I reported earlier in this book. "I still like playing it down, because I don't want to create a panic."

Trump said that the daily press briefings with members of his White House Coronavirus Task Force, led by Vice President Pence, were helping turn the tide of public opinion and making the public see his response in a more positive light.

"You know the news conferences I've been doing on a daily basis, because I think it keeps people informed and it's been good, they've gotten very good reviews but they've also gotten unbelievable ratings," he said.

The rambling, repetitious, often defensive and angry monologues eroded confidence in his grasp of the problem and his leadership. I asked Trump what his next steps were.

"My next step is I've got 20 calls waiting for me on this stuff, and I've got to get making them. Okay? That's my next steps. My next step, Bob, is I have to do a great job," Trump replied. "And I have to be very professional . . . I think that people are respecting what's happening. And I think frankly since I started doing the news conferences, it's all turned around."

He had spoken at over 10 White House Coronavirus Task Force briefings and had begun holding them daily.

"Because we've done a great job. You've got to always say one of the best parts of the great job was the shutdown of China very, very early."

Earlier in the day, Trump had given an 80-minute press briefing in which he promoted the use of the drug hydroxychloroquine as an alleged treatment for the virus. "If things don't go as planned," he said, "it's not going to kill anybody."

Studies later indicated the drug could cause serious heart problems, and the FDA in June cautioned against its use as a Covid-19 treatment due to risk of heart rhythm problems and trials that found "no benefit for decreasing the likelihood of death."

Trump used the press briefing to praise the work of administration officials, including himself. He said Food and Drug Administration commissioner Stephen Hahn had "worked like, probably as hard or harder than anybody in this—in the group, other than maybe Mike Pence or me."

When he spoke to me that evening, he remained fixated on the media's coverage of his leadership during the pandemic.

"I had no symptoms, but the press was my symptom," he said, referring to questions about whether he'd been tested for the virus.

I asked Trump about Dr. Fauci, who had become omnipresent in the lives of Americans through his media appearances since the outbreak of the virus.

"This is a war," I said. "And in many ways, he's your Eisenhower." Under President Franklin Roosevelt, Eisenhower had been Supreme Commander of the Allied Forces and planned the invasion of Normandy which led to victory in World War II.

"Well, he's a very good guy. He's done it before," Trump said of Fauci. "He's a sharp guy."

I began to ask Trump if he ever sat down alone with Fauci to get a tutorial on the science behind the virus when the president cut in.

"Yes, I guess, but honestly there's not a lot of time for that, Bob. This is a busy White House. We've got a lot of things happening. And then this came up."

No matter how busy or what other things were happening, I frankly wondered what could be more important. Trump had carved out hours to talk with me.

"Look, we had the greatest economy on earth. The greatest economy we've ever had," Trump added, overstating the strength of the U.S. economy compared to other periods in the nation's history. It reminded me of Kushner's notion that "controversy elevates message."

"And in one day, this thing came in and we had a choice to make," Trump continued. "Close everything up and save potentially millions of lives—you know, hundreds of thousands of lives—or don't do anything and look at body bags every day being taken out of apartment buildings."

"Who told you that?" I asked.

"It was me," Trump said. "I told me that."

As he led the nation through the crisis, Trump showed few signs of introspection.

"Was there a moment in all of this, last two months, where you said to yourself—you know, you're waking up or whatever you're doing and you say, ah, this is the leadership test of a lifetime?" I asked.

"No," he answered.

"No?"

"I think it might be, but I don't think that. All I want to do is get it solved."

I brought up Trump's comments at a press briefing the previous week, when he had said "I don't take responsibility at all" for the crisis.

"I don't take responsibility for this," Trump told me. "I have nothing to do with this. I take responsibility for solving the problem. But I don't take responsibility for this, no. We did a good job. The Obama administration—they were obsolete tests. And in all fairness to them, nobody ever thought in terms of millions of people."

I could find no support for Trump's claim, repeated several times in public remarks, that the Obama administration left behind "obsolete" or "broken" tests. Obama's National Security Council had left behind a 69-page document titled "Playbook for

Early Response to High-Consequence Emerging Infectious Disease Threats and Biological Incidents" that included instructions for dealing with novel influenza viruses which "would produce an estimate of between 700,000 and 1.4 billion fatalities from a pandemic of a virulent influenza virus strain." The document recommended officials in the early stages of such a pandemic check the nation's diagnostic testing capacity and the amount of personal protective equipment available for health care workers.

Complaints about a lack of preparation were universal. For two years Redfield had testified before Congress that the country was not prepared for a large health crisis. When a 2018 report on the Zika virus, West Nile virus and other diseases caused by insect bites was released, Redfield said, "We don't know what will threaten Americans next."

Shortly before midnight on March 22, Trump tweeted in all-caps, "WE CANNOT LET THE CURE BE WORSE THAN THE PROBLEM ITSELF. AT THE END OF THE 15 DAY PERIOD, WE WILL MAKE A DECISION AS TO WHICH WAY WE WANT TO GO!"

In late March, Kushner and Pence had a meeting with the data people at FEMA, the Federal Emergency Management Agency. They gave Kushner a list showing the country would need 130,000 ventilators by April 1. The message sank in. It meant possibly 130,000 people were going to die because he didn't get them a ventilator. It meant the situation soon could mirror that in Italy, where doctors were choosing who lived and who died. In Kushner's view people dying on hospital gurneys because they couldn't get ventilators was not politically survivable.

Pence saw Kushner was disturbed. "Come for a ride back," he said. So Kushner and Pence rode back to the White House together. "Jared," Pence said, "we'll figure it out."

Kushner broke the news about the ventilators to Trump, who later called it the scariest day of his life and said he told the team to "move heaven and earth" to get the ventilators.

Kushner gathered White House economists and data modelers he knew from the private sector in the Roosevelt Room. They pulled Medicare and Medicaid data and went hospital by hospital, getting the highest number of ventilators the hospital had ever billed for at one time, then aggregated the numbers on a state-by-state basis. Before FEMA sent out more ventilators, Kushner said, it would need to ask how many ventilators were in the state, how many anesthesia machines had the state converted to ventilators, and what was the state's daily utilization rate?

Kushner's team predeployed ventilators so that every time they got to about 96 hours away from running out, they sent them another 500. New York and New Jersey came close a few times on ventilators.

New York governor Andrew Cuomo was holding daily press conferences that were getting high marks, and he loudly complained about the lack of ventilators, at one point saying New York needed 40,000 more ventilators.

Trump called Kushner. Jared, why aren't you sending out more ventilators?

Cuomo was wrong, Kushner said. He and his team had checked by calling the New York hospitals. No one in New York was 96 hours away from needing a ventilator, Kushner said.

On March 26, a reporter asked Trump about the language he used to describe the virus. "I talk about the Chinese virus and—and I mean it. That's where it came from," he said. "And this was a Chinese virus."

Later that day, Trump and Xi spoke again by phone about the virus. At the start of the call, Trump discussed comments by the Chinese Foreign Ministry spokesman that the virus had been brought to China by an American soldier. This is a ridiculous comment, you know, Trump said. It was tense, and they argued.

Xi pivoted to a different topic. French president Emmanuel Macron wanted to hold a meeting of the five permanent members of the U.N. Security Council. The leaders discussed the potential meeting before the conversation moved back to the virus.

Xi said China was on the other side of its peak, and new case numbers had dropped significantly. He claimed any new cases in China were imported. Trump and Pottinger, who was listening on the call, knew this was not true at all.

Xi called the virus the common enemy and said his health minister would contact Azar, his American counterpart, to share best practices.

Trump asked Xi what was effective in fighting against the virus. What medicines and therapeutics were working for China?

Lockdowns, quarantine and social distancing were effective, Xi replied. He claimed the lockdown in Wuhan had prevented the spread of the virus to the rest of the world. Early discovery, early testing, early quarantine and early treatment were helpful, he said.

It would help, Xi added, if U.S. officials—many of whom had borrowed the "Chinese virus" phrase from Trump—adjusted their comments. He expressed concern about anti-Chinese sentiment.

Trump said that he personally and the American people loved the Chinese people and would never tolerate mistreatment of people visiting from China.

The two leaders spent the remainder of the call discussing the virus and treatments for it.

Why is the fatality rate so high in Wuhan? Trump asked.

Xi replied that it was because of the proportion of elderly people in Wuhan, and the high concentration of cases.

The call ended cordially, with Xi inviting the president and first lady to visit once the virus had passed and Trump again thanking him for the offer.

Although Xi did not make any direct threat, Pottinger thought he had suggested a cause-and-effect relationship between the tone of U.S. official statements and the degree of cooperation China would provide. He also thought it was outrageous—and part of the cover-up—that China had not provided virus samples as required by international agreement.

During the next day's briefing, Trump alluded to his call with Xi and said, "You can call it a germ, you can call it a flu, you can call it a virus. You know, you can call it many different names. I'm not sure anybody even knows what it is."

On March 27, Trump met with Pence, O'Brien, Kushner and Larry Kudlow, the chief White House economic adviser who had succeeded Gary Cohn, in the Oval Office to discuss using the Defense Production Act on 3M.

The shortage of protective face masks for medical workers was a full-blown crisis. The stockpile was about 40 million masks—1 percent of what was needed.

"On masks," Kushner said to the president, "there's no way we can scale to the capacity we need here in America in the time we're going to need it. If we want to get the product we need to get through the next couple of weeks, China is the only answer." China manufactured about 80 percent of the world's face masks. "So you've got to decide how you want to play this."

Call your contact, Trump said.

Kushner phoned Cui Tiankai, the 67-year-old, gray-haired Chinese ambassador to the United States. Cui had been in his post in Washington for an astonishing seven years. A Chinese Foreign Ministry veteran, Cui had done graduate work in the United States at Johns Hopkins, and he spoke perfect English. Kushner and Cui, both devoted networkers, had arranged the first meeting between Trump and Chinese president Xi at Mar-a-Lago in 2017. It was a useful relationship to both.

"Right now," Kushner said in a call to Cui, "we're in this situation." Trump had been publicly referring to the "Chinese virus" as conspiracy theories piled one on top of another. Given its own overwhelming virus crisis, China was restricting exports of protective medical equipment, including the masks. The 75-cent masks were one of the most effective ways to contain the virus.

Kushner proposed to Cui some reputation and national image management. "When we get out of this, there's going to be a lot of people very angry with China. And how you guys act now with a lot of the materials that are made in China is going to be looked at very carefully by the country and the world."

Kushner asked directly, "Do you hold over people's head the fact that a lot of global manufacturing of this is in the country?"

Kushner added, "So I just want to put that out there to you and let you know that this is something that's going to be watched very closely."

Kushner had a remedy. "I'm going to start working to find supply here, and I want to make sure that I'm not going to have any restrictions getting out the supply that I'm able to procure in China."

"I'm running a big, big operation," the president said when I reached him again by phone on Saturday morning, March 28.

The country had surpassed 2,000 deaths and officially had more reported cases than any other country. The day before, Trump had signed a $2 trillion pandemic response bill.

"The world is under siege, as you know," he said. "I think we're doing a good job. It's unbelievable, though." He sounded beleaguered. "What's your feeling?"

"The leadership task that's on your shoulders," I began.

"Yeah."

"People are going to be looking at this and trying to understand it a hundred years from now," I said. My question for that history was, "What are your priorities?"

"There's a lot of really fake news out," he answered, retreating to his first talking point. He complained for a time about the media.

"The question though is what—because it's on your shoulders," I tried again. "What are your priorities?"

"My priorities are saving lives," he said. "That's my only priority."

I reminded him he'd said that he discussed how this began with President Xi. "Did he have an answer?"

"Right," Trump said. "Well, I did, and I discussed it. And then I said, look, it's no longer relevant right now. We'll talk about it after it's all over. Because in the meantime we have to fix what's here. But there's no reason to get into a big argument about that now. Sometimes you just sort of say, okay, let's talk about that sometime later. They're very defensive, as they probably—as you would be."

"When we talked in February, you said there's dynamite behind every door," I said. "And this is before all of this accelerated. And I wonder if at that point did you have any inkling or intelligence that my God, we've got this storm coming?"

"Well nobody knew that a thing like this could happen," Trump said. "The best decision I made was Europe and China, closing our doors. We would've had a much bigger problem, like many times bigger than we had. We would've had unbelievable amounts of death."

"Fauci is predicting we may have 100,000 deaths in this country," I said.

"It could happen," he said. "And if we didn't do what I'm doing, you would've had a number many times that. Can you believe that?"

"How's Xi's mood?" I asked. "Because they've been clobbered also."

"They've been clobbered far worse than you read," the president said.

"I understand that it shows in North Korea they're being clobbered also." North Korea had publicly claimed it didn't have a single case of the virus.

"Like you wouldn't believe," Trump said. "We haven't had a war," he reminded me. "Okay? And then you have something like this. And this stops wars, because they've got their own war now."

"Somebody told me that the virus is just blazing through North Korea," I said.

"Yeah. A big problem. Iran is an unbelievable problem."

China had blamed American soldiers for bringing in the virus. Trump said he told President Xi, "Look, you can't do that. And you know, we had a little bit of an argument."

I understood that Trump's decision to publicly call coronavirus the "Chinese virus" had led some White House staffers to feel emboldened to criticize China even harder. Trump was worried because he knew words could cause wars. He had told them, "You can't do that shit," and stopped them fast.

The scale of the problem had clearly sunk in. Trump almost sounded like a different person.

As the end of the "15 Days to Slow the Spread" inched closer, Trump said he wanted to reopen the country for Easter. We really want to have people at church, he said.

"I'm a Catholic," Fauci said. "I went to Catholic schools. I understand the importance of Easter, but I'm a little concerned that if you want to have people go back to churches on Easter, that might not be a good idea."

I don't know, Trump said. I'd love to be able to do that. Nice, beautiful churches, he said. Beautiful mass. It's a really sunny day. Okay, Trump said. Let's get back to this and see what we're going to do.

Fauci and Birx returned a few days later, right at the end of the 15 days. They needed to extend the time of the shutdown and advocated for another 30 days to "slow the spread."

"Mr. President, that's a nonstarter," Fauci said of reopening the country for Easter. "You can't do that." After 15 days, they couldn't know if they'd had any impact. It was premature. "We've got to go to 30 more days."

Trump turned to Fauci and Birx. You guys feel really strongly about this?

Mr. President, they said, we really do need to do it. Because we may start to see a flattening of the curve, and then you'll come back and say, you know, it was a really good thing for us to do this.

Okay, we'll go with it, Trump said. I hope you guys are right.

Okay, Fauci said. I think we are.

Trump announced the 30-day extension on March 29. Fauci said modeling showed the U.S. could be in excess of a million cases and deaths could exceed 100,000 without mitigation efforts. "I mean, you could make a big sound bite about it, but the fact is it's possible," Fauci said. "What we're trying to do is not let that happen."

Trump added, "If we can hold that down, as we're saying, to 100,000—that's a horrible number—and maybe even less, but to 100,000, so we have between 100- and 200,000—we all, together, have done a very good job."

At the next day's briefing, Trump said, "Stay calm. It will go away. You know it—you know it is going away, and it will go away. And we're going to have a great victory."

THIRTY-EIGHT

<hr>

April began with dire headlines about the latest White House task force models, released March 31, predicting 100,000 to 240,000 deaths nationwide even with mitigation measures like social distancing, and 1.5 million to 2.2 million without mitigation.

Trump seemed to be on a war against rules. On April 3, when the CDC issued new guidance recommending that Americans wear masks, Trump said at the Coronavirus Task Force briefing that day, "This is voluntary. I don't think I'm going to be doing it."

The death toll in the United States had reached 7,000 and the number of new cases was rising by a staggering 30,000 each day.

"I'm feeling good," Trump added later in the briefing. "I just don't want to be doing—I don't know, somehow sitting in the Oval Office behind that beautiful Resolute Desk—the great Resolute Desk—I think wearing a face mask as I greet presidents, prime ministers, dictators, kings, queens, I don't know. Somehow, I don't see it for myself."

Away from the cameras, however, the president's mood was grim.

––––––––

"The plague," President Trump said when I reached him by phone late in the afternoon of April 5, 2020, Palm Sunday.

The president had given up on his plan to open the country by Easter. He sounded resigned, almost chastened, with a solemn tone unlike any I had heard in our previous nine interviews.

"It's a horrible thing. It's unbelievable. Can you believe it? It moves rapidly and viciously. If you're the wrong person and if it gets you, your life is pretty much over if you're in the wrong group. It's our age group."

He was 73, and I had recently turned 77.

I had prepared a list of 14 critical areas where my sources said major action was needed. My goal was to cover all 14 in our interview and find out what Trump thought and might have planned. Given the risks and hazards, I believed this could not be a standard interview. I wanted to lay it out as starkly and candidly as I could. Was he organized? Was there a plan?

"Are we going to go to full mobilization?" I asked. "People I talk to say they want that feeling of full mobilization. No one is going to say Trump did too much. There's never too much."

"I agree," he said.

Testing was the first of the 14 areas I wanted to cover. My reporting showed that Dr. Anthony Fauci, in private briefings, had been saying of the federal government's response to the coronavirus that "we aren't there yet." Officials were saying we need a "Manhattan-like project," something reminiscent of the scale and scope of the 1940s project to successfully develop an atomic bomb.

Trump has a habit of ignoring questions and attempting to redirect the conversation. At times, talking with him meant being talked at. Now Trump veered off, citing the 3,000-bed facility the U.S. military had built in the Javits Center in New York City.

"That was for regular surgeries, etc. That was for regular patients, not Covid patients," he said. "I don't know if you know that. Do you know that?"

"Yeah. Certainly. The question is—"

"But you know that's a big deal, Bob. I mean, that's a big deal." They were trying to make sure there was enough room in the hospitals for coronavirus patients.

Given the magnitude of the crisis, the Javits Center was important but did not address the national crisis. I pushed again on testing. All the health professionals said testing was key because people, particularly those without symptoms, could be isolated to prevent infecting others. Tens of millions of tests would be required, if not hundreds of millions.

"The question is, are you happy?" I asked about the scope of the federal government's response. On testing, "Is it enough?"

He did not answer. The Democratic governors, he said, would not give him enough credit in public.

"Is this full mobilization?" I pressed. "A Manhattan Project? Are we going—pardon the expression—balls to the wall? That's what people want. And people want to feel that."

He said he'd been "speaking to people all day" and indicated he was trying to get that message out through his daily news conferences. "Maybe then I'm doing a bad job of, not saying it."

That was an almost unheard-of concession, but he immediately began talking about New York governor Andrew Cuomo. "Hey look," the president said. "Cuomo asked us for 40,000 ventilators. Okay? Think of it." The most severely ill patients needed the ventilator machines to help them breathe.

"Okay," I said, "but Cuomo is not the issue."

"No, no, I know. But 40,000. I told him, you don't need anywhere near that amount. Now it's turning out that we're right." Trump was correct. When the White House individually polled the New York hospitals, far fewer were needed.

The responsibility was his, I said. "You are the one. This is a question about your leadership. And you know, I just want to know how you feel about it."

"I feel good," he said. "I think we're doing a great job." He launched into a familiar grievance. "I think we'll never get credit from the fake news media no matter how good a job we do. No matter how good a job I do, I will never get credit from the media, and I'll never get credit from Democrats who want to beat me desperately in seven months."

"If you go out and say this is full mobilization—" I said.

"I've done it. I have done it. Well look—" he said.

"Manhattan Project—"

"Well, yeah," he said.

We were speaking past each other, almost from different universes.

I turned to the second large issue on my list, the struggle to supply personal protective equipment to hospital employees and other workers. "The medical supply chain. People I talk to say they still aren't satisfied with it."

The president let out a loud sigh that can be heard on the recording.

"We're getting very few complaints," he said. "Now, I am a big fan of the hydroxychloroquine." The antimalarial drug was touted by some, including Trump, as a game-changing cure for Covid-19. "It may not work, by the way, and it may work. If it does work, I will get no credit for it, and if it doesn't work, they'll blame the hell out of me. Okay? But that's okay. I don't mind that. But we are—we have millions of—we've ordered millions of doses of the hydroxy. We've ordered millions—we have millions—we're stocked."

Later, on May 18, Trump would reveal he had been taking the drug.

"The third area, sir, is the unemployment benefits and the cash payments." Was there really a system in place that would work?

Nearly 10 million had applied for unemployment benefits—a stunning number. Congress had passed a $2 trillion stimulus package in late March that provided those on unemployment an extra $600 per week.

"I was totally opposed to the distribution of the money the way the Democrats wanted it," the president said. "They wanted it to go through unemployment insurance—you know, centers. But many of them have 40-year-old computers. I said, it'll take a long time to get there if you do that. And we have already—the money is sent. It's up to the states to deliver it."

"Okay," I said. "The fourth area is the small business loans" being given out through the Paycheck Protection Program.

"That's going really well, Bob. I mean, that—I don't know if you saw. It was opened on Friday."

"I understand. But some of the banks are not participating because they say that—"

"Well, if they don't participate we're not going to be happy with them. But Bank of America, JPMorgan Chase, they had to get straightened out. It had nothing to do with us." He had a strong point that $13 billion had been loaned in the first day, though the total allocated in the stimulus and rescue package was $350 billion and would have to be increased.

"Fifth area," I said. "Shelter in place."

"It's been very successful," he said.

"Does it need a national order? I know you're reluctant to do this."

The effort to get people to stay at home was going well, he correctly noted. "There are a lot of constitutional reasons, there are a lot of federalist reasons" not to issue a national order.

"Sixth is the food supply," I said. "Are you confident that the food supply is going to get out to people?"

"Yeah," he said. "You haven't even heard a complaint about that, Bob. I mean, it's going great. I had a big meeting with all the big suppliers on Thursday. The biggest in the world, all of them. We also had meetings with all the big department store types and all of them—from Amazon to Walmart to all of them. And they're all doing well. And they also, they have long lines going to stores because we're keeping them six feet away in the line." A month later, spiking infection rates in meatpacking plants would jeopardize the nation's meat supply.

"Seventh area, international coordination." I asked Trump if he had seen Henry Kissinger's recent op-ed in *The Wall Street Journal* headlined, "The Coronavirus Pandemic Will Forever Alter the World Order."

"I did not, no. What did he say?"

Kissinger had stressed the international nature of the crisis. "Failure," he'd written, "could set the world on fire."

"Do you have somebody who will be the focal point of coordinating with all the other countries involved in this?" I asked.

"I do. I do. We have a secretary of state named Mike Pompeo."

"And he's focused on this?" I asked.

"Oh yeah. He's very focused on it. We have more than him. We have, the entire State Department is focused on it. But honestly Bob, it's more of a local problem from that standpoint."

It was not at all clear what he meant by "a local problem," but before I could ask he cited his invocation of the Defense Production Act to get 3M to agree to ship 166.5 million N95 masks from China over three months, which Kushner had successfully pushed. Trump had faced criticism for being slow to use the DPA to force domestic manufacturers to focus on U.S. government needs, and the country was still well short of the 500 to 600 million face masks sought by the administration.

"Okay," I said. "How about the next area? What's the definition of an essential worker? People feel it's—everyone's defining it the way they want to define it. Do you have a definition or does the federal government—"

"We had a specific definition," he said. "I can give it to you if you want. But we do have a very specific definition." The Department of Homeland Security had released a 19-page advisory memo with suggested ways to identify essential workers in March, but individual states and counties differed in their definitions.

"Well, it seems loose and vague to people."

"Okay, well, I'll put it out. Maybe I'll talk about that today." He did not bring the subject up in his press briefing that night. "You know, we had a case where the churches are saying it's essential. It's a very interesting question. The churches are saying they're essential."

Some states had classified churches among the essential businesses in order to allow them the option to stay open and conduct services.

"How about air travel?" I asked. "Some people say you're just sending planes with four people on it from one city to the next and that is jeopardizing people. Is there a national policy?"

"They're mostly closed down. We have to keep some flights open for emergency purposes, but they're mostly closed down. The airlines are doing checks. We're doing checks. But they're mostly closed down, Bob. But they do have some routes. If you do what some people—you need to have at least a semblance of, a little bit—now, we check people going on, getting off. And it has not been a problem."

In March 2020 U.S. airlines carried 36.6 million passengers on scheduled flights, according to the Bureau of Transportation Statistics, about half of the 77.5 million passengers in March 2019.

In a press briefing on April 1, Trump had said he was considering taking action to regulate flights. "You have them going, in some cases, from hot spot to hot spot," he said. But ultimately, no federal government action was taken to limit domestic air travel.

"Do Fauci and Dr. Birx, do they say this is enough?" I asked if they considered air travel "leakage."

"Well, they haven't complained," Trump said. "I mean, you know—maybe I'll ask them that question, but they have not complained either."

"Okay," I said. I tried again to ask the basic unanswered question: Who is in charge of key areas? "Now who's in charge of the effort—I've talked to some people"—again the president let out a deep sigh—"who are doing very aggressive, imaginative work on vaccines and antibodies. Who's in charge of that?"

"NIH," he said. "National Institute, which is phenomenal. And they are doing it. They're in charge of it. We have a lot of potential vaccines, especially probably Johnson & Johnson. You know, NIH is doing the work but we also farm it out to many, many companies."

He was correct about Vaccine Development Services at NIH, but there was no one person clearly and publicly leading this vital government effort.

"Have you talked to Bill Gates at all?" I asked. Gates, the cofounder of Microsoft and more recently one of the world's leading experts on managing mammoth public health crises, had with his wife, Melinda, invested billions of dollars through the Bill and Melinda Gates Foundation into global development and public health initiatives. Gates had been warning about a pandemic for years. In a recent *Washington Post* op-ed, he'd written that the only way out of the crisis would be a vaccine.

"No, I have not. He—But I think I'm going to be meeting him very shortly, yeah."

The two had met several times before. In December 2016, Gates came to Trump Tower to warn the president-elect about the risks of a pandemic and encouraged him to prioritize preparing for one. In 2017, Trump told Gates he was thinking about establishing a commission to examine the "bad effects" of vaccines. "No, that's a dead end, that would be a bad thing, don't do that," Gates had told Trump.

"He's the expert," I said. "He spent billions of dollars of his own money. He says we only get out of this when we have vaccines."

Trump later announced that he was going to discontinue funding for the World Health Organization because he felt the organization had protected China during the crisis. In a tweet on April 15, Gates blasted the decision, writing, "Halting funding for the World Health Organization during a world health crisis is as dangerous as it sounds. . . . The world needs WHO now more than ever." After the tweet, Gates and the president never met, according to a Gates senior aide.

"Well, we're doing great on vaccines," Trump said. "The problem with a vaccine is a vaccine will take 13 to 14 months once you have it. Because you have to test a vaccine. As opposed to the hydroxy, you have to test it. Because the hydroxy's been out there for 25 years." Hydroxychloroquine had long been available as a treatment for malaria and arthritis, but it was still being studied as a theoretical treatment for Covid-19 when we spoke.

"Next area is China on the wet markets. Some people—I think Fauci is saying privately in briefings we've got to get China to close down their wet markets" where the virus originated in Wuhan.

"Yeah, some people are saying that," Trump acknowledged. "And that one I have not done yet. You have to understand, I just signed a massive trade deal turning everything—because China's been ripping us off for years. Like ripping us like you've never seen, economically." He did not want to jeopardize the China trade deal.

"No, I—listen, Mr. President, I understand all of that. The question is, you've got some experts like Fauci—"

"Well, I don't know," Trump said. "Fauci also said that this wouldn't be a problem, so—this disease was not going to be a problem. I was in the room when he said it, okay? So you know—"

In public, Fauci did play down the severity of the virus in late February.

Trump continued, "And some of the people that you mentioned. And you know, they turned out to be wrong on that. So you know, they can be wrong too, Bob. Right?"

"Absolutely. I think—I'm telling you as a reporter, I'll emphasize this again. They're saying they want a sense of World War II mobilization."

"All right, I got you. I understand. I got you. I think we're doing a very good job, but I've got exactly what you're saying. Now in New York the deaths have fallen for the first time. That's a big step." The day before, New York State had reported 630 coronavirus deaths. That morning it had reported 594.

"How about the small-government Republicans who, you know, are real leery of all this spending of trillions of dollars?" I asked. "Are they obstacles?"

"If I listened to them, I wouldn't have closed the country."

"Okay. How about the intelligence agencies? How's CIA director Gina Haspel doing?" I asked, trying to ascertain the role intelligence was playing in the fight against the virus. "And do you feel that you know what's going on in the world?"

"Better than any president's known in 30 years," he said, only answering the last part of the question. But he added, "I'm listening to every word you're saying."

My reporting, I repeated, showed that people wanted "full mobilization, we're at Manhattan Project level here and we're not going to stop—and I'm reporting to you what people are saying—"

"No matter what I do," he replied, "they'll always tell you bad."

"Even people who don't like you," I said, "people who are opposed to you—want this country to succeed on this."

"Well, no," he said. "I think there are some people that would rather have it not succeed. Okay? That's a big statement. There are some people that would rather have it not succeed so that they could possibly beat me in the election. All right?

"I will tell you that with straightness. There are people on the radical fringes and the left that would rather have us not succeed."

"God will never forgive them, then," I said.

"Well, maybe that's true," Trump said. "I will never forgive them."

He tried to steer the conversation back to the ventilator dispute his administration had resolved.

"But if you go to full mobilization—" I said.

"I am," he said.

"—and you tell the world and the country that's it, these are the people who are in charge of testing, of unemployment benefits, loans, the food supply, international coordination, air travel, the vaccines, China, the intelligence world—if you, if that's clear to people—"

"Right," Trump said.

"During the Nixon case," I said, "Nixon did not understand the goodwill that people feel toward a president. Now, you—that is a problem now in this country, the polarization, no question. But—"

"Yeah, but the ones that like me, like me a *lot*, okay?" Trump said.

"But people know this is a survival issue," I said. "People are talking about their kids, and they're saying, what kind of world are we going to give to our kids?"

"They're right. But when you talk about that—Nixon was an unpopular guy. I have great support out there. You don't see it, probably. All you have to do is take a look at the polls. I'm getting—I just got a 69 percent or 68 percent for the approval rating for this."

A Gallup poll in March showed that 60 percent approved of his handling of the crisis while 38 percent did not. Presidents often get bumps in their approval ratings during times of national crisis.

"I'm asking you a series of questions," I said, "based on my reporting."

"Give me a list of the things you said. Did you write them down, or not?"

"Yes, I wrote them all down."

"Just read them out. Go ahead, read them."

I read back over the list, reemphasizing all the critical areas. Trump pushed me impatiently along, item by item.

I added a final point: "People really need a sustainable income stream"—or at least a reliable way to say, "okay, at some point I'm going to get this money—whether it's unemployment benefits, cash payments, some sort of loan."

When I reached the end of the list he said, "That's good. I'm glad you told me. Many of these things are done or in great shape. But I'm glad you told me."

He was blowing off both me and the list.

Elsa, my wife, was in the room during the call. At times I raised my voice in order to be able to complete a question or press the president to answer. At one point, she told me to stop yelling. She felt my list of 14 points sounded too much like I was telling him what to do. Others, I am sure, would agree. The list represented what I had found from my reporting, as I told him several times. If I was going to write about the list—and I was sure I would—I thought it only fair to ask him about it.

I hung up, feeling distressed. Trump never did seem willing to fully mobilize the federal government and continually seemed to push problems off on the states. There was no real management theory of the case or how to organize a massive enterprise to deal with one of the most complex emergencies the United States had ever faced. Beyond being a reporter, I was worried for the country.

That same evening, Lindsey Graham spoke with Trump in a phone conversation of about 25 minutes. Graham had talked repeatedly with the president during the crisis and worried that Trump didn't want to own the coronavirus problem.

"He's got one foot in and one foot out," Graham said, describing the call afterward. "He wants to be a wartime president, but he doesn't want to own any more than he has to own."

Graham told Trump complaints from people about unemployment benefits were a state problem and not his fault, but said, "I think it's your job to fix problems, even if it's not your fault."

The real flaw, Graham said, is testing. He had talked to Fauci. "Dr. Fauci said there's 25 to 50 percent of the population with it that don't even know they have it," he said—referring to the percentage of infected people who don't have symptoms but can spread the virus to others, not the overall U.S. population. "The only way you're ever going to find out is to test. If you don't, you'll reignite the virus."

Graham said he told the president, "You need a plan. You need to explain to the country, we're not helpless against the virus. Here's the game plan to beat the virus.

"You need theater commanders like you've got in Iraq or in Afghanistan. Somebody in charge of testing. Somebody in charge of vaccines. You need a Petraeus to regain your footing. You've lost the momentum. You need a surge. Testing is the biggest flaw we have."

While Trump's job approval rating had reached the highest level of his presidency the week of this interview—about 47 percent in an average of national polls—it was beginning a downward slide as the weeks of the crisis drew on. "You need to peak in October," Graham told Trump. "You need to have the economy showing signs of life. A vaccine on the horizon. Drug therapies that work."

Graham said Biden would be "a rough opponent, but your opponent's the coronavirus."

"That's probably true," Trump answered.

"It is, Mr. President. If you fuck it up, there's nothing you can do to get reelected. If you seem to, you know, manage it well, you're pretty much unbeatable. You keep the body count down, people will see you as somebody that was successful."

As close as he was to the president, Graham felt it was hard to penetrate Trump World and find out who had influence with him. But Graham knew Trump's nature. "His biggest political threat is for people to go without a paycheck for weeks and get disgruntled, and he overreacts and tries to open up the economy too soon. That will be the end of him, because you'll have another round of the virus."

People needed their paycheck, Graham was sure. "He'll say, I'm tired of this, let's open up the economy as the answer, instead of trying to fix the state unemployment systems. If they're out of work for six weeks with no check, they're going to hold him accountable."

THIRTY-NINE

◆━━━◆

On April 6, the day after I spoke with Trump, the president began the day on a cheery note. "LIGHT AT THE END OF THE TUNNEL!" he tweeted around 8:00 a.m. Later that day, American deaths rose to 10,746. One of Trump's allies, U.K. prime minister Boris Johnson, came down with the virus and was moved into intensive care.

It was also becoming clear the virus was disproportionately affecting minority communities. Counties that are majority-Black "have three times the rate of infections and almost six times the rate of deaths as counties where white residents are the majority," *The Washington Post* reported on April 7.

In the four-week period ending April 9, more than 17 million Americans had filed for unemployment, Labor Department figures showed.

On April 10, Trump predicted the U.S. death count would be lower than the minimum predicted by the task force's models. "The minimum number was 100,000 lives, and I think we'll be substantially under that number," he said.

On April 11, the death toll from the coronavirus in the United States climbed above 20,000. The United States surpassed Italy as the country with the most coronavirus fatalities in the world.

On Sunday, April 12, Fauci was asked about a story that Trump had been too slow to act on the virus during an interview on CNN. "If you had a process that was ongoing and started mitigation earlier, you could have saved lives," Fauci said. He added: "If we had, right from the very beginning shut everything down, it may have been different. But there was a lot of pushback for shutting everything down back then."

Several hours later, on Sunday evening, Trump retweeted a tweet that suggested Fauci should be fired, sparking widespread speculation and worry about Fauci's fate. Trump later told me he had a good relationship with Fauci.

Monday afternoon, the president fought back against the criticism in a freewheeling, two-hour press briefing that began with a campaign-ad-style video touting his "decisive action" on the virus. Answering questions from reporters, Trump declined to acknowledge any mistakes and said his administration was "way ahead of schedule" in its response. When asked what he had done to prepare hospitals and ramp up testing with the extra time Trump said he bought by being ahead of schedule, the president called the reporter "disgraceful." He alternated between blaming Democratic governors for failures and claiming he had total authority over the national response. "When somebody is the president of the United States, the authority is total," Trump said. "And that's the way it's got to be. It's total."

The next day, Trump said decisions about when to reopen would be largely in the hands of the governors. The federal government would "be there to help," he said, but "the governors are going to be opening up their states. They're going to declare when."

I reached Trump at the White House about 10:00 p.m. Monday, April 13, to follow up with my questions on the 14 areas to tackle on the virus that we had gone over on April 5.

He wanted to talk about Mueller, impeachment and the news media rather than the policy details of his administration's virus response.

"But you have a series of problems," I said. I went to the list of 14 areas of issues that needed to be integrated in a national response for examples. "Testing."

"We have good testing," he said. That day, *The Washington Post* reported "shortages" of personal protective equipment, or PPE, and swabs needed to perform tests across the country. The country needed "broad, rapid tests" to reopen, the *Post* said, but in an analysis of testing numbers "over the past two weeks, the data suggest that our ability to establish such a system has become less likely, not more."

I asked if he had talked to Bill Gates yet. "You will never regret listening to somebody, sir," I said.

"Gates," Trump said, "and I saw him on some show and read something that he said. And one problem is if it was up to him, he'd keep the country closed for two years and you won't have a country anymore."

"You've got lots of economic problems" too, I said. How about the unemployment benefits and those Small Business Administration loans?

"Those are doing great, Bob."

The vaccines?

"We probably already have the vaccine," Trump said, although the science was far from definitive at the time. "You know the biggest problem though? You have to test it, so you have to make sure—it kills the virus, but you've got to make sure it doesn't kill the person. Can you imagine? You vaccinate a hundred million people and you find out it's poison, right?"

What about China, where the virus originated?

He wanted to talk about trade. "Well," he said, "nobody's been tougher. But we just made a $250 billion trade deal where they've got to buy our stuff."

As part of the Phase One trade deal in January, China had agreed to increase purchases from the U.S. by $200 billion over two years.

He said the Mueller investigation had been "an attempted takedown of the president of the United States."

"I say this to you directly," I said. "What happened in the past, you have to—it's getting in the way, I think, of you doing" your job on the virus.

"This was an attempted and failed coup," Trump said.

"I don't think that's what it is. There's a momentum," I said, to an investigation, trying to offer an analogy. "I wrote four books on George W. Bush's wars. I spent hours with Bush." He was driven by a belief that Saddam Hussein had weapons of mass destruction. There was a momentum and belief a war would be easy.

"Didn't he come out terribly in those books?" Trump asked. The four books had traced Bush's actions after 9/11 and the origins of the wars in Afghanistan and Iraq.

"The third book was called *State of Denial* because he got into denial," I said.

"He spent all that time with you," Trump said. "And you made him look like a fool, okay, in my opinion."

"No, no, no," I replied. "He had his say. He didn't object."

"I hope I'm not wasting a lot of time. Because to be honest, I can think of other things I'd rather be doing."

"I understand," I said. "And my job is to find the best obtainable version—"

"Ugh," Trump said. "And in the end you'll probably write a lousy book. What can I say? I respect you as an author. But if that's an example."

"Okay," I said. "So your big decision now is what to do with the virus."

"I'm comfortable," he said. "I'm comfortable. I'm comfortable. You won't even know if it's a good decision probably by the time you come out with the book. Maybe it'll go away. But it's possible you won't even know about it."

"But I want to describe the process," I said. I asked about Fauci and Birx and how many other experts he'd consulted.

"Well you know Fauci got it wrong," Trump replied. "Fauci said no problem in late February."

Trump was partially correct. Fauci had said on the *Today* show, "Right now the risk is still low, but this could change."

"But I like him," Trump said. "He likes me. We have a good relationship. We'll find out."

"He's become a symbol to lots of people," I said.

"Well, he is," Trump said, "but don't forget the media don't say that he got it wrong. They don't ever print that he got it wrong. If I want, I can do that—but I'm not looking to do that to him. But he did get it wrong. I got it right. I put up a wall, I put up a—basically I put up a ban on China." He was referring to his restrictions on foreigners flying into the United States from China. "I turned out to be right. Almost everybody was against me. Took a lot of heat."

As this book has shown earlier the five key national security and health officials, including Fauci, supported the restrictions.

In our interview April 13, Trump continued: "It's so easily transmissible, you wouldn't even believe it. I was in the White House a couple of days ago. Meeting of 10 people in the Oval Office. And a guy sneezed, innocently. Not a horrible—just a sneeze. The entire room bailed out, okay? Including me, by the way."

"You're risking getting it, of course," I said. "The way you move around and have those briefings and deal with people. Are you worried about that?"

"No, I'm not. I don't know why I'm not. I'm not," he said.

"Why?"

"I don't know. I'm just not."

Shifting the subject, Trump returned to one of his favorite topics. Boeing was in real trouble, he said. "It's not like somebody's going out to buy 50 planes."

"They screwed up in their process," I said. Trump too was struggling with his process. "So you've got the problem that Boeing had, magnified 10,000 times." I again told Trump his handling of the virus was, in my view, the "leadership test" of "a lifetime."

"In terms of the importance of the decision, certainly," he said, agreeing. "But Boeing, boy, what they've done to that company, you have no idea. It's hard to believe, actually."

"And so you've got your process," I said. "You make an—"

Trump blew a frustrated-sounding raspberry.

"—important point," I finished. "By the time my book comes out, I may not know the outcome. But I want to know the process."

"What's your timing?" he asked, referring to the release of the book.

"I want to come out in September or October."

"So if it's a bad book—no, think of it. If it's a bad book, you're right in front of my election. That's a beauty. That's terrible."

Trump said my last book, *Fear*, "was horrendous, but that was my fault. I would've loved to have seen you. But they didn't tell me you were calling. Now it's a much different ballgame. When you called me last time, I was under siege" with the Mueller investigation, he said. I had been unable to reach Trump for an interview for *Fear*, though I tried to make contact through six of his closest advisers. "Okay. I hope you treat me better than Bush, because you made him look like a stupid moron, which he was."

"Sir," I said, "you're going to be judged by how you handle the virus."

"I disagree," he said. "It'll be a part of it, but I've done a lot of other things too."

"It's so monumental," I said.

"I agree," he said. "It's a war. It is a war. It's like being attacked. But I'm not going to be judged entirely by that."

The next evening, Lindsey Graham appeared on Fox News and defended Trump's handling of the coronavirus crisis. "The president has overdelivered when it comes to supplies to the states, hospital beds, ventilators, you name it," Graham told host Sean Hannity.

Trump called Graham after watching the segment.

"You're your own best messenger and you're also your own worst enemy" in the daily virus press conferences, Graham said.

I'm getting nine million watching, Trump said.

"I don't doubt people are watching," Graham said. "Just control the message." People will have a hard time attacking you if you follow the advice of Birx and Fauci on health care and stay in close touch with the governors about a plan to open the economy.

I'm the one that decides everything, Trump said.

"Mr. President, all your haters would love nothing more than you make all the decisions," Graham said. He had to listen to his outside advisers on the task force he'd assembled. "The more buy-in you can get, the wider and deeper net you throw, the better outcomes you'll get."

Trump was focused on China. It was clear to Graham that Trump absolutely believed Xi had lied about the virus and personally misled him. It was hard for Trump, who liked personal relationships and liked it when heads of state were his friends. He'd felt he had a good relationship with Xi, but now he and the entire Republican Party had turned on China. Trump believed that China's decision to withhold information had put him in the bind he was in today, Graham thought.

Trump had recently had a call with Putin, who'd called China the largest out-of-control country on the planet. The wheels were turning on China, Graham saw. Trump and Putin spoke on April 9 and 10. The public statements about the calls released by the White House and the Kremlin did not mention China.

Graham viewed the next two weeks, between mid-April and May 1, as a critical time to make progress against the virus. They'd have to come up with a testing regime that could be built out quickly, he believed, or they were going to lose the whole summer.

Graham told Trump again that his opponent wasn't Biden, "It's the coronavirus." His presidency would be defined by this. He said Trump would win the election if "in October, we've got a vaccine around the corner and therapies on the shelf and we have been doing a lot of testing and there hasn't been a major outbreak and people are beginning to go to football games in small numbers and the economy's back." But "if we go too far too quick and there's another outbreak and the economy falters, you're in trouble."

As April drew on, Trump started to tell advisers he had had enough of the shutdown. We have got to reopen the country, he said. We can't do this. This is doing irreparable damage.

"I am not going to sit back and preside over the funeral of the greatest country in the world," Trump said. "You guys have to realize. You're my medical experts. But my job is to look at a lot of different factors."

The president had developed a complex relationship with Fauci, looking to him for advice even though Fauci was sometimes out of step with Trump's positions and rhetoric.

"Tony, I appreciate what you got to do," Trump told him at one point. "You got to do what you got to do. But I'm the President of the United States. I got to put a lot of factors into my decision."

Trump, at the urging of Treasury Secretary Mnuchin, finally decided the economy needed to be reopened. He sent Fauci, Birx and Redfield to work to develop a plan for reopening the country's schools and businesses.

"Okay," Fauci said, "so if that's the case we've got to have some sort of structure to how we reopen America."

"I don't know how you're going to do it," Trump said. "You guys can do what you want. You know, figure out a way to do it, but we cannot stay closed. We've got to reopen."

The president was emphatic about it, sounding almost as though he were pleading with his public health advisers.

"You know, we've got to do it," Trump said. "We've really got to do it, Deb. We've got to do it, Tony. We just got to do it."

Fauci, Birx and Redfield worked on a plan. Governors could allow schools, businesses and other public spaces to reopen in a three-phase process once their states showed a 14-day downward trajectory in coronavirus cases.

When the health experts finally brought their plan to Trump in the Oval Office, Fauci warned against the possibility governors might rush to reopen too quickly.

"We really got to be careful," Fauci said. "We can't be leapfrogging over one to get to the other. Because if we do there's going to be a danger of a rebound. And the one thing you don't want, Mr. President, is to try to open and then rebound and have to close again. Because that's going to be very embarrassing."

"I hear you," Trump said, "but I don't think that's going to happen. I think we'll be fine."

At one point, Trump asked what the transition plan should be called. Reopening America Again? Opening America Again?

"What sounds better?" Trump asked.

Everyone seemed to know that it was a marketing slogan and Trump would decide on it himself.

On April 16, Trump announced the plan developed by his medical advisers to reopen in a phased process.

"Our nation is engaged in a historic battle against the invisible enemy," Trump said. "To win this fight, we have undertaken the greatest national mobilization since World War Two. . . .

"Based on the latest data, our team of experts now agrees that we can begin the next front in our war, which we're calling 'Opening America Up Again.'"

The president's announcement was overshadowed in the next day's newspapers by grim economic news brought about by the shutdown. "U.S. Unemployment Claims Rise to 22 Million," a banner headline on the front page of *The Washington Post* read the next day. "Broad Shutdown Pushes Americans to Economic Edge" was the top headline in *The New York Times*.

Governors rushed to restart their states' economies following the release of the administration's plan, even though many did not meet the criteria for reopening.

Georgia governor Brian Kemp had on April 20 said he would allow "gyms, hair salons, bowling alleys and tattoo parlors" to open in four days.

Trump opposed the move in public. "I told the governor of Georgia, Brian Kemp, that I disagree strongly with his decision to open certain facilities which are in violation of the phase one guidelines for the incredible people of Georgia," he said at the April 22 task force briefing.

But the next day, Trump changed course and began praising governors who were reopening their states.

"You see states are starting to open up now," Trump said on

April 23, "and it's very exciting to see. I think it's very awe-inspiring. We're coming out of it, and we're coming out of it well."

By the end of April, 30 states had reopened or announced plans to reopen within the next week—even though most were showing more new cases or a higher percentage of positive tests than two weeks earlier, and therefore did not meet White House criteria for reopening.

The virus claimed the lives of more than 50,000 Americans in April alone, bringing deaths to 63,000 total. Still, the president sounded optimistic and upbeat in public.

"It's gonna go," Trump said at a meeting with industry executives on April 29. "It's gonna leave. It's gonna be gone. It's gonna be eradicated."

Relations between the United States and North Korea appeared to worsen over time. Efforts to continue negotiations among diplomats for the two countries in Stockholm in early October 2019 had resulted in failure. "If the United States is not well prepared, we don't know what terrible events will happen," North Korea's lead negotiator Kim Myong Gil said afterward. North Korea had threatened the U.S. with a "Christmas gift" in late 2019.

In March 2020, Trump had sent a letter about the coronavirus to Kim Jong Un.

Trump, speaking in an April 18 press briefing, said that Kim had replied back. "I received a nice note from him recently. It was a nice note," Trump said. "I think we're doing fine."

North Korea's Foreign Ministry, however, denied Kim had sent any such note.

In April and May 2020, Kim mysteriously disappeared for a 20-day period, prompting widespread speculation about his health and whereabouts. At an April 30 news conference, Trump declined to discuss the situation.

"Well, I understand what's going on and I just can't talk about Kim Jong Un right now," Trump said. "I just hope everything is going to be fine. But I do—I do understand the situation very well."

When Kim reemerged in late May, so too did North Korea's plans to continue developing both nuclear and conventional weapons.

State media reported that Kim had presided over a meeting in which the nation's military had set forth "new policies for further increasing the nuclear war deterrence of the country."

The state media report—accompanied by a photo of Kim sitting at a dais—added North Korea had also undertaken measures "for considerably increasing the firepower strike ability of the artillery pieces of the Korean People's Army."

Later, North Korea demolished a liaison office it shared with South Korea—a de facto embassy—and threatened to send troops into the Demilitarized Zone. The office had been closed because of the coronavirus but its destruction seemed an ominous, provocative act.

Several times, Trump underscored for me what he said he believed was his real achievement with Kim: "No war, there was no war. No war!"

Pompeo thought the U.S. was in a reasonably good position with North Korea, though there was no certainty. Pompeo noted that given all the talks and letters and back and forth, Kim never once, directly or indirectly, raised the issue of the 30,000 U.S. troops stationed in South Korea. Kim wanted them there, Pompeo concluded, because they were a restraint on China. That was, yet again, another reason to keep the troops there.

FORTY

"I've got the whole Joint Chiefs of Staff waiting for me downstairs," Trump told me when I reached him by phone around 7:00 p.m. on Wednesday, May 6. "Or at least part of them. So I'm going to have to go."

Trump spoke with me for another fifteen minutes.

I reminded him of something he'd often said to others about the touch needed on the putting green in golf: each putt differed with the weather, the conditions, the way you felt standing on the green. No two putts were the same. You always had to adjust for the shot you were going to make.

"It applies to life," Trump said. "It applies to life, and certainly to what's going on now."

"And so you have to make the calculation how to measure all the conditions" now on the virus, I said.

"That's right. You've got to figure it all out," he said, "otherwise it doesn't work out so well."

"How do you feel about that now?" I asked.

"I feel that we're doing well," Trump said. "We have six months to go." He was talking about his upcoming election, not the state of the country. Some 70,000 people had died from the coronavirus in the United States by then. "I was sailing, sailing," he said. "I was presiding over the greatest economy in the world."

I told him people I talked to were saying the presidential race between him and Biden was now a coin toss.

"You know, maybe," he said. "And maybe not."

That sounded like a good description of a coin toss.

Trump said he needed to be an optimist. "I have to be the cheerleader too. You can't have a deadhead." He added, "Plus we have tremendous stimulus. And there's a pent-up demand that's incredible." He road-tested that new optimism, saying the economy would transition and by "the fourth quarter, we're going to start to see some decent numbers, and next year we're going to have among the best numbers we've ever had, you watch."

He said he thought he would do well in the election "if I can knock out the plague substantially, so that we handle it pretty routinely—and that will happen. And if we can start going up with the economy, I think Trump's going to be very hard to beat."

I asked the president who had been the first person in January or February to alert him to the danger posed by the coronavirus.

"Well, you start seeing it, Bob. You don't have to—you start seeing it."

"When did you see it first?" I asked.

"Well, I'd say toward the end of January, if you think about it." He reminded me of his decision, announced January 31, to restrict travel from China to the United States.

I asked Trump about the state of his relationship with Dr. Anthony Fauci.

"He's a Democrat," Trump said, "but we have a good" relationship. Fauci, who has held his job since the Reagan administration, is not affiliated with any political party, according to Washington, D.C., voting records. "If there was a problem, he'd know about it. So would you."

I told Trump that my reporting showed his national security adviser, Robert O'Brien, had told him in a PDB session on January 28, "Mr. President, this is going to be the biggest national security threat to your presidency." I asked Trump if he remembered that, which in itself had to be a jolt.

"No, I don't," he said. "No, I don't. I'm sure if he said it—you know, I'm sure he said it. Nice guy."

Trump said when he instituted the restrictions on travel from China, "I did that more from what I was seeing on television and reading in the newspapers. I was reading about China."

Two days later, May 8, at a public meeting with Republican members of Congress, Trump disparaged tests and vaccines in a rambling discourse.

He noted that Katie Miller, press spokesperson for Vice President Pence, had just tested positive "out of the blue. That is why the whole concept of tests aren't necessarily great. . . . She was tested very recently and tested negative. And then today, I guess, for some reason, she tested positive."

The coronavirus is highly contagious and spreads easily, including among people who are infected but have no symptoms, which is why health professionals say testing has to be continuous.

Trump went on to disparage vaccines. "Well," he said, "I feel about vaccines like I feel about tests. This is going to go away without a vaccine. . . .

"I just rely on what doctors say. They say it's going to go— that doesn't mean this year, it doesn't mean it's going to be gone, frankly, by the fall or after the fall. But eventually, it's going to go away. The question is will we need a vaccine? At some point, it will probably go away by itself. If we had a vaccine, that would be very helpful. I'd be very happy to have a vaccine."

Redfield, for one, had told associates a vaccine was essential, and it would be a two- to three-year race to get one.

As Friday came to a close several hours later and the Sabbath drew near, Jared Kushner, apparently unaware of Trump's words, gave the fullest endorsement of testing and vaccines in private.

"I actually feel like we're turning a good corner," Kushner told an associate. "I'm feeling like we're managing through the hardest parts and we're heading in a good direction." He hoped to have 80 million tests per month available by September, but the path to get there was uncertain. To that date, May 8, only 8.4 million tests had been conducted in the U.S. since the start of the virus. "We're still figuring it out. But we're figuring out in real time."

Even as Trump vacillated on whether a vaccine was needed to beat the coronavirus, Kushner hoped to put together "an obsessive, focused effort" on vaccine development and was zeroing in on someone to lead it. He wanted to develop a structure for running a vaccine and therapeutics workstream for Trump to sign off on within the week.

The administration's policy and messaging were not settled.

"I've been living in the bunker," Kushner said. "In some ways, getting these things done with these multiagency, high-scrutiny, high-stress environments is like the game of *Frogger*," an arcade game. "You keep running through the highway, and occasionally you get hit by a couple of trucks. But you get back up, and you've just got to keep dodging through and trying to get going."

Two weeks earlier, Trump had called Kushner on a Saturday.

"Jared, I need you to get really focused on testing again, because they're killing me on testing," Trump had said. "Get your team of geniuses on it."

Kushner believed that when it came to the Trump presidency, "there's the above the waves that everyone sees, and then there's the below the waves." He operated below the waves.

He told Trump they were already working on the supply chain.

"The way you solve testing is you have to make an agreement with the governors. You make the agreement with Cuomo, because he's kind of the lead on this stuff right now. Let me call Andrew, try to make a deal."

When they spoke, Cuomo told Kushner, "Look Jared, this is unprecedented territory. We have to get to a place where we can both be saying that has never been done before at this scale. We're both doing the best we can. And we believe we have enough to open up. And the question now is, what is enough to open up?"

Cuomo had to figure out where all his public health labs were and their testing capacity. They would also need a surge of personal protection equipment for administering tests.

Kushner and his supply chain team met with Cuomo for an hour and a half at the White House on April 21 and asked what his testing goal was.

You have to understand, Cuomo said, governors have never done testing before. Nobody knows what enough is yet because we haven't designed what reopening the country looks like. Cuomo was at 20,000 tests per day and said if he could get to 45,000, he would be happy.

"Good," Kushner said. "You have our guarantee that we'll get you to 45,000 a day."

Kushner and his team repeated this with the other 49 governors, asking how many tests they wanted to get done in May and June. They worked with the governors to identify laboratory capacity in their states and promised to get them the needed supplies. When governors complained in the press about a lack of federal effort, Kushner felt it meant they weren't using all of the laboratory resources in their states.

"We probably won't know till July if everything we've done worked," he said, or how much of the economy they had held together.

"We've exploded the testing ecosystem," Kushner said. "I

think you have to grade this on the level of the complexity of the problem. If there was a magic wand you could wave and then have tests for everybody, that'd be a great thing. But that's just not how the world works."

The situation reminded Kushner of bringing exams home from school as a child to his father. He'd said he didn't care what grade Jared got, and only asked one question: Did you do the best you can? On testing, Kushner felt he had. "We've left nothing on the field on this, in the sense that I've spent every hour of my life, I've used every contact I have. I've used every idea I've had. I've tried things. I've pushed people. I made some people happy, I made some people mad. But I've done everything in my power and everything I'm capable of to get these numbers as high as possible."

But as the sun set over Washington that evening, Kushner's best was not enough. His attempt to work below the waves overlooked that many waves were caused by Trump himself.

Kushner's efforts were those of one person in an ambiguously defined role, attempting to remake parts of the government bureaucracy in the image of a streamlined corporation. This would likely be impossible without clear presidential leadership under the best of circumstances.

The Labor Department released a report on the morning of May 8 showing that 20.5 million jobs had been lost in April. The unemployment rate had soared to 14.7 percent. The death toll from the coronavirus was higher than the number of Americans killed in Vietnam. Kushner observed to Trump that the country had experienced more deaths than Vietnam and more job losses than the Great Depression, and his approval numbers had actually held very steady.

This was largely true. Trump's job approval had only fallen two points, from 47 percent to 45 percent, between late March and early May.

Kushner and White House aides Hope Hicks and Dan Scavino

had recently met for dinner. "We were just kind of sitting around saying, you know, it's amazing that we survived through all this," Kushner recalled. Trump's presidency had had so many different chapters: tax cuts, trade deals, deregulation, Mueller, impeachment, pandemic. They'd gone through four chiefs of staff and four national security advisers. "It's been an extraordinary presidency."

Kushner tried to take the long view. "I feel it's not about where you start, it's not about where you are in the middle, it's where you are at the end. And I feel like when I'm done with my time in Washington—like, this isn't my career. It's just a tour of duty to do a service for the country." Kushner said he would look back on the Mexico trade deal, moving the American embassy to Jerusalem and criminal justice reform. "I got ventilators for people who needed ventilators. I helped the president when he needed help. Made a lot of great friendships. And I was able to be a constructive person who helped move the country forward."

Kushner knew the virus might come to define Trump's presidency. "When you're with Trump, you just never know," he said. "That would be the smart-money bet, and I think this is a once-in-a-hundred-year challenge. But I really do believe that he's passed the competency test on the execution."

An abundance of evidence indicated Trump had not. The constant upheaval and deep internal contradictions remained.

On May 15—a week later, right on Kushner's schedule— Trump announced he had selected Dr. Moncef Slaoui, a former vaccine chairman at GlaxoSmithKline, to lead the vaccine effort as an overall czar.

In public comments in the Rose Garden, Slaoui provided some good news: "In fact, Mr. President, I have very recently seen early data from a clinical trial with a coronavirus vaccine. And this data made me feel even more confident that we will be able to deliver a few hundred million doses of vaccine by the end of 2020." A few days later, biotech company Moderna announced promising early results from a phase one trial. Slaoui had served on the board of Moderna until Trump announced his White House role and still had stock options in Moderna valued at over $10 million.

In his speech in the Rose Garden, Trump dubbed the vaccine effort Operation Warp Speed and said he was launching "the most aggressive vaccine project in history. There's never been a vaccine project anywhere in history like this."

But in his next breath, Trump immediately undermined his own effort.

"And I just want to make something clear. It's very important: Vaccine or no vaccine, we're back." The economy was reopening no matter what happened. "In many cases, they don't have vaccines, and a virus or a flu comes, and you fight through it."

FORTY-ONE

———◆———

At 9:18 p.m. on Friday, May 22, 2020, I reached President Trump by phone at the White House.

What about your relationship with Chinese president Xi?

"You know," Trump said to me, "I've very much hardened on China. So, I'm not happy. Let me tell you, I'm not a happy camper."

What turned you? I asked.

"I wanted people to go into China," he said, referring to the crack U.S. team of medical experts Trump, Redfield and Fauci wanted to send to investigate the virus back in January.

I said I knew he had tried twice with Xi.

"He didn't want to do it," Trump said referring to Xi. "I was okay with it. You know why? Because I figured they knew what they were doing. Okay? And they either did or they were incompetent, and either one is no good."

Trump was doing a 180-degree turn from his natural optimism. He seemed to be searching for someone to blame.

"But he stiffed you," I said, "when you look back."

"No he didn't stiff—let's say—you know, he's a prideful person," Trump said. "But he thought he was able to contain it." He added tellingly, "Or not."

Trump continued, "I think what could've happened, Bob, is it got away from them and he didn't want to contain it from the rest of the world because it would've put him at a big disadvantage. And we were already beating them very badly. You know, on trade."

Now I was utterly surprised. It had never occurred to me that Trump would think President Xi had intentionally let the virus spread.

Trump turned to the book. "You're probably going to screw me," Trump said. "You know, because that's the way it goes. Look, Bush sat with you for hours and you screwed him. But the difference was, I ain't no Bush. Boy oh boy, what a mess. I'm trying to get out of that mess that he got us into in the Middle East."

He talked about his ambitious goals for troop withdrawals and obtaining more money from countries the U.S. helped protect, as he put it, "even a little thing like getting massive amounts of money from some of these countries that were freeriding us."

At another point, Trump turned to his judicial nominations. "I'm going to be up to 280 judges very soon. A lot of them are older and we convinced many of them to go on senior leave." He meant senior status, in which judges can effectively retire but stay active on the bench with a reduced case load. This leaves a vacancy the president can fill.

"And more importantly," Trump said, "Obama gave us 142 judges when I came here. They're like golden nuggets." Republicans had controlled the Senate for the last two years of the Obama presidency and Majority Leader McConnell blocked most appointments.

"Do you ever get down?" I asked. "Do you ever feel, my God, an avalanche of one thousand problems has descended on me?"

"This is a good thing," Trump said. "I'm so busy"—and he laughed—"I don't have time to get down. Okay? It's crazy." And he immediately went off on how the United States was providing protection to Saudi Arabia but he had told the Saudis, "You've got to pay."

National Security Adviser Robert O'Brien shared Trump's suspicions about Xi and China. In a West Wing White House meeting more than two weeks later, June 11, O'Brien told an aide that China had concealed what was happening.

"They covered it up," he said, referring to the government's attempt to conceal the genetic sequencing on the virus. "One lab published it, and then it was immediately taken down and the lab was threatened."

O'Brien continued, "It appears that they closed down travel all through China so that this disease couldn't get to Shanghai or Beijing and other key cities. But at the same time they're letting other folks travel from Wuhan to all over Europe and infected Europe and infected the United States. That's not good. But whatever happened the Chinese have repurposed it into a bioweapon. And they're using it, they're attempting to take advantage of Covid to gain a geopolitical advantage over the United States and the free world, and to displace the United States as the leading power in the world."

O'Brien considered Trump's assertion that Xi "didn't want to contain it from the rest of the world because it would've put him at a big disadvantage" as "an absolutely reasonable hypothesis."

In 2020 an aggressive new approach to international relations called "wolf warrior" diplomacy had emerged from a defensive China.

O'Brien said since Covid "hit the whole world, they're using it with what they call their wolf diplomacy and for a long time they were attempting to trade PPE to get access for Huawei into countries. They were bullying countries into thanking them. They were bullying countries into saying things about the U.S. But overall, the theme is that they, as an authoritarian government, with all their surveillance state and their concentration camps and all that sort of thing, offer a better alternative for the world, a more efficient alternative, a kind of weird, nationalistic, technocratic alternative to the world that's better than liberal democracy. And Covid is an example of why the world should embrace China and Chinese values, and the Chinese form of hybrid capitalist-mercantilist-communist government."

O'Brien said, "they're taking every measure possible during this crisis to displace the United States. And we've got a hell of a fight on our hands.

"They covered up a lot about this virus because they want to present this model of ruthless efficiency," he said.

For example the Chinese have said that somewhere between 4,000 and 15,000 people in China died from the virus. O'Brien said he believed that the true number was in the 100,000 range, about the same as in the U.S. in late May.

O'Brien described an apocalyptic wasteland gleaned from social media, before it was removed by government censors. "They welded people into their apartments. They eventually came in a couple weeks later and pried open the doors and opened up, there were a lot of elderly people that died of dehydration and starvation. There were all kinds of people that hung themselves out their windows."

O'Brien concluded the consequences were dire. "If we lose our economic edge and we lose our economic might and stay closed for too much longer, we might be in a position where we couldn't stay ahead or maybe we'd get behind and couldn't catch up."

For CDC chief Redfield the Chinese failure to close down international flights was disastrous. He told colleagues the United

States had silently filled with Covid-19 infections "from Italy, Spain, Germany, France, Great Britain, Belgium." All this late-winter travel brought clusters of Covid to the United States. "Also unknown to us that probably half of those clusters weren't even symptomatic, so you couldn't find them" with airport screening.

"It was difficult to understand how China had aggressive travel restrictions within China, and yet did not move to any travel restrictions" for people who wanted to leave China and go abroad, Redfield said.

"If there could have been one major, global action that could've really saved hundreds of thousands of lives, it's if they had just shut down their out-of-China travel at the same time they shut down their intra-China travel.

"They really started moving in the latter part of January. That's where they quarantined people. That's where they shut down the city. That's where they stopped the trains. They really locked down all of Wuhan at one point. I think they quarantined over 11 million people. You couldn't go from Wuhan to Beijing, but you could go Wuhan to London."

FORTY-TWO

———— ◆ ————

On May 25, a Minneapolis police officer was caught on video with his knee on the neck of George Floyd for eight minutes and 46 seconds, torturing and killing Floyd, a 46-year-old Black man. A massive wave of angry protests erupted in more than 2,000 cities and towns on a scale not seen in America since the Civil Rights Movement and the Vietnam War. "Black Lives Matter" extended its reach as a rallying cry against racism and police brutality.

While most of the protests against police misconduct and racial inequality were peaceful, television news was filled with chaotic scenes of rioting, looting and buildings set afire in major cities.

In Washington, D.C., a fire was set in the basement nursery of the historic St. John's Episcopal Church, 1,000 feet from the White House, on Sunday, May 31. Following the fire, the church had been boarded up. A city curfew set by D.C. mayor Muriel Bowser was scheduled to begin the next day, June 1, at 7:00 p.m.

Trump, in a phone call with governors that afternoon, stressed the need to use force against the demonstrators. He wanted an energetic crackdown.

"You have to dominate," Trump said. "If you don't dominate, you're wasting your time. They're going to run all over you, you'll look like a bunch of jerks. You have to dominate, and you have to arrest people, and you have to try people and they have to go to jail for long periods of time."

That day, hundreds of mostly peaceful protesters gathered in the area around Lafayette Square, a seven-acre public park between St. John's Church and the White House.

At around 6:30 p.m., without apparent provocation, officers in riot gear suddenly advanced on the protesters, tossing riot control devices into the crowd that created loud explosions, sparks and smoke. Videos show officers pushing protesters to the ground, shooting some with rubber projectiles and spraying others with a chemical agent. Authorities shot "pepper balls"—projectiles containing a powdered chemical that irritates the eyes and nose—at the protesters. Officers on horseback pushed protesters further away from Lafayette Square.

"I didn't see any provocation that would warrant the deployment of munitions," Mayor Bowser said afterward.

It was a jarring display of militarized government forces against those exercising their First Amendment rights to assemble.

At 6:48 p.m., just minutes after forces dispersed the protesters, Trump began a speech in the White House's Rose Garden about the unrest sweeping across the country.

"All Americans were rightly sickened and revolted by the brutal death of George Floyd," Trump said. "My administration is fully committed that, for George and his family, justice will be served. He will not have died in vain. But we cannot allow the righteous cries and peaceful protesters to be drowned out by an angry mob.

"The biggest victims of the rioting are peace-loving citizens in our poorest communities, and as their president, I will fight to keep them safe. I will fight to protect you. I am your president of law and order, and an ally of all peaceful protesters."

Trump spent most of the seven-minute address promising to combat what he described as "riots and lawlessness that has spread throughout our country." He recommended that each governor deploy the National Guard "in sufficient numbers that we dominate the streets."

"If a city or a state refuses to take the actions that are necessary to defend the life and property of their residents," he said, "then I will deploy the United States military and quickly solve the problem for them."

After his Rose Garden address, at about 7 p.m., Trump left the White House grounds. A coterie of advisers followed, including Secretary of Defense Mark Esper, Chairman of the Joint Chiefs General Mark Milley in a camouflage uniform, White House chief of staff Mark Meadows, O'Brien, Attorney General Barr, Kushner and Ivanka. The president walked the 1,000 feet north through Lafayette Square to St. John's, known as "the Church of the Presidents."

When the president reached the church, Ivanka pulled a Bible out of her white handbag and handed it to her father.

Trump stood in front of the church for about two minutes, holding the Bible awkwardly and waving it around.

"Is that your Bible?" a reporter asked.

"It's a Bible," Trump answered.

A reporter asked the president what his thoughts were.

"We have a great country," he said. "That's my thoughts."

It appeared the president had walked to the church to give photographers and cameramen an opportunity to take his picture with the burned church and a Bible as props.

After a few moments, Trump motioned to his advisers and Meadows, Barr, Esper, O'Brien and Press Secretary Kayleigh McEnany walked over to join him in standing in a line in front of the church.

"I am outraged," the Episcopal bishop of Washington, Mariann

Edgar Budde, said afterward. "Everything he has said and done is to inflame violence."

"This evening," Episcopal Church Presiding Bishop Michael Curry said, "the President of the United States stood in front of St. John's Episcopal Church, lifted up a bible, and had pictures of himself taken. In so doing, he used a church building and the Holy Bible for partisan political purposes."

Later, the White House and the U.S. Park Police defended the dispersal of the crowd, citing "violent protesters." Footage of the protest shows that at least two protesters threw water bottles at the police.

About three hours later, two helicopters operated by the D.C. Army National Guard hovered over the remaining protesters. The helicopters flew as low as 45 feet—below the heights of some buildings—creating wind speeds equivalent to a tropical storm, snapping thick tree limbs, swirling the air with dust and broken glass. Many protesters ran for cover in panic and confusion. The use of helicopters to disperse civilians is a common tactic in war zones.

Mattis broke his long-held silence, issuing a statement.

"When I joined the military, some 50 years ago," Mattis wrote, "I swore an oath to support and defend the Constitution. Never did I dream that troops taking that same oath would be ordered under any circumstance to violate the Constitutional rights of their fellow citizens—much less to provide a bizarre photo op for the elected commander in chief, with military leadership standing alongside. . . .

"Donald Trump is the first president in my lifetime who does not try to unite the American people—does not even pretend to try," he continued. "Instead, he tries to divide us. We are witnessing the consequences of three years of this deliberate effort. We are witnessing the consequences of three years without mature leadership."

Trump responded with a series of tweets later that evening. "I didn't like his 'leadership' style or much else about him, and many others agree," Trump tweeted about Mattis. "Glad he is gone!"

Soon after, Mayor Bowser had "Black Lives Matter" painted in giant yellow letters on the street leading to Lafayette Square and the White House.

Protests against racial injustice and inequities continued to fill streets across the country in the weeks that followed.

Two days after his law-and-order speech, Trump returned my call. It was the morning of June 3.

"Hi, Bob, how's the book? Am I keeping you busy enough?"

"You give me new chapters," I said.

"Yeah. It's law and order, Bob, law and order. We're right where I want."

"Do you have a few minutes to—"

"Law and order, Bob." He launched into his talking points about how the economy would start to get better, how the states that were reopening were strong, and how the administration was doing very well on vaccines and therapeutics for the virus.

"And we're going to get ready to send in the military slash National Guard to some of these poor bastards that don't know what they're doing, these poor radical lefts." And he added pointedly, "Of course, you're a poor radical left to an extent, I guess."

I asked if Trump had watched the George Floyd tape.

"Yeah, I saw it. It was terrible. I thought it was a terrible thing. I've said it—" He reminded me that in an earlier speech in Florida for a NASA and SpaceX rocket launch, he had talked about George Floyd. He had devoted eight minutes to Floyd.

Where did you watch it? Did he watch the whole thing, or just parts of it?

"Sure I got to watch it. Everybody did. All you need was a television. I watched it numerous times. I mean, mostly I was in the White House, upstairs, because I don't get to watch much television during the day. I mean, upstairs. And I watched it. It's been on, it's been on a lot. No, it's a terrible thing, and strong feeling toward it. I don't like it at all. I'm very unhappy about it. And action has been taken and it will be taken, and it will be dealt with. And I think the riots are—I put it out in Minneapolis. That was the worst one of all. They were ripping down the city. They're all liberal Democrats, every one of them is a liberal Democrat. Hard to believe, right?"

"How did you decide, okay, I'm going to give that law-and-order speech?"

"It was very easy for me to decide," he said. "Because I looked and there was no law and order. And the radical left Dems and the Democrat—they're all Democrat mayors or governors. I mean, every one of them. Every one of them. Every one where there's weakness is that. So that was an easy speech for me to write. Usually I write them and/or substantially adjust them."

"Did somebody help you?"

"Yeah, I get people. They come up with ideas. But the ideas are mine, Bob. The ideas are mine. Want to know something? Everything's mine. You know, everything is mine."

I asked about his walk to St. John's and the treatment of the protesters there.

"It's total bullshit," he said. "They didn't use tear gas."

Firsthand witnesses, including reporters, and videos showed law enforcement officers using pepper spray, smoke canisters and pepper balls to disperse the crowd.

"Well," Trump said, "these nice, wonderful people tried to burn down the church the day before. You know, they were all saying, these were nice people. Well, they weren't nice people. They were rough people. And the day before, they tried to burn down the church. And so now the Republicans are all on my side.

By the way, I had a big night last night. We won all of—every race that I endorsed. And I'm 64 and 0 this congressional cycle, 64 and 0 on endorsements. Both wins, and wins in primaries. And many of them were losing before I endorsed."

At the time it was true.

"And so the idea of standing there with the Bible, that's quite a photo," I said.

"It's my idea. Nobody else. And a lot of people loved it."

"A lot of people did," I acknowledged. "And I'm sure a lot of people don't."

"Perhaps."

"Why did you decide to use the Bible as a symbol?" I asked.

"Because I thought it was terrible that they tried to rip down a church that was built simultaneously with the White House, and whose first parishioner was James Madison. And I thought it was a terrible thing, and a terrible symbol that they could do such a thing. And made a strong statement, and people loved it. Other than the radical left, people loved it. And by the way, they ought to appreciate it, but they tried to knock it as much as possible."

News reports said he had been rushed to the emergency White House bunker, called the Presidential Emergency Operations Center (PEOC) on May 29. "Did you go down in the bunker?"

"For a period," Trump said. "I had a choice. And it was really more of an inspection than anything else. Because they wanted me to inspect it. It was a very minor event, and I just went down to inspect it. It was, first of all, it was during the day, where there was no problem during the day at all.

"You know," Trump continued, "when people get rambunctious, it happens during the night. This was during the day, long before there was any darkness. And they said, would you like to inspect it now? Would you like to go down? I said, oh, I'll go down. And then they write a fake piece in *The New York Times*, like I'm sitting in a bunker. That was during the day and it was the inspection, the second time I've ever seen it."

"Were you there a long time, or just looking around?"

"Fifteen minutes. Just looking around. Looking around, came right up—it was during the day."

"It's not exactly a cozy place, is it?" I said.

"No, it's just—you know, it was really, you're supposed to go and inspect it. And I did. And I did it. They said this would be a good time. I said, why? They said, well, we got people outside, but there's no problem. It was, I think 4:00, 5:00 in the afternoon. It was during the day. It was beautiful."

"Who suggested that you inspect it?" I asked.

"Huh? One of the Secret Service guys said, you don't have to do it now—I didn't have to go down—it was, I went down as an inspection. And they said I went down. And the reason I went down as an inspection was, it was appropriate to do because I had to go down and inspect it anyway. And I got—and they made it sound like I was in there. Not that there'd be anything wrong— plenty of people have been. Not a big deal. Not a big deal. And down there's not a big deal. But I was only there for 15, 20 min- utes. And it was more walking around, looking at things."

"I see. And you didn't go again?" I asked.

"No, I didn't go again. I went one time, very quickly. It was an inspection, and they made it sound like it was—again, Bob, it was during the day."

"Listen, that's why I'm asking," I said.

Attorney General Barr would later say on Fox News that it was not an inspection. "Things were so bad that the Secret Service recommended the president go down to the bunker."

"There were very few people during the day," Trump went on. "There were almost no protesters."

The police had violently broken up the June 1 protest.

"No," Trump said, "that's only if you watch CNN and if you watch MSDNC. But—or you read *The New York Times* or your favorite newspaper, *The Washington Post*. Uh, outside of that, the people are very unhappy. These are arsonists, they're thugs, they're anarchists and they're bad people. They're bad people. Very bad people. Very dangerous people.

"Even the peaceful protesters?" I said. "There are a lot of peaceful protesters."

"There are not many. I'll tell you what. Not many. These are very well-organized thugs. You'll be seeing that when it comes out. These are very well-organized. Antifa's leading it. These are very well-organized events. Very well-organized."

Antifa, an abbreviation for "Anti-fascist," is a decentralized movement. It is not an organization and does not have a leader or membership dues.

"Well," I said, "we're going into the election. Everyone keeps asking, suppose it's a close election, and it's contested? What are you going to do? Everyone says Trump is going to stay in the White House if it's contested. Have you—"

"Well, I'm not—I—I don't want to even comment on that, Bob. I don't want to comment on that at this time."

Trump referenced the book I was working on about him. "If I have a fair book, it's going to be a great book. Did you see the book they wrote about Trump and Churchill? Did you see it? It just came out." He was referring to *Trump and Churchill: Defenders of Western Civilization*, by Nick Adams, a conservative commentator. "And he gave me a rating as one of the greatest presidents ever."

Trump turned to his future. "The economy, I'll do it again. It's already started. By September, October, the economy will start heading up. And once it starts heading up, and in big numbers, we're going to have a phenomenal following year. But by September, October—maybe sooner—but by September, October, you'll start to see tremendous jumps in employment and GDP. And by October it'll be really big. And the numbers will be announced and I'll win the election. Watch. Better than where I was before. Better. Where I was riding high."

I returned to the immediate story of the massive protests. "You bought ownership of the whole problem," I said, "the racial tensions, by making your declaration of law and order."

"Law and order, that's right," he said. "I'll take my chances. It would be an honor to get a good book from you, but that probably won't happen, but that's okay, too. Thanks, Bob."

◆ ◆

FORTY-THREE

After Trump stood in front of the church waving a Bible Lindsey Graham privately said that night, "I've never been more worried than I am right now." In Graham's view, Trump could have chosen three ways to respond to the racial unrest unleashed by the George Floyd murder: "George Wallace, Robert Kennedy or Richard Nixon."

Graham believed Trump had chosen Wallace, the firebrand former Alabama governor, who embodied defiant resistance to civil rights. In his inaugural address Wallace had promised "segregation now, segregation tomorrow, segregation forever." In 1963 he stood in the door at the University of Alabama to block two Black students from enrolling.

Trump had poured gasoline on the tensions. Graham wished Trump would, instead, "appoint a presidential commission to deal with policing and race. And then get tough on the protesters." The key was to redefine the way police interacted with their communities.

Graham wondered, "Do you really want to deploy the active-duty military against Americans unless you have to? The military has a lot of respect from everybody. Do you really want to get them in the middle of this shitshow?"

"Right now his presidency's very much at risk," Graham said. "This thing has the potential now to eat him alive."

But at the moment Trump and Graham were not talking. Trump wanted Graham, as chairman of the Senate Judiciary Committee, to call former president Obama as a witness in his investigation of the origins of the Russia investigation and allegations the Obama administration had spied on the 2016 Trump campaign.

Graham had refused publicly, saying, "I understand President Trump's frustration, but be careful what you wish for."

But the freeze-out did not last long. Trump and Graham needed each other, or at least their cherished phone dialogue. In a series of phone calls through the first two weeks of June, Graham presented a grim assessment directly to Trump.

"Right now," Graham told Trump, "if the election were held, you would lose."

Trump disagreed vociferously, saying he didn't believe that at all.

The photo op in front of the church backfired, Graham said.

Again Trump disagreed strongly.

The anti-police movement no doubt was overreaching, Graham said. Trying to defund the police or banning them from a stretch of occupied streets in downtown Seattle was untenable. "Some of these people are just insane," Graham said. "But you've got to be more than the law-and-order guy. You're going to have to be the guy that puts points on the board for the country."

Graham knew Trump's Democratic opponent Joe Biden better than probably any Republican. He had been close friends with the former vice president, traveled the world with him, and publicly praised him as a thoroughly decent human being. "I don't think you can disqualify Joe Biden," Graham told Trump. "You can make people have doubts about him. But you need to show you can solve problems."

Graham said he had doubts about a heavy law-and-order campaign similar to Nixon's in 1968. "Richard Nixon was the challenger, not the incumbent." As the incumbent president, Graham said, Trump had to show he could govern, make changes and improve the lives of people—examples of points on the board.

Never shy about sharing his ideas, Graham had a three-part plan: police reform through an executive order, a massive infrastructure bill to rebuild roads and schools, and—an old Graham favorite—protect DACA, Deferred Action for Childhood Arrivals.

DACA, put in place by Obama, protected more than 700,000 undocumented young adults who had been brought to the United States as children. They were called "Dreamers." The Trump administration had ended the program, and the matter was in the courts.

"But if you could solve the DACA problem, or make an incredible effort to solve it," Graham told Trump, "then that becomes your criminal justice reform for the Hispanic community."

Graham told Trump he believed the Democrats would overplay their hand. "If it weren't for the Democratic Party, the Republican Party would fold," Graham said. "They always keep us in the game. They're able to throw us a lifeline. So this defund the police, occupation of Seattle and this crazy shit is going to put you back in the game. But you have to solve problems. You've got to show that your presidency is worth voting for because you can get something done. So go big on infrastructure. Deal with DACA. And do police reform."

Graham pushed: "Piling up a series of field goals and maybe a touchdown to grab the lead in the fourth quarter" was the way to win.

Trump wasn't buying it. In golf every player had a favorite club he wanted to hit, especially under pressure, and Graham knew that the president wanted to use his "go-to shot" of division. He argued that labeling Trump's opponents and enemies and out-tweeting Biden would not work here. Trump had to deliver.

The president still was not buying.

Graham was also pushing to get $3 to $4 billion for the Global Alliance for Vaccines and Immunization to distribute a Covid-19 vaccine in the developing world if the United States ever came up with one. Graham was also trying to get another $3 to $4 billion to buy the vaccine. Good policy and good politics, he figured.

Former president George W. Bush, a big promoter of aid to the developing world, called Graham.

"You tell the president if he does this," Bush said, "it'll really help him a lot."

"I will," Graham said. "Would you want to talk to Trump?"

"No, no," Bush said. "He'd misconstrue anything I said." Trump regularly criticized Bush.

"Yeah," said Graham, "you're probably right. President Trump can be a handful, but he's a smart guy."

Graham, who was running for reelection himself and had a large stake in the outcome for Trump and the Republican Party, made his rounds. He called Trump's campaign manager Brad Parscale.

"Trump's problem is all about tone," Parscale said. "There's no revolting against Trump policy out there." They needed a softer Trump. "Police reform and softening him up, and policy initiatives that would soften him up is what we need to do."

Parscale added, "Police reform is really as much about moderate whites as it is about the African American community politically." He said that police reform would help with suburban women as would DACA and infrastructure, anything that improves hope for the economy.

In another conversation, Trump told Graham that he wanted to go higher than $3 trillion for another economic stimulus and recovery package.

"Don't worry about the base," Graham said. "Nobody elected you as a fiscal conservative." He tried to reinforce his plan. "Just imagine the combination of police reform—bipartisan. DACA—bipartisan. Infrastructure—bipartisan. Stimulus—bipartisan. A growing economy. All before November."

A big infrastructure package would give the country a needed facelift, Graham said. No other Republicans would spend the needed money. Not George W. Bush and not Graham's great friend, the late John McCain.

Trump seemed to be listening.

"The virus could undercut everything I just talked about," Graham said.

"Why'd you tell me that?" Trump said.

"It's just true."

Trump said again that it was all unfair that this was dropped on him.

"Well, it's unfair to everybody. It's part of being president. Things happen."

They agreed that there was no way to shut down the country again even as virus outbreaks were causing great alarm in lots of southern and western states.

The infection rates—the number of cases—didn't worry Graham that much. The majority of people had mild symptoms, and many had no symptoms at all. "What I care about is how many people go in the hospital and the number of deaths due to the virus. Can you control the infections so that you don't overrun the hospitals?"

So much hinged on the vaccines. Trump's opponent was now fear, Graham told Trump.

On police reform, Graham advised. "You've got to push your base." That would mean "pissing cops off," he said and perhaps supporting a file-sharing system—so if one cop was fired from one police department, that record would follow him to the next—and making it easier to fire police officers.

Trump had initially resisted criminal justice reform, known as the First Step Act, reforming prisons and sentencing passed by

Congress and signed into law in 2018, but Kushner had pushed it hard and it passed with large bipartisan majorities. It was working politically so Trump now clung to it. Graham realized Trump rewrote the history on that and said he had always been for it.

Graham told Trump that the photo-op at St. John's Church didn't help his cause much.

"Christians loved it," Trump said.

"Well, I'm not a good Christian," Graham said, "but I'm a Christian. And I particularly didn't love it. I think most people don't like waving the Bible. Mr. President, that just didn't work."

Though they had started out as opponents in 2016 when Graham had run for president, Graham had come to genuinely like Trump. It was not just the political advantage that accrued from a public friendship with a president, or the influence Graham wielded with Trump by staying in his orbit with frequent phone calls and golf outings. Trump could have a consequential presidency despite all the drama, and Graham wanted to remain a Trump ally. If the president considered someone an ally, he would accept their criticism. He would never accept criticism if he came to see them as an enemy.

"But it's all at risk now," he told Trump candidly. Part of the question was whether Trump could respond to the political and emotional stress. After the George Floyd murder, Graham believed there was no going back politically. He did not believe Trump needed to show a conversion on the road to Damascus on race, but he did need to define the problem more honestly.

"It's a once-in-a-lifetime chance to reenergize America," Graham told Trump. "If you do these three things right"—DACA, police reform and infrastructure—"you will have a more consequential presidency and you are more likely to get reelected. If you try to be the law-and-order president alone, you're going to lose."

FORTY-FOUR

The first six months of 2020 had been a taxing time for Fauci, who was trying to balance what he believed was the obligation to provide the public with accurate medical information and advice necessary to fight Covid-19 with some of Trump's less than helpful statements and attitudes.

In Fauci's view some of Trump's early decisions had been his finest hours—restricting travel from China (January 31) and Europe (March 11) and asking sick Americans to stay home and all to practice good hygiene with his initial "15 Days to Slow the Spread" (March 16) and then extending it for another 30 days (March 29). The president had stepped up to the task and had listened to Birx, Redfield, himself and others.

When Trump engaged in wishful thinking about the virus, musing it would disappear on its own, Fauci at least could correct the record on television.

Then on April 7 Trump said of the virus, "It will go away." He had said that many times before but on that day, Mark Meadows, in his first week as White House chief of staff, had installed a new White House press secretary, Kayleigh McEnany. A 31-year-old unbending Trump campaign spokesperson and Harvard Law School graduate, McEnany limited Fauci's television appearances.

Under the system, all the networks and cable news outlets had to submit a request for a Fauci interview in writing to the Department of Health and Human Services, who then in turn would pass it to the White House for approval. It was like the requests were disappearing into a black hole. No action, no response. One in ten of the requests would be approved so it would not look like Fauci was being completely muzzled.

On April 17, in the middle of what was supposed to be the 30-day extension of the "15 Days to Slow the Spread," Trump tweeted "Liberate Minnesota," "Liberate Michigan," and "Liberate Virginia," expressing support for a subversion of his own guidelines. Fauci's jaw dropped. He asked his colleagues, What was going on?

The answer was obvious. The Finest Hours were over. The White House and Trump were laser-determined to open up the country. That was Plan A. There was no Plan B, an essential, Fauci believed, when dealing with a virus that was out of control.

Fauci gave an interview to *Science* magazine and said that when things were said at the Coronavirus Task Force press conferences which were not factual, "I can't jump in front of the microphone and push him down."

That was as edgy as Fauci got in public though he often adopted a challenging tone with the president at the daily task force press conferences.

After the president said once again that the virus would disappear, Fauci decided he had better be the skunk at the picnic at the next task force meeting, which was held in the Oval Office and was supposed to be confidential.

"We need to be careful," Fauci said, intentionally addressing not just Trump but the other task force members who were present. "This is not going to just disappear. It's not going to go away by itself. It's going to be up to us." They had to continue to mitigate and find a vaccine.

"I know a guy who got sick," the president responded, repeating an anecdote they had all heard before, changing the subject and overpowering the session.

"The president is on a separate channel," Fauci later told others. Trump's leadership was "rudderless."

Another time Fauci made an appeal to others in the Oval Office after the president had strayed from the facts in the press briefing. "We can't let the president be out there being vulnerable," Fauci said, "saying something that's going to come back and bite him."

Pence, chief of staff Mark Meadows, Kushner and aide Stephen Miller tensed up at once. It was palpable to Fauci. It was as if they were saying you can't be talking to the president that way. They were an unyielding fortress around the president.

Often when Fauci challenged Trump on something he had said, Trump would jump in and change the subject. Fauci marveled at Trump, who would hopscotch from one topic to another. "His attention span is like a minus number," Fauci said privately.

Trump seemed interested in one outcome. "His sole purpose is to get reelected," Fauci told an associate. Fauci was particularly disappointed in Kushner, who talked like a cheerleader as if everything was great.

Fauci tried to preserve the candor but with the gentle touch.

"Mr. President," he said another time, "I really would be careful about saying it that way. They are going to come back and criticize you."

"Who gives a shit?" Trump replied. "They criticize me no matter what I do anyway." Trump never invited Fauci or the other medical professionals to brief him in detail or provide a tutorial. Nor did Fauci ever ask for extended time or time alone with the president.

Fauci gave high marks to Matt Pottinger for realizing China's deceit. Going back to late January, Fauci and Pottinger had a serious conversation about how China had covered up the 2003 SARS epidemic, not telling the public the truth for three months after the outbreak. Fauci publicly said China had been "egregiously nontransparent" during SARS.

For Pottinger, the new virus fit the old pattern. China was doing it again. "They're the source of it," Pottinger said. "You know you can't believe anything they say. I know them. I was a reporter there. They're all lying. They're full of crap. It's worse than they're really saying."

Pottinger said he had a doctor friend in China with impeccable credentials and access to solid information who was passing it on. The doctor said, "Don't believe their numbers. They're all lying to you."

Fauci thought Pottinger was talking as if the sky was falling and way overstating the case against China. "We got to be more aggressive in trying to control it," Pottinger told Fauci, "because countries like Singapore and Taiwan have been able to control it by being very aggressive in shutting things down." Hong Kong had done the same.

When the pandemic later exploded, Fauci said, "Wait a minute. Matt was right all along. This thing is really out of control."

Despite Trump's ambivalent public statements that he thought the virus would dissipate with or without a vaccine, the push for a vaccine was nonstop. As part of Operation Warp Speed, drug companies were being prepaid billions of dollars to manufacture millions of doses of drugs that might not pass trials or even be used. The design was to ensure the drug companies immediately would have the supply after a new vaccine was approved.

In an Oval Office task force meeting at 4:00 p.m. on June 2, Moncef Slaoui, the new vaccine czar and head of Operation Warp Speed, and all the others told the president that December was the earliest a vaccine might be ready. More likely it would be January, February or March 2021.

"Can't we get a vaccine earlier?" Trump asked. "What about the fall? How about in September and October?"

The answer was no.

Fauci said the president might hear or read about the Chinese or the Brits or others claiming they could get a vaccine in September or October. But that would not be one that cleared the stringent U.S. regulatory hurdles. It would be almost impossible to prove such an early vaccine would be safe and effective.

Trump called me unexpectedly on Friday, June 19, at 10:30 a.m. We had not spoken for over two weeks.

I said I was finishing a draft of this book, and was running into some roadblocks with his calls with Chinese president Xi Jinping.

"I had very good calls with him," Trump said, "but since they sent us the plague I'm not so thrilled with them, okay?"

I reminded him he had previously told me this. But my reporting showed that some of his aides were suggesting something more sinister. "There's some evidence that this is quite dark and nefarious. That they're allowing—allowed the virus to spread. What do you think?"

"I'm the one that said that louder and clearer than anybody," Trump said, "if you want to know the truth. I'm the leader of that group. Because I think they could have kept it—Now, it is starting up in Beijing, which is interesting. Because I was saying—but, you know, they've got a problem in Beijing."

"What are they up to?" I asked. "What's their motive?"

"I think they could have done a hell of a lot better job stopping it coming out to the rest of the world, including the United States and Europe," Trump said.

"Do you think they intentionally let it come to the United States and the rest of the world?" I asked.

"There's a possibility. I don't say they did, but there's certainly a possibility." He added, "But it came to Europe, the United States and the rest of the world. Yep."

"If they actually did this intentionally, President Trump—"

"The ink wasn't dry on my great deal on trade," he said. "They're buying a lot of stuff. And they're—by the way, they are buying. And that's one of the things I watch every day. They're buying a lot. They're buying tremendous amounts of farm product and stuff. But the ink wasn't dry when the plague came in."

Two days earlier, *The Wall Street Journal* had published an excerpt of former national security adviser John Bolton's book, *The Room Where It Happened*. In it, Bolton wrote of a meeting between Trump and Xi: "Trump then, stunningly, turned the conversation to the coming U.S. presidential election, alluding to China's economic capability and pleading with Xi to ensure he'd win. He stressed the importance of farmers and increased Chinese purchases of soybeans and wheat in the electoral outcome."

Trump went on. "Bob, watch what happens, okay. Remember, I told you, the stock market is close to an all-time high and we're not finished with the pandemic yet. I have—I have a rally tomorrow night in Oklahoma. Over 1.2 million people have signed up. We can only take about 50, 60 thousand. Because, you know, it's a big arena, right? But we can take 22,000 in one arena, 40,000 in another. We're going to have two arenas loaded. But think of that. Nobody ever had rallies like that."

"Your reaction to the protests?" I asked, switching subjects.

"I think that the weak liberal Democrats have handled their cities very badly. And I think the strong people have handled it very well. You'll see what happens in Oklahoma. You'll see what happens in Oklahoma. We're all set."

"We share one thing in common," I said. "We're white, privileged. My father was a lawyer and a judge in Illinois. And we know what your dad did. And do you have any sense that that privilege has isolated and put you in a cave, to a certain extent, as it put me—and I think lots of white, privileged people—in a cave? And that we have to work our way out of it to understand the anger and the pain, particularly, Black people feel in this country?"

"No," Trump said. "You really drank the Kool-Aid, didn't you? Just listen to you," he said, his voice mocking and incredulous. "Wow. No, I don't feel that at all."

"You don't?"

"I've done more for the Black community than any president in history with the possible exception of Lincoln," repeating one of his favorite lines. He had said so publicly at least five times by that point in 2020 alone.

"I don't think it's the Kool-Aid, Mr. President, I think there is a reality out there that Black people feel. And part of our job is—I mean, you and I talked about this some months ago, that you're governing in an environment where there are two Americas—"

"Yep," he said. "And by the way, Bob, it's been that way for a long time. Longer than when I've been here. It's been that way under Obama and it's been that way a long time. There was great division under Obama. It was a much more silent division, but there was tremendous hatred and tremendous division, more than there is now."

"You're convinced of that?"

"Yeah. I am."

In the 2016 election, Trump had clearly seen and used those divisions—the seething undertow of rage and resentment.

"Look, we talked about this," I said. "We talked about history's clock, remember that?" Six months earlier in December I had referenced Barbara Tuchman's famous 1962 book *The Guns of August* about how World War I had been an accidental war. I had described the beginning of Tuchman's book to Trump: a scene about the old order not realizing it was dying on history's clock.

"And I said my analysis was that you came and seized history's clock when you were elected. And that the Democrats and your party, the Republicans, did not know what was going on in America. Remember that? Agree with that?"

"Sure," Trump said. "I do. I do. It's still true. It's still true about, you know, the Democrats and many people in the Republican Party. But I know what's going on. I know what's going on."

"There's been a shift," I said. "And it's substantial. And it's, I think, incumbent on white, privileged people like myself, like you, to say—and I don't think this is Kool-Aid. I think it is understanding points of view that may not come to us naturally."

"But I don't have to be there to understand a point of view," he said. "I don't have to be Black to understand the Black point of view. I don't have to have gone through personal slavery in order to understand the horrible atrocity that people have suffered. I don't have to. You know, I don't have to put myself in that position. I can fully understand it without being in that position."

"Do you consider it an atrocity?"

"Oh, absolutely," he said. "Slavery? Absolutely."

"And what's happened after, up to this day, that we do not have a system of equality and equal opportunity?"

You can hear him exhale on the tape. "Well—"

"I'm pushing," I said.

"It's gone on for a hundred years, Bob."

"Sure, but—"

"It's been going on for a hundred years plus," he said.

"You see what I'm asking?"

"I fully do. No, it's very fair. It's been going on for a hundred years plus. It's been going on for a long time. And we've made a lot of progress in a lot of different ways. And a lot of progress is being made as we speak—I mean right now. More than you would even think. But this has been going on for many, many years. Many, many years."

"We've talked about this," I said. "Your job is to bring people together?"

"I agree," he said. "But before I can bring them together, sometimes you have to bring them to a point. We've made a lot of progress in the last short period of time. Don't forget. Until the Chinese plague came in, we had the lowest unemployment in the history of this country for African Americans. We had the lowest unemployment numbers by far, African American. We had the lowest for Asian, Hispanic too. But we had the best employment numbers in the history of our country. And then we got hit with the plague. Now here's what's happening. I'm building up the economy." He said the recovery would not just be a "V" shape but and almost an "I"—apparently meaning straight back up. "Look at the job numbers, look at the retail sales numbers. Look at these numbers that are coming in. Wait till you see the third quarter, how good it's going be, when your book comes out."

I wanted to move beyond the economic numbers. He did not.

"Look at the numbers," he said and repeated. "We had the highest employment numbers in history two weeks ago. We had the best retail sales numbers increase in history two days ago. In history, Bob."

"But this—"

"Wait till you see the numbers come in," he said.

"For people out there struggling, for people—"

"Yeah, but they won't be struggling for long, Bob. They're struggling because we had to turn it off. Because if I didn't turn it off, we would have lost three million lives instead of 150,000, or whatever the final number will be. But it will be in that vicinity.

We would have lost three million lives. And you know what? That's not acceptable, three million lives."

I didn't know what projections he based that figure on.

"Okay," I said. "Let me ask this question, please. Bear with me on this, because I think it's one of the pillars of trying to understand. And if I'm a Black man out there, how am I going to say to myself, ah, President Trump understands my plight, my pain? And he is—the numbers, yes. I understand the work on the economy."

"Wait till you see—by the third quarter," he said. "By the time your book—well, I don't know when your book is coming out. But by the election, we will have some of the greatest numbers released by any country. And it's already happening, Bob. Unless some crazy thing happens."

"But do you think that the person out there wants the president to understand how they feel?"

"I do. Let me just tell you, I passed criminal justice reform. Obama couldn't get it done—I passed opportunity zones. Obama and all these people that came before me, not only Obama, couldn't get it done. Nobody could get done what I got done. I got prison reform done. I got criminal justice reform done. I got—forget all about the good economic numbers, which will be just as good in a very short—because I turned it off and then I turned it back on."

"Have you won the hearts of minorities and Black people in this country who feel pain and anguish and are angry? Have you won their hearts? That's my question."

"Okay, you ready?" he asked. "Yes. I did, prior to the plague coming in. But now a lot of those jobs that were, were won—the Black people had the lowest unemployment numbers in history!"

"Okay, but they're, if you're—"

"They had the best jobs! They were making more money than they ever made!"

"You look at the polls, you look at the protests, and you talk to people—" I said.

"They'll be employed very soon, Bob. It's all coming back. They're going to be employed. Okay—before the plague, they had the best numbers ever. Everybody was doing great. They were getting tremendous increases. They were making more money and people were happy. When the plague came in from China, that was the—then a lot of people lost jobs. Those jobs are all coming back. Black people will all be employed very soon, just like they were before. And the numbers will even be better."

"But as you know and as you've said, the murder of George Floyd triggered something in people," I said. "Not just Black people, minorities, but in white people—who are saying, you know, like I'm trying to say, I think I've been a privileged white person. I know you have been, right?"

There was a three-second pause in the conversation. "No?" I prompted.

"I don't get into that argument," he said. "I've done a good job for Black people. I've done the best job of any president since Lincoln."

"Now, here's the other question," I said.

"I don't get into that," he said. "I—you know—there's no point to getting into it. All I can do is what I'm doing. I have done the best job of any president of the United States history, other than Abraham Lincoln, for Black people. I got criminal justice reform, I got Black colleges and universities."

"Have you won their hearts?" I asked. "Because this is a business of the heart." I wondered, did he not understand?

"I'll let you know that at the end of my term, when they get their jobs back," the president said. "By the end of the year you're going to see numbers like nobody's ever seen before. And it's already happened, Bob. Two days ago, you had the greatest retail sales numbers in history, Bob." The percentage increase between

April and May was indeed the largest since the Commerce Department began tracking retail sales, although it was not the highest amount.

Trump went on, "Now, they're all saying Trump was right. It's beyond a 'V.' In fact, the market's up today almost 200 points. We're ready to set a record on the stock market, and the pandemic is ending, it's weaving its way out—and by the way, we're going to have a vaccine soon and we're going to have therapeutics soon. Hey, Bob, could I call you later so I can get to these generals to make sure everything's good?"

I said I still wanted to push on some of these questions.

"I don't mind," he said. "I hope you're truthful. If you're truthful, you're going to write a great book. And if you're not truthful, you're going to hit me."

I called him again that night. He did not call back. I wondered if that might be the last conversation we'd have.

FORTY-FIVE

◆————◆

Trump returned my call three days later, June 22 at 8:15 p.m. "I just got to the White House, and I'm watching a—an event go down where they're trying to rip down a statue in Washington, D.C., and we're stopping them with great force, I think."

Protesters were trying to tear down the Andrew Jackson statue in Lafayette Square. As we spoke, police began to push protesters away from the still standing statue with tear gas and batons. "I'll let you know," Trump said. "But it's terrible what's going on. Terrible."

"What do you think of all that?" I asked.

"I think it's a disgrace. I think it's disgraceful. And it's—you know, it's been going on for a long time, indirectly. But it's gotten more direct. And I've stopped them. On the federal basis I've stopped them strongly. But some of these states are, in some cases, foolish. In some cases, weak."

He wanted to talk about his rally in Tulsa, his first in 60 days, which had been held over the weekend. Less than half of the arena was filled and Trump had to stare into rows of empty blue seats, the focus of most media coverage.

"It just came out, that the headline, quote, 'Trump Rally Gives Fox News the Largest Saturday Night Audience in Its History,'" he read to me. "I'd say that's not bad, even by your standard, right?

"For two weeks," he said, "these people did nothing but talk about, if you go there it's going to be a death chamber. You'll die, essentially. They basically said horrible, horrible things about, don't go there, don't go. Don't go. The networks. You know, the fake news. Then we had protesters there who were quite violent."

Tulsa's top public health official had said he wished the event could be postponed, calling it a "huge risk factor." All the accounts I found said there was very little violence.

"The first empty seats I've ever had," he said.

How long did you work on your speech? I asked. "You're using the teleprompter on that, you have to?"

"Maybe 25 or 30 percent teleprompter," he said. "The rest was ad-lib. How long have I worked on it? It's a very interesting question. I guess my whole life I've worked on it, right? No, when you think of it. No, I didn't work on it. I just tell—I tend to be able to tell stories when I get up to a microphone."

Turning to the virus, he said China "could have stopped it. I believe they could have stopped it."

First Lady Melania Trump came in and briefly joined the call.

"Honey, I'm talking to Bob Woodward," Trump said.

I mentioned the new book, *The Art of Her Deal* by Mary Jordan, a colleague of mine at *The Washington Post*. "So they did that book on you," I said, "and they're giving all kinds of credit to you for knowing how to live with this man."

Melania laughed.

"I didn't know this," Trump said. "What book is this? I want to read this one." He told her that I was doing a book on him. "It'll probably be atrocious, but that's okay."

I wanted to ask more about the protesters.

"I think you probably think they're wonderful people," Trump said.

I made an argument for listening. "I, as a reporter, have to understand, how people reach conclusions, what their emotions are—"

"Okay. I'm okay with that."

"You have to step out of your own shoes," I said.

"Yeah."

"Don't you?"

"Yeah, you do," Trump said. "But you can see things even from your shoes."

I laughed. "Okay."

"I don't think you necessarily have to be there." You can see it from both ways, he said.

In our previous conversation, the president had accused me of drinking the Kool-Aid when I asked him about the idea of white privilege and the anger and pain of Black people.

"My question to you," I said, "and this is the Kool-Aid question, do you understand people who feel passionately—I mean, the Black Lives Matter movement is real. There are a lot of people who are angry and feel pain. You were saying, hey look, I can't be those people. That's quite true. But I think it's really important to step out of your shoes."

"That's okay," he said. "I get it. I'm okay with that."

I reminded him I had my tape recorder on.

"That's okay. I don't mind. You can have it on. I'm a straight shooter."

I said I thought people wanted to hear "the president talking to Black people in this country about what you understand they've gone through. And, you know, we can get to what your remedy is and what you're going to fix. But do you understand you're a person of white privilege just like I am? And the question is, can somebody like you—because of your position—step out and say, you know, I've got some breaks, I've had advantages? There are people out there who have not, and I understand their anger and their fierce, fierce resentment of people like you and people like me."

"I feel I do understand it," Trump said. "But if I didn't understand it, I would not have done criminal justice reform that nobody was able to do but me. I would not have done opportunity zones which have had a tremendously positive impact on areas that were absolutely dying. I would not have funded long-term historically Black colleges and universities," known as HBCUs. "But I wouldn't have done it if I didn't understand it. In other words, if I was not extremely sympathetic to the cause and the plight of what they've gone through, of what, you know, African Americans and the Black community has gone through, I would not have done, you know, a vast amount of money for historically Black colleges and universities."

In December 2019, Trump had signed a bill continuing $255 million in annual funding to HBCUs and other schools serving primarily minority students.

"The question is," I asked, "What's in your heart? I think people want to understand that you understand. What's the essence of your responsibility as president?"

"I think the essence of my responsibility is to do a good job for all communities."

"Suppose I had 10 Black Lives Matter people here as a focus group. And I said, here's President Trump. And this is what President Trump wants to say to you about how he can step out of his shoes, to understand what life is like in your shoes. And what are you going to say?"

"I'm somebody that likes to get things done rather than talk."

"Sometimes when you get in these things," I said, "You have to lay it on yourself. And there's no bigger 'yourself' in this country than you, as president. And I'm not trying to get you to say something you don't feel. I'm asking whether you can understand the plight, struggle, pain of people—I mean it's real. It's been an awakening for me, if I may say that, at my age. I'm older than you—77. To see that they are saying, it's been a raw deal, and I've not liked it, and it's a form of oppression. It's a new form of slavery that has occurred in this country that you're president of. And I want to make sure I understand what you want to say to them. You understand that?"

"Yeah, I do, Bob. I think this. I think that I have some wonderful—what I can do best is get things done. And I have some wonderful things that I'm going to be doing for the Black community in the United States. And I did a lot of it until the Chinese virus hit us so hard."

"If a member of my focus group said to you, President Trump, do you understand me, what would you say?" I asked.

"I would say that I really believe I do. And that's why I've done so much for the Black community." He gave his list again.

"Do you think there is systematic or institutional racism in this country?" I asked.

"Well, I think there is everywhere," Trump said. "I think probably less here than most places. Or less here than many places."

"But," I asked, "is it here in a way that it has an impact on people's lives?"

"I think it is. And it's unfortunate. But I think it is."

He had at least said it.

"But there's a spiritual dimension to this," I said, "where I think people want somebody to get up and say, hey, I get it. I really am moving toward getting my feet in your shoes. I know you wouldn't like this, but remember Hillary Clinton went on a listening tour? Do you need to go on a listening tour and listen to people?"

"I think I listen to people—I think I listen to people all the time. I like to listen to people. I hear what people are saying. I'm able to get things done economically. And that's a very big part of the problem. I'll tell you what—had we been allowed to carry on that great economy. Had we not gotten hit by this artificial situation—it was an operation like a patient gets operated on. And now we're starting all over again. Well, yeah, pretty much. Had I not built a strong foundation for the country, you wouldn't be able to have the kind of numbers that were announced last week on jobs, et cetera, et cetera."

Trump seemed to be referring to the June 5 jobs numbers, which was the most recent information released by the Bureau of Labor Statistics. While tens of millions were still out of work, 2.5 million jobs had been added in May.

"I do hear what people are saying. I do understand what they're saying. And I'm doing things about it. Including, including economic things. It could heal a lot of—a lot of hearts. A good economy can take care of a lot of problems.

"Nothing gets rid of all of them, Bob. Nothing. Problems can disappear. And that's what I'd like to do."

"You remember when Bob Costa and I came and talked to you before you got the nomination in 2016?" I asked. "They were doing renovation on your hotel. And this is when you said to us:

'I bring out rage in people. I bring rage out. I always have. I don't know if it's an asset or a liability. But whatever it is, I do.' Is that true?"

"Yes," Trump said. "Sometimes. I do more things than other people are able to get done. And that, sometimes, can make my opponents unhappy. They view me differently than they view other presidents. A lot of other presidents that you've covered didn't get a lot done, Bob."

"What do you think of your Justice Gorsuch, who kind of led the charge against you on LGBTQ issues?" Neil Gorsuch had just authored a 6 to 3 opinion ruling that the Civil Rights Act protects gay and transgender people from workplace discrimination.

"Well, it's the way he felt, it's the way he felt," Trump said.

"It was against your administration's position," I said.

"Yeah," Trump said, "but this is the way he felt. And, you know, I want people to go the way they feel. I mean, he felt he was doing the right thing. I do think it opens—I do think it opens the spigots for a lot of litigation."

"Suppose," I asked, "Donald Trump was on the Supreme Court, how would he vote on this? I don't see you voting against freedom for more people—"

"I don't want to comment," he said.

I asked about his poll numbers that showed he was in trouble against Biden.

"You see different polls than I do," he said. "I think we're doing fine. The campaign hasn't really started. It's starting, you know, over the next few weeks."

He returned to the Tulsa rally, "with the Chinese virus in the room," as he put it. There were empty seats, he said, because people said, "Hey, I'll watch it on television. And they did, because it was a very big night. And a tremendous night, even bigger on online."

He shifted to his recent graduation speech at West Point. "I made a very good speech and they refused to cover it. They covered that and they were saying, maybe he has Parkinson's" because of the way he shuffled slowly down a steep ramp "inch-by-inch. And literally—you know, you've done that, where you have a steep surface, and I had very slippery shoes. Believe it or not. If you have leather shoes, they're very slippery on the bottom. I'm covered very, very unfairly. Including polls."

In 2016, he said, "I had a poll, the *Washington Post*-ABC poll, two weeks out, two and a half weeks out, I was 14 points behind. And I knew it wasn't true. I knew it wasn't true. We complained about it. And I think that—but it was *Washington Post*, your favorite newspaper, and ABC. And you remember, they came out with a poll, two weeks, and I said, there's no way."

This was basically correct. An ABC poll had Clinton ahead by 12 points.

Trump was traveling far down memory lane. "How do you rate that election, Bob, 2016? Was that one of the great of all time, or was it? It's hard to—people consider that to be a moment in history like no other. What's your feeling on that? Even though you don't call yourself a historian."

In 2016, I had said Trump could win.

"I think I'm in much better position than I was then," Trump said, "because I've done a lot. I also think I have a much weaker opponent." He turned to Hillary Clinton. "Whether you like her or not, she's a horrible human being, but whether you like her or not, she was smart. Very smart. And very devious, very tricky, very smart. And you said you're 77, 78. That means you're the same age as Joe. But it hasn't hit you. It may someday. But it has hit Joe. And you know that. I mean look, you see. You see what's going on. It's a weird deal. He couldn't do it in prime time. I used—remember, I used to call him One Percent Joe.

"Hold on, let me see something." He was watching television or getting some news. "I'm just seeing something coming across the—oh, that's funny."

I didn't know what it was, and he didn't say. What's debating Biden going to be like? I asked.

"I think he did at least even against Bernie," Trump said. "I was surprised that he was able to get through that debate. And he didn't win it but he didn't lose it. You know, it was a pretty even debate. And you know, I was surprised. So you never know what happens."

"Yeah," I agreed.

"You never know what happens," he said again, returning to memory lane. "But let's see what happens. I've had some very good debates. I wouldn't be talking to you if I didn't have good debates. You know that. My best debate was probably the second debate with crooked Hillary. I mean that was probably—that was a great debate."

The second debate, held on October 9, 2016, had been somewhat overshadowed by the release of the *Access Hollywood* tape two days before.

I reminded Trump that on our last call we had talked about historian Barbara Tuchman's book about World War I and history's clock. "And the whole business of what happened in 2016," I said. "And you came along, and the Democrats and your own party had no idea what was going on in America."

"Yep," he said. "Got them by surprise, Bob. Caught them by surprise. I'll get them by surprise again, Bob. You watch."

"Where's history's clock?" I asked.

"Well, we're going to find out. I've done a lot. China set me back. I was sailing. I told you, I feel so differently toward the whole thing with China. This is such a terrible ordeal for the world. Not only just us, for the whole world."

I said that some experts said "if you were going to imagine a virus that would attack with such efficiency and be so lethal on somebody's lungs, you could not have designed a better one. And there's some people who think that they manipulated this, as you know."

"Oh, sure I've heard that," Trump said. "I've heard many theories. I've also heard that it was incompetence. I have heard that it was a mistake. I've heard mistake, I've heard incompetence, and I've heard, you know—"

"Manipulation?" I asked. "And what's the reality? Because that's important."

"Well," he said, "I think we may find the reality at some point. But right now, nobody knows for sure."

"If they engineered this and intentionally let it out into the world—" I said.

"Well how come they got hit so hard?" Trump asked.

"They couldn't control it. I think they didn't realize what it was. And your experts can't get the real numbers from them."

"That's right," he said. "But the numbers are substantial. Very, very substantial."

"We are at one of these pivot points in history," I said. "And you are in charge."

"I had the greatest economy that we've ever had," Trump said mournfully. "Stock market hit all-time highs in history. I was riding so high, the market was riding so high."

The stock market had been climbing steadily since 2009—regularly hitting new highs—until the coronavirus-related shutdowns resulted in a historic crash in February 2020. At the time of our interview, the markets were showing signs of recovery.

The question, he said, was, "Can we take this all the way to that very special date of November 3rd?"

FORTY-SIX

◆

Trump called me unexpectedly on Wednesday, July 8, before his day of meetings with Mexican president Andrés Manuel López Obrador.

"I'm so busy," Trump said. "I don't have time to breathe." I don't think he intended any reference to George Floyd.

"This will be our 17th conversation for this book," I said.

"All I ask for is fairness," Trump said. "And, you know, I'm sure I won't get it, but that's okay. I'm used to that. But I do ask for fairness because nobody's done what I've done. Nobody. Did you get the new list of new things that were added on?" It was a long, boilerplate list of dozens of large and small matters, and I said I did receive it.

What, I asked, was he trying to accomplish in the two speeches he had just given over the Fourth of July weekend, one at Mount Rushmore and the other at the White House?

Both painted divisive portraits of some citizens threatening the country—a kind of reemergence in tone of "American carnage" from his inaugural address. As best I could tell, presidents of both parties universally gave unifying and inspiring speeches on July 4—a freebie of goodwill. "In the Mount Rushmore speech you talk about a new far-left fascism," I said. He had said there was "a merciless campaign to wipe out our history. Angry mobs are trying to tear down statues of our Founders," and "this left-wing cultural revolution is designed to overthrow the American Revolution."

I said, "There's some people who represent that kind of anger, the radical left. But it's not much."

The next day, in the White House speech, Trump had said that like the American heroes who defeated the Nazis, "We are now in the process of defeating the radical left, the Marxists, the anarchists, the agitators, the looters."

I said there were no Marxists left.

"No," Trump said, "that's wrong, Bob. Black Lives Matter, what they do is they literally have it in their website that they're Marxists."

One of the cofounders claimed in 2015 that she and other organizers of Black Lives Matter were "trained Marxists." It was not, however, on their website. The Black Lives Matter phrase has been adopted as a reformist slogan by the broader social movement for racial justice.

"What are you saying to people?" I asked the president. "In the second speech you said 'our movement,' referring to your movement and your base. 'Never forget, we are one family and one nation.'"

"Right," Trump said.

"Black Lives Matter people look at all of this and they say they're not being invited in. That you've put up a wall around your base. And the question is, what's your intent?"

He didn't answer but said, "I have done more for the Black community than any other president other than Abraham Lincoln."

I said that Lyndon Johnson certainly had done more. The passing of the 1964 Civil Rights Act was a monumental achievement. It outlawed discrimination based on race, religion or sex, further mandated the desegregation of schools, the prohibition of racial discrimination in employment and protections against the unequal application of requirements for voter registration.

"But it's about the heart," I said.

"I have done a tremendous amount for the Black community," Trump said. "And, honestly, I'm not feeling any love. As soon as the China virus came in—as soon as the plague, China virus, came in—as soon as it came in—those poll numbers all of a sudden started inching back" down "8 or 9 or 10 percent. And I don't understand that. I don't. Because nobody blames me for the virus."

Of course, many people, and perhaps history, might blame him for mishandling the crisis.

"It's a matter of the heart and the spirit," I said. "Are you saying to people who are Black Lives Matter, who are minorities in this country, you are welcome here?"

"The door is very wide open," he said. "I want to include all people. I want to include all Americans. The door is absolutely open." And he went back to his talking points about all he had done for Black Americans.

"So, what's your goal here?"

"My goal is to do a great job as president," he said. He talked about numbers, jobs growth. He seemed not to understand that I was trying to ask about outreach and healing.

"You'll do a third book in the next year," he said. "Next year's going to be a fantastic year. Watch."

"As you know," I said, "the virus is on fire. Absolutely on fire."

"It's only on fire because of our testing. Because we're testing 40 million people," he said.

But the percentage of positive tests was also going up—a key indicator of trouble.

Trump also said that the death rate was down.

I reminded Trump that Fauci had said publicly earlier in the week that "it's a false narrative to take comfort in a lower rate of death" because with the huge growth in cases the death rate would go up in a matter of weeks.

He didn't answer but recycled his arguments with Fauci.

"The question is, where are we now?" I asked.

"We're in great shape," Trump said. "Most of the country is headed absolutely away from the virus. We're totally set with our hospitals. We're totally set."

"Okay, but it's on fire, sir," I said.

"Because we did 40 million people, anybody that has the sniffles—any kid that has a little bit of a cold, they test positive. And it's going to go away in two days. It's frankly, it's ridiculous."

I was surprised that Trump was trivializing a positive test in a child as he continued to criticize his public health officials.

"Have you called Tony Fauci in and sat him down in the Oval Office?" I asked.

"He couldn't win that argument with me," Trump said. "He cannot win that argument." If he hadn't acted, he said, "We would have had three million dead instead of 130,000 as of today." Trump was correct. The travel restrictions on China and Europe and the initial shutdowns did save lives.

"As a citizen, somebody who lives here," I said, "I'm worried as I can be about this whole thing."

"Don't worry about it, Bob. Okay?" Trump said. "Don't worry about it. We'll get to do another book. You'll find I was right."

"What I've learned in the world of Trump is news cycles don't last very long," Kushner said on Monday, July 13, as he reviewed the overall Trump strategic picture with a top staffer.

"He's had a string of bad luck," Kushner said, especially with the virus. "He'll get a couple of breaks along the way, and when he does, hopefully we'll take advantage of them. So he's getting ready for the fight and his head's getting in the game. It's also about just getting his head out of D.C. Right? D.C. is filled with a lot of traps."

Meanwhile the public polling across the board showed Biden beating Trump by double digits and winning the battleground states. Kushner's three separate private polls, however, painted a much more favorable picture. He did his own data with big samples. "Our polls basically show that he's either ahead or in the margin of error in all the states he won last time."

Kushner continued, "The whole thing with polling is it's about getting likely voters, number one, as opposed to registered voters. Public polling is using registered voters, not likely, and they're definitely skewing the turnout model. And so we believe it is a different race than other people believe."

So it was similar to 2016. Trump voters simply were more enthusiastic and highly motivated. Kushner's turnout model reflected a much higher percentage of Trump voters going to the polls.

"Biden's had about as good a couple months as he could get, being hidden," Kushner said. "And so at some point there's going to be a real discussion of him." Biden's reliance on Bernie Sanders's and Elizabeth Warren's liberal ideas amounted to a "long political suicide note," Kushner said.

"The goal" with Trump, Kushner said, "is to get his head from governing to campaigning."

When I learned about this, I was incredulous. In the midst of the largest public health crisis in a century, Kushner thought it was time to turn to campaigning?

But the virus was all about governing. It could not be campaigned away.

"I think," Kushner continued, "that for five years"—since Trump started to run—"he basically was on offense. And then for four and a half months"—since the virus exploded—"he was on defense. And the goal is to get him back to offense."

The offense soon appeared. First, the White House released a document listing the number of times Fauci had been wrong in his predictions about Covid-19, a highly unusual and, from a health point of view, irresponsible effort to undermine the chief of infectious diseases. Fauci had privately acknowledged he was not by any means always correct. But polling showed that he was trusted by at least twice as many people as Trump.

Second, on Tuesday, July 14, Trump took an early opportunity to attack Biden in what was billed as a press conference in the Rose Garden on China. Instead he spoke for 57 minutes and mentioned Biden 30 times before taking questions for six minutes. Because Trump was reading from some text or notes, he looked down many times and the speech had none of the fire and passion of his rally performances.

New York Times Chief White House Correspondent Peter Baker wrote in an article that appeared on page 17, "Even for a president who rarely sticks to the script and wanders from thought to thought, it was one of the most rambling performances of his presidency."

Third, on Wednesday night, July 15, Trump replaced Brad Parscale as his campaign manager, demoting him to a senior adviser. Trump was still angry about the low-attendance, empty-seat rally in Tulsa and the poor public poll numbers.

This effectively ended Parscale's hope for a movie, a new cash haul from Republicans who might want his expertise in a 2024 presidential race and a place in the campaign manager hall of fame.

Trump named Bill Stepien, a longtime political aide, his new campaign manager. Kushner considered Stepien one of the most talented political operatives around. They were close, and Kushner's control of the campaign would continue.

Trump called me unexpectedly on the morning of Tuesday, July 21. The reason, he said, was "to say hello. How are you doing?" I turned on my recorder and we held our 18th interview for about half an hour. The manuscript for this book was due to my publisher this day.

"Things are getting bad," I said, "aren't they?"

"Bad in what way?" he asked as if he was surprised.

"The virus," I said. New daily cases were at about 60,000, with deaths near 1,000 each day.

"Well, it's flaring up. It's flaring up all over the world, Bob. By the way, all over the world. That was one thing I noticed last week. You know? They talk about this country. All over the world, it's flaring up. But we have it under control."

"What?" I said. He noticed last week? The virus had been out of control for months.

Texas and Florida were being hit, he said. But his ambivalence was on full display in the next sentence: "But we have it under control. We have it absolutely—I believe it's—but it's a tough, there's no question."

"What grade would you give yourself on the handling of the coronavirus?" I asked.

"Well, I think I'd give myself a very good grade because what we've done—you know, we were totally—when I took over, there was nothing, there were no provisions." No one was prepared for this.

"What have you learned about yourself?" I asked.

Once again he returned to Mueller's investigation. "I was fighting the fake Russia thing."

I asked again about the virus. "When we started talking in December, if I said to you we're gonna have a virus that comes and kills 140,000 people in this country, you would think I was smoking something," I said.

"Well, you know all my life I've heard the word pandemic," he said. "But somehow you never think of that as a modern-day thing that could happen."

"But it's happened," I said. "Biden is not really your opponent. The virus is your opponent. Do you agree?"

"Well, I think that's largely true," he said. "It's the virus and it's a radical left group of people, and it's the media. The media is my opponent, regardless of anything. No matter how well we do, they will say we didn't do well."

"But 140,000 people have died," I said.

"But we have a much bigger country," the president said. "If you look at China, they have many more people that died. They just don't report it. If you look at Russia, if you look at India—"

The U.S. at this time had the eighth-highest per capita death rate.

"Jared said you are getting back on offense," I said. "Is this the strategy—back on offense?" I listed the examples of the previous week—attacking Biden in the Rose Garden, the White House attack on Fauci and the removal of his campaign manager.

"I have a very flexible strategy, Bob. I've had it for a long time. My whole life has been flexible strategy and I've done very well. And I had it in the last campaign, too. I was very flexible. I changed campaign managers three times."

"Is it offense now? Or is it governing?" I asked. "You understand why I'm asking?"

"I won the last campaign in the last four weeks. But I would really say I won it in the last week. I did rallies, I did many, many things in the last week."

"Okay, but is it offense, or is it governing?"

"I think it's really both. It's a combination of governing and a political campaign. We have 105 days. Now, to me, 105 days is a very long time. . . . It's an eternity."

"In July, it's not clear what the plan is," I said.

He mentioned immigration, health care and DACA.

I returned to the virus and recalled for him a discussion we had in April about a "strategy and a matrix and a roadmap" for him to lead.

"Well, I am leading. But, you know, you have a lot of great leaders around the world and their countries are stymied. We're not stymied. But you have a lot of great leaders around the world, and this has affected them very, very powerfully."

What about the plan? I asked.

"I've got 106 days," he said. "That's a long time. You know, if I put out a plan now, people won't even remember it in a hundred—I won the last election in the final week."

"No, no," I said. "But it's not just put out the plan, it's execute it, isn't it?"

"No. I am executing. You'll see it starting. I've already started. But you will see things being signed—documents being signed, not just—this isn't just a plan, this is getting it done. I will have immigration done. I will have health care done.

"I think we're going to have vaccines soon," he said. "I think we already have them. But they're in tests. And you'll see them being announced over the next month. Now would you view that as a game changer?"

I again asked for the grade he would give himself.

"I give ourselves an A. But the grade is incomplete, and I'll tell you why. If we come up with the vaccines and therapeutics, then I give myself an A-plus."

"I've talked to lots of your predecessors," I said. "I never talked to Nixon, but I talked to many, many of them. They get philosophical when I ask the question, what have you learned about yourself? And that's the question on you: What have you learned about yourself?"

Trump sighed audibly. "I can handle more than other people can handle. Because, and I'll tell you what, whether I learned about it myself—more people come up to me and say—and I mean very strong people, people that are successful, even. A lot of people. They say, I swear to you, I don't know how it's possible for you to handle what you handle. How you've done this, with the kind of opposition, the kind of shenanigans, the kind of illegal witch hunts."

"It's a tough job," I acknowledged.

"Tougher for me than probably just about anybody," he said. "I would think."

"People are worried about the virus," I said.

"I know that, Bob. But the virus has nothing to do with me. It's not my fault. It's—China let the damn virus out."

"But you have the problem," I said. "And the question is, what's the plan? How are you going to lead?" In November, I continued, "The question is we're going to look back and we're going to say, end of July, August, September, October, what happened with the virus?"

"I have opposition like nobody has. And that's okay. I've had that all my life. I've always had it. And this has been—my whole life has been like this. In the meantime, right now, I'm looking at the White House. Okay? I'm staring right at the walls of the White House." It seemed to be his way of reminding me that he was the president.

He continued, "We've got 105 days. Let's see how it turns out. I was unlucky with the virus."

"But you got it," I said. "The country's got it. And the world's got it. But you're in charge of the country. . . . You're in charge of the national interest."

"Will I get credit for it?" he asked. "Probably not. But I'll take credit."

"Presidents have power," I said. "Extraordinary power. And people are leaning on you."

"They do have extraordinary power," Trump said. "But in my case, they never accepted it. And they never accepted this president, because they're a bunch of dishonest people. And they spied on my campaign and we caught them. They spied before and after I won. And we caught them. And we caught them cold. Let's see what happens."

I talked about how in my business we try to understand people.

"You don't understand me," he said. "You don't understand me. But that's okay. You'll understand me after the election. But you don't understand me now. I don't think you get it. And that's okay."

He wanted to make sure I had the list of his accomplishments.

But on the issues before you, I said, "You know what number one is? The virus. Number two's the virus. Number three is the virus."

Then he displayed his ambivalence about his role again. "No, no," he said first and then added, "I agree with that." Then he added, "But that was thrown upon me when we were riding high. The election was over. I was going to win easily. And all of a sudden we got hit with the China virus. And now I'm working my ass off." And he abruptly said, "So long, Bob. Good luck."

Seven hours later, Trump gave a long statement at his first Coronavirus Task Force press conference in three months. He spoke alone at the White House. No Pence, Fauci or Birx. He also shifted tone. Everything was not rosy with the outlook for the virus.

"It will probably, unfortunately, get worse before it gets better," Trump said injecting an unusual dose of realism. "Something I don't like saying about things, but that's the way it is."

Previously Trump had been reluctant to wear a mask. "Get a mask," he said. "Whether you like the mask or not, they have an impact. They'll have an effect and we need everything we can get."

His comments were a tacit acknowledgment that his previous approach had not worked, and that, in fact, the virus was much worse.

The day was a microcosm of Trump's presidency, veering from "We have it under control" to "worse before it gets better," all in the span of a few hours. It was just the most recent example—and the last before this book went to press—that Trump's presidency was riddled with ambivalence, set on an uncertain course, swinging from combativeness to conciliation, and whipsawing from one statement or action to the opposite.

EPILOGUE

————◆————

After I finished reporting for this book on President Trump, I felt weariness. The country was in real turmoil. The virus was out of control. The economy was in crisis with more than 40 million out of work. A powerful reckoning on racism and inequality was upon us. There seemed to be no end in sight, and certainly no clear path to get there.

I thought back to the conversation with Trump on February 7 when he mentioned the "dynamite behind every door," the unexpected explosion that could change everything. He was apparently thinking about some external event that would affect the Trump presidency.

But now, I've come to the conclusion that the "dynamite behind the door" was in plain sight. It was Trump himself. The oversized personality. The failure to organize. The lack of discipline. The lack of trust in others he had picked, in experts. The undermining or the attempted undermining of so many American institutions. The failure to be a calming, healing voice. The unwillingness to acknowledge error. The failure to do his homework. To extend the olive branch. To listen carefully to others. To craft a plan.

Mattis, Tillerson and Coats are all conservatives or apolitical people who wanted to help him and the country. Imperfect men who answered the call to public service. They were not the deep state. Yet each departed with cruel words from their leader. They concluded that Trump was an unstable threat to their country. Think about that for a moment: The top national security leaders thought the president of the United States was a danger to the country.

Trump said the intelligence people needed to go back to school. The generals were stupid. The media was fake news.

Trump had spent so many years undermining people who challenged him. Not only his opponents but those who worked for him and for the American public.

And here was the problem: By undermining so many others not only had he shaken confidence in them but he had shaken confidence in himself. This was particularly apparent when the country most needed to feel the government knew what it was doing in an unprecedented health crisis.

Jared Kushner, Trump's son-in-law, maybe had it more right than he knew when he said understanding Trump meant understanding Alice in Wonderland.

Trump talked a lot. Almost incessantly. So much that he weakened the microphone of the presidency and the bully pulpit, and too many people no longer trusted what he said. Half or more of the country seemed to be in a perpetual rage about him, and he seemed to enjoy it.

I think of Robert Redfield knowing that the virus fight would not be merely six months or a year, it would be two to three years. Of Trump repeatedly saying the virus would disappear or blow away. And of the enormous wearing down of public health officials to not stray too far from the president's message.

I close out this book with a belief that almost anything can happen in the Trump presidency—anything. Lots could get better or worse or much worse. It is unlikely lots could get much better. For the moment, in the middle of the summer, the virus, the economy, and the internal political divisions define Trump. The intensity of those divisions is at its height.

The concentration of power in the presidency has been growing for decades and the power of the president might be at an all-time high under Trump. Trump uses it especially in dominating the media.

Trump has talked very tough, often in a way that unsettles even his supporters. But he has not imposed martial law or suspended the Constitution, despite predictions of his opponents. He and his attorney general, William Barr, have several times challenged the traditional rule of law. Unnecessarily, in my view. Using the justice system to reward friends and pay back enemies is petty and Nixonian. Constitutional government might seem wobbly at times, and that could change overnight. Still, democracy has held.

But leadership has failed. What did Trump want to accomplish? What were his goals? Too often he seemed not to know himself. Decision by tweet, often without warning to those charged with executing his policies, was one of the biggest sticks of dynamite behind the door.

His relationship and letters with North Korean leader Kim Jong Un outlined in detail here were not by the foreign policy establishment playbook. But as Trump says repeatedly we had no war. That was an achievement. Diplomacy should always be worth a try. It may have been worth it. Where it goes next is one of the imponderables of the Trump era. Is Trump's and Kim's mutual pledge of fealty—the "fantasy film"—sustainable as Kim is more threatening? "We'll see," as Trump says all the time.

The shadowy presence of Trump's son-in-law, Jared Kushner, is another imponderable. Highly competent but often shockingly misguided in his assessments, Kushner's role is jarring. Was there no one else to act as chief of staff? Trump's friends are mostly others with money or social standing. Or those who liked to talk on the phone at night. Was there no real friend who shared Trump's interest in governing who could help and be called to service?

Senator Lindsey Graham, Trump's First Friend in the Senate, has often been portrayed as embarrassingly and shamelessly subservient to the president, but actually at times provided wise counsel, urging Trump to take a strategic view.

On January 28, 2020, when Trump's national security adviser and his deputy warned Trump that the virus would be—not might be, but would be—the biggest national security threat to his presidency, the leadership clock had to be reset. It was a detailed forecast, supported by evidence and experience that unfortunately turned out to be correct. Presidents are the executive branch. There was a duty to warn. To listen, to plan, and to take care.

For a long time Trump hedged, as did others, and said the virus is worrisome but not yet, not now. There were good reasons to ride both horses, but there should have been more consistent and courageous outspokenness. Leading is almost always risky.

The virus, the "plague," as Trump calls it, put the United States and the world in economic turmoil that may not be just a recession, but a depression. It is a genuine financial crisis, putting tens of millions out of work. Trump's solution is to try to recreate what he believes is the economic miracle he created in the pre-virus time. Democrats, Republicans and Trump did agree to spending at least $2.2 trillion on recovery, which will create its own future problems with growing deficits. The human cost has been almost unimaginable, with more than 130,000 Americans killed by the virus by July and no real end in sight.

The deep-seated hatreds of American politics flourished in the Trump years. He stoked them, and did not make concerted efforts to bring the country together. Nor did the Democrats. Trump felt deeply wronged by the Democrats who felt deeply wronged by Trump. The walls between them only grew higher and thicker.

My 17 interviews with Trump presented a challenge. He denounced *Fear*, my first book on him, as untrue, a "scam" and a "joke," calling me a "Dem operative." Several of those closest to him told him that the book was true, and Lindsey Graham told him that I would not put words in his mouth and would report as accurately as possible.

Trump decided, for reasons that are not clear to me, that he would cooperate. To his mind, he would become a reliable source. He is reliable at times, completely unreliable at others, and often mixed. I have tried to guide the reader as best I can. But the interviews show he vacillated, prevaricated and at times dodged his role as leader of the country despite his "I alone can fix it" rhetoric.

As America and the world know, Trump is an overpowering presence. He loves spectacle.

Trump is a living paradox, capable of being friendly and appealing. He can also be savage and his treatment of people is often almost unbelievable.

In a time of crisis, the operational is much more important than the political or the personal. For tens of millions the optimistic American story has turned to a nightmare.

My wife, Elsa Walsh, who had worked for years as a reporter for *The Washington Post* and then as a staff writer for *The New Yorker*, and I spent endless hours sifting through the story of the Trump presidency, talking intensely for the last year. What was the remedy, the course that could have been taken? we asked. Was there a way to do better?

Elsa suggested looking at a previous president who wanted to speak directly to the American people, unfiltered through the media, not just during troubling times but during a major crisis. The model was Franklin D. Roosevelt. Over his 12 years as president, FDR gave 30 fireside chats. His aides and the public often clamored for more. FDR said no. It was important to limit his talks to the major events and to make them exceptional. He also said they were hard work, often requiring him to prepare personally for days.

The evening radio addresses concerned the toughest issues facing the country. In a calm and reassuring voice, he explained what the problem was, what the government was doing about it, and what was expected of the people.

Often the message was grim. Two days after Japan's December 7, 1941, surprise bombing attack on Pearl Harbor, FDR spoke to the nation. "We must share together the bad news and the good news, the defeats and the victories—the changing fortunes of war. So far, the news has been all bad. We have suffered a serious setback." He added, "It will not only be a long war, it will be a hard war." It was a question of survival. "We are now fighting to maintain our right to live among our world neighbors in freedom and common decency."

FDR invited the American people in. "We are all in it—all the way. Every single man, woman and child is a partner in the most tremendous undertaking of our American history." Japan had inflicted serious damage and the casualty lists would be long. Seven-day weeks in every war industry would be required.

"On the road ahead there lies hard work—grueling work—day and night, every hour and every minute." And sacrifice, which was a "privilege."

Japan was allied with the fascist powers of Germany and Italy. FDR called for a systematic "grand strategy."

A few months later in another fireside chat he asked Americans to pull out a world map to follow along with him as he described why the country needed to fight beyond American's borders. "Your government has unmistakable confidence in your ability to hear the worst, without flinching or losing heart."

For nearly 50 years, I have written about nine presidents from Nixon to Trump—20 percent of the 45 U.S. presidents. A president must be willing to share the worst with the people, the bad news with the good. All presidents have a large obligation to inform, warn, protect, to define goals and the true national interest. It should be a truth-telling response to the world, especially in crisis. Trump has, instead, enshrined personal impulse as a governing principle of his presidency.

When his performance as president is taken in its entirety, I can only reach one conclusion: Trump is the wrong man for the job.

Note to Readers

Nearly all interviews for this book were conducted under the journalist ground rule of "deep background." This means that all the information could be used but I would not say who provided it.

The book is drawn from hundreds of hours of interviews with firsthand participants and witnesses to these events. Nearly all allowed me to tape-record our interviews. When I have attributed exact quotations, thoughts or conclusions to the participants, that information comes from the person, a colleague with direct knowledge, or from government or personal documents, calendars, diaries, emails, meeting notes and other records.

I interviewed President Trump 17 times on the record for this book—in one case, I took handwritten notes and the other 16 were recorded with his permission.

Source Notes

The information in this book comes primarily from my deep background interviews with firsthand participants and witnesses. Additional source notes follow:

PROLOGUE

xvii   *"How concerned are you":* "Interview: Sean Hannity Interviews Donald Trump at Mar-a-Lago," February 2, 2020. Available on YouTube.

xvii   *That morning, even National Security Adviser O'Brien: Face the Nation* transcript, CBS, February 2, 2020.

xviii   *About halfway through:* "Remarks by President Trump in State of the Union Address," U.S. Capitol, February 4, 2020, WhiteHouse.gov.

xviii   *When I later asked the president:* Interview with President Donald J. Trump, May 6, 2020.

xviii   *"I wanted to always play it down":* Interview with President Donald J. Trump, March 19, 2020.

xviii   *"Now we've got a little bit":* Interview with President Donald J. Trump, February 7, 2020.

xix   *The president had also said:* Interview with President Donald J. Trump, December 13, 2019.

xx   *While discussing* Fear *on television: CBS Sunday Morning,* CBS, September 9, 2018.

CHAPTER ONE

4   *Trump had promised in the campaign:* "Transcript of the Second Debate," *The New York Times*, October 10, 2016.

5   *"All I can say is he is the real deal":* "Trump Calls Mattis 'The Real Deal' After Meeting," *The Hill*, November 19, 2016.

CHAPTER TWO

7   *Records show Tillerson made more:* Federal Election Commission, Itemized Receipts, FEC.gov.

8   *Exxon had a 30 percent interest:* "ExxonMobil in Russia," ExxonMobil, March 30, 2020.

CHAPTER THREE

16   *On December 1, in Cincinnati:* Dan Lamothe, "Trump Picks Retired Marine Gen. James Mattis for Secretary of Defense," *The Washington Post*, December 1, 2016.

19   *He characterized his difference:* George P. Shultz, *Turmoil and Triumph: My Years as Secretary of State* (New York: Scribner's, 1993), p. 650.

CHAPTER FOUR

26   *When the* Access Hollywood *tape:* @SenDanCoats, "Donald Trump's vulgar comments are totally inappropriate and disgusting, and these words have no place in our society," 10:16 a.m., October 8, 2016, Twitter.com.

28   *"I fear if we do not unite":* Marsha Coats, "Unity Makes the Impossible, Possible," Indiana GOP News Release, May 19, 2016.

33   *Six months earlier, as a civilian:* Carla Marinucci, "Ex-Military Leaders at Hoover Institution Say Trump Statements Threaten America's Interests," *Politico*, July 15, 2016.

33   *He thanked Trump and Pence:* "Secretary of Defense Ceremonial Swearing-In," C-SPAN, January 27, 2017.

33   *The travel ban, which began:* Jenna Johnson, "Trump Calls for 'Total and Complete Shutdown of Muslims Entering the United States,'" *The Washington Post*, December 7, 2015.

34   *On March 19, 2017,* The Washington Post: Lisa Rein and Juliet Eilperin, "White House Installs Political Aides at Cabinet Agencies to Be Trump's Eyes and Ears," *The Washington Post*, March 19, 2017.

34   *In early April, Trump ordered:* See Bob Woodward, *Fear: Trump in the White House* (New York: Simon & Schuster, 2018), Chapter 18.

35   *Mattis sent a memo:* Ibid., p. 161.

CHAPTER SIX

42 *In the CIA's reexamination of its role:* See Bob Woodward, "With CIA Push, Movement to War Accelerated," *The Washington Post*, April 19, 2004.

CHAPTER SEVEN

45 *Trump was "steaming, raging mad":* Philip Rucker, Robert Costa, and Ashley Parker, "Inside Trump's Fury: The President Rages at Leaks, Setbacks and Accusations," *The Washington Post*, March 5, 2017.

48 *"Dear Director Comey, While I greatly":* Special Counsel Office, "The Mueller Report," DOJ, Vol. 2 p. 65.

49 *In July 2016, Comey had usurped:* "Statement by FBI Director James B. Comey on the Investigation of Secretary Hillary Clinton's Use of a Personal E-Mail System," July 5, 2016, FBI.gov.

50 *"I do not understand his refusal":* Rod J. Rosenstein, "Subject: Restoring Public Confidence in the FBI," May 9, 2017.

51 *Comey was in Los Angeles speaking:* James Comey, *A Higher Loyalty* (New York: Flatiron Books, 2018), p. 263.

51 *"FBI Director James Comey Is Fired by Trump":* Michel D. Shear and Matt Apuzzo, "Director James Comey Is Fired by Trump," *The New York Times*, May 9, 2017.

51 *"In Trump's firing of James Comey":* Peter Baker, "In Trump's Firing of James Comey, Echoes of Watergate," *The New York Times*, May 9, 2017.

51 *The White House put out a statement:* Statement from the Press Secretary, WhiteHouse.gov, May 9, 2017.

52 *The next morning, Wednesday, May 10:* Andrew G. McCabe, *The Threat* (New York: St. Martin's Press, 2019), Chapter 7. See McCabe's book for a full account of the call.

53 *The Democratic governor Terry McAuliffe:* D'Angelo Gore, "Clinton's Connection to FBI Official," *FactCheck.org*, October 25, 2016; and "Trump Wrong About Campaign Donations," *FactCheck.org*, July 26, 2017.

CHAPTER EIGHT

55 *On May 11, two days after:* Michael S. Schmidt, "In a Private Dinner, Trump Demanded Loyalty. Comey Demurred," *The New York Times*, May 11, 2017.

56 *The conversation was "chaotic":* *A Higher Loyalty* (New York: Flatiron Books, 2018), p. 239.

56 *In an interview with NBC: NBC Nightly News*, "Watch Lester Holt's Extended Interview with President Trump," NBC, May 11, 2017.

57 *Under the current regulations:* Under the previous statute—which was enacted after Watergate in 1978 and allowed by Congress to lapse in 1999 after the Clinton impeachment—the independent counsel was specifically

mandated to "advise the House of Representatives of any substantial and credible information . . . that may constitute grounds for an impeachment." Under the regulations now governing special counsel investigations, including Mueller's, the special counsel has no mandate or explicit authority to advise Congress of information which may potentially constitute grounds for impeachment.

58   *About two hours later,* The New York Times: Michael S. Schmidt, "Comey Memo Says Trump Asked Him to End Flynn Investigation," *The New York Times*, May 16, 2017.

61   *On May 17, 2017, in a one-page order:* Office of the Deputy Attorney General, "Appointment of Special Counsel to Investigate Russian Interference with the 2016 Presidential Election and Related Matters," May 17, 2017.

61   *When Trump was informed:* Special Counsel's Office, "The Mueller Report: The Report of the Special Counsel on the Investigation into Russian Interference in the 2016 Presidential Election," U.S. Department of Justice, Volume 2, p. 78.

61   *In line with Rosenstein's assurances:* Terri Rupar, "Trump Reacts to Special Counsel's Appointment," *The Washington Post*, May 17, 2017.

61   *On Thursday morning shortly after 10:00:* @RealDonaldTrump, "With all of the illegal acts that took place in the Clinton campaign & Obama Administration, there was never a special counsel appointed!," 10:07 a.m., May 18, 2017, Twitter.com.

62   *In some respects that day:* See Bob Woodward, *Fear: Trump in the White House* (New York: Simon & Schuster, 2018), Chapter 20.

63   *Later, during a House Judiciary Committee:* "Live coverage: Tensions Mount as Rosenstein Grilled by GOP," *The Hill*, June 28, 2018.

CHAPTER NINE

64   *If Kushner could not find:* Amir Tibon, "Trump to Kushner: If You Can't Produce Middle East Peace, Nobody Can," *Haaretz*, January 20, 2017.

67   *"Your Excellency, Mr. President":* "Remarks by President Trump and President Abbas of the Palestinian Authority in Joint Statements," May 23, 2017, WhiteHouse.gov.

CHAPTER ELEVEN

75   *After months of apprehension:* See Bob Woodward, *Fear: Trump in the White House* (New York: Simon & Schuster, 2018), Chapter 22.

76   *General Brooks said in a provocative:* General Vincent K. Brooks, "Combined Statement on Alliance Response," United States Forces Korea, July 4, 2017.

76   *In case anyone missed the message:* United States Forces Korea, "ROK-US Alliance Demonstrates Precision Firing Capability in Response to North Korean Missile Launch," July 28, 2017.

79 *On September 22, Trump tweeted:* @RealDonaldTrump, "Kim Jong Un of North Korea, who is obviously a madman who doesn't mind starving or killing his people, will be tested like never before!," 6:28 a.m., September 22, 2017, Twitter.com.

79 *The following day, North Korean foreign minister:* Michelle Nichols, Yara Bayoumy, and Phil Stewart, "North Korea Says Rockets to U.S. 'Inevitable' as U.S. Bombers Fly Off North Korean Coast," Reuters, September 23, 2017.

79 *Trump responded later that day:* @RealDonaldTrump, "Just heard Foreign Minister of North Korea speak at U.N. If he echoes thoughts of Little Rocket Man, they won't be around much longer!," 11:08 p.m., September 23, 2017, Twitter.com.

81 *"He was totally prepared," Trump told me:* Interview with President Donald J. Trump, December 13, 2019.

82 *"If I weren't president, we would have":* Interview with President Donald J. Trump, December 30, 2019.

82 *"It would've been a bad war, too":* Interview with President Donald J. Trump, February 7, 2020.

CHAPTER TWELVE

83 *Trump had undermined:* @RealDonaldTrump, "I told Rex Tillerson, our wonderful Secretary of State, that he is wasting his time trying to negotiate with Little Rocket Man . . ." 10:30 a.m., and ". . . Save your energy Rex, we'll do what has to be done!," 10:31 a.m., October 1, 2017, Twitter.com.

88 *He called the economic, cultural and political awakening:* "Remarks by President Trump to the National Assembly of the Republic of Korea," November 7, 2017, WhiteHouse.gov.

CHAPTER THIRTEEN

90 *He now had his "mighty sword":* Joshua Berlinger, "Making North Korea Great Again. How Realistic Are Kim's New Year Plans?," CNN, January 19, 2018.

91 *"Along with President Trump," Chung said:* "Remarks by Republic of Korea National Security Advisor Chung Eui Yong," March 8, 2018, WhiteHouse.gov.

92 *Evan S. Mediros, an Asia expert:* Mark Landler, "North Korea Asks for Direct Nuclear Talks, and Trump Agrees," *The New York Times*, March 8, 2018.

92 *Nearly two years later:* Interview with President Donald J. Trump, December 5, 2019.

92 *"I loathe Kim Jong Il":* See Bob Woodward, *The War Within* (New York: Simon & Schuster, 2008), p. 431.

93 *The most recent episode:* Nichole Gaouette and Joshua Berlinger, "Tillerson Says US Won't Set Preconditions for North Korea Talks," CNN, December 13, 2017.

93   *A White House spokesman pushed back:* Matt Spetalnick and David Brunnstrom, "White House Says Not Right Time for North Korea Talks, Despite Tillerson Overture," *Reuters*, December 13, 2017.

94   *In fact, the day before the surprise:* Nick Wadhams, "U.S. Is a 'Long Way' from Talks with North Korea, Tillerson Says," *Bloomberg*, March 8, 2018.

94   *"If he came here, I'd accept him":* Nick Gass, "Trump: I'll Meet with Kim Jong Un in the U.S.," *Politico*, June 15, 2016.

96   *"Mike Pompeo, Director of the CIA":* @RealDonaldTrump, "Mike Pompeo, Director of the CIA, will become our new Secretary of State. He will do a fantastic job! Thank you to Rex Tillerson for his service! Gina Haspel will become the new Director of the CIA, and the first woman so chosen. Congratulations to all!," 8:44 a.m., March 13, 2018, Twitter.com.

96   *It had earlier leaked out:* Shane Savitsky, "NBC: Tillerson Called Trump a 'Moron,' Almost Resigned," *Axios*, October 4, 2017.

97   *Speaking to reporters on the South Lawn:* "Trump Answers Questions on Rex Tillerson and Mike Pompeo: Full Transcript," *The New York Times*, March 13, 2018.

97   *"This can be a very mean-spirited town":* Gardiner Harris, "Tillerson Says Goodbye to 'a Very Mean-Spirited Town,'" *The New York Times*, March 22, 2018.

98   *"Tillerson Ousted as Trump Silences":* Mark Landler, Maggie Haberman and Gardiner Harris, "Tillerson Ousted as Trump Silences Dissent in Cabinet," *The New York Times*, March 14, 2018, p. A1.

100   *"Dear Chairman Kim," Trump wrote:* Letters between President Donald J. Trump and Kim Jong Un obtained by the author.

100   *Kim's letter was more enthusiastic:* Ibid.

100   *Trump later told me with pride:* Interview with President Donald J. Trump, December 13, 2019.

102   *"We want to thank Kim Jong Un":* "Remarks by President Trump at Arrival of Americans Detained in North Korea," May 10, 2018, WhiteHouse.gov.

CHAPTER FOURTEEN

103   *"I respect the decision":* Video: "Sen. Graham, I Believe Clinton Operatives Emailed DOJ," *America's News HQ*, Fox News, May 18, 2017, video.foxnews.com.

103   *In April 2018, Graham cosponsored:* See Mike Memoli and Frank Thorp V, "Senate Judiciary Committee Passes Bill to Protect Mueller," *NBC News*, April 26, 2018.

103   *The president called White House Counsel Don McGahn:* "The Mueller Report: The Report of the Special Counsel on the Investigation into Russian Interference in the 2016 Presidential Election," U.S. Department of Justice, Volume 2, p. 86.

105   *"You can see evidence in plain sight":* State of the Union transcript, NBC, February 17, 2019.

CHAPTER FIFTEEN

This chapter is primarily based on letters between President Donald J. Trump and Kim Jong Un obtained by the author.

107   *"The model, if you look at that model"*: "Remarks by President Trump and Secretary General Stoltenberg of NATO Before Bilateral Meeting," May 17, 2018, WhiteHouse.gov.

107   *North Korea's vice foreign minister*: Joshua Berlinger, "North Korea Warns of Nuclear Showdown, Calls Pence 'Political Dummy,'" CNN, May 24, 2018.

108   *"Holy shit," the president later told me*: Interview with President Donald J. Trump, December 13, 2019.

108   *Trump later said he found Kim*: Ibid.

108   *By the end of the meeting*: "Joint Statement of President Donald J. Trump of the United States of America and Chairman Kim Jong Un of the Democratic People's Republic of Korea at the Singapore Summit," June 12, 2018, White House.gov.

108   *"We will be stopping the war games"*: "Press Conference by President Trump," Capella Hotel, Singapore, June 12, 2018, WhiteHouse.gov.

109   *"Just landed—a long trip"*: @RealDonaldTrump, "Just landed—a long trip, but everybody can now feel much safer than the day I took office. There is no longer a Nuclear Threat from North Korea. Meeting with Kim Jong Un was an interesting and very positive experience. North Korea has great potential for the future!," 5:56 a.m., June 13, 2018, Twitter.com.

109   *In a second tweet, Trump added*: @RealDonaldTrump, "Before taking office people were assuming that we were going to War with North Korea. President Obama said that North Korea was our biggest and most dangerous problem. No longer—sleep well tonight!," 6:01 a.m., June 13, 2018, Twitter.com.

109   *"Saying it doesn't make it so"*: Karen DeYoung and John Wagner, "Trump and Kim Declare Summit a Big Success, but They Diverge on the Details," *The Washington Post*, June 13, 2018.

CHAPTER SIXTEEN

112   *On February 13, 2018, Dan Coats*: U.S. Government Publishing Office, "Full Transcript for Senate Hearing 115-278, Open Hearing on Worldwide Threats," hearing before the Select Committee on Intelligence of the United States Senate, February 13, 2018, Intelligence.Senate.gov.

112   *Under the headline, "Russia Is targeting"*: Ellen Nakashima and Shane Harris, "Russia Is Targeting 2018, Top Spies Warn," *The Washington Post*, February 14, 2018, p. A1.

112   *In its front-page story*: Matthew Rosenberg, Charlie Savage, and Michael Wines, "Russia Sees Midterm Elections as Chance to Sow Fresh Discord, Intelligence Chiefs Warn," *The New York Times*, February 13, 2018.

113   *"They said they think it's Russia":* "Remarks by President Trump and President Putin of the Russian Federation in Joint Press Conference," Presidential Palace, Helsinki, Finland, July 16, 2018, WhiteHouse.gov.

113   *Former Republican House Speaker Newt Gingrich:* @NewtGingrich, "President Trump must clarify his statements in Helsinki on our intelligence system and Putin. It is the most serious mistake of his presidency and must be corrected—immediately," 5:15 p.m., July 16, 2018, Twitter.com.

113   *John O. Brennan, the former CIA director:* @JohnBrennan, "Donald Trump's press conference performance in Helsinki rises to & exceeds the threshold of 'high crimes & misdemeanors.' It was nothing short of treasonous. Not only were Trump's comments imbecilic, he is wholly in the pocket of Putin. Republican Patriots: Where are you???," 11:52 a.m., July 16, 2018, Twitter.com.

113   *Coats, some 16 months into the job:* Director of National Intelligence, "Statement from DNI Coats," July 26, 2018, DNI.gov.

114   *Actually, Russia had about 1,600:* Hans M. Kristensen and Matt Korda, "Status of World Nuclear Forces," Federation of American Scientists, April 2020, FAS.org.

114   *Just before opening a question-and-answer session:* "A Look Over my Shoulder: The DNI Reflects and Foreshadows," Aspen Security Forum transcript, July 19, 2018, AspenSecurityForum.org.

115   *Coats made a public apology:* Zeke Miller, "Top U.S. Intelligence Official Coats Says He Meant No Disrespect to Trump Over Putin Summit," Associated Press, July 21, 2018.

116   *The NSA and CIA had evidence:* The names of the two counties have not been previously reported.

117   *So on August 2, Coats:* "Press Briefing by Press Secretary Sarah Sanders and National Security Officials," the White House, August 2, 2018, WhiteHouse.gov.

119   *In one meeting, Trump handed:* This article appeared in the print version of *USA Today* on September 14, 2018. Much of the information contained in it is currently available online at: Samantha Maffucci, "Who Is Dan Coats' Wife? New Details on Marsha Coats," September 14, 2018, YourTango.com.

119   *Representative Devin Nunes, the Republican chairman:* Charlie Savage and Sharon LaFraniere, "Republicans Claim Surveillance Power Abuses in Russia Inquiry," *The New York Times,* January 19, 2018.

119   *Unmasking was routine:* The National Security Agency processed 10,012 unmasking requests in 2019.

120   *To others, Trump said that Nunes:* Eli Watkins, "Trump Suggests Medal of Freedom for Rep. Devin Nunes," CNN, October 11, 2018. Trump initially suggested the Medal of Honor, which is a military award, and corrected himself that it should be the Medal of Freedom, a civilian award.

CHAPTER SEVENTEEN

126   *In September 2015, Xi had said:* "Remarks by President Obama and President Xi of the People's Republic of China in Joint Press Conference," White House Rose Garden, September 25, 2015, ObamaWhiteHouse.archives.gov.

CHAPTER EIGHTEEN

131   The New York Times *would later call him:* Helene Cooper, "How Mark Milley, a General Who Mixes Bluntness and Banter, Became Trump's Top Military Adviser," *The New York Times*, September 29, 2019.

133   *"I consider myself the most reluctant person":* Jim Mattis and Bing West, *Call Sign Chaos* (New York: Random House, 2019), p. 197.

CHAPTER NINETEEN

138   *Back in Washington on Wednesday:* @RealDonaldTrump, "We have defeated ISIS in Syria, my only reason for being there during the Trump Presidency," 9:29 a.m., December 19, 2018, Twitter.com.

138   *Later that day, Trump released:* @RealDonaldTrump, "After historic victories against ISIS, it's time to bring our great young people home!," 6:10 p.m., December 19, 2018, Twitter.com.

139   *Mattis figured that Kelly:* Annie Karni and Maggie Haberman, "John Kelly to Step Down as Trump, Facing New Perils, Shakes Up Staff," *The New York Times*, December 8, 2018.

139   *Nine months earlier, Mattis:* @RealDonaldTrump, "Mike Pompeo, Director of the CIA, will become our new Secretary of State. He will do a fantastic job! Thank you to Rex Tillerson for his service! Gina Haspel will become the new Director of the CIA, and the first woman so chosen. Congratulations to all!," 8:44 a.m., March 13, 2018, Twitter.com.

141   *"One core belief I have always held":* Daniel Bush, "Read James Mattis' Full Resignation Letter," *PBS NewsHour*, December 20, 2018, PBS.org.

143   *At 5:21 p.m. Trump tweeted:* @RealDonaldTrump, "General Jim Mattis will be retiring, with distinction, at the end of February, after having served my Administration as Secretary of Defense for the past two years. During Jim's tenure, tremendous progress has been made, especially with respect to the purchase of new fighting . . ." and ". . . equipment. General Mattis was a great help to me in getting allies and other countries to pay their share of military obligations. A new Secretary of Defense will be named shortly. I greatly thank Jim for his service!," 5:21 p.m., December 20, 2018, Twitter.com.

143   *But three days later, Trump said:* @RealDonaldTrump, "I am pleased to announce that our very talented Deputy Secretary of Defense, Patrick Shanahan, will assume the title of Acting Secretary of Defense starting January 1, 2019.

Patrick has a long list of accomplishments while serving as Deputy, & previously Boeing. He will be great!," 11:46 a.m., December 23, 2018, Twitter.com.

143 *At a cabinet meeting the next day:* Maggie Haberman, "Trump Says Mattis Resignation Was 'Essentially' a Firing, Escalating His New Front Against Military Critics," *The New York Times*, January 2, 2019.

143 *Later he called Mattis:* @RealDonaldTrump, "Probably the only thing Barack Obama & I have in common is that we both had the honor of firing Jim Mattis, the world's most overrated General. I asked for his letter of resignation & felt great about it. His nickname was 'Chaos,' which I didn't like, & changed to 'Mad Dog' . . ." and ". . . His primary strength was not military, but rather personal public relations. I gave him a new life, things to do, and battles to win, but he seldom 'brought home the bacon.' I didn't like his 'leadership' style or much else about him, and many others agree. Glad he is gone!," 9:02 p.m., June 3, 2020, Twitter.com.

143 *When I asked Trump about Mattis:* Interview with President Donald J. Trump, December 5, 2019.

CHAPTER TWENTY

144 *His interim Top Secret security clearance:* See Andrew Desiderio, "Whistleblower: White House Overruled 25 Security Clearance Denials," *Politico*, April 1, 2019. Also see "Summary of Interview with White House Whistleblower on Security Clearances," April 1, 2019, memo linked to in the article.

147 *John Kelly had a less-flattering assessment:* Bob Woodward, *Fear: Trump in the White House* (New York: Simon & Schuster, 2018), p. 286.

CHAPTER TWENTY-ONE

148 *Dan Coats launched the new year:* Director of National Intelligence, "Strategy Promotes Integration, Innovation, Partnerships, and Transparency for the 17 Intelligence Elements," January 22, 2019, DNI.gov.

148 *The strategy warned about "weakening":* "National Intelligence Strategy of the United States of America 2019," DNI.gov.

148 *A week after releasing the strategy, Coats gave:* U.S. Government Publishing Office, "Full Transcript for Senate Hearing 116-75, Open Hearing: Worldwide Threat Assessment of the U.S. Intelligence Community," hearing before the Select Committee on Intelligence of the United States Senate, January 29, 2019, Intelligence.Senate.gov.

149 *Fred Fleitz, president of the Center for Security Policy:* See @LouDobbs, "#DrainTheSwamp—@FredFleitz: I would fire Dan Coats because of his assessment. This intelligence service has evolved into a monster that is second-guessing @POTUS all the time. @realDonaldTrump has to stop these unclassified worldwide threat briefings. #MAGA #TrumpTrain #Dobbs," 7:48 p.m., January 29, 2019, Twitter.com.

149 *Lou Dobbs, host of the show:* Ibid.

149 *Trump tweeted: "The Intelligence people seem":* @RealDonaldTrump, "The Intelligence people seem to be extremely passive and naive when it comes to the dangers of Iran. They are wrong! When I became President Iran was making trouble all over the Middle East, and beyond. Since ending the terrible Iran Nuclear Deal, they are MUCH different, but . . ." 8:50 a.m. and ". . . a source of potential danger and conflict. They are testing Rockets (last week) and more, and are coming very close to the edge. There economy is now crashing, which is the only thing holding them back. Be careful of Iran. Perhaps Intelligence should go back to school!," 8:56 a.m., January 30, 2019, Twitter.com.

149 *"If we write a report based":* John Bowden, "Senate Intel Chairman: 'We Don't Have Anything' to Prove Collusion Between Trump Campaign and Russia," *The Hill*, February 7, 2019.

149 *Trump celebrated on Twitter:* See multiple @RealDonaldTrump tweets and retweets about Burr, February 7–25, 2019, Twitter.com.

150 *Chris Ruddy, the CEO of Newsmax:* "Sen. King Warns Against Dismissing Intelligence Director for Disputing Trump," CNN, July 28, 2019.

150 *A front-page story in* The Washington Post: Shane Harris, Josh Dawsey and Ellen Nakashima, "President Losing Faith in Coats, Aides Say," *The Washington Post*, February 20, p. A1.

CHAPTER TWENTY-TWO

154 *The result was a compromise:* "The Mueller Report: The Report of the Special Counsel on the Investigation into Russian Interference in the 2016 Presidential Election," U.S. Department of Justice, Volume 2, p. 2.

155 *The core finding of the Mueller report:* "Read Attorney General William Barr's Summary of the Mueller Report," *The New York Times*, March 24, 2019.

156 *Mueller wrote in his report:* "The Mueller Report: The Report of the Special Counsel on the Investigation into Russian Interference in the 2016 Presidential Election," U.S. Department of Justice, Volume 2, p. 2.

156 *However, Muller wrote:* Ibid.

156 *"Based on the facts":* Ibid.

156 *Barr said in his letter:* "Read Attorney General William Barr's Summary of the Mueller Report," *The New York Times*, March 24, 2019.

157 *At 4:46 p.m. that afternoon, Trump:* "Remarks by President Trump Before Air Force One Departure," Palm Beach, Florida, March 24, 2019, White House.gov.

158 *Trump walked onto the South Lawn:* Video: "Trump: 'America Is the Greatest Place on Earth,'" *The Washington Post*, March 24, 2019.

159 *"Mueller Finds No Conspiracy":* Matt Zapotosky and Devlin Barrett, "Mueller Finds No Conspiracy," *The Washington Post*, March 25, 2019, p. A1.

159   *"In* The New York Times *the banner headline:* Mark Mazzetti and Katie Benner, "Mueller Finds No Trump-Russia Conspiracy," March 25, 2019, p. A1.

159   *A news analysis in* the Times: Peter Baker, "Burden Lifts, Leaving Trump Fortified for the Battles to Come," March 25, 2019, p. A1.

159   *On March 27, Mueller wrote:* "Special Counsel Mueller's Letter to Attorney General Barr," *The Washington Post,* May 1, 2019.

160   *"We staffed the Department of Justice":* Molly Finnegan, "Read Rod Rosenstein's Full Resignation Letter," *PBS NewsHour,* April 29, 2019, PBS.org.

160   *"You put the power and authority":* Brett Samuels, "Hirono Rebukes Barr During Hearing: 'You Should Resign,'" *The Hill,* May 1, 2019.

161   *Several days later, more than 700:* Matt Zapotosky, "Trump Would Have Been Charged with Obstruction Were He Not President, Hundreds of Former Federal Prosecutors Assert," *The Washington Post,* May 6, 2019.

161   *In an April 2019 column:* Michael Smolens, "Public Has Mueller-Report Fatigue and Wants to Move On," *San Diego Union-Tribune,* April 18, 2019.

161   *In a March 2020 opinion issued:* See *Electronic Privacy Information Center v. United States Department of Justice and Jason Leopold* and *Buzzfeed, INC. v. United States Department of Justice.*

163   *Mueller testified before the House:* "Transcript of Robert S. Mueller III's Testimony Before the House Judiciary Committee," *The Washington Post,* July 24, 2019.

164   *Barr and Trump had defined the report:* @RealDonaldTrump, "The Democrats were trying mightily to revive the badly & irrevocably tarnished Witch Hunt Hoax until Robert Mueller put on the greatest display of ineptitude & incompetence that the Halls of Congress have ever seen. Truth is, he had no facts on his side. Nothing he could do!," 4:15 p.m., July 27, 2019, Twitter.com.

164   *Trump later told me:* Interview with President Donald J. Trump, December 30, 2019.

CHAPTER TWENTY-THREE

166   *In an open letter to Trump:* William H. McRaven, "Revoke My Security Clearance, Too, Mr. President," *The Washington Post,* August 16, 2018.

166   *Trump had blasted back: Fox News Sunday* transcript, Fox, November 18, 2018.

CHAPTER TWENTY-FOUR

168   *Trump began following a series:* The series of 14 columns were published in *The Hill* beginning in March 2019. For details, see "The Hill's Review of John Solomon's Columns on Ukraine," *The Hill,* February 19, 2020.

169   The New York Times *just released:* Maggie Haberman, Julian E. Barnes, and Peter Baker, "Dan Coats to Step Down as Intelligence Chief; Trump Picks Loyalist for Job," *The New York Times,* July 28, 2019.

169 *On the sixth hole:* @RealDonaldTrump, "I am pleased to announce that highly respected Congressman John Ratcliffe of Texas will be nominated by me to be the Director of National Intelligence. A former U.S. Attorney, John will lead and inspire greatness for the Country he loves. Dan Coats, the current Director, will . . ." and ". . . be leaving office on August 15th. I would like to thank Dan for his great service to our Country. The Acting Director will be named shortly," 4:45 p.m., July 28, 2017, Twitter.com.

CHAPTER TWENTY-FIVE

This chapter is primarily based on letters between President Donald J. Trump and Kim Jong Un obtained by the author.

175 *Trump had his own version of events:* Interview with President Donald. J. Trump, December 13, 2019.

176 *The summit was reported:* David E. Sanger, "Collapse of Talks Exposes Perils of 1-to-1 Diplomacy," *The New York Times*, March 1, 2019, p. A1.

177 *While in Japan on June 29:* @RealDonaldTrump, "After some very important meetings, including my meeting with President Xi of China, I will be leaving Japan for South Korea (with President Moon). While there, if Chairman Kim of North Korea sees this, I would meet him at the Border/DMZ just to shake his hand and say Hello(?)!," 6:51 p.m., June 28, 2019, Twitter.com.

178 *"Would you like me to come in?":* Interview with President Donald J. Trump, December 5, 2019.

178 *"I want to thank you," Trump said:* "Remarks by President Trump and Chairman Kim Jong Un of the Democratic People's Republic of Korea in 1:1 Meeting," Panmunjom, Inter-Korean House of Freedom, June 30, 2019, WhiteHouse.gov.

179 *"A Ratings-Minded President":* David Nakamura, "A Ratings-Minded President Gets the Shot He Wanted," *The Washington Post*, July 1, 2019, p. A1.

181 *"I got a very beautiful letter":* "Remarks by President Trump Before Marine One Departure," August 9, 2019, WhiteHouse.gov.

CHAPTER TWENTY-SIX

This chapter is primarily based on an interview with President Donald J. Trump on December 5, 2019.

186 *It costs the United States approximately:* Office of the Under Secretary of Defense (Comptroller)/Chief Financial Officer, "Operation and Maintenance Overview, Fiscal Year 2020," March 2019, Defense.gov.

187 *Exit polls showed:* Jon Huang, Samuel Jacoby, Michael Strickland, and K. K. Rebecca Lai, "Election 2016: Exit Polls," *The New York Times*, Nov. 8, 2016.

CHAPTER TWENTY-SEVEN

This chapter is primarily based on an interview with President Donald J. Trump on December 13, 2019.

190 *The vote to impeach was 23 to 17:* Mike DeBonis, John Wagner and Toluse Olorunnipa, "House Set for Historic Floor Vote Next Week After Committee Approves Two Articles of Impeachment Against Trump," *The Washington Post*, December 13, 2019.

191 *We turned to North Korea:* Simon Denyer, "North Korea Warns United States of an Unwelcome 'Christmas Gift,'" *The Washington Post*, December 3, 2019.

192 *It was actually 50 percent:* Trump's 2016 presidential campaign spent $398 million. Clinton's campaign spent $798 million. The media analysis firm mediaQuant estimated Trump received about $5 billion in earned media exposure, compared to $3.2 billion earned media for Clinton's campaign.

CHAPTER TWENTY-EIGHT

This chapter is primarily based on an interview with President Donald J. Trump on December 30, 2019.

199 *Early in the interview I mentioned:* David Frost, *"I Gave Them a Sword": Behind the Scenes of the Nixon Interviews* (New York: William Morrow, 1978), p. 269.

199 *In the rough transcript:* See "Telephone Conversation with President Zelenskyy of Ukraine," July 25, 2019, transcript, declassified September 24, 2019, WhiteHouse.gov.

201 *Trump was referring to Biden's:* See video and transcript, "Foreign Affairs Issue Launch with Former President Joe Biden," Council on Foreign Relations, January 23, 2018, CFR.org.

202 *Schiff led into his heavily paraphrased account:* See Lori Robertson, "Schiff's 'Parody' and Trump's Response," *FactCheck.org*, October 1, 2019.

206 *Trump's best-known recent apology:* See Robert Farley, "Trump's Rare Apology," *FactCheck.org*, December 12, 2017.

CHAPTER TWENTY-NINE

208 *The Senate had confirmed 187:* Russell Wheeler, "Judicial Appointments in Trump's First Three Years: Myths and Realities," Brookings, January 28, 2020, Brookings.edu.

CHAPTER THIRTY

212 *"My concern is that there are always emerging":* See video, "Dr. Anthony Fauci '58 Visits Regis," Regis High School, June 27, 2019, Regis.org.

212 *Redfield, 68, an expert:* See Chinese news release linked to in the "China—Original 2919-nCov news thread: weeks 1–4" on FluTrackers.com.

213 *The CDC's first formal report:* "China Pneumonia of Unknown Etiology Situational Report," CDC, January 1, 2020. Document obtained by the author.

214 *On January 2, the second CDC:* "China Pneumonia of Unknown Etiology Situational Report," CDC, January 2, 2020. Document obtained by the author.

215 *"Hong Kong, Taiwan, Singapore":* "China Pneumonia of Unknown Etiology Situational Report," CDC, January 3, 2020. Document obtained by the author.

217 *By January 5, according to the CDC:* "China Pneumonia of Unknown Etiology Situational Report," CDC, January 5, 2020. Document obtained by the author.

218 *The situational report for January 6:* "China Pneumonia of Unknown Etiology Situational Report," CDC, January 6, 2020. Document obtained by the author.

218 *One* Bloomberg News *story, dubbing it:* "China Will Rack Up Three Billion Trips During World's Biggest Human Migration," *Bloomberg News,* January 20, 2020.

218 *The CDC report also noted:* "China Pneumonia of Unknown Etiology Situational Report," CDC, January 6, 2020. Document obtained by the author.

218 *On January 7, he stood up:* "2020 Pneumonia of Unknown Etiology Situational Report," CDC, January 7, 2020. Document obtained by the author.

219 *The January 8 situational report:* "2020 Pneumonia of Unknown Etiology Situational Report," CDC, January 8, 2020. Document obtained by the author.

219 *The CDC situational report for January 13:* "Novel Coronavirus (nCoV) 2019 Situational Report," CDC, January 13, 2020. Document obtained by the author.

220 *On January 15, the CDC Situational Report:* "Novel Coronavirus (2019-nCoV) Situational Report," CDC, January 15, 2020. Document obtained by the author.

CHAPTER THIRTY-ONE

This chapter is primarily based on interviews with President Donald J. Trump on January 20 and January 22, 2020.

223 *About two minutes after our call:* @RealDonaldTrump, ". . . And they say you can add 7% to 10% to all Trump numbers! Who knows?," 1:53 p.m., January 20, 2020, Twitter.com.

223 *The national average of presidential job approval:* "President Trump Job Approval," *RealClearPolitics,* January 20, 2020.

223 *"It's one person coming in from China":* Matthew J. Belvedere, "Trump Says

He Trusts China's Xi on Coronavirus and the US Has It 'Totally Under Control,'" CNBC, January 22, 2020.

223   *"We think it is going to be handled":* Alexandra Alper, "Trump Says U.S. in 'Great Shape' with Plan for Coronavirus," Reuters, January 22, 2020.

227   *In a fact check, the Associated Press:* Calvin Woodward and Robert Burns, "AP FACT CHECK: Trump Inflates Value of Saudi Arms Deal," Associated Press, November 21 2018.

228   *Although Trump has repeated:* Russell Wheeler, "Judicial Appointments in Trump's First Three Years: Myths and Realities," Brookings, January 28, 2020, Brookings.edu.

229   *According to a tally kept:* Juliet Eilperin and Darla Cameron, "How Trump Is Rolling Back Obama's Legacy," *The Washington Post*, published March 24, 2017, and updated January 20, 2018.

230   *On January 24, Chinese scientists:* Chaolin Huang, Yeming Wang, Xingwang Li, et al., "Clinical Features of Patients Infected with 2019 Novel Coronavirus in Wuhan, China," *The Lancet*, January 24, 2020, Vol. 395, Issue 10223, TheLancet.com.

231   *A new impeachment sensation appeared:* Maggie Haberman and Michael S. Schmidt, "Money to Ukraine Tied to Inquiries Bolton Book Says," *The New York Times*, January 27, 2020, p. A1.

233   *Press Secretary Stephanie Grisham said:* "Statement from the Press Secretary Regarding the President's Coronavirus Task Force," January 29, 2020, WhiteHouse.gov.

233   *In a Michigan speech January 30:* "Remarks by President Trump at a USMCA Celebration with American Workers," Warren, Michigan, January 30, 2020, WhiteHouse.gov.

235   *The German report, printed as a letter:* Camilla Rothe, Mirjam Schunk, Peter Sothmann, et al., "Transmission of 2019-nCoV Infection from an Asymptomatic Contact in Germany," *The New England Journal of Medicine*, January 30, 2020, NEJM.org. See also Matt Apuzzo, Selam Gebrekidan, and David D. Kirkpatrick, "How the World Missed Covid-19's Silent Spread," *The New York Times*, June 27, 2020.

237   *"This is a serious health situation":* "Press Briefing by Members of the President's Coronavirus Task Force," January 31, 2020, WhiteHouse.gov.

237   *"We still have a low risk":* Ibid.

237   *"Today President Trump took decisive action":* Ibid.

237   *"Administration Elevates Response to Coronavirus":* Erica Werner, Yasmeen Abutaleb, Lenny Bernstein, and Lena H. Sun, "Administration Elevates Response to Coronavirus," *The Washington Post*, February 1, 2020, p. A1.

237   *In The New York Times, the news:* Michael Corkery and Annie Karni, "Declaring Health Emergency, U.S. Restricts Travel from China," *The New York Times*, February 1, 2020, p. A1.

237   *Despite the conclusive evidence:* Interview with President Donald J. Trump, March 19, 2020.

238   *On May 6, he told me:* Interview with President Donald J. Trump, May 6, 2020.

CHAPTER THIRTY-TWO

239 *"What he did was not perfect"*: "Full Transcript: Mitt Romney's Speech Announcing Vote to Convict Trump," *The New York Times*, February 5, 2020.

240 *While he said Trump's behavior*: "Alexander Statement on Impeachment Witness Vote," Office of Lamar Alexander, January 30, 2020, Alexander .Senate.gov.

240 *"Let me be clear, Lamar speaks"*: Sheryl Gay Stolberg and Carl Hulse, "Alexander Says Convicting Trump Would 'Pour Gasoline on Cultural Fires,'" *The New York Times*, January 31, 2020.

240 *"I believe that delaying"*: Joseph Morton, "Sasse Says Delaying Aid to Ukraine Was 'Wrong,' but Not Grounds for Removing Trump from Office," *Omaha World-Herald*, February 4, 2020.

244 *The official press release*: "Representatives of Coronavirus Task Force Brief Governors at NGA," February 9, 2020, HHS.gov.

244 *The next day, President Trump said publicly*: See "Remarks by President Trump at the White House Business Session with Our Nation's Governors," WhiteHouse.gov; Transcript of *Trish Regan Primetime*, Fox Business; and "President Trump Rally in Manchester, New Hampshire," C-SPAN, all February 10, 2020.

244 *Fauci attended a public conference*: "Public Health Grand Rounds at the Aspen Institute Presents Coronavirus: The New Pandemic?," February 11, 2020. Video available at AspenInstitute.org.

245 *At an event a week later*: Transcript, "Threats to Global Health and Bio Security," Council on Foreign Relations, February 18, 2020, CFR.org.

246 *I reached President Trump by phone*: Interview with President Donald J. Trump, February 19, 2020.

246 *Six days earlier, Attorney General Bill Barr*: Anne Flaherty, "Barr Blasts Trump's Tweets on Stone Case: 'Impossible for Me to Do My Job': ABC News Exclusive," ABC, February 13, 2020.

247 *Barr made the comments after*: @RealDonaldTrump, "This is a horrible and very unfair situation. The real crimes were on the other side, as nothing happens to them. Cannot allow this miscarriage of justice!," 1:48 a.m., February 11, 2020, Twitter.com.

247 *In early 2020, with 80 million*: According to two actively maintained Wikipedia pages that track public Twitter and Facebook metrics: "List of Most-Followed Twitter Accounts" and "List of Most-Followed Facebook Pages," En.Wikipedia.org.

248 *Earlier that day he had tweeted*: @RealDonaldTrump, "Internal REAL Polls show I am beating all of the Dem candidates. The Fake News Polls (here we go again, just like 2016) show losing or tied. Their polls will be proven corrupt on November 3rd, just like the Fake News is corrupt!," 12:10 p.m., February 19, 2020, Twitter.com.

250 *The report released by the group*: "Report of the WHO-China Joint Mission on Coronavirus Disease 2019 (COVID-19)," 16–24 February 2020, WHO.int.

250 *The WHO report contained a stark:* Ibid., p. 19.

251 *"We have it very much under control":* "Remarks by President Trump Before Marine One Departure," February 23, 2020, WhiteHouse.gov.

251 *The next day he tweeted:* @RealDonaldTrump, "The Coronavirus is very much under control in the USA. We are in contact with everyone and all relevant countries. CDC & World Health have been working hard and very smart. Stock Market starting to look very good to me!," 4:42 p.m., February 24, 2002, Twitter.com.

251 *"The disruption to everyday life":* "Transcript for the CDC Telebriefing Update on COVID-19," CDC.gov, February 25, 2020.

252 *"Viral Crisis in U.S. Is Deemed Likely":* Pam Belluck and Noah Weiland, "It 'Could Be Bad': Viral Crisis in U.S. Is Deemed Likely," *The New York Times*, February 26, 2020, p. A1.

252 *"Threat to Americans called 'inevitable'":* Erica Werner, Yasmeen Abutaleb, and Lena H. Sun, "Coronavirus Will Spread in U.S., CDC Says," *The Washington Post*, February 26, 2020, p. A1.

252 *"When you have 15 people":* "Remarks by President Trump, Vice President Pence, and Members of the Coronavirus Task Force in Press Conference," February 26, 2020, WhiteHouse.gov.

254 *In testimony before the House:* "HHS Secretary Azar Testifies on President's 2021 Budget Request," C-SPAN, February 27, 2020.

254 *Later that day at a rally in South Carolina:* Rem Rieder, "Trump and the 'New Hoax,'" FactCheck.org, March 3, 2020.

254 *"So, Dr. Fauci, it's Saturday":* *Today* show video, "Dr. Fauci on Coronavirus Fears: No Need to Change Lifestyle Yet," NBC, February 29, 2020.

255 *At the Coronavirus Task Force briefing:* "Remarks by President Trump, Vice President Pence, and Members of the Coronavirus Task Force in Press Conference," February 29, 2020, WhiteHouse.gov.

CHAPTER THIRTY-THREE

257 *"He's crazy . . . and it's kind of working":* Peggy Noonan, "Over Trump, We're as Divided as Ever," *The Wall Street Journal*, March 8, 2018. Several months after that column, Trump posted a tweet denouncing Noonan as "the simplistic writer for Trump Haters."

258 *He paraphrased the cat:* The Cheshire Cat said: "It doesn't matter which way you go . . . if you only walk long enough."

258 *In the book, Whipple:* Chris Whipple, *The Gatekeepers* (New York: Broadway Books, 2018). *The Gatekeepers* shows the immense power and responsibility entrusted to those who have held the unelected, unconfirmed position and argues "[t]he framers of the Constitution never envisioned anything like it."

258 *Adams, the creator of the* Dilbert *comic:* Scott Adams, *Win Bigly: Persuasion in a World Where Facts Don't Matter* (New York: Portfolio/Penguin, 2018).

258 *Kushner said that Scott Adams's approach:* "Remarks by President Trump in State of the Union Address," U.S. Capitol, February 4, 2020, WhiteHouse. gov.

259 *A hair-splitting, fact-checking debate:* In some ways, Trump was applying to the presidency the same approaches he used in his career as a New York real estate developer. In his 1987 bestseller *The Art of the Deal*, Trump wrote: "People want to believe that something is the biggest and the greatest and the most spectacular. I call it truthful hyperbole. It's an innocent form of exaggeration—and a very effective form of promotion."

260 *Earlier in February:* Interview with President Donald J. Trump, February 7, 2020.

CHAPTER THIRTY-FOUR

264 *A DHS report said the wall:* Julia Edwards Ainsley, "Exclusive–Trump Border 'Wall' to Cost $21.6 Billion, Take 3.5 Years to Build: Internal Report," Reuters, February 9, 2017.

265 *But Customs and Border Protection (CBP) said:* See Eugene Kiely, Brooks Jackson, Lori Robertson, et al., "FactChecking the State of the Union," *FactCheck.org*, February 5, 2020; and U.S. Customs and Border Protection, "CBP/USACE Border Wall Status as of January 24, 2020," linked to in the article.

266 *"Cumming District is a disgusting":* @RealDonaldTrump, ". . . As proven last week during a Congressional tour, the Border is clean, efficient & well run, just very crowded. Cumming District is a disgusting, rat and rodent infested mess. If he spent more time in Baltimore, maybe he could help clean up this very dangerous & filthy place," 7:14 a.m., and "Why is so much money sent to the Elijah Cummings district when it is considered the worst run and most dangerous anywhere in the United States. No human being would want to live there. Where is all this money going? How much is stolen? Investigate this corrupt mess immediately!," 7:24 a.m., July 27, 2019, Twitter.com.

266 *"This seems, Mick," Wallace said:* Fox News Sunday transcript, Fox News, July 28, 2019.

CHAPTER THIRTY-FIVE

271 *The main headline in* The New York Times: Matt Phillips, "Coronavirus Fears Drive Stocks Down for 6th Day and into Correction," *The New York Times*, February 27, 2019, updated February 28, 2019.

271 *The day before, Trump had said during remarks:* "Remarks by President Trump in Meeting with African American Leaders," February 27, 2020, WhiteHouse.gov.

CHAPTER THIRTY-SIX

273 *"We're dealing with an evolving situation":* Video, "Dr. Fauci: Coronavirus Now at 'Outbreak' and 'Likely Pandemic Proportions,'" MSNBC, March 2, 2020.

274 *Speaking at the CDC, Trump promised:* "Remarks by President Trump After Tour of the Centers for Disease Control and Prevention," Atlanta, Georgia, March 6, 2020, WhiteHouse.gov.

274 *"We're not blind where this virus is":* Ibid.

275 *After this became public, Bolsonaro:* Lisandra Paraguassu, "Brazil's Bolsonaro Says Coronavirus Is Not All the Media Makes It Out to Be," Reuters, March 10, 2020.

275 *On March 9, with the stock market reeling":* @RealDonaldTrump, "So last year 37,000 Americans died from the common Flu. It averages between 27,000 and 70,000 per year. Nothing is shut down, life & the economy go on. At this moment there are 546 confirmed cases of CoronaVirus, with 22 deaths. Think about that!," 10:47 a.m., March 9, 2020, Twitter.com.

275 *The New York Times headline the morning:* Matt Phillips, Peter Eavis, and David Enrich, "Markets Spiral As Globe Shudders Over Virus," *The New York Times*, March 10, 2020, p. A1.

275 *The Times wrote it was:* Live update, "Wall Street Bounces Back from Monday's Plunge," *The New York Times*, March 10, 2020.

275 *In remarks to reporters following:* "Remarks by President Trump After Meeting with Republican Senators," U.S. Capitol, March 10, 2020, White House.gov.

276 *In January before the restrictions:* Anne Schuchat, "Public Health Response to the Initiation and Spread of Pandemic COVID-19 in the United States, February 24–April 21, 2020," CDC Morbidity and Mortality Weekly Report, May 8, 2020.

276 *Nearly 140,000 had come from Italy:* Ibid.

277 *"Everyone is pro-tree," Benioff said:* Lisa Friedman, "A Trillion Trees: How One Idea Triumphed Over Trump's Climate Denialism," *The New York Times*, February 12, 2020.

277 *That afternoon, the World Health Organization:* "WHO Director-General's Opening Remarks at the Media Briefing on COVID-19," March 11, 2020, WHO.int.

277 *"This is the most aggressive":* "Remarks by President Trump in Address to the Nation," Oval Office, March 11, 2020, WhiteHouse.gov.

278 *Peggy Noonan wrote the next day:* Peggy Noonan, "'Don't Panic' Is Rotten Advice," *The Wall Street Journal*, March 12, 2020.

279 *Testifying before Congress, Fauci said:* Glenn Kessler, "What Did Dr. Anthony Fauci Say About Coronavirus Testing 'Failing'?," *The Washington Post*, March 18, 2020.

279 *The Dow Jones fell 10 percent:* Emily Cochrane, Jeanna Smialek, and Jim

Tankersley, "Worst Rout for Wall Street Since 1987 Crash," *The New York Times*, March 13, p. A1.

279   *A giant chart on the front page:* See Caitlin McCabe and Caitlin Ostroff, "Stocks Plunge 10% in Dow's Worst Day Since 1987," *The Wall Street Journal*, March 12, 2020.

279   *On March 13, Trump declared:* "Remarks by President Trump, Vice President Pence, and Members of the Coronavirus Task Force in Press Conference," March 13, 2020, WhiteHouse.gov.

279   *Shortly after, Google tweeted:* @Google_Comms, "Statement from Verily: 'We are developing a tool to help triage individuals for Covid-19 testing. Verily is in the early stages of development, and planning to roll testing out in the Bay Area, with the hope of expanding more broadly over time," 5:16 p.m., March 13, 2020, Twitter.com.

CHAPTER THIRTY-SEVEN

282   *Asked about his frequent assertion:* "Remarks by President Trump, Vice President Pence, and Members of the Coronavirus Task Force in Press Briefing," March 16, 2020, WhiteHouse.gov.

283   *In a tweet on March 16, Trump wrote:* @RealDonaldTrump, "The United States will be powerfully supporting those industries, like Airlines and others, that are particularly affected by the Chinese Virus. We will be stronger than ever before!," 6:51 p.m., March 16, 2020, Twitter.com.

284   *"This thing is a nasty—it's a nasty situation":* Interview with President Donald J. Trump, March 19, 2020.

285   *Just two days before, at the task force briefing:* "Remarks by President Trump, Vice President Pence, and Members of the Coronavirus Task Force in Press Briefing," March 17, 2020, WhiteHouse.gov.

286   *"If things don't go as planned":* "Remarks by President Trump, Vice President Pence, and Members of the Coronavirus Task Force in Press Briefing," March 19, 2020, WhiteHouse.gov.

287   *Studies later indicated the drug:* "FDA Cautions Against Use of Hydroxychloroquine or Chloroquine for COVID-10 Outside of the Hospital Setting or a Clinical Trial Due to Risk of Heart Rhythm Problems," June 15, 2020, FDA.gov.

288   *I brought up Trump's comments at a press briefing:* "Remarks by President Trump, Vice President Pence, and Members of the Coronavirus Task Force in Press Conference," March 13, 2020, WhiteHouse.gov.

288   *Obama's National Security Council had left behind:* Executive Office of the President of the United States, "Playbook for Early Response to High-Consequence Emerging Infectious Disease Threats and Biological Incidents," undated, available on DocumentCloud.org.

289   *Shortly before midnight on March 22:* @RealDonaldTrump, "WE CANNOT LET THE CURE BE WORSE THAN THE PROBLEM ITSELF. AT THE

END OF THE 15 DAY PERIOD, WE WILL MAKE A DECISION AS TO WHICH WAY WE WANT TO GO!," 11:50 p.m., March 22, 2020, Twitter .com.

290 *"I talk about the Chinese virus":* "Remarks by President Trump, Vice President Pence, and Members of the Coronavirus Task Force in Press Conference," March 26, 2020, WhiteHouse.gov.

292 *During the next day's briefing, Trump alluded:* "Remarks by President Trump, Vice President Pence, and Members of the Coronavirus Task Force in Press Conference," March 28, 2020, WhiteHouse.gov.

293 *"I'm running a big, big operation":* Interview with President Donald J. Trump, March 28, 2020.

296 *"I mean, you could make a big soundbite":* "Remarks by President Trump, Vice President Pence, and Members of the Coronavirus Task Force in Press Briefing," March 29, 2020, WhiteHouse.gov.

296 *Trump announced the 30-day:* "Remarks by President Trump and Members of the Coronavirus Task Force in Press Briefing," March 30, 2020, WhiteHouse.gov.

CHAPTER THIRTY-EIGHT

This chapter is primarily based on an interview with President Donald J. Trump on April 5, 2020.

297 *On April 3, when the CDC issued:* "Remarks by President Trump, Vice President Pence, and Members of the Coronavirus Task Force in Press Briefing," April 3, 2020, WhiteHouse.gov.

302 *I asked Trump if he had seen:* Henry A. Kissinger, "The Coronavirus Pandemic Will Forever Alter the World Order," *The Wall Street Journal*, April 3, 2020.

303 The Department of Homeland Security had released: "Advisory Memorandum on Identification of Essential Critical Infrastructure Workers During COVID-19 Response," March 28, 2020, CISA.gov.

303 *In March 2020 U.S. airlines carried:* "March 2020 U.S. Airline Traffic Data (Final)," June 11, 2020, BTS.gov.

303 *In a press briefing on April 1:* "Remarks by President Trump, Vice President Pence, and Members of the Coronavirus Task Force in Press Briefing," April 1, 2020, WhiteHouse.gov.

304 *In a recent* Washington Post *op-ed, he'd written:* Bill Gates, "Bill Gates: Here's How to Make Up for Lost Time on Covid-19," *The Washington Post*, March 31, 2020.

304 *In December 2016, Gates came to Trump Tower:* See Betsy McKay, "Bill Gates Has Regrets," *The Wall Street Journal*, May 11, 2020.

304 *In 2017, Trump told Gates:* Josh Keefe, "Is Donald Trump an Anti-Vaxxer? Bill Gates Said President Asked Him if Vaccines 'Weren't a Bad Thing,'" *Newsweek*, May 18, 2018.

305 *In a tweet on April 15, Gates blasted:* @BillGates, "Halting funding for the World Health Organization during a world health crisis is as dangerous as it sounds. Their work is slowing the spread of COVID-19 and if that work is stopped no other organization can replace them. The world needs @WHO now more than ever," 11:17 a.m., April 15, 2020, Twitter.com.

307 *A Gallup poll in March showed:* Jeffrey M. Jones, "Trump Job Approval at Personal Best 49%," Gallup, Inc., February 4, 2020.

309 *While Trump's job approval rating had reached:* "President Trump Job Approval," *RealClearPolitics*, January 20, 2020.

CHAPTER THIRTY-NINE

311 *"LIGHT AT THE END OF THE TUNNEL!":* @RealDonaldTrump, "LIGHT AT THE END OF THE TUNNEL!," 7:55 a.m., April 6, 2020, Twitter.com.

311 *Counties that are majority-Black:* Reis Thebault, Andrew Ba Tran, and Vanessa Williams, "The Coronavirus Is Infecting and Killing Black Americans at an Alarmingly High Rate," *The Washington Post*, April 7, 2020.

311 *In the four-week period ending April 9:* Heather Long and Andrew Van Dam, "America Is in a Depression. The Challenge Now Is to Make It Short-Lived," *The Washington Post*, April 9, 2020.

311 *"The minimum number was 100,000 lives":* "Remarks by President Trump, Vice President Pence, and Members of the Coronavirus Task Force in Press Briefing," April 10, 2020, WhiteHouse.gov.

312 *"If you had a process that was ongoing":* State of the Union transcript, CNN, April 12, 2020.

312 *Several hours later, on Sunday evening:* Katie Shepherd, John Wagner, and Felicia Sonmez, "White House Denies Trump Is Considering Firing Fauci Despite His Retweet of a Hashtag Calling for His Ouster," *The Washington Post*, April 13, 2020.

312 *Answering questions from reporters:* "Remarks by President Trump, Vice President Pence, and Members of the Coronavirus Task Force in Press Briefing," April 13, 2020, WhiteHouse.gov.

312 *The federal government would "be there to help":* "Remarks by President Trump in Press Briefing," April 14, 2020, WhiteHouse.gov.

313 *I reached Trump at the White House:* Interview with President Donald J. Trump, April 13, 2020.

313 *That day,* The Washington Post *reported "shortages":* Philip Bump, "The Reality of Coronavirus Testing Continues to Differ from Trump's Claims," *The Washington Post*, April 13, 2020.

317 *"The president has overdelivered":* Video, Lindsey Graham appearance on *Hannity*, Fox News, April 14, 2020.

320 *"Our nation is engaged in a historic battle":* "Remarks by President Trump, Vice President Pence, and Members of the Coronavirus Task Force in Press Briefing," April 16, 2020, WhiteHouse.gov.

320 *"U.S. Unemployment Claims Rise to 22 Million":* Philip Rucker, Josh Dawsey,

and Yasmeen Abutaleb, "U.S. Unemployment Claims Rise to 22 Million," *The Washington Post*, April 17, 2020, p. A1.

320 *"Broad Shutdown Pushes Americans to Economic Edge":* Patricia Cohen, "Broad Shutdown Pushes Americans to Economic Edge," *The New York Times*, April 17, 2020, p. A1.

320 *Georgia Governor Brian Kemp had on April 20:* Jeff Amy, "Kemp Says Some Shuttered Businesses Can Reopen Friday," Associated Press, April 20, 2020.

320 *"I told the governor of Georgia":* "Remarks by President Trump, Vice President Pence, and Members of the Coronavirus Task Force in Press Briefing," April 22, 2020, WhiteHouse.gov.

320 *"You see states are starting to open up now":* "Remarks by President Trump, Vice President Pence, and Members of the Coronavirus Task Force in Press Briefing," April 23, 2020, WhiteHouse.gov.

321 *"It's gonna go," Trump said at a meeting:* "Remarks by President Trump and Vice President Pence in Roundtable with Industry Executives on the Plan for Opening Up America Again," April 29, 2020, WhiteHouse.gov.

321 *"If the United States is not well prepared":* "North Korea's Top Nuclear Negotiator Warns of 'Terrible Events' if Talks with U.S. Resume Without Shift," Reuters, October 7, 2019.

321 *North Korea had threatened the U.S.:* Joshua Berlinger, "North Korea Warns US to Prepare for 'Christmas Gift,'" but No One's Sure What to Expect," CNN, December 5, 2019.

321 *"I received a nice note from him":* "Remarks by President Trump and Members of the Coronavirus Task Force in Press Briefing," April 18, 2020, White House.gov.

322 *"Well, I understand what's going on":* "Remarks by President Trump on Protecting America's Seniors," April 30, 2020, WhiteHouse.gov.

322 *State media reported that Kim had presided:* Choe Sang Hun, "Kim Jong Un Moves to Increase North Korea's Nuclear Strength," *The New York Times*, May 24, 2020.

322 *Later, North Korea demolished:* The building was demolished on June 16, 2020.

CHAPTER FORTY

This chapter is primarily based on an interview with President Donald J. Trump on May 6, 2020.

325 *He noted that Katie Miller:* "Remarks by President Trump in Meeting with Republican Members of Congress," May 8, 2020, WhiteHouse.gov.

328 *The Labor Department released a report:* Employment Situation News Release, "The Employment Situation—April 2020," U.S. Bureau of Labor Statistics, May 8, 2020, BLS.gov.

328 *Trump's job approval had only:* "President Trump Job Approval," *RealClear Politics*, January 20, 2020.

329   *In public comments in the Rose Garden, Slaoui:* "Remarks by President Trump on Vaccine Development," May 15, 2020, WhiteHouse.gov.

CHAPTER FORTY-ONE

This chapter is primarily based on an interview with President Donald J. Trump on May 22, 2020.

CHAPTER FORTY-TWO

This chapter is primarily based on an interview with President Donald J. Trump on June 3, 2020.

337   *"You have to dominate," Trump said:* Transcript, "READ: President Trump's Call with U.S. Governors over Protests," CNN, June 1, 2020.

337   *At around 6:30 p.m., without apparent provocation:* Carol D. Leonnig et al., "Barr Personally Ordered Removal of Protesters Near White House, Leading to Use of Force Against Largely Peaceful Crowd," *The Washington Post*, June 2, 2020; Alex Horton et al., "A Low-Flying 'Show of Force,'" *The Washington Post*, June 23, 2010; and Carol D. Leonnig, "Park Police Spokesman Acknowledges Chemical Agents Used on Lafayette Square Protesters Are Similar to Tear Gas," *The Washington Post*, June 5, 2020.

337   *"All Americans were rightly sickened":* "Statement by the President," Rose Garden, June 1, 2020, WhiteHouse.gov.

338   *"Is that your Bible?":* Zach Montague, "Holding It Aloft, He Incited a Backlash. What Does the Bible Mean to Trump?," *The New York Times*, June 2, 2020.

338   *"I am outraged":* Michelle Boorstein and Sarah Pulliam Bailey, "Episcopal Bishop on President Trump: 'Everything He Has Said and Done Is to Inflame Violence,'" *The Washington Post*, June 1, 2020.

339   *"This evening," Episcopal Church Presiding Bishop:* "Presiding Bishop Michael Curry's statement on President Trump's Use of St. John's, Holy Bible," Episcopal News Service, June 1, 2020, EpiscopalNewsService.org.

339   *"When I joined the military, some 50 years ago":* Jeffrey Goldbert, "James Mattis Denounces President Trump, Describes Him as a Threat to the Constitution," *The Atlantic*, June 3, 2020.

340   *"I didn't like his 'leadership'":* @RealDonaldTrump, ". . . His primary strength was not military, but rather personal public relations. I gave him a new life, things to do, and battles to win, but he seldom 'brought home the bacon.' I didn't like his 'leadership' style or much else about him, and many others agree. Glad he is gone!," 9:02 p.m., June 3, 2020, Twitter.com.

342   *News reports said he had been rushed:* Michael D. Shear and Katie Rogers, "Trump and Aides Try to Change the Narrative of the White House Protests," *The New York Times*, June 3, 2020.

343   *"Things were so bad that the Secret Service":* Chris Strohm, "Barr Says Secret

Service Told Trump to Go to White House Bunker," *Bloomberg News*, June 8, 2020.

CHAPTER FORTY-THREE

347   *Graham had refused publicly:* Andrew Desiderio, "Graham Shoots Down Trump's Call for Obama's Testimony on Russia Probe Origins," *Politico*, May 14, 2020.

CHAPTER FORTY-FOUR

This chapter is primarily based on an interview with President Donald J. Trump on June 19, 2020.

352   *Then on April 7 Trump said:* "Remarks by President Trump, Vice President Pence, and Members of the Coronavirus Task Force in Press Briefing," April 7, 2020, WhiteHouse.gov.

353   *On April 17, in the middle of:* @RealDonaldTrump, "LIBERATE MINNESOTA!," 11:21 a.m., "LIBERATE MICHIGAN!," 11:22 a.m., "LIBERATE VIRGINIA, and save your great 2nd Amendment. It is under siege!," 11:25 a.m., April 17, 2020, Twitter.com.

353   *Fauci gave an interview:* Jon Cohen, "'I'm Going to Keep Pushing.' Anthony Fauci Tries to Make the White House Listen to Facts of the Pandemic," *Science*, March 22, 2020.

355   *Fauci publicly said China:* "Threats to Global Health and Bio Security," Council on Foreign Relations, February 18, 2020, CFR.org.

357   *In it, Bolton wrote of a meeting:* John Bolton, "John Bolton: The Scandal of Trump's China Policy," *The Wall Street Journal*, June 17, 2020.

358   *"I've done more for the Black community":* Trump's claim that he has done more for the Black community than any president other than Abraham Lincoln has been widely refuted by historians. See Linda Qiu, "Trump's False Claim That 'Nobody Has Ever Done' More for the Black Community than He Has," *The New York Times*, June 5, 2020.

CHAPTER FORTY-FIVE

This chapter is primarily based on an interview with President Donald J. Trump on June 22, 2020.

365   *"It just came out, that the headline, quote":* See Brian Flood, "Trump Rally Gives Fox News Largest Saturday Night Audience in Its History," *Fox News*, June 22, 2020.

365   *Tulsa's top public health official:* Stetson Payne, "Tulsa Health Department Director 'Wishes' Trump Rally Would Be Postponed as Local COVID Cases Surge," *Tulsa World*, June 13, 2020.

369   *Trump seemed to be referring to the June 5 jobs numbers:* Employment Situation News Release, "The Employment Situation—May 2020," U.S. Bureau of Labor Statistics, June 5, 2020, BLS.gov.

369   *"You remember when Bob Costa and I came":* See Bob Woodward, *Fear: Trump in the White House* (New York: Simon & Schuster, 2018); and Bob Woodward and Robert Costa, "Transcript: Donald Trump Interview with Bob Woodward and Robert Costa," *The Washington Post*, April 2, 2016.

370   *In 2016, he said, "I had a poll":* An ABC News tracking poll released October 23, 2016, two weeks before election day in 2016, showed Clinton had a 12-point lead over Trump. *The Washington Post* was not involved in the poll. *See*: Gary Langer et al., "Clinton Vaults to a Double-Digit Lead, Boosted by Broad Disapproval of Trump," ABC News, October 23, 2016.

371   *In 2016, I had said Trump could win:* See "Bob Woodward on the Final Stretch of Election 2016," *The O'Reilly Factor*, Fox News, October 19, 2016. Available on YouTube.com.

CHAPTER FORTY-SIX

This chapter is primarily based on an interview with President Donald J. Trump on July 8, 2020.

374   *Both painted divisive portraits:* See "The Inaugural Address," U.S. Capitol, January 20, 2017, WhiteHouse.gov.

375   *He had said there was "a merciless":* "Remarks by President Trump at South Dakota's 2020 Mount Rushmore Fireworks Celebration," July 4, 2020, WhiteHouse.gov.

375   *The next day, in the White House:* "Remarks by President Trump at the 2020 Salute to America," July 5, 2020, WhiteHouse.gov.

375   *One of the cofounders:* Yaron Steinbuch, "BLM Co-founder Describes Herself as 'Trained Marxist,'" *New York Post*, June 25, 2020.

375   *It was not, however:* BlackLivesMatter.com, July 8, 2020.

377   *I reminded Trump that Fauci:* Orion Rummler, "Fauci: 'False Narrative' to Take Comfort in Lower Coronavirus Death Rate," *Axios*, July 7, 2020.

EPILOGUE

Trump has some real accomplishments that are not understood. The NAFTA replacement, called the USMCA, fully is a success. Robert Lighthizer, the trade representative, negotiated a middle path between globalism and Trump's protectionism with Canada and Mexico. The trade agreement passed in 2019 with the votes of 90 percent of both the House and Senate. It is full of progressive pro-worker and pro-environmental provisions. Jared Kushner played a key role in the endless negotiations.

Trump has a compelling case that the trade deficit of some $500 billion with China is a ripoff. Trump's view is supported by no less a financial authority than

Warren Buffett, the most successful investor of all time and one of the richest people in the world. In a November 10, 2003, *Fortune* magazine article called "America's Growing Trade Deficit Is Selling the Nation Out from Under Us," Buffett and *Fortune* editor-at-large Carol J. Loomis demonstrated how a continuing, large trade deficit with another country is a wealth transfer that could drain all the financial assets from a country that allows the deficit to persist year after year.

391   *"We must share together the bad news"*: Transcript, "Fireside Chat 19: On the War with Japan," UVA Miller Center, December 9, 1941.
391   *"Your government has unmistakable confidence"*: Transcript, "Fireside Chat 20: On the Progress of the War," UVA Miller Center, February 23, 1942.

Acknowledgments

My gratitude to Jon Karp for giving this book the benefit of his fully engaged, big-picture and brilliant editing skills while simultaneously stepping into his new role as CEO at Simon & Schuster. This is my 20th book at Simon & Schuster—my first without my editor, the late Alice Mayhew, and the first in decades without the late CEO Carolyn Reidy. As CEO, Jon is already carrying forward their traditions of excellence and aggressive editorial independence. He is now the Senior CEO Wonder.

At Simon & Schuster, I thank the following: Kimberly Goldstein, Maria Mendez, Richard Rhorer, Julia Prosser, Stephen Bedford, Irene Kheradi, Lisa Erwin, Lisa Healy, Lewelin Polanco, Kate Mertes, Richard Shrout, W. Anne Jones, and Elisa Rivlin.

Although copy editor Fred Chase was unable to join my assistants and me in Washington because of the pandemic and we missed his endless in-person energy and cheer, the book benefited enormously from his unflagging dedication and attention to detail virtually and from a distance.

Carl Bernstein remains a source of endless ideas and insight.

Although we don't always agree, our regular discussions enhanced my understanding of politics and the White House.

My thanks to executive editor Marty Baron at *The Washington Post*, who continues to guide the paper with just the right touch, and managing editor Cameron Barr. Special extended thanks to Steven Ginsberg, the *Post*'s national editor.

The *Post*'s owner, Jeff Bezos, is rich, steely and tough—the perfect and necessary combination for survival in 21st-century journalism. He has led the *Post* to a place of financial profitability and stability.

My gratitude to Robert Costa, Philip Rucker, Ashley Parker, Carol Leonnig, Josh Dawsey, Tom Hamburger, Rosalind Helderman, David Fahrenthold, Karen Tumulty, Robert O'Harrow, Amy Goldstein, Scott Wilson, Peter Wallsten, Dan Balz, Lucy Shackelford, Dave Clarke, Toluse Olorunnipa, David Nakamura and countless others at the *Post*.

Thanks to many old colleagues and friends at the *Post* or once there, including Don Graham, Sally Quinn, David Maraniss, Rick Atkinson, Christian Williams, Paul Richard, Patrick Tyler, Tom Wilkinson, Leonard Downie Jr., Marcus Brauchli, Steve Coll, Steve Luxenberg, Scott Armstrong, Al Kamen, Ben Weiser, Martha Sherrill, Bill Powers, Carlos Lozada, Fred Hiatt, John Feinstein and Fred Ryan.

Writing a book on Trump, the White House and an unfolding pandemic isn't possible without following and learning from the reporting done by *The Washington Post*, *The New York Times*, *The Wall Street Journal*, CNN, NBC, AP, Reuters, *Axios* and *Politico*.

Many thanks to lawyer, counselor and friend Robert B. Barnett, who is always present, always loyal and always wise.

Evelyn, Steve and I are grateful for the care and kindness of Rosa Criollo.

Special thanks to these friends: Michael Newman, Linda Maraniss, Richard Snyder, Jamie Gangel, Danny Silva, Andy Lack,

Betsy Lack, Tom Brokaw, Rita Braver, Carl Feldbaum, Anne Swallow, Jen Young, David Greenberg, Suzanne Nossel, Seymour Hersh, Richard Cohen, Steve Brill, Tom Boswell, Wendy Boswell, Judy Kovler, Peter Kovler, Ted Olson, Lady Olson, Karen Alexander, Brendan Sullivan, Bill Nelson, Jim Hoagland, Jane Hitchcock, Robert Redford, Katharine Weymouth, Mike Allen, Glenn Kessler, David Remnick, David Martin, Gerald Rafshoon, Cheryl Haywood, George Haywood, Jim Wooten, Patience O'Connor, Christine Kuehbeck, Ken Burns, David Woodward, Wendy Woodward, Lynn Keller, Sue Whall, Harry Rhoads, Bernie Swain, Klair Watson, Kevin Baine, Catherine Joyce, Jon Sowanick, Bill Slater, Carey Greenauer, Don Gold, Kyle Pruett, Marsha Pruett, Therese McNerney, Veronica Walsh, Mickey Cafiero, Grail Walsh, Redmond Walsh, Diana Walsh, Kent Walker, Daria Walsh, Bruce McNamara, Josh Horwitz, Ericka Markman, Barbara Guss, Bob Tyrer, Sian Spurney, Michael Phillips, Neil Starr, Shelly Hall, Ali Matini, Dr. William Hamilton, James Vap, Joan Felt, Ken Adelman, Carol Adelman, Tony D'Amelio, Joanna D'Amelio, Matt Anderson, Jenny Taylor, Brady Dennis, Jeff Glasser, Bill Murphy, Josh Boak, Rob Garver, Stephen Enniss, Steve Milke, Chris Haugh, Pat Stevens, Bassam Freiha, Jackie Crowe, Chauncey Foust, Brian Foley, Cyrille Fontaine, Dan Foley, Betty Govatos, Barbara Woodward.

Elsa Walsh, my wife, has played an extraordinarily pronounced role in this book. She is a brilliant and clear-eyed editor who had the stamina to stick with a seemingly unending editing process. I repeatedly showed new chapter drafts—or redrafts—to her. "How many times have I seen this?" she would ask. I had to answer honestly that I had lost count. She always gave more, gave the most. Often pages had as many of her handwritten notes as they did typed words. There were always reasons, which it often took me time to realize. Her work enhanced every scene and can only be described as devoted.

Several times, in several different forms, she uttered the dreaded editor's mantra: "You're not saying what you mean." She would then help me find what I meant, or should mean. Still a disciple of Henry James's notion about the importance of kindness, she is always gentle. I will never be able to thank her enough for her contributions to my work and our life together. This is the 16th book in the last 39 years we have been together. I still have not been able to get the complete answers to questions such as, How does she know? Where does this intellect come from? All I know for sure is that she remains the love of my life.

Photography Credits

Index

Insert photos are indicated by Plate number. Terms beginning with numbers are alphabetized as if spelt-out; 3M, for instance, is listed in the Ts.

About the Author

BOB WOODWARD is an associate editor at *The Washington Post*, where he has worked since 1971. He has shared in two Pulitzer Prizes, first for the *Post*'s coverage of the Watergate scandal with Carl Bernstein, and second as the lead reporter for coverage of the 9/11 terrorist attacks. He has authored or coauthored 19 books, all of which have been national nonfiction bestsellers. Thirteen of those have been #1 national bestsellers.